JESUS, REVOLUTIONARY OF PEACE

A Nonviolent Christology in the Book of Revelation

PATERNOSTER BIBLICAL MONOGRAPHS

Full listings of all titles in both Paternoster Biblical and
Theological Monographs appear at the close of this book

PATERNOSTER BIBLICAL MONOGRAPHS

JESUS, REVOLUTIONARY OF PEACE

A Nonviolent Christology in the Book of Revelation

Mark Bredin

Foreword by Richard Bauckham

MILTON KEYNES · COLORADO SPRINGS · HYDERABAD

First published 2003 in Paternoster Biblical and Theological
Monographs by Paternoster

Paternoster is an imprint of Authentic Media
9 Holdom Avenue, Bletchley, Milton Keynes, Bucks, MK1 1QR
1820 Jet Stream Drive, Colorado Springs, CO 80921, USA
OM Authentic Media, Medchal Road, Jeedimetla Village,
Secunderabad 500 055, A.P., India
www.authenticmedia.co.uk
Authentic Media is a division of IBS-STL UK, a company limited by guarantee
(registered charity no. 270162)

09 08 07 06 05 04 03   7 6 5 4 3 2 1

British Library Cataloguing in Publication Data
A catalogue record for this book is available from the British Library

ISBN 978-1-84227-153-7

Typeset by M.R. Bredin
Printed and bound in Great Britain
for Paternoster
by Nottingham Alpha Graphics

Paternoster Biblical Monographs

Series Preface

One of the major objectives of Paternoster is to serve biblical scholarship by providing a channel for the publication of theses and other monographs of high quality at affordable prices. Paternoster stands within the broad evangelical tradition of Christianity. Our authors would describe themselves as Christians who recognise the authority of the Bible, maintain the centrality of the gospel message and assent to the classical credal statements of Christian belief. There is diversity within this constituency; advances in scholarship are possible only if there is freedom for frank debate on controversial issues and for the publication of new and sometimes provocative proposals. What is offered in this series is the best of writing by committed Christians who are concerned to develop well-founded biblical scholarship in a spirit of loyalty to the historic faith.

Series Editors

For Fran, Hannah and Charis

Contents

Foreword

It can safely be said that no other book in the New Testament has suffered so seriously from misinterpretation as the book of Revelation. Like the book itself the history of its interpretation both inspires and appals. At stake in the struggle over the interpretation of Revelation that has been going on, with more or less awareness of the key issues, in the Revelation scholarship of the last few decades is not just the correct reading of this or that passage or the elucidation of this or that mystery of meaning in this complex work, but the central message of the whole book and the whole theological and ethical thrust of its teaching. Mark Bredin's is a significant new voice in this interpretative struggle.

In his study of the figure of the human Jesus in Revelation several distinctive angles of vision converge in an exciting way. He brings to his study a Gandhian understanding of non-violence and a Girardian suspicion of redemptive violence, not as prejudicial but as heuristic approaches by which to highlight what is ideologically remarkable in Revelation's presentation of Jesus' victory by non-violent witness. He also approaches the text from the perspective of the Hebrew Bible and early Jewish traditions, recognizing and appreciating John's deep immersion in these traditions, and arguing that his engagement with them includes creative transformation of key images and motifs. Finally, he keeps in the forefront of his study of Revelation the image of the revolutionarily non-violent Jesus of the Gospels and the rest of the New Testament, an image which is too often left aside as interpreters enter the apparently so different world of the last book of the New Testament. Bredin invites us to see in Revelation, not a betrayal of that Jesus, but a powerful expression of the impact of that Jesus in a world dominated by military and economic violence. He brings to the fore the earthly and human aspect of Revelation's Jesus, the Jesus who bore faithful witness in his life and his suffering to the point of death, and who requires his followers to follow in precisely that way of non-violent witness. In ways that others have adumbrated but few have pursued so consistently, and none have developed so fully, he argues that the Jesus of Revelation never becomes unfaithful to this faithful witness he bore in his earthly life and death - a witness to which non-violence, as well as non-cooperation with evil, is integral. The controlling christological image of the slaughtered Lamb remains the controlling image even when the apparently so militaristic image of the Rider on the white horse fills the vision in chapter 19. Revelation's Jesus appears not as a violent revolutionary, but as a revolutionary against the forces of violence.

This is a bold and engaging thesis with much that is fresh to offer any reader ready to engage in their own struggle with the meaning and message of Revelation.

Richard Bauckham
Professor of New Testament Studies and Bishop Wardlaw Professor
University of St Andrews, Scotland

Acknowledgements

Through theological study I have come to meet and know inspiring and energizing people. People who live adventurously and have encouraged me, by their example, to take up the challenge of faith seeking understanding.

I wish, in particular, to express my gratitude to Professor Richard Bauckham, both for his help, as my supervisor while this work was in preparation, and for his generosity in contributing the foreword. Our many long walks in the Scottish hillsides have been a joy to me and without him I would have missed much of this beautiful countryside. His supervision and friendship, also, made the difficult task of writing a PhD and changing it into a book a less daunting one. His engagement with biblical scholarship and theology has challenged me to relate biblical teaching with the theological challenge. Thanks also to Margaret Barker who has been so open and generous with her time and encouragement. Her hospitality, good food, good coffee and inspiring and humorous conversation have much lightened the load of scholarship. Our long phone calls and discussions were extremely helpful to me. She continues to be a support and inspiration to many young and older scholars alike. I would also like to express my appreciation to all those who are dedicated to the cause of nonviolence in writing and action. In particular, Professor Willard Swartley, whose correspondence and writing have added much to my reflections and thinking about nonviolence and the gospel in recent years. Also, Wilfrid Harrington O.P. who kindly read and offered his commendation to this book.

I am indebted to the Rev. Charles Bradshaw, Rev. Roy Pape, and Dr. John Hey who stirred and challenged my early theological explorations and gave generously of their time.

I thank the Paternoster team of Anthony Cross and Jeremy Mudditt who have patiently helped me and encouraged me with getting this book ready for publication.

Finally, the debt to my wife Fran and our daughters Hannah and Charis is enormous. It is only right that this book should be dedicated to them. Without their support I would never have begun or completed this work. They have been patient while competing with the Book of Revelation for my time, and refreshed and inspired me with their own creative lives.

Mark Bredin
St Andrews, April 2003

Abbreviations

Adv.Haer	Irenaeus *Adversus omnes Haereses*(Against All Heresies)
Ann	Tacitus' Annals of Rome
BDB	Brown-Driver-Briggs-Gesenius Hebrew-English Lexicon
b. Sanh	Babylonian Talmud tractate Sanhedrin
b. Sotah	Babylonian Talmud tractate Sotah
b. Yoma	Babylonian Talmud tractate Yoma
CD	Damascus Rule
Dom	Suetonius' Domitian in The Twelve Caesars
EH	Eusebius' Ecclesiastical History
Ep (see Pliny)	Pliny's (the Younger) Epistles
Ex. R.	Midrash Rabbah on Exodus
6 Ezra	Chapters 15-16 of 4 Ezra
Frag.Targ	Fragment Targum
Gen. R	Midrash Rabbah on Genesis
Ant	Josephus' Antiquities
Jub	Jubilees
LAB	*Pseudo-Philo*, Liber Antiquitatum Biblicarum
LXX	Septuagint
MT	Massoretic text of the Hebrew Bible
M.Tamid	Mishnah tractate Tamid
NH	Pliny's (the Elder) Natural History
Num. R	Midrash Rabbah on Numbers
PH	Melto's Paschal Homily
Pliny Ep	Pliny (the Younger) Epistles
Ps.Jon	Targum Pseudo-Jonathan
Ps. Sol	Psalms of Solomon
RH	Dio Cassius' Roman History
Sib.Or	Sibylline Oracles
Tacitus Hist	*Tacitius' Histories*
Test. Ben	Testament of Benjamin
Test. Jos	Testament of Joseph
Test. Mos	Testament of Moses
Vesp	*Suetonius' Vespasian in The Twelve Caesars*

Introduction

When you get down to the nitty gritty, everything rests on violence in the end. *Iris Murdoch*

It is a bad outlook for the world if the spirit of violence takes hold of the mass mind. Ultimately it destroys the race. *Mohandas Gandhi*

There is no doubt that the human race has progressed technologically. Sadly, we cannot make such a claim regarding our move towards the reign of *shalom* on our planet. There is little if any evidence to support a view that we have journeyed far beyond our Neanderthal ancestors. As Cato says in Iris Murdoch's novel *Henry and Cato*: 'everything rests on violence in the end'. The only difference is that the so-called civilized nations are violent in more sophisticated and thorough ways than their ancestors. In spite of this, throughout history, figures have appeared proclaiming and living love and forgiveness. They have warned that violence will ultimately destroy humanity. Jesus of Nazareth was such a man. Sceptics point out that men fight more wars in Jesus' name than for any other. They are also quick to point out that the Book of Revelation and its portrayal of Jesus are both vengeful and violent. They might even say that many Christian churches support violent governments. It is not difficult to find examples of Christian leaders praying for victory over their enemies.

As that may be, Jesus has also inspired men and women to teach love and forgiveness in their lives. The twentieth century has produced great figures such as Mahatma Gandhi, Martin Luther King, Archbishop Oscar Romero, Dorothy Day, Dominique Barbé, and Archbishop Desmond Tutu (to name but a few). Each of them was influenced by Jesus' teaching and example. Eminent New Testament scholars and theologians such as John Howard Yoder, Jürgen Moltmann, Stanley Hauerwas, Walter Wink, James Douglass and Ched Myers have all argued for an understanding of Jesus as a non-violent revolutionary.

Revelation in particular draws forth the wrath of humanists and non-violent Christians who see it as a violent book. Yet others have attempted to show that its violence is legitimate. Still others suggest that its violence is the violence that the world brings upon its own head and not something that God causes.

The purpose of this study is to contribute to the debate by assessing whether Jesus is a figure of vengeance or a figure of compassion in Revelation. I believe this is an important exegetical task for advancing our understanding of Revelation and the figure of Jesus in it. If biblical exegesis is part of the theological task of faith seeking understanding, then exegesis must inform our understanding of God's salvific work in creation. I hope that this study will move forward our understanding of how God works for the transformation of all creation.

PART ONE

Setting the Scene

In Part One I will provide the preliminaries that are necessary for setting the scene for Parts Two and Three. I will define what I mean by 'non-violence' in chapter 1. In chapter 2 the credibility of understanding Jesus as a non-violent revolutionary will be assessed. My approach for establishing my argument will be discussed in chapter 3. This will explain how I propose to examine Revelation, its social setting, and the sacred traditions that John depended upon. With the increase in approaches to biblical texts it seems only right to define quite clearly what distinguishes my approach to the text. In chapter 4 I will look at the work of other scholars as they deal in different ways with the elements of violence and vengeance in Revelation.

CHAPTER 1

Nonviolence

Never be said of us: we had no war to wage. *Evelyn Underhill*

Peace is life itself. But by peace I do not mean life of passivity. I do not mean a life without action because sometimes we have to act a lot to bring peace. *Aung San Suu Kyi*

Introduction

In this chapter I will outline my understanding of the term 'nonviolence' through examining the work of the great nonviolent activist and martyr Mahatma Gandhi. Gandhi (1869-1948), more than any person in the twentieth century, encapsulated in his writings and life the ideology of nonviolence. It is an ideology that I propose will lead to an important understanding of the Jesus of the Book of Revelation.

Gandhi's nonviolence was active and pacifism was far from his mind. Nonviolence is the witness that an activist gives. It demands non-cooperation with a system that advocates violence. It means accepting suffering and death rather than using violence.

Himsa and Ahimsa

Himsa means that which is contrary to truth and God. More specifically it means 'violence', that which is opposed to life. It meets force with force and hatred with hatred. The Jesuit activist Ignatius Jesudasan, in his helpful study of Gandhi, observes that for Gandhi 'the root of the evil of violence was the want of a living faith in a living God'. The opposite of *himsa* is *ahimsa* and it expresses the idea of nonviolent suffering love.[1] It is the truth of humankind's nature which desires peace, justice, order, freedom and personal dignity. Gandhi could say that '*ahimsa* is truth (*satya*)'.[2] Gandhi wrote that the nearest approach to *satya* is through 'love'.[3]

---

1 Jesudasan (1984):95-96, 159; Gandhi writes: 'No man has ever been able to describe God fully. The same is true of ahimsa' (11—45). Note that all quotes from Gandhi, unless otherwise stated, are from the two-volume edition of Nonviolence and War (1948). The reference in brackets refers to the part of the book the quote can be found in.
2 Quoted in Jesudasan (1984):95. Later in Gandhi's life he used satya instead of God (see Parekh (1997):26; Hick (1999):191 discusses Gandhi's understanding of truth as God.

Those who do not pursue the way of sacrificial love do not know absolute truth and therefore do not know God. In other words, the whole of creation is centred on selfless love so when we hold fast (*agraha*) to *satya* we live in 'harmony with the nature of existence and reality'.[4] Therefore Gandhi could write:[5]

> Belief in nonviolence is based on the assumption that human nature in its essence is one and therefore unfailingly responds to the advances of love (1—175).

Thomas Merton, who has done so much in drawing Christians to the work of Gandhi, pointed out that Gandhi thought it impossible to face death and suffering without hatred unless there is a belief in God.[6] So Gandhi believed that when we pursue nonviolence and the way of selfless love we live close to God. Without God we cannot live the life of a suffering servant. Gandhi fervently writes of his personal journey towards God:

> I claim to be a passionate seeker after truth, which is but another name for God. In the course of that search the discovery of non-violence came to me (1—282).

Written some two thousand years before Gandhi, the author of the First Epistle of John would surely have welcomed Gandhi's insights. In his epistle love (Greek: *agape*) is possible only when God is the centre of a person's life for 'God is love' (1 Jn. 4.8). This New Testament writer shares much with Gandhi in terms of *agape* and *ahimsa*. The ultimate command is to love one another (3.11). Evil is personified in the first murder committed by Cain with Abel as the victim, who was righteous before God (3.12). Not to have *agape* is to abide in death (3.14). Even to hate is to murder (3.15). In 3.16 the high point of *agape* is to die for another. The author of 1 John had a strong sense that Jesus laid down his life for humanity.[7] In the same verse all who have *agape* are to do the same. Gandhi's *ahimsa* means readiness to die for others.

Tapasya

Another important and connected term in Gandhi's thought is the idea of *tapasya*. Gandhi was strongly concerned to convert people to nonviolence. *Tapasya* expresses his understanding of how this is achieved. It expresses penance, mortification, expiation and self-suffering. Gandhi believed that unless someone is prepared to suffer at the hands of the violent, then there is no way of bringing about

---

3 Quoted in Jesudasan (1984):94.
4 Sharp (1979):288; Hick (1999):191-199.
5 All quotes of Gandhi, unless otherwise stated, come from Gandhi's two-volume edition of Nonviolence in Peace and War (1948).
6 Merton (1996):109.
7 The Greek has 'brother'. This might suggest that the author is only concerned with loving those in one's own community. But this must surely refer to all humanity.

a feeling of penance and mortification from the violent oppressor.[8] Suffering without retaliation (1—272) brings about the transformation of those committed to *himsa*:

> Those who die unresistingly are likely to still the fury of violence by their wholly innocent sacrifice (1—278).

Jesudasan comments that in Gandhi's thought 'submission to pain is the very nature of love that is *ahimsa*'.[9] Gandhi almost utters 1 John's test of one who has *agape*: 'By this we know love (*agape*), that he laid down his life for us; and we ought to lay down our lives for our brethren' (3.16). Gandhi writes:

> The test of love is *tapasya* and *tapasya* means self-suffering.[10]

It follows that martyrdom is an important component of being a *satyagrahi* (one who holds on to truth) for Gandhi. The nonviolent activist and writer Ellacuría perceptively picks up on many Christians who pay lip service to the idea of nonviolence but don't really live it because they fall short of being ready to suffer and die. He writes that being a nonviolent supporter:

> does not mean that they [supporters of nonviolence] leave the 'dirty' work to others, counting themselves among the 'pure' who do not get their hands dirty. It is rather a question of giving the fullest and most comprehensive witness to the fact that life is above death, and that love is stronger than hate.[11]

The martyred Roman Catholic priest Dominique Barbé wrote of the power that suffering and death has on the oppressor: 'death of the righteous one has a curious power. It moves the noblest fibers of the human heart'.[12] Barbé is not attempting to explain the way it influences people, but that evidence shows that a martyr's death can have a profound influence. He points out that the death of an innocent martyr needs to be remembered and proclaimed to keep alive the love and compassion the martyr showed.[13] There is no greater way of remembrance than that of being ready to die. A powerful example of nonviolent resistance is the seven Vietnamese Buddhist martyrs who died in 1963. They are martyrs to their people because they set fire to themselves as a protest against the government's banning of Buddhist worship. Hope and Young in their book on peace activists write that their actions

---

8 Jesudasan (1984):96-97, 161. See also Douglass (1969): 48-76 where he looks at Gandhi's understanding of Jesus as the suffering servant of Isaiah 52.13-53.12.
9 Jesudasan (1984):96.
10 Quoted in Jesudasan (1984):96.
11 Ellacuría (1988):77.
12 Barbé (1989):59; see also Sobrino (1990):127 who discusses the salvation that martyrs bring.
13 Barbé (1989):59.

welded a fierce unity in the populace.[14] Thich Nhat Hanh, the Vietnamese Zen monk and nonviolent activist, comments that the actions of his friends were not suicide. It was sacrifice. Suicide is the resignation of hope in life. The immolations were affirmations of hope, and an effort to save life'.[15] Their actions had a visible affect upon their own people. Liberation theologian Sobrino likewise writes: 'the fact that hope arises and re-arises in history shows that history has a current of hope running through it which is available to all. The bearers of this current of hope are the crucified peoples'.[16] In his book on Gandhi, Parekh observes that suffering love moves the heart. It is the best way to transform the heart of one committed to *himsa*. He quotes Gandhi:

> I have come to this fundamental conclusion that if you want something really important to be done, you must not merely satisfy the reason, you must move the heart also. The appeal of reason is more to the head, but the penetration of the heart comes from suffering. It opens up the inner understanding in man. Suffering is the badge of the human race not the sword (xlviii. 189).[17]

A *satyagrahi* aims to live the most difficult and radical of teachings: he considers his oppressor a fellow human and not an enemy. The task of the *satyagrahi* is to lead the oppressor away from *himsa* and towards the nonviolent God.[18] The *satyagrahi's* suffering love and moral nobility disarms his opponent and weakens his feelings of anger. He moves the heart of his oppressor by his readiness to suffer and die. His uncomplaining *suffering* denies his opponent the pleasure of victory by gaining public support.[19] Sobrino thoughtfully puts it that when someone is ready to suffer and die for another, she or he is giving the other the gift of 'love'.[20] This readiness to suffer and die is essential to Gandhi's understanding of atonement.

Gandhi does not believe that atonement is the removal of sin. The hope of the nonviolent activist is to show the oppressor the truth about violence. We might consider the Johannine imagery of the sons of light bringing light to the sons of darkness. Once the light invades the darkness, there is no excuse for the violent. They have seen the horror of their violence. The nonviolent revolutionary is God's witness who leads the violent to self-understanding and at-one-ment with God.[21] The act of dying is an act on behalf of the murderer that brings light to the darkness of the world of the violent. The martyr's love has an impact on the oppressor that

---

14 Hope and Young (1977):189.

15 Hope and Young (1977):190 quotes the words of Thich Nhat Hanh in his words to Martin Luther King. See Wink (1992):192-193 who considers both Gandhi and Thich Nhat Hanh as exemplars of the third way.

16 Sobrino (1990):127.

17 In Parekh (1997):55.

18 Parekh (1997):55.

19 Parekh (1997):56.

20 Sobrino (1990):127.

21 Jesudasan (1984):110.

brings light to those ignorant of their violence. When the ignorance is removed and the oppressor continues and even intensifies the action of violence, the oppressor will receive no atonement.

Gandhi, always the realist, acknowledged that there are those who will persist in their violence even when they experience and begin to know *satya* (truth). Gandhi believed that the rejection of the martyr's witness would lead to his or her own violent death: 'what is gained by the sword will also be lost by the sword (1—212).[22] The reality for Gandhi was that the rejection of nonviolent truth would mean the escalation of violence. He wrote: 'It is a bad outlook for the world if the spirit of violence takes hold of the mass mind. Ultimately it destroys the race' (II—75). Such is the lot that is so often graphically described in early Jewish and Christian writings. Schillebeeckx expresses a view that Gandhi would have liked: 'God does not take vengeance; he leaves evil to its own, limited logic!'[23] Violence is the punishment. This profound truth has implications to the one who knowingly lives and gains by violence. The person committed to *himsa* lives apart from the controlling principle of life, which is God.[24] For the compassionate Gandhi, there could be no greater punishment, as also was the case for Jesus. Compassion must be the reaction to anyone who lives a life separated from *ahimsa*.[25]

Identification with Sin

Gandhi's journey towards nonviolence raised for him the question of sin. Gandhi was too aware that human nature always sees the sin in the other. Gandhi's time with Christians and his reading of the Sermon on the Mount would have been influential. The Christian spirit is caught up in the words of confession and words which express Gandhi's thoughts: 'if we say we have no sin we deceive ourselves and the truth is not in us'. Gandhi would surely have been moved by Jesus' words to the crowd who had caught the woman in the act of adultery: he who is without sin let him cast the first stone (John 8.7). Gandhi was aware of Jesus' teaching on the mount when Jesus said 'how can you say to your brother, "let me take the speck out of your eye" when there is the log in your own eye' (Mt. 7.4-5; Lk. 6.41-42). Gandhi took Jesus' teaching on sin seriously. Gandhi took an essential Christian doctrine and reminds us of the importance of identifying our sin and sharing the sins of the world. Gandhi taught that a *satyagrahi* should never think that he or she is beyond sin:

---

22 In II—59 Gandhi speaks of the sword of the satyagrahi as being love.

23 Schillebeeckx (1990):138-139 also Harrington (1993):234.

24 Wink (1992):69 speaks of the evil that can be transformed. It is the 'brute lust for annihilation. It is the sedimentation of thousands of years of human choices for evil'.

25 Hick (1974):355 makes the point that human sufferings are self-regarding, but Jesus' suffering was for humanity.

sin of one is the sin of all. And hence it is not up to us to destroy the evil doer. We should, on the contrary, suffer for him.[26]

The *satyagrahi* therefore must bear the order of *himsa* in his or her life and indeed suffer its consequences. There is no place for blaming the sinner and killing him or her. One must live with its evil. The alternative is to project our sin and violence on to some 'other'. The one we blame is then destroyed either by God or those who have projected their sin on to their enemy. Dominique Barbé comments that we can destroy the enemy so that peace might be achieved; yet this peace will not reign for long because the true cause of strife has not been recognized. The people deceive themselves.[27] Barbé therefore did not teach the violent overthrow of an oppressive government. He taught that the violent revolutionary overcomes the oppressive regime and becomes a new oppressive force. It follows that the spiral of violence continues. In the Gandhian tradition, *ahimsa* conquers not by rooting out the one who has been blamed for the violence, but by dying at the hands of the violent. Gandhi would have been aware of the Buddha's teaching in the *Dhamaparda*: 'hate never dispelled hate. Only love dispells hate'.[28]

Walter Wink, who writes profoundly on nonviolence in the Gospels, recognizes the significance of the doctrine of the fall in Genesis 2 for our understanding of sin: all share the same sin. Such is the teaching of Gandhi. Wink spells out that since we belong in the world of *himsa*, and contribute to its existence, we do not even recognize it as evil. Redemption is a slow process of awakening and we never fully distinguish what *himsa* is.[29] We are all in the dark to some extent. This explains why Gandhi avoided the idea of having an enemy: 'In the dictionary of *satyagraha* there is no enemy' (1—216). We simply do not know who is the enemy. The log in our eye may be bigger than the speck in our brother's eye. How then can we fully see?

Nonviolent Revolution

Satish Kumar, the editor of *Resurgence* an important journal promoting Gandhian nonviolence, acknowledges that the world we live in is ruled by the principle of *himsa* (violence). He asserts that that there can be no just or redemptive violence. Violence is violence and nothing more. Kumar's insight that violent revolution is a contradiction in terms is an important one. If revolution implies an overall shift from one state to another, then what is the change if the revolution is violent?[30] There is no transformation. The rule of *himsa* is transferred from oppressor to victim who now becomes the inflictor of *himsa*. As Caird writes: 'Evil wins its success by contagion. Whenever a man responds to an injury with retaliation, or imitation, sin

---

26 Quoted in Jesudasan (1984):109.
27 Barbé (1989):12.
28 Shambhala Pocket Classic edition (page 1).
29 Wink (1992):68-73.
30 Kumar (1969).

has gained control of two lives in the place of one'.[31] In early Jewish and Christian literature the rule of Satan is transferred from one superpower to another (cf. Rev. 18). There is no distinction between Babylon and Rome. They are different representatives of *himsa*. True revolution is a shift from the old rule of violence to that of nonviolence. It is the change from the order of Satan to the order of God.[32] This involves a transformation rather than elimination. Gandhi put it succinctly:

> A non-violent revolution is not a programme of seizure of power. It is a programme of transformation of relationships (II—8).

Again Gandhi wrote:

> Satyagraha believes not in destruction but conversion (II—149).

However, the word 'revolution' is intimately associated with violence. It is a subversive term and is connected with suspect and dangerous people. In our present climate, 'revolutionary' and 'terrorist' go together. People are torn between supporting America and supporting terrorism. President George W. Bush presents this dilemma to the people of the world, yet many know that the choice is not so clear-cut. In fact the true choice we are presented with is violence or nonviolence. Terrorists, revolutionaries and governments of the world are driven to seize power or hold on to power. *Satyagraha* is the Gandhian term for revolution and a term that I prefer to use from that of 'revolution'. It is subversive and its followers are dangerous. That is why Jesus, Gandhi, Martin Luther King, Archbishop Romero, Barbé and many others were killed. They said 'no' to the violent revolutionaries and 'no' to the violent oppressors. They said 'no' to maintaining or seizing power. Thich Nhat Hanh movingly tells of being suspected by the Marxist Viet Cong and by the American authorities because he and his monks refused to support either group during the Vietnam War. They supported the way of *Satyagraha*. My aim is to demonstrate that the book of Revelation is the literature of *Satyagraha*. A *satyragrahi* seeks to win over opponents and not to destroy them. A *satyagrahi* seeks to persuade his or her opponent, through reasoning, through suffering and finally, when all else fails, through non-cooperation (11—53).[33]

Jesus the Satyagrahi

Gandhi was a great follower of Jesus. The Jesuit priest Ignatius Jesudasan has attempted to show the influence of Jesus on Gandhi and hints at Gandhi's Christology. With little doubt, the most significant influence of Jesus on Gandhi is his understanding of *satyagraha*. Jesus lived all the stages of the *satyagrahi* - a

---

31 Caird (1955):2 and also (1987):170.
32 Kumar (1969):10-25.
33 Jesudasan (1984):97.

revolutionary in the real sense, one who sought a change from *himsa*. Gandhi held nothing back when he wrote of Jesus:

> Jesus was the most active resister known perhaps to history. This was non-violence par excellence (II—19).

Gandhi could not speak more highly of Jesus than he does here. Jesus is nothing less than a man who had divine status. He had this status because his life was based on the principles of *satyagraha*.[34] Jesus was connected with the ultimate truth (*satya*) that is just another name for God. Jesus was totally obedient and true to God his father. Gandhi's understanding was rooted in the cross:

> Jesus, a man who was completely innocent, offered himself as a sacrifice for the good of others, including his enemies, and became the ransom of the world. It was a perfect act (II—166).

Jesudasan writes:

> The dynamism of the cross is to bring the inflictor to recognize with the victim the unity of all in Christ. The dynamism of non-violence is to move the inflictor to recognize with the victim their common humanity. To bring about this recognition of faith, suffering is necessary.[35]

Sobrino points out that Jesus and the faithful martyrs create realities and values opposed to violence, by their faithful suffering. They bring light to the violent which hopefully leads them out of the darkness of their violence.[36] Gandhi saw that the importance of the cross is exemplary and if those who follow his way are not prepared to suffer, Jesus' action was in vain:

> Jesus lived and died in vain if he did not teach us to regulate the whole of life by the eternal law of love (1—181).

James Douglass in his important book on Gandhi also emphasizes the centrality of the cross and the effect it has:

> The logic of non-violence is the logic of crucifixion and leads the man of non-violence into the heart of the suffering Christ. The purpose of non-violence is to move the oppressors to perceive as human beings those whom they are oppressing.[37]

---

34 See Jesudasan (1984):113.
35 Jesudasan (1984):116.
36 Sobrino (1997):53.
37 Douglass (1969):71

Summary

Gandhi longed passionately for total victory for his understanding of truth. *Satyagraha* achieved through suffering, witness and non-compromise was the only way of transformation. Gandhi believed that the struggle between violence and nonviolence was connected with a conflict between the ultimate principle, *satya*, upon which the cosmos is formed, against violence which is alienated from the ultimate principle, *satya*. It was a religious understanding affecting every area of life and politics. In killing, one is estranged from *satya*. It is better to die than to kill. Gandhi looked to Jesus as the supreme example of nonviolence. At the cross suffering love received its fullest expression even to Gandhi who did not consider himself a Christian.[38]

---

38 Douglass (1969):71.

CHAPTER 2

Jesus the Nonviolent Teacher
and Activist

God has not called me to be successful, he has called me to be faithful. Mother Teresa

Introduction

In this chapter I will consider Jesus in the Gospels and the bond that exists between Jesus and Gandhi. The perceptive works of nonviolent writers and activists Walter Wink and Ched Myers will be particularly helpful in this respect. Also, René Girard's important mimetic theory and his proposal that Jesus rejected scapegoat sacrifice will be examined.

I think it is fair to say that many studies in Revelation neglect to remember that John, the writer of the Book of Revelation, was above all other things, concerned to make Jesus real and relevant to himself and those to whom he wrote. John the devotee and follower of Jesus reflected on the beloved traditions of his people as well as the troubling and alarming particulars that challenged them. Yet studies in Revelation exhibit more interest in the exalted and coming Christ. I believe that this is at the cost of the Jesus who lived, taught and died. The exalted, coming Christ is indeed prominent in Revelation. But we need to understand this exalted Christ as the Jesus who lived, taught and died. Christ on the throne of God is the slaughtered Lamb. The humanity of Jesus is emphasized throughout Revelation in the fourteen occurrences of the name 'Jesus', and in the presentation of Jesus as a human witness whose witness his followers must continue.

Revelation and the early Jesus Sayings

It is likely that John had knowledge of what Jesus did and taught. John would have been part of a prophetic tradition that relied upon early sayings of Jesus that were central to the forming of the Synoptic tradition.[1] Richard Bauckham points out that

---

1 Bauckham (1993a):93; Hill (1971-72):406-411; Aune (1983):274-288, has emphasized the prophetic nature of the book; for a summary of current views regarding the nature of Revelation as prophecy see Aune (1997):lxxv-lxxvi; Mazzaferri (1989) argues that Revelation is not at all an apocalypse but belongs to the genre of Old Testament prophetic writings; Fekkes (1993) has also emphasized the nature of Revelation as prophecy.

the words of Christ reported in Revelation are not present in the Synoptic tradition. Rather, Revelation reflects more John's concern with Jesus being appropriate to the situation of the churches (see 1.17-3.22; 16.15; 22.7, 12-16, 20).[2] John would draw upon sayings of Jesus that were appropriate to his community.

Nonviolent Teaching among the Sayings of Jesus[3]

Many knew of Jesus' teachings as they circulated throughout the New Testament world. Paul's letters do not often depend upon traditions regarding what Jesus taught. Yet one such text that does is Romans 12.14-21, especially vv.14 and 17. The teachings of Jesus Paul echoes here are particularly applicable to this discussion on how to behave towards one's persecutor: 'Bless those who persecute you; bless and do not curse them' (Rom. 12.14; cf. v.17 and Lk. 6.28a and Mt. 5.44). Paul points to a non-violent approach to those who opposed and hated the followers of Jesus. In Ephesians 6.10-18, there is a call for nonviolence and resistance to the forces of evil (cf. 1 Pet. 2.21-24). Revelation 13.10 likewise echoes the sayings of Jesus in regards non-violence: those who fight with the sword will die by it (cf. Mt. 5.39-42; 26.52)

Walter Wink, as a New Testament exegete, influenced heavily by Gandhi, argues that Jesus is an exemplar of the Third Way. He defines the Third Way as a specific kind of non-violence. He writes: 'Human evolution has provided the species with two deeply instinctual responses to violence: flight or fight: Jesus offers a third way: a nonviolent direct action'.[4] Wink discusses four gospel texts that present Jesus as a nonviolent teacher: 1) turn the other cheek (Mt. 5.39);[5] 2) give the undergarment (Mt. 5.40);[6] 3) go the second mile (Mt. 5.41);[7] 4) do not resist evil (Mt. 5.39).[8] In the first example, Wink concludes that 'the person who turns the other cheek is saying, in effect, "Try again". Your first blow failed to achieve its intended effect'.[9] With the second example, Wink makes the point that the oppressed person is in mind, one who is 'squeezed dry by the rich'.[10] The setting is that the indebtedness

---

2 Bauckham (1993a):93.

3 Brandon (1967) argued that Jesus was involved with Jewish resistance movements against Rome. He argued that Jesus and his disciples sympathized with the ideas of the Zealot movements; for a detailed critique see Hengel (1971); also Bammel and Moule (eds.)(1984); Horsley (1987):326 comments: 'Jesus was apparently a revolutionary, but not a violent political revolutionary'. Desjardins (1997):11 concludes: 'The NT strongly promotes peace and it strongly promotes violence'. Desjardins 117 points out that there is no evidence that Jesus was a violent revolutionary activist. Also more recently Klassen (1999):131-149.

4 Wink (1992):175; see also (1991):5-28.

5 Wink (1992):175-177.

6 Wink (1992):177-179.

7 Wink (1992):179-184.

8 Wink (1992):184-186.

9 Wink (1992):176.

10 Wink (1992):178.

of the poor to the rich was so extreme that they might even be stripped of their outer garments. Wink suggests that Jesus ridicules the situation by suggesting that the poor person strips naked. In so doing, he satirizes the oppressor. Possibly such an action would show the madness of a system that leaves a group so impoverished.[11] In the third example, Wink comments that Jesus is not supporting the enemy. The action of going another mile would throw the soldier off balance. The victim deprives his oppressor of the response he expects, namely, reluctance and refusal. The soldier did not expect the man or woman to go an extra mile.[12] In the fourth example Jesus says: μὴ ἀντιστῆναι τῷ πονηρῷ - 'Do not resist evil' (Mt. 5.39); the Greek 'to resist' ἀντιστῆναι contains the idea of 'set against' especially in battle. Josephus uses it for violent struggle fifteen out of seventeen times.[13] Wink concludes that the phrase means in this case that Jesus is teaching that people should 'not react violently'.[14]

Ched Myers' study on Jesus as a nonviolent resister and martyr in Mark's Gospel also needs mentioning. Myers argues that Mark develops certain Old Testament traditions to build up his portrayal of Jesus.[15] He recognizes the suffering servant echoed in Mark 10.45, with its message that the cross is 'the embodiment of the way of non-violence'.[16] Myers writes: 'it is the only Messiah Mark proclaims. The way of non-violence'.[17] Gandhi too interprets non-violence as the way of witness to God: 'It shall be proved by living it in their lives with utter disregard of the consequences to themselves'.[18] Myers says of Jesus: 'in the footsteps of "Second Isaiah" he understood the cost of telling the truth and of calling the people to account before the vision; he was prepared to be "despised and rejected, a man of sorrows"' (Isa. 53.3).[19]

René Girard

A discussion about Jesus as a teacher of non-violence would be incomplete without some mention of the French literary scholar René Girard and his mimetic theory. Girard believes that people blame others for the violence in themselves. This 'other' Girard calls 'the victim' whom we kill believing that we are rooting out violence and creating peace.[20] In the tradition of the scapegoat we lay all our sins upon the scapegoat and send it out into the desert. Girard uses the word 'sacrifice' to express

---

11 Wink (1992):179.
12 Wink (1992):182. There may be an echo of this in James 5.6.
13 See references in Wink (1992):185.
14 Wink (1992):185. See also Wright (1996):291.
15 Myers (1988):97-99 and on Isaiah 124-127, 173, 302, 309, 363, 378, see also discussion in Dear (1990):26-50.
16 Myers (1988):279.
17 Myers (1988):279.
18 Myers (1988):279ff. In Gandhi's complete works 1, 122.
19 Myers (1988):445.
20 Williams (2000):163.

the idea of killing.[21] Alison expresses it well: 'we are all, always and everywhere, immensely violent creatures, and the only way which we have to control this violence is the search for collective unanimity against a victim'.[22]

Mimetic theory understands humans as absolutely dependent on the other. The child eats quickly because he imitates the speed at which his father eats. The girl plays with dolls because she copies what other girls do, even though she might not like dolls.

Desire is connected with imitation. If we did not imitate we would not desire to be like somebody. The child in the playground desires what the other has. She does so because she imitates the other child in the playground. Imitation is central to the way humans grow. We can imitate in a good way or a bad way. Those who have been loved are more likely to love others. Those who have not been loved are less likely to love. Rather they seek to manipulate and control others. There are obviously various levels within this. Through imitation, we learn to desire what the other has. We desire to be like the other and have what they have. The adolescent boy desires his friend's first girlfriend in the same way that he desired his toy car in the playground. The friend boasts about his girlfriend and the friend desires her. Girard is quick to point out that the driving force of imitation is to possess the other. It is a relationship of 'rivalry' in which human beings are placed. The adolescent son quarrels with his father, the one he admires, over something insignificant. But the real cause is much deeper and is concerned with the son becoming a man and challenging his father's status over him. The son wants to be like his father. But that involves conflict. The son must challenge his father's decision so that he can show that he is his own man.

Girard points out that the true causes of quarrels and wars are often forgotten and replaced by something insignificant. The quarrel may occur over some small point. The two do not sit down and say 'sorry', and acknowledge that the real cause is that you have what I want. The quarrel is solved another way, according to Girard. A third party is blamed so that the friendship can be maintained. Alison uses the helpful example of the young pupil desiring what his teacher has. They dispute on some vital point of scholarship. They resolve their conflict by blaming the visiting professor.[23] The visiting professor is condemned for sowing seeds of contention among them and she must be sacrificed. She is the scapegoat whom they cast out believing they will establish peace. But for how long? According to Girard, 'a very little time'. Violence will return.

Girard observes that the human tendency to scapegoat for the sake of peace is present in mythology. Rome's beginnings are founded on the myth that the righteous Romulus killed his unrighteous brother Remus and so Rome was founded. The victim, Remus, was the cause of the violence that prevented the formation of

---

21 I think 'sacrifice' can be misleading. Sacrifice can mean many different things. A parent can make sacrifices for their children.
22 Alison (1996):21.
23 Alison (1996):21.

Rome. Romans did not want to know that Rome was founded on rivalry and murder. Girard writes:

> People do not wish to know that the whole human culture is based on the mythic process of conjuring away man's violence by endlessly projecting it upon new victims. All religions are built on this foundation, which they then conceal, just as a tomb is built around the dead body that it conceals.[24]

Girard believes that the Bible breaks from this mythology. It rehabilitates victims that myths would regard as justly immolated.[25] Certain high points in the Bible are perceived such as the suffering servant song of Isaiah 53.[26] In Isaiah 53 the speakers confess that the victim (the servant) is innocent and was unjustly sacrificed. Jesus is the highest point to which Isaiah 53 points. Jesus is the innocent victim of a group in crisis, which, for a time at any rate, is united against him. Unlike the classic myth, Girard writes: 'the passion is presented as a blatant piece of injustice. Far from taking the collective violence upon itself, the text places it squarely on those who are responsible for it. It lets the violence fall upon the heads of those to whom it belongs'.[27]

Girard is concerned with the non-violent God of the Bible and hopes that mimetic theory enables us to understand the mimetic spirit of the mob and to move away from it and identify with the victim. Jesus calls his followers to imitate him. They must come out of the mob. His way is against the mimetic spirit of the mob. A crucial text for Girard is the Matthean allegory of the sheep and goats (Mt. 25.31-46). Girard puts it simply: 'When we identify with the person in need or who has been victimized, we encounter the Son of Man, Jesus Christ'.[28] We must see the violence in ourselves so that we can identify with the victims of history.

In sum, Girard believes that the New Testament replaces the violent God of the past with a non-violent God whose demand is for nonviolence and not scapegoat sacrifice. The Christ of the Gospels dies against sacrifice. Jesus' life and teaching challenges the scapegoat sacrifice as the way of maintaining peace. The way of Jesus is not to resolve the conflict by sacrificing a third person, (the scapegoat), by driving that victim into oblivion with our sins on its head. There is only the idea of the death and suffering we are prepared to undergo to show their violence (as in Gandhi's thought). Girard writes:

---

24 In Williams (2000):163.
25 In Williams (2000):272.
26 In Williams (2000):274.
27 In Williams (2000):165.
28 In Williams (2000):279.

A nonviolent deity can signal his existence to mankind only by becoming driven out by violence - by demonstrating that he is not able to remain in the Kingdom of violence.[29]

Conclusion

Wink and Myers have been inspired by the ideas of Girard. Wink concludes from his exegesis of the Gospels that Jesus is a non-violent revolutionary. Myers shows that Mark uses the Old Testament, especially Isaiah 40-55, to portray Jesus as a nonviolent revolutionary. He gains victory by nonviolent means. Girard's mimetic theory provides an important insight into the causes of violence. It opens up the strange new world of the Bible. The Bible is at odds with the classic myth that justifies the violence and scapegoat sacrifice of another for the good of the many. It rehabilitates the innocent and rejects the culture of scapegoat sacrifice. These important works of Wink and Myers on the Jesus of the Gospels and Girard's pioneering mimetic theory, and of course Gandhi, inspire us to look at Jesus anew considering these intellectual labours. I hope to show that the Book of Revelation points to the Jesus of the Gospels: Jesus is a nonviolent revolutionary of peace.

I have so far defined what I understand by the term nonviolence. Moreover, there is enough about Jesus to lead us to consider Jesus as a revolutionary of peace. Something now needs to be said about the particular way I will approach Revelation and its Jesus.

---

29 In Williams (2000):193.

CHAPTER 3

Intertextuality and Conflict

The life of the word is contained in its transfer from one mouth to another, from one context to another context, from one social collective to another, from one generation to another generation. *Mikhail Bakhtin*

Introduction

In a preliminary discussion some explanation of the approach that I intend to use in establishing my argument needs to be given. I prefer to think of this work as historical biblical exegesis. I hope to put forward Revelation's understanding of Jesus and not one set by ideology. Historical biblical exegesis uses many approaches in reaching its various destinations. This work will also employ many insights in approaching biblical texts.

I will join an increasing number of biblical exegetes in using the term 'intertextuality' to explain my approach to the Book of Revelation. My understanding of 'intertextuality' is expressed well by O'Day:

> Intertextuality refers to the ways a new text is created from the metaphors, images, and symbolic world of an earlier text or tradition. The interaction between a received text and a fresh social context brings a new textual and symbolic world into being.[1]

Intertextuality understands that an author is a reader and reflector upon tradition. Intertextuality is a postmodern concept that tends to ignore the fact that conflict within society affects the development of texts. Post-modern readings understand the world as consisting only of texts relating to each other.[2] Those who emphasize the significance of conflict in society tend to focus more on the relationship between the socio-economic contexts and texts. My way combines these approaches. The intertextual process is the development of tradition through conflict between different interpreters. Bakhtin shows that the relationship between the social and literary contexts is an important one in understanding literature. He discerns language as occurring in specific social situations between specific groups and individuals. There are no final and unquestionable positions as language develops

---

1 O'Day (1990):259.
2 Sommer (1996):487 expresses this approach when he writes: 'Intertextuality thus becomes less a name for a work's relation to particular prior texts than a designation of its participation in the discursive space of culture...'

through the process of dialogue.[3] The Book of Revelation develops out of dialogue with others as it seeks to set forth its understanding and to persuade others of its claims.

Intertextuality

No text can be read as an isolated unit. This is an important insight of intertextual approaches to literature. Literature is part of a complex of texts. But the particular circumstances of any group present new challenges for each new generation and result in the development of the group's ideology contained within its texts. Greene recognizes that the new text defines itself through the rewriting or modernizing of a past text. In this way, the new sets itself as a true successor.[4]

Moyise helpfully adopts Thomas Green's work on 'forms of imitation' in understanding Revelation.[5] Green discerns that when a text uses earlier texts it is a form of imitation. He believes that four forms of imitation explain the way a text uses its earlier text: reproductive, eclectic, heuristic and dialectic.[6] The latter two are of interest in this discussion about how Revelation imitates its earlier texts. In the *heuristic imitation*, the new work defines itself through the rewriting or modernizing of a past text. The new is not an imitation of the old. It is its true successor.[7] In the *dialectical imitation*, there is a tension between the text and its earlier text. Green observes that a struggle between texts and eras occurs. It is a struggle that an author often fails to resolve and the tension is discernible.[8]

The insights of intertextuality are important in historical approaches to literature. What we know about the author is only what is set down in the text to help the reader associate to specific intertexts that the reader should relate to, in order to understand the author's intentions. Imagine reading an Irish novel and the phrase 'you Fenian' appears. The term means different things. If directed to a Catholic by a Protestant it is a negative term. Yet if a Catholic uses the term it would be a positive one. The intent of this phrase can only be grasped when we understand the term against the history of social conflict between Catholics and Protestants in Ireland. How the listener sees the term depends on the listener's perspective.

According to Moyise the purpose of an intertextuality study is to explain how the earlier text continues to speak through the new work and how the new work forces new meaning from its pre-text.[9] The main inspiration for Revelation is the Old Testament. Myers makes the important point that intertextuality is rarely

---

3 Allen (2000):211.

4 Greene (1982):16-19, 37-53; Worten and Still (1990):11 write: every quotation distorts and redefines the "primary" utterance by relocating it within another linguistic and cultural context'. See Moyise (1995):112.

5 Moyise (1995):118-120.

6 Moyise (1995):118.

7 Moyise (1995):119.

8 Moyise (1995):120.

9 Moyise (1995):111.

straightforward because references are most often implicit. The author assumes the audience is familiar with the tradition and will catch the allusion.[10] Scholars risk being too cautious in seeing the parallels between texts. They miss the process of interpretation and conflict that underlies the text. Identical phrases in two or more texts cannot be the only criteria for establishing a relationship between texts.[11] Often the reader can only understand the text when the earlier text/s are appreciated.

Conflict

Malina remarks that change is all around us and people define changing situations through their system of symbols. Communities adapt and change their systems of symbols to protect their members within their worldview.[12] The writer of Revelation reads and reflects upon the Old Testament in an environment of conflict and change. He presents Jesus to his contemporaries in the language and imagery of the Old Testament. His claims are persuasive only if they develop out of their shared traditions.

George Lindbeck

Lindbeck talks of religion as providing a set of systems that give meaning and shape the entirety of life and thought of a community.[13] Lindbeck calls the sacred traditions that give meaning to a community its 'cultural-linguistic system'. Communities find meaning and identity in their sacred texts. They are the lenses through which one understands the world.[14] But as conflict dominates life in the community, the sacred texts are open to diverse interpretation.

We need to study the traditions of the Jewish people and early Christians. They spell out what shaped the group's life and thought and gave meaning. This takes priority over the particular social setting. I stand close to Lindbeck in this matter. Tradition is more important than the social setting for understanding a text. Nevertheless, given the nature of conflict that exists in society, the social setting is important. Traditions are open to interpretation. Discussion and conflict arise over the true interpretation of tradition in response to the challenge of any particular circumstance. I will put more emphasis throughout this work on the element of *responding to situations* that Lindbeck advocates. Therefore, exegesis does mean a careful consideration of a text's social setting.

Historical considerations are my primary concern. My interest with intertextuality is to further those considerations. This is in contrast to an understanding of

---

10 Myers (1988):97.
11 Pfister (1985):26-30 has defined six qualitative criteria for judging the intensity of intertextual relationships. 1. Referentiality; 2. Communicativity; 3. Auto-reflexivity; 4. Structurality; 5. Selectivity; 6. Dialogibility.
12 Malina (1983):20-22; Larkin (1994):25.
13 Lindbeck (1984):33.
14 Lindbeck (1984):34.

intertextuality that sets aside historical questions. My interest is not in the relationship between texts that the present reader sees. My concern is with what John and his readers are likely to have noticed. The practice of intertextuality came as a response to the needs of their situation. John and his readers were well aware of the needs of their community and with the need to develop their traditions in response to their particular circumstances. Traditions and narratives are authoritative and control the way a group sees their own particular environment. Within the same movement are different ways of seeing a particular situation. We account for the different ways of interpretation through the need to develop tradition in response to the particular threat that society presents.

Familiarity with the sacred traditions and the social context is important for gaining historical understanding of a text. The sacred traditions of the Jewish religion need close examination. Such consist of the Old Testament and later interpretations of it. Aune points out that 'the precursor texts which the ancient reader would have assumed have been lost and are consequently unknown to us'.[15] Reconstruction can only be imperfectly realized. Nevertheless, the texts we do have improve our knowledge of John's sacred traditions in spite of the lost texts. We better understand the thought of a writer when we have some knowledge of the writer's sacred texts. We need to establish, as best we can, the particular issues that challenged synagogue and church members in the late first century when John wrote the Book of Revelation.[16] The synagogue and church shared the same traditions and narratives. They also faced in different ways the effects of Roman rule. Rome presented its own particular challenges to synagogue and church.

Revelation is a Response to Roman Policy

John opposed compromise with Rome. The crucial source in his opposition to Rome was his sacred traditions. Members of the churches may not have shared John's understanding of Jesus or his attitude towards Rome. They shared the same religious system, but they could oppose the other with the same traditions. Social circumstances challenged them to make sense of their heritage. The challenges to each member depended on how they interpreted their sacred ways in response to Rome. If challenged to offer a sacrifice to a Roman deity, the outcome would depend on how the member responded. Clearly, if this were the case most would refuse and there would be a persecution. The more difficult situation is that of Rome challenging the member by letting them believe that they could conform and still be part of their community. This is the greatest threat. Does a member attend a banquet held in honour of the emperor or not? No doubt both synagogue and church members met the challenges in different ways. In this work, I will examine John's understanding by considering his tradition, particular circumstances and understanding of Jesus and the kinds of attitudes John was in dialogue with.

---

15 Aune (1991):143.
16 I will be discussing the dating of Revelation later in chapter 9.

Concluding Remarks

Intertextuality is a valid term in historical exegesis. Karl Barth's hermeneutical axiom was: 'consider well'. When we approach Revelation we must consider the it as part of a process of development of sacred tradition. John considered well the teachings of Jesus and the depository of Jewish tradition. He was profoundly moved and his very being was challenged. He needed to make sense of his faith in Jesus against the backdrop of an intra-Jewish debate and Roman policies in the provinces. John's self-understanding is dominated by the figure of Jesus and his teaching. John interprets the teachings, life and death of Jesus in a way that had integrity for himself and his sacred traditions. Fundamental to understanding Revelation is appreciating the traditions upon which John drew and the particular social issues that challenged him, both from the synagogue and from Rome. Intertextuality is not a term John was familiar with, but it is a term that expresses something he did. If John's traditions, and Jesus' teachings are to have any meaning, John repeated and rethought what they meant. I approach Revelation as an important tradition that also needs to be considered well, and rethought.

CHAPTER 4

Interpretations of Revelation

No part of the Bible has aroused greater controversy. From early times, Christians have disagreed about its status as scripture. While some of its readers regard it as the most wonderful book in the Bible, others question its right to be there at all. *Arthur W. Wainwright*

Introduction

In this chapter I will consider ways in which Revelation has been understood in terms of violence and vengeance. I will set out the view that Revelation's Jesus is distant from the nonviolent Jesus of the Gospels. Two recognizable responses are: (1) a justification of the violence in the book. (2) Jesus of Revelation is the same Jesus who teaches love and forgiveness in the Gospels.

I do not intend to give a detailed exegetical discussion at this point in my work on the merits and demerits of response (1) that is contrary to my argument. Such will be undertaken when examining the texts in detail. Nevertheless, some points will be raised in terms of whether violence and vengeance can ever be justified.

Revelation: Horror of the New Testament

D.H. Lawrence called Revelation a reinforcement of envy on the part of the 'have-nots';[1] H. Bloom comments that 'resentment, not love is the teaching of the Revelation of St. John the Divine. It is a book without wisdom, goodness, kindness, or affection of any kind'.[2] A.N. Whitehead writes of its 'barbaric elements'. W.D. Davies comments on Revelation's teaching about the political authorities as 'an abortive hatred that can only lead, not to their redemption, but to their destruction'.[3] Preisker comments: 'the Revelation of John manifests a virtuosity of hatred and satisfies itself with the punishment coming to the enemies'.[4] C.J. Jung sees Jesus in the opening vision of Revelation as a figure of fear, not love: 'This apocalyptic "Christ" behaves rather like a bad-tempered, power conscious "boss"'.[5] Jung sees the 'outburst of long pent-up feelings such as can frequently be observed in people

---

1 See discussion of Lawrence in Wainwright (1993):199-200.
2 Bloom quoted by Wainwright (1993):113-114; see Bloom (1988):1-5.
3 Quoted by Klassen (1966):301.
4 Quoted by Klassen (1966):301.
5 Jung (1965):123.

who strive for perfection' in the author of Revelation.[6] Wink comments that John abandons 'Jesus' teaching on love of enemies and the liberation of women. Male domination of women remains intact, and it is not even clear that women will be permitted in the New Jerusalem - so deep is this author's misogyny'.[7] Selvidge writes: 'The book of Revelation advocates terrorism and, like the ancient prophets, it justifies the complete annihilation of the other in order to bring into existence a new social order... Revelation advocates the total destruction of a people who are presently in power'.[8] M. Waldmann sees Revelation as an exception to the rest of the New Testament due to its violence,[9] while R. Völkl comments that hatred is condoned and encouraged in Revelation.[10] Even W. Barclay was alarmed by Revelation's call to rejoice over fallen Babylon in Revelation 18.20 thus lamenting that the book does not represent the way that Jesus taught.[11]

We see above a broad consensus of views regarding Revelation from D.H. Lawrence to William Barclay. Such views are startling in contrast to the claims I am attempting to make in my book. There has been no shortage of scholarly and less-than-scholarly responses to the above. It is important to look at some of these.

Response One

This is probably the most dominant response.[12] Yarbro Collins accepts that Revelation is 'flawed by the darker side of the author's human nature'.[13] Nevertheless, she believes Revelation is a healthy work in which emotions of fear and pity are purged through a process of catharsis.[14] Yarbro Collins acknowledges that Revelation 'is an explicit rejection of the militant option'.[15] She argues that John intensifies resentment against Rome. John predicts the destruction of the hearers' enemies by God in the last days.[16] This has a cathartic effect and is considered healthy. Yarbro Collins follows Jung in this understanding of the dark side of human nature and his reading of Revelation.

We need to ask whether this is the best integration of the evidence – not what we think John might or might not have done. John knew of Jesus' teaching of love and

---

6 Quoted in Klassen (1966):301.

7 Wink (1992):99; also Garrett (1992):377-382; Pippin (1992) and Selvidge (1992 and 1996).

8 Selvidge (1996):275.

9 Quoted in Klassen (1966):301.

10 Quoted in Klassen (1966):301.

11 Barclay (1976):vol.2 165.

12 Representatives of this view are many and varied. Charles (1920):133, the blood on the garments is the blood of the enemy; Swete (1922):252; Ladd (1978):254; Mounce (1977):344.

13 Yarbro Collins (1984b):172.

14 Yarbro Collins (1984b):152.

15 Yarbro Collins (1977):247.

16 Yarbro Collins (1984b):154.

compassion towards his enemies. It seems odd that he would encourage hatred of them and hope through God's destruction of them. We need to explore whether John has really abandoned the teacher of mercy and compassion. If he has, then we can accept the views stated above that Revelation teaches violence. This interpretation has not really responded to the above, it has merely justified violence on the basis of redemptive violence.

Schüssler Fiorenza and Yarbro Collins defend the violence, hatred and vengeance of Revelation with their argument that those who attack the desire for vengeance, as seen, for example, in Revelation 6.9-11, only do so insofar as such people do not suffer unbearable oppression and are not driven by the question of justice.[17] Such likewise is the reading of M. Volf followed by J.L. Coker. Coker notes the importance of pacifism in Volf's reading of Revelation: 'Volf's vision is of a "not yet" eschatology in which Christ will some day return to violently vanquish the forces of evil. Christians can live peaceably in this violent and unjust world because they know that ultimately God's justice and vengeance shall reign'.[18] Coker comments that those who react against a vengeful God must come from 'the quiet of a suburban home'.[19]

This line of argument does not excuse the above claims that Revelation is violent and vengeful. It simply justifies violence. Violence and vengeance is something 'to desire'. This falls into the category of Girard's understanding of classic myth. It is saying that one group or an individual can have hatred for another. They can hope for the violent death of their supposed oppressor because they feel oppressed. This does not take into account how difficult it is to know how much John or his audience suffered. Perhaps they had courted persecution.[20] It should also be remembered that there are examples of suffering individuals and groups who are imprisoned for their witness for peace and justice and who do not seek vengeance against their captors, for example, Gandhi, Luther King, and the Vietnamese Buddhists who torched themselves during the Vietnamese war as an act of conscience against the government.[21] Such people do not come from 'the quiet of a suburban home'.

Vengeance may well be a legitimate cry of rage against the oppressor. Nevertheless, it is difficult sometimes to distinguish the victim from the oppressor. A study of warfare would reveal this. It can be said that there are very few, male or female, or any of the various classes and peoples, that have not experienced

---

17 Yarbro Collins (1984b):170; Schüssler Fiorenza (1981):84-85.

18 Coker (1999):266; such a reading resembles Bultmann's reading (1955):vol.2, 175 of Revelation which he reacts to because it is more like a Jewish apocalypse insofar as the present is simply seen 'as a time of temporariness, of waiting'. Missing is the "between-ness" of Christian existence i.e. that Christ has brought believers into a new beginning.

19 Coker (1999):267.

20 For this view see Thompson (1990):191-197, who argues that the work comes from a 'cognitive minority' with its own way of looking at life and the book provides a 'deviant knowledge'.

21 See accounts of witnesses in the struggle for peace and justice in Dear (1990).

humiliation, failure, injustice and depression. War and violence, put simply, occurs between people because someone wants what the other has. People in comfortable suburbia are driven to desire more just as those are who have absolutely nothing. We do not justify someone's violence because they desire something.

Revelation, in this perspective, does not call believers to take up arms. But it does call them to believe that God will carry out his vengeful acts against their perceived oppressors. Rowland rightly warns: 'All too easily the human ego can demand satisfaction of its needs in the promotion of a good cause with the result that the cause itself can become subordinated to that need'.[22] In the light of this, this argument cannot be said to defend or excuse the above attacks.

Summary

The view of Revelation from this perspective does not really differ in its reading of Revelation from that to which it responds. The violence of Revelation is present. This perspective differs in its estimate of the importance of Revelation. Revelation is justified on the basis of a redemptive vengeance ideology. This is an ideology I am not persuaded by and one that I believe cannot be harmonized with the Jesus of the New Testament elsewhere. If there is a call for the punishment of Rome in Revelation, then I will accept the view of D.H. Lawrence and others. This is the crux of this work: can Revelation be understood in terms other than of a violent God who kills people because they belong to a certain social group?

Response Two[23]

G.B. Caird (1966)

In Revelation people are given the opportunity to repent (6.1-8; 8.6-12; 11.13). Caird writes:

> For unless God is to acknowledge defeat by abandoning his world to the destructive forces of evil, he must provide a way of stopping men from endlessly producing the means of their own destruction and must release them from the tyranny of demonic powers they themselves have brought into being.[24]

Caird allows that there will be some who will not repent (cf. 20.12): 'For such people [the violent] the presence of God could be nothing but a horror from which they, like the earth they made their home, must flee, leaving not a trace behind. For

---

22 Rowland (1993):38.
23This is not an exhaustive study. There are many other scholars that I could have looked at. Especially Hayes (1996):169-185 and Boring (1986).
24 Caird (1984):295-296.

them there remains only the annihilation'.[25] Caird further comments: 'In justice to John let it be noted that the "lake of fire" is not for men, as it is for the demonic enemies of God, a place of torment'.[26]

Nonviolent ideology dominates Caird's position with its hope for the transformation of evil. Caird distinguishes between Satan and humankind. He emphasizes that the nations are deceived by Satan (see Rev. 12.12).[27] It is Satan's power that must be destroyed. Caird is careful in his discussion: 'it would be a mistake to suppose that, because John speaks of evil in vast cosmic symbols, he therefore believed in mythical demonic powers operating independently of human wrongdoing'.[28] He writes: 'Satan himself owes to human sin his right to appear in heaven and to thwart the merciful purposes of God by his accusations'.[29] Wink observes that the Dragon in Revelation 12 is embodied in one empire after another.[30] Caird like Wink is fully aware of the self-destructive nature of evil. The Dragon seduces the nations. But it is not the Dragon that perishes in the self-destructive process. Wink writes: 'Violence can liquidate the current regime, but not the Dragon, who leaps upon its exorcists and possesses them each in turn'.[31] The Dragon is destroyed when violence comes to an end.

On the one hand humankind is to blame, while on the hand, Satan is the source. This tension should not cause us problems in terms of the ancient Jewish and Christian writers. Supernatural forces were understood to be the source of human sin. But such powers were not an excuse for human sin. Ancient Jewish and Christian writers believed that when a person did well, the Spirit of God inspired the person. That person is responsible for his or her own good deed. People attacked Jews in Nazi Germany because Nazi propaganda deceived them. But we do not excuse their actions. They are held responsible.

Caird's reading of Revelation draws much from Farrer. Farrer used the phrase 'the rebirth of images' to explain the relationship between Revelation and Old Testament passages. Revelation re-worked Old Testament passages both deliberately and unconsciously.[32] A clear example is Caird's understanding of Revelation 5.5, he writes: 'What John hears is couched in the traditional messianic imagery of the OT; what he sees constitutes the most impressive rebirth of images he anywhere achieves'.[33]

---

25 Caird (1984):260.
26 Caird (1984):260.
27 Caird (1984):300.
28 Caird (1984):293.
29 Caird (1984):293.
30 Wink (1992):91.
31 Wink (1992):92.
32 Farrer (1949).
33 Caird (1984):73.

W. Klassen (1966)

The apparent gloating of the saints over the fall of Babylon in Revelation 18.20 interests Klassen. He argues that John does not in fact present them as a spiteful set of believers gloating over Babylon's suffering. They are rather rejoicing in the outcome of God's cause.[34] The text might suggest that the saints are rejoicing over the violence Babylon is suffering, but they are rather celebrating Babylon's fall as the fall of Satan. It is the end of violent nations. The faithful witnesses have brought about the transformation away from violence. Satan has nowhere left to dwell. Satan cannot exist unless fed by human violence and greed. We must remember that at this stage in Revelation the majorities have repented of their violence (Rev. 11.13). Babylon's fall is self-inflicted and empowered by the violence of those who reject the witness of Jesus and his followers. John may be thinking of civil war. Violence destroys itself and there is no one to represent Satan. In this sense, Klassen points out that the saints rejoice in God's cause. Victory is not gained through violence.[35] Klassen understands that the victory is John's *theologia crucis* (theology of the cross). Faithful suffering gains victory.

J. Sweet (1979)

The Lamb is not 'a lion in sheep's clothing'.[36] Jesus as Lamb is the complete contrast to the second beast (13.11). The second beast uses trickery and violence to make people worship the beast. Sweet puts it well: 'this is indeed a dragon in sheep's clothing. It is a deliberate parody of the spirit of the Lamb, whose only power is that of the sword which issues from his mouth'.[37] Sweet at times tends towards Jung's analysis when accounting for the negative aspects of Revelation. John's desire for vengeance is due to his personal situation and psychology.[38] But Sweet's exegesis is a different story. He interprets vengeance texts in the light of the Lamb figure. Sweet adds much to our understanding of Revelation 6.9-11. He notices that the vengeance sought by the martyrs under the altar does not result 'in the punishment of individual enemies but in the "judgment of the great harlot" who deceives the nations (17.1-19.2)'.[39] Jesus as the shepherd of the nations with a rod of iron draws Sweet's comments that perhaps the rod of iron is a shepherd's crook to those who respond (cf. 7.17) and an iron bar to those who do not.[40] Sweet quotes Caird favourably in acknowledging that evil is not threatening people from outside, it is that which humanity contributes.[41]

---

34 Klassen (1966):304.
35 Klassen (1966):305-306.
36 Sweet (1979):51.
37 Sweet (1979):51.
38 Sweet (1979):42-44, .50.
39 Sweet (1979):141; cf. Caird's observation (1987):260 of the 'lake of fire'.
40 Sweet (1979):96.
41 Sweet (1979):168.

W. Harrington (1993, 1995)

Harrington argues against Yarbro Collins. Jesus as Divine Warrior is transformed by the dominant suffering Lamb image.[42] Victory has been 'won by suffering, not by inflicting hurt'.[43] He comments further: 'He is worthy precisely as the slain Lamb, as the crucified One. Like Paul and Mark, John, too, in his manner, proposes a *theologia crucis*'.[44]

Harrington observes that the violent imagery is mythological. The battle of Armageddon is not an historical but a mythical battle.[45] Harrington suggests that the mythological language explains John's observations of society as violent. The four riders in Revelation 6.1-8 express 'the mindless folly of war'.[46] The violent depiction of the destruction of the violent in Revelation 19.17-21 shows not the literal eschatological consequences. Harrington quotes Schillebeeckx: 'The evil have excluded themselves from communion with the living God - excluded themselves from life. They no longer exist. But there is no shadow kingdom of hell next to the eternally happy kingdom of God'.[47] Harrington develops his understanding of evil in line with Schillebeeckx. Evil is the lack of good. 'Good', it follows, will be the principle upon which the cosmos is created. Evil is non-existence. It denies all that exists. Those who engage in violence share and expand the power of evil and choose to be separated from God. This is the path to non-existence expressed in Revelation 19.17-21 (see chapter 15).

Harrington contributes significantly to exegesis in developing the importance of Farrer's idea of the rebirth of Old Testament imagery in Revelation. He believes that if we examine Revelation's re-birthing of Old Testament imagery we will appreciate the reversal of a violent messianic expectation.[48] In his discussion of the rider in 19.11-17, he comments that instead of the rider being the violent, crushing warrior of Isaiah 63, 'might not John, in a startling rebirth of images, be challenging his hearers/readers to reinterpret the imagery to which he and they are heirs? John has reversed the image of Isaiah'.[49]

R. Bauckham (1993)

Bauckham proposes that Revelation is a Christian war scroll.[50] His work is not unlike Yarbro Collins' study of martyrdom in holy war tradition. Instead of God

---

42 Arguments for this are made in 1993 and 1995.

43 Harrington (1995):59.

44 Harrington (1993):87-88.

45 Harrington (1993):229.

46 Harrington (1993):92.

47 Harrington (1993):234.

48 There are great similarities at this point with Bauckham.

49 Harrington (1993):192.

50 Bauckham (1993a):213.

gaining a military victory, it would be gained by martyrdom.[51] Bauckham does not accept the model of catharsis to excuse the conquering/vengeance aspect of Yarbro Collins' Revelation. The warfare metaphor is re-interpreted in the light of the suffering witness theme. Martyrdom is not one that brings about vengeance as in Yarbro Collins' view (cf. *T. Mos.*10), but brings about salvation. He observes, for example, that John reinterprets the military conquering Lion with a slain Lamb.[52] Bauckham points out that John draws upon Old Testament motifs other than that of holy war; for example, he thinks it quite plausible that John recalls the lamb led to the slaughter in Isaiah 53.7.[53]

Bauckham's work reflects independently Barbé's *theology of conflict* with its nonviolent reading of the Bible as well as Wink's understanding of Israel's development from submission to holy war to prophetic peacemaking.[54] The essence of messianic holy war tradition is that the righteous will conquer by violence (cf. especially 1QM14). Barbé observes that this tradition exists in all societies and in the Old Testament. He observes developments from this in the Old Testament similarly to Wink. Barbé draws upon the work of Girard who contrasts the story of Cain and Abel in Genesis 4.1-25 with that of the Roman myth of Romulus. Romulus slaughters his brother Remus. Cain slaughters Abel. Romulus, unlike Cain, is justified and exalted. Rome is founded.[55] Barbé sees elements in Isaiah 53 as 'reinforcing the evolution we perceive in the Bible toward a new way of making peace'.[56] The Lamb is not the good looking, powerful, strong hero but represents 'suffering'. Barbé writes: 'By the suffering of the righteous victim, the community becomes conscious of the evil it harbors in its bosom'.[57] Bauckham's reading suggests that Revelation is representative and a high point of Barbé's evolution and reconscientization of the mechanisms of conflict with a new nonviolent conception of God: 'Jesus has already defeated evil by sacrificial death. He has delivered God's people, but they are from all nations, not only Jews'.[58] Bauckham sees Jesus as providing a model of active resistance for his followers: 'Christians are called to participate in his war and his victory - but by the same means as he employed: bearing the witness of Jesus to the point of martyrdom. It is misleading to describe this as "passive resistance": for John it is as active as any physical warfare and his use of holy war imagery conveys this need for active engagement in the Lamb's war'.[59] Gandhi, too, saw the battle against oppression as a war. Wink observes this point in Gandhi: 'Gandhi insisted that no one join him who was not willing to take

---

51 Yarbro Collins (1977):243, 248-252.
52 Bauckham (1993a):214; this is also emphasized by Caird (1984):73 and Sweet (1979):125.
53 Bauckham (1993a):215.
54 Wink (1992):188.
55 Barbé (1989):25.
56 Barbé (1989):46.
57 Barbé (1989):46.
58 Bauckham (1993a):215.
59 Bauckham (1993a):234.

up arms to fight for independence'.[60] Bauckham's and Harrington's discussions develop Jesus as the Third Way more than the previous thinkers. Wink points out: 'one cannot pass directly from the "flight" to Jesus' Third Way. One needs to pass through the "fight" stage'.[61]

Finally, it is apparent from the above that Bauckham, like Caird and Sweet, is indebted to Farrer for his concept of the rebirth of images.[62]

J.N. Kraybill (1996)

Kraybill understands Revelation as nonviolent and active.[63] What he means by active is the testimony that followers of Jesus give, although he nowhere refers to 'witness' or 'testimony'. It seems the witness is in non-cooperation and readiness to suffer and be martyred. Supporting Tertullian's reading of Revelation 18.4, Kraybill writes: 'John was adamant that disciples of Jesus Christ must withdraw from exchange with Rome on every level, including trade'.[64] Kraybill acknowledges that non-cooperation would lead the witness into an economically difficult situation.[65] Non-cooperation was therefore difficult, and further was hindered by the fact that many were well off. He observes rightly that the threat to the Christian communities of Asia Minor was the internal desire to conform rather than 'external pressure in the way of persecution'.[66]

Kraybill's understanding of victory is rooted in a *theologia crucis* (theology of the cross). He points out that Revelation 'parts dramatically from the Jewish tradition of heroic armed revolt against imperial oppression'. Rather, 'in Revelation it is a Lamb "standing as if it had been slaughtered" (5.6) that leads God's people to triumphant celebration on Mount Zion'.[67] Picking up on Revelation 13.10, 'if you kill with the sword, with the sword you must be killed', he comments that the saints must endure with patience and nonviolence. Kraybill observes that John structures his work on the two polarities of 'beast' which signifies greed and idolatry resulting in non-existence in the lake of fire, and 'Lamb' which points to hope and love resulting in the New Jerusalem.[68] The beast is represented in the violence and oppression that proceed from Rome's rule. It 'violated Christian standards of love and justice'.[69] Such love and justice run through Revelation and this is reflected in its soteriology. Kraybill observes that Revelation 'never suggests that people who

---

60 Wink (1992):187.
61 Wink (1992):187.
62 Bauckham (1993a):178.
63 Kraybill (1996):202.
64 Kraybill (1996):29.
65 Kraybill (1996):30.
66 Kraybill, 91996):197.
67 Kraybill (1996):201.
68 Kraybill (1996):202.
69 Kraybill (1996):200.

co-operated with idolatrous pagan institutions are beyond redemption'.[70] Kraybill comments that 'people who love greed and violence more than the kingdom of God will have excluded themselves'.[71]

Kraybill reflects more the work of Yarbro Collins when he observes the joy of the saints at the fall of Babylon.[72] He comments in the same interpretative way as Yarbro Collins: 'The bile of the book pours out as a catharsis of emotion, offered to God as the only one capable of redressing the situation'.[73] This cannot be harmonized with Christian values of love and compassion. Kraybill's work does not engage with Klassen's view that the joy comes from seeing God's rule being established rather than the self-destruction of human lives. Kraybill's reading of the four horses in Revelation 6.1-8 certainly suggests that Kraybill acknowledges the self-destructive nature of violence when he observes that 'they are evil agents of Roman oppression' and that the red horse is the horse of 'civil war'.[74]

Summary and Conclusions

Some believe that the Jesus of the Gospels is different from the Jesus of Revelation. One response justifies the more violent aspects of Revelation in favour of justifiable violence.[75] It maintains that Revelation's presentation of Jesus is a move away from the Jesus of the Gospels who taught love and forgiveness. Revelation looks to God to deal violently with the oppressors. The witnesses are ready to suffer so that God will punish those who inflict suffering. Its non-violence is a strategy to bring about God's vengeance. It is nonviolence but not in the way that I define it. It may not call upon believers to kill their enemies, yet it does hope that God will slaughter their enemies.

Another response emphasizes the slain Lamb in Revelation. The war metaphor is rebirthed in the light of suffering witness. Revelation offers another way of perceiving and resisting the world. It implores people to confront the dominant power, but in such a way that seeks their conversion rather than their destruction. Nonviolence is the essence of Revelation's understanding of God and his creation. Nonviolence is not a strategy. It is a way of transformation to wisdom and life from ignorance and death. Revelation transforms scapegoat ideology of the righteous destroying the unrighteous into the conviction that all can be righteous.

The above review demonstrates that Revelation can be read in a way that corresponds to Gandhian nonviolence. It is surprising that such concurrence has not been celebrated or commented on before. Gandhi would have missed the subtlety of Revelation and would not have been inspired by it in the same way that it failed to inspire D.H. Lawrence and others. New Testament exegetes can miss this subtlety

---

70 Kraybill (1996):203.
71 Kraybill (1996):203.
72 Kraybill (1996):205.
73 Kraybill (1996):205.
74 Kraybill (1996):147.
75 A phrase that Wink uses (1992):17-31.

and rebirthing of tradition. This work hopes to develop and celebrate a reading of Revelation that corresponds to Gandhian nonviolence.

The witness of Jesus and his followers through suffering and death can lead the heart of the violent away from the ignorance of their violence. This is atonement in the nonviolent sense. The witness of the nonviolent reveals the ordering principles of the cosmos: love and forgiveness. The witness then rejects those who reject the witness.

In Part Two, I will examine the religious traditions that would have influenced John and the social setting of Revelation.

PART TWO

Establishing the Contexts

I will attempt to establish the literary and social contexts against which John wrote the Book of Revelation. I will pay particular attention to understanding the Old Testament and later Jewish traditions that would seem to have influenced John in his writing. The ways of God and the ways of the world will be seen as very different in these traditions and to which John was drawn. The world is the plunderer and will suffer the consequences of its plundering way. Close attention will be given to Domitian who reigned during the time John lived and composed the Book of Revelation.

CHAPTER 5

The Way of God
and the Way of the Nations

Violence is any day preferable to impotence. There is hope for a violent man to become nonviolent. There is no such hope for the impotent. *Mohandas Gandhi*

The fool is his own enemy. The mischief he does is his own undoing. How bitterly he suffers. *Teaching of the Buddha in the Dhammapada*

Introduction

My task in this chapter is to become sensitized to the pool of traditions from which John drew inspiration. As the title of the chapter suggests, my concern is with the way of God, and the way of the nations. Old Testament tradition saw Israel as needing to live according to the ways of God. Consequently, in the Old Testament there are traditions that are hostile to the nations who did not live according to the covenant of God and abused Israel. I will bear in mind my major concern of demonstrating that Revelation is the work of a nonviolent revolutionary about Jesus the revolutionary of peace. I will therefore probe traditions of Israel rejoicing and hungry for the destruction of its enemies and ask why John used them.

It is worth dwelling for a moment on the well-known fact that the Old Testament and Jewish literature contain violent and vengeful traditions. Marlin Miller quotes Jacob Neusner:

> The Torah knows nothing of not resisting evil and does not value either the craven person, who submits, or the arrogant person, who holds that it is beneath one's dignity to oppose evil. Passivity in the face of evil serves the purpose of evil. The Torah calls eternal Israel always to struggle for God's purpose; the Torah sanctions warfare and recognizes legitimate power.[1]

Neusner made these comments in the context of saying why he is not a disciple of Jesus. Neusner misunderstands Jesus if he believes Jesus teaches that religious duty is to give way to evil. Nonviolence does not mean giving way to evil. It believes that evil will be punished. It understands that God is the ultimate judge who punishes evil. I believe that much in the Old Testament seeks justice against the violent

---

1 Miller (2000):36.

plunderers. I would not suppose to say that it is nonviolent literature. That would be an argument too difficult to make. But the warrior heart of the Old Testament contains the seeds of the nonviolent warrior who is supremely represented in the figure Jesus and in the Book of Revelation. Remember that nonviolence desires justice. Gandhi observed that a true nonviolent attitude begins with a hunger to see oppression and violence eradicated. There must be the heart of a 'fighter' in the nonviolent revolutionary and not the heart of one who flees and compromises. John's tradition is the tradition of a 'fighter' who seeks for justice for the victims of violence. Retaliation is a response of a nonviolent activist. True retaliation against violence can only be nonviolent.[2]

The Old Testament is a broad and diverse collection of writings. Biblical traditions often look for the violent end of their enemies. God, for example, commands Israel to seize another's land and destroy all that is in it. The most conspicuous biblical war texts refer to *ḥerem* in which all defeated peoples are committed to destruction (the most extreme example of this is in Deut. 20.16-17; cf. Deut. 7; Num. 21.2-3).[3] There are also the oracles against the nations that look for God's vengeance (Ps. 9.12). Such often embarrass our modern sensibilities. But Israel's hope for the overthrow of its enemy is often linked to its loyalty to God. Unfortunately, such loyalty did not always lead Israel to see its own violence and corruption. It frequently confused loyalty with the violent overthrow of its enemy and not their transformation. In so doing, Israel's violence is constantly repaid by violence. God's concern is for the innocent victim of the powerful. God commands Israel to be just and a blessing to all nations.

Plundering and Plundered in the Old Testament

In this section, I will trace the theme of plunder through the Old Testament. This theme is important for our understanding of Revelation and particularly the list of plundered items in Revelation 18.12-13, which will be considered in chapter 10. The powerful nations plunder and then are plundered. Violence is repaid by violence. If Israel keeps God's covenant, she will not be plundered and in return will be wealthy with the plunder of the violent.

Israel

> The People of Israel had also done as Moses told them, for they asked of the Egyptians jewellery of silver and gold, and clothing; and the LORD had given the people favour in the sight of the Egyptians, so that they let them have what they asked. Thus they despoiled the Egyptians (Ex. 12.35-36).

---

2 Weaver (2001):49.

3 Niditch (1993):28-55 points out that 'the dominant voice in the Hebrew Bible treats the ban not as a sacrifice in exchange for victory but as a just and deserved punishment for idolaters, sinners, and those who lead Israel astray or commit direct injustice against Israel' (45).

These plundered goods form the material from which Israel's consecrated items are made (Ex. 25-28).[4] The covenantal curses promised that wealth was a blessing from God if his people kept his covenant (Lev. 26 and Deut. 28). A faithful Israel will conquer its enemies (Lev. 26.7), but a faithless Israel will become desolate (Lev. 26.31-33). These texts establish the milieu for much that is seen throughout the Bible. Israel is very rich in the merchandise that she plundered from Egypt (1 Kgs. 10 and 2 Chr. 1.16). David provided Solomon's wealth through plunder (1 Sam. 30.20; 2 Sam. 8.7, 11; 1 Kgs. 7.51; 1 Chr. 22.5, 14) and Solomon built the temple from these plundered goods. King Jehoshaphat had great riches because he did what was right in God's eyes (2 Chr. 17.5; 18.1). The nations feared Jehoshaphat and paid him a tribute of silver (2 Chr. 17.10-11). The nations came to fight against Judah. Yet they fled leaving cattle, goods, clothing and precious things as spoil for Judah (2 Chr. 20.25).

However, rebellious Israel did not keep the covenant and so suffered for her disobedience. Hosea declares that the more Israel gains the more altars she builds to other gods. Her heart is false (10.1-2). He declares that her wealth will be plundered by Assyria (10.6; see Ezek. 23.7). More precisely Hosea points out that Israel's sin is failing to worship God and to keep God's covenant and she is a murderer (4.2; see Ezek. 22.5, 29). Hosea announces that Israel is greedy (7.14). She did not thank God for her wealth. She decked herself with rings and jewellery to worship Baal and she played the harlot (2.13; see Jer. 4.30; Ezek. 23.40). Israel did not obey The LORD's demands for justice and did not have a fair economic policy (Lev. 25.35-38; see Amos 2.7 and elsewhere). Following Israel's failure, Hosea testifies:

> They [Israel] shall return to the land of Egypt, and Assyria shall be their king (11.5).

Hosea proclaims that Israel is rejected as a nation of priests (4.6). This is a reversal of the privileged status of priesthood promised by God (Ex. 19.6; see Zech. 14.20-21; Jer. 23). A priest is one who has much wealth (Isa. 61.6, 10) and Assyria will seize that wealth (Ezek. 23.7). Israel suffers violence and becomes a victim as a result of living by violence. Raymond Schwager observed four classifications of texts that speak in different ways about divine violent retribution.[5] We see in the Old Testament that punishment for plunderers and aggressors is to endure the violence they have inflicted (Isa. 50.11; Ps. 7.13-17; Prov. 8.36; 26.27). Schwager writes:

> God threatens death for the sinner. But in so doing, God himself in no way becomes violent. He only drives the guilty from his presence. The punishment consists in God's

---

4 Schoff (1920):111 what is plundered from Egypt becomes the items which form Israel's sacred traditions. This will be seen to be important especially in chapter 10.

5 Schwager (2000):61-62 1) God appears as an irrational being killing or wanting to kill without apparent reason. 2) He reacts to evil deeds perpetrated by humans, and himself takes revenge. 3) He punishes evil doers by delivering them in his anger to other (cruel) human beings. 4) The wicked are punished by their deeds' recoiling on themselves.

abandoning humankind to the desires of its heart. People punish one another and hide themselves from God's face.[6]

Israel becomes a victim of its own crime. Such is the fate of humanity as it hides its face from justice and love. The mischief it does is its own undoing (see opening quote). But as Schwager has observed self-punishment and punishment at God's hands are not two distinct realities. The two in fact go together.[7]

Assyria

God uses Assyria to chastise Israel for her unfaithfulness. Assyria causes Israel to bear the violence she has inflicted and plunders Israel of her wealth as she plundered. But Nahum and Habakkuk proclaim that Assyria, too, will be plundered because she plundered (Nah. 2.9; cf. Isa. 27; Nah. 3.1; Hab. 1.16, 2.6). Assyria's sin of plunder is analogous with harlotry, murder, theft and sorcery. Nahum describes Assyria as a sorcerer who beguiled the people of God (Nah. 3.4):

Because of the multitude of harlotries of the seductive harlot, The mistress of sorceries, Who sells[8] nations through her harlotries, And families through her sorceries (Translation NKJ).

Assyria is a harlot who has relations for political and monetary profit. Fraser connects sorcery with luxury and trade suggesting that this underlies v.4:

after her conquests Nineveh endeavoured to build herself up as a centre of world commerce. Presumably, this was for the sake of the wealth and luxuries to be gained thereby. She approached people with her wares. She deceived them by her lies. She enervated them with her luxuries.[9]

Nahum considers the number of merchants:

You increased your merchants more than the stars of the heavens (3.16).

Nahum's reference to trade in v.16 suggests that this should be also recognized in v.4. Therefore, Assyria improved trading by deceiving the nations. This resulted in some growing rich (especially merchants), and many becoming poor.[10] Israel's identity as God faithful was under threat because of this. The Israelite people were tempted to compromise for profit from Assyria's wealth. This led Israel to forget the covenant she made with the LORD. In other words, Israel did not care about justice.

---

6 Schwager (2000):70.

7 Schwager (2000):65.

8 NRSV translates 'enslaved'. This is not necessary. The verb clearly is מכר 'to sell'.

9 Fraser (1979):766.

10 Ezekiel 28.5 makes the connection between trade and violence more explicit (see discussion below).

Ezekiel recounts the sorcerer who seeks profit by deceiving God's people. She held the power of life and death (13.19). Those who listened to her lies lived and the faithful died. The sorcerer was also Assyria. Assyria did what the sorcerer did in Ezekiel 13. She weakened the principles of righteousness that Israel was commanded to keep (13.22). The prophet Ezekiel longs for the sorcerer's fall (13.23).

Philip Esler discusses the significance of the sorcery accusation for the first century CE in a way that is helpful for understanding accusations of sorcery against any enemy, whether Assyria or Rome. He comments: 'An accusation of witchcraft or sorcery made by a community will generally function to clarify and affirm social relations'.[11] Nahum accuses the outsider (i.e. Assyria) of sorcery. He establishes his community's boundaries over against Assyria.[12] Assyria is an outsider and is therefore depicted as threatening the prophet's community. Sorcery represents what attacks the vulnerable goodness of the community by way of an outside power.[13] As Esler writes: 'witchcraft comprised moral judgement. To say "It is witchcraft" was virtually synonymous with saying "It is bad"'.[14] Girard's theory of how groups find a scapegoat to resolve intra-group conflict also resonates with this and explains the blaming and labelling.[15]

The fall of Assyria gave rise to hope for Israel:

> Because you (Assyria) have plundered many nations, all the remnant of the peoples shall plunder you, for the blood of men and violence to the earth, to the cities and all who dwell therein (Hab. 2.8).

Here we glimpse the theme of salvation which the prophet anticipates. Israel will be restored with all its wealth and violence will be visited upon the violent.

Judah

Jeremiah describes how Babylon plundered Judah's wealth because of its sin (20.4-5; cf. 5.17, 28). Judah disobeyed God and did not execute justice. She failed to keep God's covenant (Lev. 26 and Deut. 28; see Jer. 22.13-14; cf. 17.11; Ezek. 12.19-20; 17.19-23; 22.25; 22.29; 34.17-22 and many others). Ezekiel describes the wealthy of Judah as fat sheep as he critiques Judah's economic policies (34.17-22). Taylor suggests that the fat sheep are the bullying merchant classes. They have seized for themselves all the good things. The lean sheep are the victims of the merchant

---

11 Esler (1994):141.
12 Esler (1994):14 accusing those within one's own community of sorcery views the accused as belonging to a rival faction. This is indeed seen in Ezekiel 16.17-23. Note also the accusations made by the Elder Pliny which associates magic and Jewish rites and customs (*NH*. 30.11).
13 Esler (1994):141.
14 Esler (1994):139.
15 Also Niditch (1993):25.

class.[16] We read of those who have the best, but instead of sharing, they prevent the rest from having what they have. The poor must eat what the rich tread on. Merchants are those who pick from the poor the best of the lands' resources leaving little for the rest. The merchants' existence is due to the excessive needs of the landed property. Ezekiel attacks Judah's wealthy for allowing an economic system to operate that could dispossess a people of their basic rights.

Tyre

Ezekiel calls Tyre a wealthy, trading nation (27.3) who becomes arrogant to such an extent that she claims to be a god (28.2, 9). Her craving for more and more through trade leads to violence (28.5; cf. 26.17). Tyre was involved in Jerusalem's destruction (26.2). Tyre, like Israel and Assyria, is a harlot (Isa. 23.14-15) who will be plundered by her enemies as she plundered (Ezek. 26.12; cf. 28.7). Tyre becomes a city devoid of joy where there is no music or song (26.13). Joel describes why Tyre will fall (3.5-6). Because of what she has done, her violent deeds will revisit her (3.7). Tyre's fall will result in Judah's salvation and the restoration of its wealth (Joel 3.8; cf. Ezek. 28.6, 9, 13, especially v.16; Hab. 2.8).

Babylon

Jeremiah proclaims that Babylon will plunder Judah of its wealth (20.4-5; cf. Ezek. 16.37-39). Nebuchadnezzar filled his belly with Judah's delicacies (Jer. 51.34; cf. 2 Kgs. 25.7-8). Jeremiah has ancient Israelite luxury in mind (cf. 1 Kgs 10; 2 Chr. 1.16). This was taken from the Israelites because of their violence, exploitation and blasphemy (Jer. 15.2; 17.3; 20.4-5; Ezek. 12.19-20 and others). 2 Kings tells of the king of Babylon's destruction of the Jerusalem temple. The bronze, silver and gold vessels of the temple were carried away (25.7-8). 2 Chronicles describes how they were deposited in the king of Babylon's temple (36.7; cf. Jer. 52.12-13). The insult is heightened as the plunderer not only seizes the sacred symbols, but also uses them to enhance and empower its own.

Ezekiel tells us that through trade with Babylon Judah accrued much wealth. It whored itself for gain (16.29). Ezekiel's portrait of Babylon as a merchant nation links plunder with trade. Babylon seduced the all too willing Judah by profit. We have seen how Nahum saw the intimate relationship between trade and plunder (3.4, 16). There are many ways to destroy a culture. It is not just achieved through a military army. Seduction by wealth and the power that goes with it can persuade the strongest to neglect their tradition. Trade and commerce conceal the suffering that otherwise is not so easily hidden if the oppressor were an army of military soldiers.

Isaiah 40-55 describes how Babylon's gain leads to its fall. Babylon is arrogant and claims divine status. Babylon boasts: 'I am, and there is no one besides me' (47.8). Babylon will in one day lose its children. Dramatically Babylon shall be as a widow (47.9). All its sorceries and enchantments will not prevent its fall (also Isa.

---

16 Taylor (1969):221; Eichrodt (1970):473.

13.16-17; Jer. 51.37 is reflected in Lev. 26 and Deut. 28). The sorcery in Isaiah 47.8 may be compared with Nahum 3.4. We have seen that Nahum links plundered wealth to trade and sorcery. Nahum was alarmed at the attack on Judah's identity.[17] He saw that Judah's place as God's faithful was challenged by its desire for power and profit. A foreign military army could not be any more effective.

There comes again the hope of salvation. Isaiah writes:

> but you shall be called the priests of the LORD, people shall speak of you as the ministers of our God; you shall eat the wealth of the nations, and in their riches you shall glory (Isa. 61.6; also Isa. 58.12; Jer. 17.24; Ezek. 39.10; Nah. 2.2 contrast with Ezek. 21.26 and Hos. 4.6).

A time is expected when all Israelites will be priests. They will be privileged and the foreign nations will keep them in wealth. The prophet says that the LORD will clothe the priests with salvation, righteousness, garlands and jewels (Isa. 61.10). Wealth is intimately connected to salvation. Israel, for example, lost its wealth when its people lost their status as priests (see Hos. 4.6; cf. Ezek. 21.26). The Hebrew word connected with wealth throughout the Old Testament is 'עֵדֶן' (see Isa. 47.8). The word is closely related to Eden and the temple in Jerusalem. Salvation for Israel is tied up with such a place. Adam and Eve were placed in the 'garden of Eden'. LXX adds that it was a place of luxury, daintiness (LXX Gen. 2.15).[18]

The Jerusalem Temple was a place of lavishness and a place of paradise like Eden (Ezek. 36.35). Margaret Barker observes the similarities between the two (Gen. 2 with Ezek. 40.31, 24; 41.17-18; 47.1-12).[19] The garden is associated also with the holy mountain again linking Eden with the place of the Temple (Ezek. 28.14). Each superpower had its own Eden that was plundered at some point. It is the items connected with a nation's sacred traditions that are plundered. A nation believes its sacred place to be the place of perfection and joy. Unfortunately, this is understood as achievable only by might and power. Such a hope dominates throughout the Old Testament.

The Persians

Haggai ministered during the second year of the Persian king Darius (1.1). He proclaimed against the nations:

> For thus says the LORD of hosts: Once again, in a little while, I will shake the heavens and the earth and the sea and the dry land; and I will shake all nations, so that the treasures of all nations shall come in, and I will fill this house with splendour, says the LORD of hosts. The silver is mine, and the gold is mine, says the LORD of hosts (Hag. 2.6-8; cf. vv.21-23).

---

17 However, this is not to suggest that the art of magic is not present in the two texts. This important point is that sorcery was hated within the Old Testament. See Esler (1994):139.

18 Vulgate also adds to MT: '*et posuit eum in paridiso voluptatis...*'

19 Barker (1991):69. Also Fishbane (1985):370-371.

Haggai sees the fall of Persia during its time of economic upheaval (1.6). This attack is timeless and could be directed against any of the previous superpowers. Zechariah directed his attack specifically against Persia at the same time as Haggai (chapters 1-8). The prophets condemn Persia for the violence it has committed against God's people. It is compared to the other violent, plundering superpowers (Zech. 1.15). The LORD declares:

> Behold, I will shake my hand over them, and they shall become plunder for those who served them (Zech. 2.9).

The plunderer who is at ease will become plunder. Haggai teaches that the fall of the nations brings the hope of restoration for God's people including the restoration of its wealth (2.7-9).

The Greeks

The author of Zechariah 9-14 probably belongs to the time of the Hellenistic empires (9.13). The author proclaims that the day of the LORD is coming. At that time, the spoil taken from Israel will be given back (14.1). This means the plundering of Greece.

Daniel writes of the plunder of wealth and riches during the fall of Persia and the rise of Greece (11.2b-39). Using older traditions, the southern king will plunder the king from the north (11.8-9). Such items of plunder are used to honour foreign gods (11.38). The king of the north will gain control:

> He shall become the ruler of the treasures of gold and of silver, and all the precious things of Egypt...(11.43)

Trust not the Ways of the World in the Old Testament

I have considered Israel and Judah in their relations with the other nations and paid particular attention to this relationship in terms of the theme of plunder and being plundered. I will now extend my consideration of the attitude of the Old Testament towards Israel's enemies to looking at how God's people are called to be separate from the nations.

Psalm 49 Attitudes towards Wealth

> Why should I fear in times of trouble, when the iniquity of my persecutors surrounds me, those who trust in their wealth and boast of the abundance of their riches? Truly no one can ransom their lives or give to God the price of their lives (vv.5-7).

The faithful suffer under the foreign empire. Eaton writes: 'Under the heathen empires, apostasy and unscrupulousness often offered an Israelite the easiest road to high office and wealth; poverty and piety thus belonged together'.[20] The Psalm strengthens group moral against the onslaught of the seductive rich empire - apostasy must be rejected. The psalmist describes what will happen to the rich: Death shall be their shepherd (v.14). No one can carry anything to the grave (v.17). However, the fate of the faithful will be different. There is hope that God will vindicate beyond the bounds of human flesh (v.15; cf. Pss. 16.10; 73 and 78). Russell writes:

> the problem of the prosperity of the wicked and the suffering of the righteous turns the psalmists' thoughts to that of continuing fellowship with God at whose right hand there are "pleasures for evermore" (Ps. 16.11). There is certainly no clearly defined doctrine of a life beyond death encountered here, but at best only a glimmering of hope.[21]

This Psalm sets Israel against its enemies. Its enemies trusted in wealth and power. The psalmist is alarmed at Israel wanting to be like the nations and pursuing wealth and power rather than trusting in God. Greed made Israel follow foreign idols.[22] Closely connected with desire for profit is the need for having a mighty army like the superpowers.

An Army like the Nations

The people of Israel wanted a king like the other nations whom they saw as powerful and rich (1 Sam. 8.5). The Israelites believed that having a king like them meant that they too would be strong and wealthy. The Israelites desired to be like the nations who did not walk in the way of the covenant. They sought profit and perverted justice (1 Sam. 8.3). The people of Israel desired the same things as the nations: power and wealth. These desires led to conflict and violence. Ezekiel tells us that Israel desired Assyrian warriors clothed in purple (Ezek. 23.5-6). Israel believed that they needed a mighty army to be powerful and wealthy.[23] It had forgotten that wealth came through trusting in God and practising justice. Hosea accuses the people of Israel of putting their trust in horses and chariots and entering into military pacts (12.2; see 5.13; 7.11-12; 8.9; 9.3; 10.4; 11.5; 14.4).[24] Micah condemns Jerusalem for introducing the war chariot (1.13; see 5.9)[25] while Isaiah attacks Israel for making military pacts and trusting in war chariots (31.1). Hosea declares to Israel that God will not deliver Israel by bow, nor by sword, nor by war, nor by horses, nor by horsemen (1.7; see Mic. 5.9). Jeremiah counsels that Israel must submit to the enemy army (21.8-9). Schwager comments that this is equivalent to being asked to renounce military power.[26]

---

20 Eaton (1967):134.
21 Russell (1960):144; Bauckham (1998):80-95.
22 Schwager (2000):79.
23 Schwager (2000):78.
24 Schwager (2000):113.
25 Schwager (2000):114.
26 Schwager (2000):115.

In sum, we see that there is a move towards a nonviolent God. God's people must not be like the nations who put their trust in military might.

Plundering and Plundered in Later Jewish Literature

My selection is limited to texts that embody developments of the Old Testament. I am particularly concerned with literature that is representative of the Palestinian setting and its ideas. We need to remember that John was at home in the ideas that these texts represent. This will be helpful when I examine Revelation in chapter 10 and more fully in Part Three.

1 Enoch

The language of the prophets' oracles against the nations is important for *1 Enoch*. It expresses the vitality of the oracles at a time later than the Old Testament prophets. The above themes are especially prominent in the *Epistle of Enoch* (chapters 91-105).[27] The bulk of the epistle resembles the Old Testament prophets with threats of judgement upon sinners, and encouragement for the faithful.[28] Those who have grown rich by sin will be destroyed (94.7). The author condemns the rich for relying on wealth (94.8). They gained it by violence and plunder (94.9; 97.8; 97.9-10; 99.13; 102.9). The lot of the wealthy is suffering (103.5).

Chapter 101 portrays God warning the unrighteous that he can destroy them. The unrighteous may well be the merchants:

> they are seized by fear, for they will discharge all their valuable property - the goods that are with them - into the sea (101.4-5; cf. Ezek. 27.35).[29]

The fate of the wealthy and all those who assisted them will be similar to those wealthy nations that have gone before:

> Your cry [of the righteous] shall be heard... For all your tribulations shall be demanded for investigation from the authorities - from everyone who assisted those who plundered you...There shall be a fire for you (104.3-4).

In *1 Enoch 63*, the lot of the kings, rulers, and landlords is described as they acknowledge their oppression with shame before the exalted Son of Man:

> Our souls are satiated with exploitation money which could not save us from being cast into the oppressive Sheol (63.11).

---

27 Nickelsburg (1972):112-130 provides an excellent discussion of the epistle and gives a detailed comparison between *1 Enoch* 104 and Deuteronomy 28 which suggests the importance of this chapter.
28 Barker (1988):30.
29 All translations of *1 Enoch* are found in Charlesworth vol. 1 unless otherwise stated.

2 Baruch

The temple destruction by the Babylonians is described in chapter 80. Yet the ancient reader was invited to compare it with the plunder of the temple in 70 CE. The author expresses confusion why those who have plundered are not themselves plundered (82.3; cf. 4 Ezra. 3.33). Later the text tells us the enemy, in spite of her beauty, will fall (82.7). The author of 2 Baruch is concerned that Judah does not compromise with the enemy and that the enemy's beauty and her delights do not beguile Judah. He demands that Judah fixes its eyes on God's promises (83.5). The writer is not interested in naming the particular enemy, Rome. He has traced the theme of plunder and violence from the beginning. All ruling nations are the same. The text is ostensibly about the Babylonians, but indirectly about the Romans. For the author, those who keep the covenant will be rewarded by the restoration of what has been plundered and their enemies will fall.

Commentary on Habakkuk (1QpHab)

This commentary on Habakkuk from Qumran is directed against Roman rule. Rome is the plunderer but the attack could be directed against any ruling nation. Chaldeans have been replaced with Kittim:

> The Kittim...they shall gather in their [defeated] riches, together with all their booty (6.5).

A significant line from the commentary is the attack on the Wicked Priest who compromised with the ruling nation. The priest lives off the wealth of the rulers, as did the merchants:

> he forsook God and betrayed the precepts for the sake of riches. He robbed and amassed the riches of men of violence who rebelled against God, and he took the wealth of the peoples... (8.10).[30]

Later the last priests of Jerusalem are condemned:

> the last priests of Jerusalem, who amass money and wealth by plundering the people. But in the last days, their riches and booty shall be delivered into the hands of the army of the Kittim (9.5-6).

War Scroll (1QM)

The Qumran war scroll is a prophetic narrative against the Romans that describes the ultimate war between God and the forces of darkness. God's people will be victorious against their enemy with God fighting for them in the same way that God

---

30 See discussion regarding the identity of the wicked priest and the exact issues of conflict in VanderKam (1994):102-104. VanderKam does not pick up on the issue of compromise.

fought against Egypt. The plunder of expensive items is an expectation. The seven priests of Aaron are dressed in battle raiment made from fine linen, which will be embroidered with blue, purple and scarlet thread (7.10). God will gather the spoils. There will be a multitude of cattle in the fields. Silver, gold and precious stones will be restored to God's people (12.10). It is a time when the faithful will be clothed with glorious jewels (12.15; notice the close Old Testament parallels: Jer. 4.30; 10.4; Hos. 2.13; Ezek. 16.10; 28.13; and 4 Ezra 15.46).

Trust not the Ways of the World in Later Jewish Literature

An Army like the Nations

We have observed that Old Testament traditions expressed some hostility to the use of weapons of war. This was particularly prominent in the prophetic corpus. True faith was to trust in God. Many faithful Jews opposed the use of weapons and chariots; rather they believed that God would deliver them from their enemy.[31]
This tradition can also be traced into later Jewish literature.

Psalm of Solomon 17

Many ignore the anti-war theme of this psalm. There is no doubt that the psalmist understands that there will be a day of reckoning. The wicked will become victims of their own violence (vv.24-25). The messiah is not portrayed as a military figure. He is compassionate (v.32). The psalmist specifically states that the messiah will not rule by war and fear. In fact, during his reign, there will be no war (v.33b): 'he will not rely on horse and rider and bow'. This idea of the future messiah develops from prophetic traditions about not trusting in war chariots and horses (see above). The messiah trusts in God and exercises justice according to God's covenant. The spiral of violence is ended and there is no plundering or being plundered. His way is not the way of the world.

4 Ezra 13

The messiah achieves victory by revealing to violent men the evil of their thoughts (v.31, 38). Sinners are condemned by their own thoughts. It is their violence that will destroy them (v.31). The messiah does not conquer by lifting up his hand, nor by sword, nor any instrument of war (v.9). Those who belong to the messiah are 'peaceful' (v.12).

---

31 Such a tradition emerges during the second world war when Hasidic Jews refused to defend themselves against their enemies. Hasidic trust in the LORD also accounts for their antagonism towards Zionism after the second world war.

Summary of Findings

I have investigated Jewish traditions that attack the foreign nations since Revelation also was antagonistic to the ways of the ruling nations. In particular, the ways of the people of the world are summed up by words such as pillage and aggrandizement. I have contrasted this way with the way of God and how God's people should relate to the foreign nations. The following have been observed.

The prophets declared that worldly greatness and success are measured in terms of wealth that leads to arrogant claims of divinity (Isa. 47.8; cf. Ezek. 28.9). Such worldly success leads the powerful to loot the weak. With their power and wealth, they seduce the defeated by their beauty and riches urging the conquered to join them in their godless reign. The prophets urge the people of Israel not to participate in the ruling nation's sin and reign of violence and self-enhancement. They hope that fidelity to God's covenant will lead to the renewal of Israel as a great nation: a people of priests who are well satisfied. God punishes by means of another nation. It has been seen that those who live by violence will fall by it. 'Trusting in God and not in military force and material goods' is the battle cry of a faithful Jew.

The traditions I have examined exhibit little concern with a specific enemy. The great nations are the previous great nations. This typology correlates the new historical event with the older one. This encourages hope among the faithful insofar as making connections with the past leads to a sense of belonging to those who have gone before. A pattern emerges: the superpowers are like the previous superpowers. Babylon, as did its predecessors, committed violence while seizing for themselves the position of God. They made sacred temples and gods from the booty of their violence and continued to crave more while careless of the suffering they caused. This way of violence is seen throughout the Old Testament and is prominent in *1 Enoch* (especially chapters 91-105) and in the Qumran commentary on Habakkuk and elsewhere. Buying and selling also is seen as a subtle form of plundering. This will be of particular interest when I examine Revelation 18 in chapter 10.

Conclusions

1. God hates injustice in all its forms. Violence is not simply physically abusing another; violence is a principle contrary to the covenant of God.
2. Those who gain unjustly through the hardship of another will themselves be plundered.
3. Redemption means the return of what has been plundered. An Edenic existence is hoped for when there will be peace and wealth. The hope is nationalistic. Those who live according to the covenant of God will live in peace.
4. The prophetic tradition regards injustice from the perspective of previous acts of injustice. Tradition is enriched with aspects of the new setting. The prophet, for example, sees the suffering caused by trade and this leads the prophet to denounce the merchant class.
5. Wealth is only condemned if the possessor forgets that the wealth is God's gift (Deut. 8.7).

6.   Holy war runs through the tradition, with the idea that God will act and destroy his enemies, but often by the next conquering violent power.[32] Tradition also depicts the punishment as violence being heaped upon the head of the violent (Ps. 7.15-16). The idea of self-punishment appears in over seventy places in the Old Testament.

The above six categories represent key prophetic understandings of the way God works and the way he expects people to live. I will demonstrate that John drew inspiration and understanding from them. He also rebukes his own people and the ruling nation of his own time. In comparing the Gandhian *ideal*, nonviolence would embrace all six categories. The traditions I have looked at are nationalistic. The idea of transforming the enemy is not prominent. But this does not mean that it is not present in the tradition. Israel is to be a light and blessing to the nations.[33] Israel constantly rebelled against God. God's concern for the victim is something that is distinctive. The LORD is not the god of the powerful. Especially in the Old Testament, traditions reveal God not as one who directly punishes, but who rather leaves people to suffer the consequences of their own actions. In the Old Testament are the seeds of the nonviolent God that we see emerging in the New Testament. It is a God who cares about the injustice that is practised on earth. He is outraged at the way groups oppress groups. In his dealings with Israel, what emerges is that Israel will only be content when it keeps God's covenant. In practising justice, peace will be established. But this peace can only be established by confronting the abuses by which the nations live. This is why Gandhi believed that it was better to be violent than condone the abuses with cowardice. Gandhi was right to say that there is more hope for the violent becoming nonviolent than for the careless person who does nothing except to stand by passively. The violent passion to see justice established (as we see in the Old Testament) I believe, with Gandhi, can become nonviolent passion. Nonviolence is not possible unless there is outrage at injustice. Revelation fully understood such outrage, as we will see. At this early stage in my argument, I suggest that justice was a key reason motivating John to denounce the violent of his time. John drew upon the above holy war traditions. John was outraged at the injustice perpetrated by Rome. For him, like the prophets, there is only one outcome for those who persecute and deceive. They will suffer their own violence. Later I will examine this theme in more detail in terms of Revelation.

---

32 However, there are exceptions (Dan. 7; Joel 3; Zech. 14).
33 We will see this in chapter 7.

CHAPTER 6

Faithful Witness through Martyrdom

In the last chapter we looked at Jewish traditions that stood against the powerful ruling classes. Israel's ruling classes were duly condemned for being careless of the poor and for oppressing the needy. The tyrant was told that he would fall by his tyranny. The message proclaimed to Israel was to be faithful to God's covenant. In so doing God would deliver the faithful from the powerful oppressor. Trusting in God was the hallmark of the faithful.

Nonviolence and Martyrdom

The nonviolent activist believes victory is gained through dying and not killing. It is not, therefore, surprising that martyrdom is considered something a nonviolent activist must be ready to endure. An important aspect of witnessing is martyrdom. In this chapter martyrdom will be considered as an act of faithful witness. I believe that insights from sociology and social anthropology can expedite a fuller understanding of the mindset of one who is prepared to die for a belief rather than kill for it. I believe John represents one such. E. and A. Weiner have provided an excellent study of martyrdom in the Jewish tradition and I will draw upon their work.

Function of Martyrdom

Sociologists and social anthropologists point out that central to understanding martyr-mindedness is the world-view from which the martyr comes. The Weiners point out that the potential martyr depends on a cultural-linguistic system that informs his or her identity and therefore motivates the individual or group to act in a certain way.[1] John, for example, developed and selected his tradition in such a way as to encourage the faithful to bear witness to God before the nations even to death.[2]

---

1 Weiners (1990):67. This is illustrated well when the mother exhorts her seven sons to die for the law. The author emphasizes that the speech was made in her own tongue (2 Macc. 7.21, 27).
2 Weiners (1990):53. 'Martyrdom is a social event intimately connected with the formation of groups and the strengthening of group identity'.

JUSTIFICATION

A devotee must justify his or her own religious group's beliefs by emphasizing the continuity between their present moment and the traditions that are so dear to their group.[3] Such justification can operate at several levels. It involves the use of proverbs, moral maxims and traditional wisdom that have been transmitted through story, myths and folklore.[4] Demonstrating to the group member that he or she must be ready to be martyred means using traditional stories about heroes who showed readiness to suffer and die for their beliefs. The devotee tells stories about ancient heroes from the community's tradition. In so doing, he or she encourages individuals to be ready to die when their way of life is challenged.[5] To this extent, the martyrs may not necessarily be responding to a particular situation. Rather, the group defines its situation through its narratives.[6] This is seen in many situations of conflict in our world today. Surely if the Irish were not so good at telling traditional stories the social boundaries between Protestants and Catholics would not exist as they do today!

HERITAGE

Following on from the previous section, we can surely agree that the development of any society or group depends on its loyalty to its heritage. Bruce Malina through his extensive anthropological explorations of the Mediterranean world concludes: 'Our ancestors passed down to us the set of lines they inherited, and with this we find ourselves in a cultural continuum that reaches back to the sources of our cultural heritage'.[7] It follows that martyrdom is in part the result of a received tradition, which can be added to in each succeeding period.[8] The cultural heritage and the narratives emphasize the differences of beliefs between the group and the ruling power.

CHALLENGE AND RESPONSE

When a person perceives that their actions reproduce the ideals of their group, they expect others in the group to acknowledge this. Anthropologists say that they are given honour. Some anthropologists understand that society is like a game of 'challenge and response'. It is a bit like table tennis. One hits the ball to one's opponents who responds by returning it. The one who fails to return the ball loses.

---

3 Berger (1990):40.

4 Berger (1990):31-32; related to this is the theory of social control. See Weiners (1990):16 and Riddle (1927 and 1931).

5 Weiners (1990):15. This what they call the 'theory of narration'.

6 Malina (1981):21-22 points this out in terms of his symbolic model. Behaviour is organized around expectations that are attached to objects that are of value to the tradition. Berger (1986):100 writes that a social situation is what it is defined to be by its participants.

7 Malina (1981):26; also Berger (1986):101 that our lives are in part dominated by those men of old who have been dead for generations.

8 This is referred to as the theory of cultural heritage and is associated with Turner (1974). See discussion in Weiner (1990):16.

They call this challenge-response game.[9] Consider this game in terms of honour. When the honour of a group is challenged, it can be seen that the challenger seeks to establish its honour over the group it challenged. In challenging the honour of the group, the challenging group attacks the truth and validity of the other.[10] From the perspective of Revelation, John presents the church as the challenger. The faithful witness challenges the principles of the ruling Empire and so upholds God's honour. The attacks on the church are the beast's response (cf. Rev. 11).[11] Revelation challenges values of the Empire such as greed and violence. Martyrdom establishes the social boundaries and prevents the group from apostasy. The greatest fear is apostasy for the church where members are seduced by success and power. Martyrdom is one way the church challenges the values of society and bears witness to the values that God represented such as love and forgiveness. The Weiners point out:

> the martyr makes believable those abstract principles that lie at the root of human connectedness, such as kinship, religious belief, national or ethnic solidarity or the more universal principle of "humanity". We are forced to take note of the martyr's conviction because it appeared true, valid and convincing enough to warrant self-sacrifice.[12]

Martyrdom strengthens the community and validates its convictions to the enemy. In so doing, it hopes to persuade them of its claims.

OUTSIDERS AND DEVIANTS

In situations of conflict, the dominant group labels the outsider with derogatory names and epithets. John, for example, saw himself and the followers of Jesus as 'deviants'. They were not of this world and were rightly labelled 'deviants' by Rome and the synagogue. They jeopardized the interests and social standing of the Roman Empire and the synagogue.[13] Malina and Neyrey note that the 'deviant label' derives from the perception of the labellers.[14] Such labellers are known as 'agents of censure'. In the case of Revelation 2.9-10, the synagogue members are the agents whom John perceives as disseminating a viewpoint to gain respectability in the eyes of Rome. The outside group develops a number of strategies to neutralize the label. The most appropriate form of neutralization for this discussion on martyrdom is to embrace the deviant label and so condemn the labeller. John, for

---

9 Malina (1981):30.

10 Weiner (1990):53; Riddle (1926-27):264-265 writes also that the function of martyrologies and apocalyptic literature is for social control of the threatened group.

11 Oakman (1993):12 writes: 'fundamental to an appreciation of John's theology is the identification of his concern for God's honor. From the standpoint of the Seer, God's honor has been offended by the course of earthly developments'.

12 Weiner (1990):52.

13 Malina and Neyrey (1991):100.

14 Malina and Neyrey (1991):102; see also Barclay (1995):115.

example, does not wish to placate the synagogue or the Roman authorities. John sets himself against the synagogue simply on the basis that he sees the synagogue in collusion with Rome.[15] John embraces the label 'outsider'. Those who were not outsiders are insiders and therefore traitors. The outsider, who is dangerous and a threat to the *status quo*, transforms this perception into a badge of honour.[16] John encourages his group to acknowledge their position as outsiders. One way of so identifying with the deviant label is through readiness to die for the beliefs that they hold and for which they have been labelled 'deviant'. Readiness to die in this setting is encouraged by the group's ability to draw from tradition people who have been ready to die and suffer for their beliefs. In this way martyrdom is not the deviant act of isolated individuals, but as the Weiners comment, 'the quintessential expression of the group's values'.[17] Malina and Neyrey write that 'it becomes an honor to have been rejected and condemned by such "morally reprehensible" people'.[18] They observe that the deviant label is redirected to the labeller. John, for example, accuses the synagogue of being 'a synagogue of Satan' and denies it the honoured title of 'synagogue of Jews'. Presumably, the synagogue had accused John and his followers of not being Jews because they were against the *status quo* that the synagogue enjoyed. But this very *status quo* becomes the reason for which John condemns the synagogue for not being Jews. This strategy is connected with those who resist an oppressing force by refusing to use violence. Readiness to die rather than use violence is a way of condemning the condemners. The martyr refuses to imitate the condemners because their actions of violence are those that condemn them. Gandhi made the same point when commenting that nonviolence is truly revolutionary because it is contrary to the violence of the oppressors. It is possible that the condemners will become admirers of the condemned because they are prepared to die rather than kill. In the case of Gandhean nonviolent action martyrdom is better than taking life. Honour is gained in death.

If martyrdom or accounts of martyrdom are common in a group's traditions, the group will be dedicated and focused on witnessing to their beliefs through martyrdom. If a member does not, he or she invalidates the honour of the martyrs in their tradition and becomes a coward in the eyes of their own community. This is a powerful motive for encouraging readiness to die, especially for the first-century Mediterranean dwellers who saw themselves as interrelated to others.[19] It is self-evident that such individuals test this interrelatedness in terms of the demands and expectations of others within their group who can grant or withhold honour.[20]

---

15 Argument is made more fully regarding Revelation 2.9-10 in Bredin (1998):160-164 and in chapter 10 of this book.
16 Weiners (1990):57.
17 Weiners (1990):57.
18 Malina and Neyrey (1991):109.
19 Malina (1990):55.
20 Malina (1981):55.

THE HOPE OF LIFE

We have already seen some factors that motivate a martyr. The significance of any religion depends upon the credibility of the banners it puts in the hands of its members as they stand before death.[21] Such banners are the narratives and traditions of its heritage. In the case of Jews and Christians, it is biblical traditions. Such encourage believers to think that death will result in either life in the continuance of the community or some form of life after death. The resurrection of the crucified Jesus was a very powerful incentive for the followers of Jesus to witness to the world by word and in readiness to die. The martyr hoped for his or her own resurrection. John did not fear martyrdom because Jesus was raised from the dead. If Jesus had not been raised, we would have to question whether John would have been so ready to be martyred. It is possible that a movement would have continued after Jesus' death and would have had a profound impact on the lives of many. But it is difficult to see that without the resurrection followers would have been so inspired to do what they did. The hope that martyrdom would keep Jesus' teaching and life a living reality would perhaps have inspired others to faithful witness before the oppressor as well as the hope of eternal life.

Traditions about Faithful Witnesses

Social groups find meaning in their traditions. Indeed these are more important than the specific situations they find themselves in. It is their oral and written traditions that provide the assurance. This is illustrated by a modern example, racists would not be prepared to die or be arrested for killing black people if they had not grown up within the tradition of white supremacy. It follows, therefore, that John would make a selection from his traditions. Particularly important would be narratives relating to victory over the enemy through voluntary death or suffering. Such would motivate the inheritors of the tradition to stay firm until death in the hope of victory. The Weiners observe three characteristics that define such a narrative: 'The martyr's motive is clear and noble, the dramatic confrontation is fully played out in the public arena, and there are the authorized versions of the hero's death'.[22] John draws upon such faithful witness traditions before the enemy in order to encourage steadfastness until death in memory of those who have gone before them as well as their conviction that they are on the side of justice.

Before I discuss more specifically Old Testament traditions about faithful witness, I need to consider briefly those who believe we must look elsewhere for such traditions. I agree with those who argue that martyrdom is developed through reflection on Hebrew traditions in the light of the social context.[23] But others argue

---

21 Berger (1990):51.
22 Weiner (1990):12.
23 Fischel (1946-47); Löhse (1955); Downing (1963); Frend (1965); Lampe (1981).

that the idea of martyrdom developed in the Greek hero cults.[24] There is little doubt, since the work of Martin Hengel, that Judaism during the Hellenistic period was influenced by Greco-Roman culture. Yet there is little evidence or reason to suggest that John would appropriate the very ideas he hated except in opposition to them.[25] Rather he draws upon his own traditions as long as there is sufficient material; especially material that attacks the rich, ruling oppressor.[26] Indeed there is considerable evidence of antagonism to Greco-Roman culture and its oppression among Jews.[27] It could be argued that all nations and individuals will respect and entertain the idea of sacrificing life for a cause, whether it be for a religious belief or, for example, to save the life of a child being attacked by a wild beast. There is surely nothing new about such a social phenomenon. However, this is neither motivated by the need to maintain social control nor to persuade the antagonist of the validity of one's truth claims, as it is the case in Revelation and Jewish tradition. Isolated examples of heroism, as is the case in Greek culture, do not encourage a community to be prepared to suffer and die for their beliefs and neither do they encourage social control or persuade the antagonist as in the case of John.[28] John must persuade his listeners and readers to be prepared to die for their heritage and in so doing remember those who have suffered and died for being Jewish. John does so by identifying and developing appropriate martyr narratives in his tradition. The heir must honour those who have gone before, lest their ancestors be seen to have died in vain. The Weiners note the importance of a group martyr view:

> The martyr's sacrifice implies that, according to the group's norms, this is the ideal demonstration of conviction. A loyal member is defined by implication as a person willing to sacrifice him or herself just as the martyr did. In other words, at the initial

---

24 Brox (1961); Campenhausen (1964); S.K. Williams (1975); Wengst (1987); Seeley (1989 and 1990); Bowersock (1995).

25 What Barclay calls oppositional acculturation (1996):97.

26 It is interesting to note in Chaim Potok's novel *My Name is Asher Lev* (Penguin, 1972) that the young Hasidic artist appropriates the hated Christian symbol of the cross in order to comprehend his own suffering as a Jew. For him there was no other symbol. However, such an appropriation is abhorrent to the Hasidic community. John's attitude is similar, he would not use overt foreign ideas. I agree with Bauckham (1995):91 and others that Jews and Christians were influenced by the culture of the Greco-Roman world. However, the dominant background is Jewish, especially regarding a text so thoroughly anti-Rome as Revelation. Yet, there is Hebrew tradition that is more compromising to the ruling nations, which presented some Jews with a reason for compromising with Rome. Thus, the dispute within Judaism (including John) remains one of divergent interpretations of a common religious heritage. John remains revolutionary and reactionary to the ruling nation; see Barclay (1996):82-98 regarding levels of assimilation.

27 Barclay (1996):97.

28 It could be so argued with Socrates. But he hardly represents a tradition, just an example of a philosopher's actions, and his death is connected with the immortality of the soul.

stages of group formation, martyrdom sets standards for praiseworthy acts that become standards for continued group membership.[29]

In the light of this, it is likely that John's model for exhorting his people to be faithful witnesses will be found in Jewish traditions relating to people who suffered and died as faithful witnesses. I will show that it was not difficult to forge continuity between the Old Testament figures who were prepared to die for their faith and John's setting. I contend that if John had not been able to draw upon Old Testament examples of those who were prepared to die for their faith, it is unlikely he would have been able to prepare others to die for their faith.

Summary

Martyrdom as a social phenomenon has been discussed against modern social and anthropological studies. Martyrdom accentuates the differences between a group's own culture and language and that of the antagonistic culture. The martyr persuades his or her own adversary of the validity of their truth claims. A writer such as John would not knowingly borrow from traditions that were perceived as idolatrous. More likely is the need to develop intertextually themes and traditions from one's own culture and language. A martyr is a martyr because he or she has been prepared to be one because of his or her own traditions. In the next two chapters, I will examine traditions about Jewish heroes in the Old Testament and later Jewish traditions. These heroes are those who bore witness to the one true God of Israel and were prepared to suffer and die for their beliefs.

---

29 Weiner (1990):58.

CHAPTER 7

Faithful Witnesses in the
Old Testament

During times of universal deceit, telling the truth becomes a revolutionary act.
George Orwell

Introduction

In chapter 6 I considered martyrdom as a way of witnessing to the powerful. In Revelation, Jesus and his followers are portrayed as 'faithful witnesses'. In this chapter I will consider traditions about 'faithful witnesses' in the Old Testament. This is a preliminary to studying the faithful witness themes as they occur in Revelation itself.

I consider that people who have been put to death by their enemies for their beliefs are faithful witnesses. But a faithful witness can also be one who has not chosen to die but still does so because of a belief. Many, for example, have died violently in Ireland while sitting in a bar shot by unknown gunmen. Such figures bolster the imagination of many from both sectarian communities of Ireland. They become martyrs who died with honour. Faithful witnesses who have died for their beliefs are good examples to those within their community. Black people who died anonymously in South Africa during the apartheid period remain martyrs for the cause of Black emancipation in addition to the better-known figures such as Steve Biko. Those who are ready to die often do so hoping that other people's faith in what they died for will be strengthened by their deaths.

Witnesses who Suffer

My examination of the Old Testament will be concerned with possible Second Temple understandings. I will examine the Old Testament as the completed sacred written corpus of the Jewish community. This study will not ponder the possible earlier strata of tradition that might or might not underlie the text as we have it. The Old Testament was not a disparate mixture of writings for the religious community as the biblical historian of tradition sometimes treats it. The sacred book inspired and vitalized individuals within the community from childhood to death. As they studied and heard the Old Testament, they frequently drew connections from one text to another - often this involved seeing a close relationship between earlier contexts and their own. The Jewish exegete of the first century CE allowed different biblical texts to inform each other. My discussion will respect relationships between texts that were presupposed and seen by the ancient reader and student. My overall concern is of course what it meant to John to read the stories of faithful witnesses in his Scriptures.

My criterion for selecting witnessing figures is that they suffered for their people vicariously. In some cases, through their readiness to suffer and die such figures gained a victory for that which they witnessed to. The highest expression is the figure of the servant songs found in Isaiah 40-55 (especially Isa. 52.13-53.12). The author of these songs was influenced by stories about Moses, Jeremiah, and Ezekiel. These songs in turn stirred the imagination of the writer of Daniel 7 in his depiction of the son of man and the wise ones in Daniel 11. The pierced one of Zechariah 12.10 also comes from the same fountain of tradition. The three heroes of Daniel 3 must be considered because in this story we read the closest account in the Old Testament to a martyr narrative as defined by sociologists. They are truly figures ready to die for their faith in the God of Israel. Their willingness to die strengthened the community. My choice of Psalm 73 and its expression of suffering and of the need to be ready to stay firm to God's covenant is an important message. My particular interest is the theme of eternal life that the Psalm presents. The idea that death is preferable to apostasy is indeed a premise that needs consideration in a discussion on martyrdom and one that would have influenced the first-century mind. Again, readiness to die has an impact on the onlookers

Moses

My study of faithful witnesses begins with Moses. The Deuteronomist tells us that God establishes his people Israel with the making of a covenant on Sinai with Moses.[1] He is faithful to God's commandments but suffers because of the constant rebellion of Israel (Ex. 6.9; 14.11; 15.24; 16.2-3; 17.2-4; 32) as he communicates God's testimonies to the people (Ex. 33.9-11). Moses was a very important figure for Jews of the first century and the New Testament writers tell us Jesus met Moses (Mt. 17.1-13; Mk. 9.2-13; Lk. 9.28-36).

Moses appears to be ready to die for his people (Ex. 32.30-33).[2] He intercedes on behalf of Israel so that they would not be punished and seems to offer his life for them.[3] Hengel considers this text a rare occurrence of the idea of the giving of one's life to atone for the guilt of others in the Old Testament.[4] Yet Hengel's reading is not without its problems. The evidence that Moses offers his life is based on the following words: 'blot me I pray thee, out of thy book which thou hast written' (Ex. 32.32b). If God does not forgive his people, Moses no longer wishes to live. Presumably, if they are forgiven, Moses will live. However, it is unlikely that the atonement will be achieved by Moses' sacrifice. Rather Moses only wishes to die

---

1 Traditions about the suffering of Moses depend on the Deuteronomist's editing which is contemporary with Jeremiah and Ezekiel. See Von Rad (1975):276.

2 North (1956):54; von Rad (1977); Hyatt (1983); Seitz (1989).

3 Hengel (1981):78.

4 Hengel (1981):8.

with his people and seeks atonement by intercession and not by sacrifice.[5] Intercessor is a key attribute of Moses.[6] Another tradition states that Moses, because of Israel's rebellion, lays prostrate before the LORD for forty days and forty nights with no bread or water in order that the LORD would not punish his people (Deut. 9.18). Moses suffered and was prepared to die through lack of food and water, in order to persuade God to forgive them. Therefore, there is no suggestion on the basis of Exodus 32.32 that he offered his life as a sacrifice. If God does not forgive them, he rather wishes to die with his people.[7] My reading neither reduces the importance of the text, nor denies that the text could be read in later tradition as Moses offering his life.

Moses suffers for his people when he prays: 'Let me cross over to see the good land beyond the Jordan, that good hill country and Lebanon' (Deut. 3.25). He declares to the people that: 'The LORD was angry with me on your account, and would not hearken to me' (Deut. 3.26; also Deut. 1.37 and 4.21-22). Moses bears the sin of his people in his punishment by forfeiting entering the Promised Land. Thanks to Moses, Israel enters the land while Moses takes upon himself the punishment due to Israel.

The faithful witness, Moses, is called to challenge the oppressor, Egypt. He proclaims God's word commanding Pharaoh to free the Israelites. If Egypt continues to persecute the Israelites, they too will suffer the consequences of their violence. Martyred liberation theologian and activist Barbé observed how Exodus reverses the classic myth of the mightiest and strongest as the victors: 'The expelled, the sacrificed, are the sources of new life, a new community, when one would have expected them to be simply incriminated and annihilated'.[8] Moses is God's witness to Egypt declaring that Israelite oppression must end. History is viewed here from the perspective of the innocent victim. God condemns the oppressor through Moses. Justice for Israel against Egypt is not achieved through violence. Barbé pointed out that liberation is not achieved through Moses killing the Egyptian guard as in Exodus 2.14. Moses declares to the Israelites 'the LORD will fight for you, and you have only to keep still' (Ex. 14.14). Moses gives an important testimony to his people that they must trust God for their survival as a people. This is not a message that would fall upon eager ears. A first-century reading of Moses would consider and remember how Israel relied on the king of Syria rather than trusting in God as 2 Chronicles 16 recounts. Such a reading would also know the story of how God acts against Israel's enemies, that as well as drowning the Egyptians he set enemy against enemy (2 Chr. 20.23). Moses proclaims an important message early in Israel's history: trust in God. But as the Bible testifies, Israel did not always trust God and suffered as a result. Moses' unpopular message led to the suffering of

---

5 Williams (1975):103; see Lyonnet (1970):123; van Henten (1997):61.
6 This interpretation is confirmed by TDOT VII, 294-5 - כפר can be understood as an act of intercession.
7 Meeks (1967):204.
8 Barbé (1989):36.

Moses and is the same message Moses was only too willing to die for. It is not difficult to recognize the dangers Moses faced when approaching the Pharaoh to ask him to free Israel. The Pharaoh could well have put Moses to death.

In sum, Moses is an example of a faithful witness. He proclaimed a message that called for obedience to God in spite of all the risks that entailed. Moreover, he suffered with his people and bore their punishment.

Faithful Witnesses in the Eighth and Seventh Centuries BCE

The tradition of Moses as a faithful witness continues into the eighth and seventh centuries. The three Major Prophets and the twelve Minor Prophets are the key figures during this period. Like Moses, they were confronted by God and driven to declare the word of God. Von Rad perspicaciously observes the possible consequences of that call: 'The logical end of the process which here began [i.e. in his call] was martyrdom for the prophet, if Yahweh so willed it'.[9] As a consequence of being called to witness to God, Amos, Hosea, the author of Isaiah 1-39 and Micah are set apart from their contemporaries and know loneliness.[10] Although there is no account of them being martyred or beaten, they suffered, like Moses, because of their radical application of the law to their generation, their message of justice and peace and their attacks on those who lived by violence (Isa. 1.11-17; Mic. 6.6-18; Amos 5.21-24).

JEREMIAH

The call of Jeremiah to prophesy that his nation would be destroyed is dated about 627 CE (1.6). Von Rad writes: 'The connection between witness-bearing and suffering is of course still closer and more logical in the case of Jeremiah...who is the martyr *par excellence* of the Old Testament'.[11] Jeremiah, like Moses, experienced rejection and faced death because of the unpopularity of his message. In a poignant verse, Jeremiah compares himself to a powerless lamb led to the slaughter (11.19). He was abused (15.10; 20.1-6), his life was threatened (18.18; 26.11), he endured loneliness (15.17) and he was beaten (20.1-2). Christopher Seitz suggests that, like Moses, Jeremiah must also suffer the same fate. He suffers because of the sins of his generation.[12] Moses sees the Promised Land (3.15-18), yet he must die away from the land. Similarly, Jeremiah is taken to Egypt against his will (43.1-7).[13] Jeremiah experiences the sins of Israel as his own.

---

9 Von Rad (1975):77.

10 Von Rad (1975):177.

11 Von Rad (1975):310; Spieckermann (1998):253-254 sees the origins of vicarious suffering in the priestly atonement procedures and in the prophets' intercession for the people. The concept of vicariousness was accomplished in the seventh and sixth centuries in the figures of Amos, Jeremiah and Ezekiel with the cult providing the theological framework.

12 Seitz (1989):11.

13 Seitz (1989):12.

Jeremiah's appointment is not just to proclaim God's message to Israel. He is also a 'prophet to the nations' (1.5). Jeremiah declares the words of God to his people that the nations shall bless themselves in him and in him shall they glory (4.2b). The well-being of the nations depends on Israel turning to God (4.1-2a). Jerusalem is the centre of redemption, a theme that we will see occurring elsewhere (3.17). Israel must cease from their evil ways. They must deal justly with their neighbours and no longer oppress the alien, orphan and widow. They must desist from violence and when they do the nations will not follow evil (7.4-11).

EZEKIEL

Von Rad writes about Ezekiel: 'His very appointment as the responsible watchman resulted in his having to discharge his office at the risk of his own life (Ezek. 33.1f)'.[14] Ezekiel is to bear the punishment of his people (4.5). Von Rad comments that 'the office with which the prophet is charged deeply affects the sphere of his personal life, and causes him to suffer; and here the suffering is expressly vicarious'.[15] Von Rad compares Ezekiel and the suffering figure in Isaiah 52.13-53.12 and this will be helpful when I discuss the song of the suffering servant in Isaiah 52.13-53.12. He further writes concerning Ezekiel 4.4-5:

> One can hardly fail to notice here the presence, in embryo, of thoughts which are later fully developed in Is. LIII, which, too, probably has a prophetic figure in mind...he Ezekiel tradition seems to have contributed to the development of the picture of the Servant of Yahweh who takes the guilt of the many upon himself.[16]

Brownlee also argues for a close relationship between Ezekiel 3.22-5.17 and the suffering servant of Isaiah 40-55.[17] He comments that the servant songs of Isaiah must have convinced admirers of Ezekiel that the songs really described Ezekiel.[18] It is certainly possible to show that later interpreters read Ezekiel 4.4-5 vicariously. For example, the Babylonian Talmud so understood it: 'God chastised Ezekiel in order to wipe away the sins of Israel' (*b. Sanh.* 39a).

Ezekiel proclaims the testimony of God to his people. His unpopular message states that God condemns his people for their violence against the oppressed. Ezekiel declares that violence leads to violence, and those who plunder will be plundered (12.19-20; 22.25, 29), and they will bear their own sins (14.10, 14). Ezekiel announces that God does not wish to destroy the wicked but hopes for their transformation (33.11). In 33.20 those who accuse God of being unjust are addressed by God's witness, each will be judged according to the way they live (cf. 2.23; 14.10,14). Yet there remains the hope of an Eden-like world (36.35).

---

14 Von Rad (1975):274-275.
15 Von Rad (1975):275.
16 Von Rad (1975):275; Cooke (1936):52; Zimmerli (1949):117; Reventlow (1998):37.
17 Brownlee (1986):51-52.
18 Brownlee (1986):52.

THE SUFFERING SERVANT IN ISAIAH 40-55

Isaiah 40-55 has been dated as early as the rise of Cyrus in 553 BCE and as late as the return of the exiles to Jerusalem. It is likely that the author/s of these chapters was aware of the witness Jeremiah and Ezekiel bore in their lives. Jeremiah and Ezekiel, as well as Moses' ministry, are significant for an appreciation of these songs. The first-century Jewish reader and listener would be fully sensitive to the themes they share: suffering, carrying the burden of a people and the risk of martyrdom.

Israel is charged to be God's witnesses to the nations:

> I have given you as a covenant to the people, a light to the nations, to open the eyes that are blind... (42.6-7; cf. 45.22; 49.6; 55.4; 56.6-7; 60.3, 14; 66.23).

Here is the idea common in the Old Testament, that all the nations will be blessed because of Israel (see Gen. 12.1-4; 22.18; 26.4 Pss. 2.10-11; 72.17; Isa. 2.2-4; 19.24; Jer. 3.17; 4.2; 25.7-8; Mic. 4.1-3; Zeph. 3.8-10; Zech. 14.16; Mal. 1.11).[19] The prophet announces that there will be a restoration of Israel's fortunes and Israel will be a witness to the nations that they might confess the LORD (40.1-11).

The servant is called a 'witness' in Isaiah 43.9-12 and 44.8-9 who takes his place in the law-court (43.9-12). The law-court image is popular in the Old Testament for presenting the ways in which God works (1 Sam. 24.15; Pss. 9.4; 43.1; 140.12; Lam. 3.58; Mic. 7.9). Caird comments that the popularity is connected with the fact that only in the law-court did the Israelites experience a systematic quest for truth governed by rules of procedure. Truth was for them something to be discovered and maintained in court.[20] The setting in 43.9-12 is the court in which all the nations and peoples are brought together and questioned regarding 'former things' (v.9b). Israel knows about such things for they have been revealed to them (40.21, 28; 41.27; 43.10; 44.8). The nations' witnesses are tested as to whether they speak the truth (v.9c). In v.10a, God's witness is introduced: 'you are my witnesses, says the LORD, and my servant whom I have chosen'. V.10b introduces the purpose of the calling of Israel, i.e. to be a servant. The purpose of being 'called a servant' is that 'you' (plural) might know and believe in the LORD. The 'you' refers back to 'you' at the beginning of v.10. The LORD has chosen Israel that Israel might believe so that they would testify to the nations. Witnesses of the nations were expected to testify (v.9c). The sense is, therefore, that the witnesses of the LORD must also testify to what God has done. The function of the witness is that of litigant. The role of the litigant in the ancient court was not to convince the judge and jury, but to convince the adversary, so placing a finger on his lips (Job 40.4). However, before

---

19 Whybray (1990):31-32 argues that this is a significant theme in Isaiah 40-55, but the consensus still supports von Rad (1977):139, although when commenting on 49.6 he writes: 'each man in his own way is to act as Yahweh's instrument to bring about the nations' recognition of Yahweh's universal sovereignty'. Gelston (1992):377-398 makes a thorough defence of the universalism of Isaiah 40-55.

20 Caird (1980):158.

Israel can testify, they must know the truth that is the purpose of their calling.[21] Consequently, I read with NEB rather than the NRSV for its translation of v.9c:

> Let them produce witnesses to prove their case, or let them listen and say: "That is the truth".[22]

If the witnesses of the nations cannot do as they are asked, then God is commanding them to be silent and accept what the LORD's witnesses testify. This is said more explicitly: 'Their witnesses neither see nor know' (44.9).

In the second song (49.1-6), the servant is described having a mouth like a sharp sword (49.2). This comparison indicates the function of a mouthpiece for the LORD by connecting senses of words that are proper to another, like sharp words.[23] The servant is God's emissary in bringing the nations to salvation: 'I will give you as a light to the nation that my salvation may reach to the end of the earth' (v.6b). Seitz writes of the calling of Israel to be a witness in Isaiah 40-55: 'The unit is not so much the account of a call as a report of one who had been called, and who is here commissioned for a new task'.[24] This new task is to be God's witness to the nations and for which the servant suffers (v.4).

In the third song (50.4-9), the servant has the disciple's tongue to help the weary with a word (v.4).[25] The song points to the faithfulness of the witness in speaking God's word, which results in maltreatment from his enemies (vv.5-6). However, the servant is confident that he will be vindicated (v.8). The suffering servant experienced affliction not unlike that of Jeremiah or of many other figures in Israel's experience.[26]

In the fourth song (52.13 - 53.12) the identity of the suffering servant is a source of much debate in modern Old Testament scholarship as it was among ancient Jewish and Christian scholars. The text does not make clear who is intended by the suffering figure. Von Rad suggested a Moses typology underlying the suffering figure: 'Moses is designated the Servant of God, indeed, he stands there as the prophetic prototype'. Later he observes of Moses: 'He too acts as mediator between Jahweh and Israel, he suffers, and raises his voice in complaint to Jahweh, and at

---

21 See von Rad's brief discussion (1977):249.

22 Observe the NRSV: 'Let them bring their witnesses to justify them, and let them hear and say, It is true'. The NEB contrasts the witnesses of the nations to that of the faithful witness.

23 Whybray (1990):137; Caird (1980):146.

24 Seitz (1996):234.

25 The NRSV has 'the tongue of a teacher'. The Hebrew suggests the tongue of those who are taught. The context of the verse suggest 'teacher' as it is a teacher who helps the weary with a word.

26 Seitz (1996):238; von Rad (1975):253; Eissfeldt (1964):341 writes: 'the Ebed is...the ancestor and representative of the people, endowed with the prophetic title of honour, servant, and thus thought of as a prophet. As such, as was indeed the task and fate of the prophets, for example Jeremiah, he has to work upon the people and to suffer for the people'.

last dies vicariously for the sins of his people'.[27] The Exodus themes underpinning Isaiah 40-55 also suggest that a Moses-type figure is being pressed in Isaiah 52.13-53.12 and that a new Moses and a new Exodus are hoped for.

The servant is rejected and acquainted with grief (53.3). God smote and wounded him for the sins of Israel (53.4). Likewise, Moses is maltreated for he could not enter the Promised Land because of the sins of the people (Deut. 1.37; 4.21). The exclusion from the land because of the sins of the people may be alluded to in Isaiah 53.8. In 53.7 the servant is compared to a lamb led to the slaughter, again heightening the vulnerable and humble personality of the servant:

> He was oppressed, and he was afflicted, yet he did not open his mouth; like a lamb that is led to the slaughter, and like a sheep that before its shearers is silent, so he did not open his mouth.

Chavasse sees in these verses an allusion to the rebellion of Israel against Moses narrated in Numbers 14.5, 16.22, 16.45, and 20.6. This is unlikely, however, as Aaron is also in the same position as Moses in Numbers. We would not say it is an allusion to the rebellion against Aaron. However, Moses' humility is a characteristic, for example, when rebuked by Aaron and Miriam (Num. 12.3).[28] Yet it is unlikely that the poet has in mind only the figure of Moses. Arguments can be made for a selection of Israelite heroes for the role of suffering servant.[29]

Comparing Isaiah 53.7 and Jeremiah 11.19 shows interesting similarities. Jeremiah like the suffering servant compares himself to a lamb led to the slaughter.[30] The same Hebrew words are used for 'to slaughter' and 'to lead'. Although there is a different Hebrew word for 'sheep', the connection of words occurs nowhere else in the Old Testament, thus raising the possibility of a literary relationship between Jeremiah and Isaiah 40-55. North urges caution, however, regarding Jeremiah: 'although his claims are in some respects attractive, it cannot be said that he suffered uncomplainingly. The most that can be said is that he contributed something to the portrait (liii.7, cf. Jer. xi.19)'.[31] The important point for my discussion is that Jeremiah is a suffering witness who lived in fear of his life because of the witness he was called to give.

As well as Jeremiah traditions, Brownlee posits traditions relating to Ezekiel underlying suffering servant traditions. He writes:

---

27 Von Rad (1975):261; North (1956):53-55; Chavasse (1964):152-163.

28 Chavasse (1964):155-156.

29 For a good assessment of the various suggested identities of the suffering servant see North (1956).

30 This thesis has a long pedigree. The tenth-century Jewish writer, Saadyah Gaon, suggested this connection on the basis of Jeremiah 11.19; also Ibn Ezra who finds Gaon's proposal attractive. For a summary of more modern approaches see North (1956):41.

31 North (1956):192; Reventlow (1998):31.

Tentatively, one may propose that Second Isaiah returned from the Babylonian Exile, himself leading a new Exodus, and that there he learned of Ezekiel's career from traditions alive on the soil of Palestine. Out of these traditions—together with Second Isaiah's acquaintance with the careers of God's great servants Moses, David, Job, and Jeremiah—the portrait of Yahweh's Servant emerged.[32]

As fascinating as the identity of the suffering servant is to the biblical scholar, it is nevertheless important to remember that Isaiah 52.13-53.12 is a key martyrological text. For Nickelsburg in his important 1972 study these verses were central for Jews in interpreting their tradition in a way that was relevant during a period of extreme crisis. This is a crucial claim for my argument. It allowed for 'the exaltation of the persecuted ones and the impending judgement of their persecutors'.[33] The presentation of the servant is my concern.

Isaiah says that the servant made of himself an offering for sin (53.10b).[34] He bore the sin of many and made intercession for their transgressions (53.12c). The idea of vicarious atonement is prominent. Identifying the interpretative framework for Isaiah 40-55's understanding of vicarious atonement is complex. The important point, for the purpose of this chapter, is that another person, through intercession, vicarious suffering and death, can atone for sin.[35] Quoting Cook, Wheeler Robinson made the interesting connection between vicarious suffering and the idea of group solidarity.[36] The idea of suffering until death rather than forsaking the truth claims of his social group would be a response to a challenge made to the group. Suffering by one would benefit others in their group. Suffering for the benefit of social solidarity is one plausible understanding of Isaiah 52.13-53.12. But we must not forget that the servant is also a witness to the nations.

As well as this understanding, I believe that the insights of Girard and Schwager can elucidate the text. We must not forget that the servant is innocent. He is wounded and smitten even though he did nothing to deserve it. We cannot say that the servant bears the sins of his accusers for the text states clearly that he is innocent. He bears the sins in the eyes of those who afflict him. For them he indeed bears the penalty of their sin. They see that in condemning him, they have come to recognize their crime. He is a light shining in their darkness. The author states that the suffering servant has borne the sin of many by being afflicted by God. God

---

32 Brownlee (1986):52.

33 Nickelsburg (1972):81.

34 The Hebrew is uncertain. NEB translates: 'and [God] healed him who had made himself a sacrifice for sin'. The NRSV seems to suggest that the servant was made a sacrifice for sin: 'When you make his life an offering for sin'.

35 Clements (1998):51 suggests as much. He believes that the text reflects the experience of defeat and exile. Therefore, without the temple there could be no sin-offering to guarantee the continuance of a holy relationship to God. Isaiah 40-55 states that God will accept the sufferings of the Servant-Israel, especially the unnamed prophet who becomes the scar by which the restored nation will be purified; also Hanson (1998):19.

36 Wheeler Robinson (1955):85. 'The idea of vicarious atonement...was latent in the ideas of group-solidarity...'

sought the salvation of the peoples and did so through his faithful witness i.e. the suffering servant. The witness' faithfulness to God is that which leads to his affliction by the violent onlookers (hence afflicted by God). But his exaltation (52.13) reveals to the onlookers the innocence of the witness and the truth of his testimony (hence he allows them to see the truth thus bearing their sins away).

The role of the suffering servant as a witness to the nations and those within their own tradition is discernible. The nations will see and have understanding because of the servant (52.15).[37] The difficult word יזה from the verb נזה meaning 'to sprinkle' in v.15a has caused problems for translators. Brownlee interprets the verse as the many nations being sprinkled for cleansing.[38] נזה signifies a sprinkling of blood, oil or water either with one's finger (Lev. 4.6) or a sprinkler (Lev. 14.7). The sprinkling was for cleansing (Lev. 4.6; 16.14; cf. 1 Pet. 1.2; Heb. 9.13-14). Young examines a possible first-century CE understanding of Isaiah 52.15. This first-century example might suggest that the Isaiah 52.15 was understood and heard as the nations being cleansed. The example is Acts 8.30-37 where Philip interprets the suffering servant to the eunuch who then wishes to receive baptism, i.e. the sprinkling of water (8.37). It is possible, but not certain, that the eunuch wished to receive baptism when he heard, from Philip, that the nations had received something similar in Isaiah 52.15.[39] This fits the context of the servant being a teacher of wisdom to the nations. LXX however translates נזה as θαυμάσαναι (to wonder at) and not to sprinkle.[40] In this case, the subject of the verb would be 'the many nations'. Thus, the nations will be in wonder because of him. Later, the fruits of the servant's mission are stated:

> [the servant] shall see the fruit of the travail of his soul and be satisfied; by his knowledge shall the righteous one, my servant, make *many* to be accounted righteous (53.11).[41]

The above reading of Isaiah 52.15 is in line with Isaiah's concern with the servant being a light to the nations. Waterman points out that the servant's future exaltation results from his suffering.[42] Nickelsburg points out that the 'servant is exalted in the presence of kings and the nations'.[43] The servant is associated with the Hebrew word ישכיל (52.13), which suggests one who teaches rather than prospers in this

---

37 Wheeler Robinson (1955):83 points out that the nations were impressed by the way he humiliated himself and confronted them in his silent suffering (52.15).

38 Brownlee (1964):208.

39 Young (1954):199-206.

40 Vulgate agrees with MT.

41 Seitz (1996):239, briefly connects 53.11 with 52.15.

42 Waterman (1937):32; Wheeler Robinson (1955):84; Watts (1998):138.

43 Nickelsburg (1972):24. Nickelsburg is right to read Isaiah 52.13-15 in this way. Later I will observe that Revelation 11 is strongly influenced by Isaiah 52.13-15. The two witnesses are exalted in the presence of those who had hurt them.

context.[44] Apostasy is ripe among the Israelites/nations whom the servant helps through his teaching, but suffers because of his witness to them (53.6).[45] Wheeler Robinson offers an interesting interpretation: 'they [the nations] see that Israel has suffered what the other nations deserved'.[46] The servant is not passive as the lamb metaphor suggests. The lamb is a deviant, outside normal behaviour. His humiliation and his silence before his oppressors are his active responses. In humiliation, he gains victory. This might explain why he impresses the nations. Those who respond with amazement feel shame. They behave with respect before the one they have caused to suffer. Their violence against the servant should be the violence they should receive as punishment for their wickedness. The witness, Israel, reveals to the nations the end consequence of violence. It is a violent death.

SUFFERING SERVANTS IN DANIEL

We can see in the Book of Daniel the use of Old Testament traditions applied to the author's particular situation.[47] This is seen in the use of suffering servant traditions as well as the influence of holy war tradition. Brownlee observed in the Old Testament a development in Jewish theology from holy war to martyrdom when he writes: 'to suffer martyrdom is to engage in Holy War'.[48] As we read in Daniel about those who are ready to die for their faith, Brownlee's observations are of particular interest.

The narrative relating to Shadrach, Meshach and Abednego in Daniel 3 resembles a martyr narrative, except that the three heroes do not die. The potential martyr's motive is clear:

> If it be so, our God whom we serve is able to deliver us from the burning fiery furnace; and he will deliver us out of your hand, O king. But if not, be it known to you O king, that we will not serve your gods or worship the golden image which you have set up (Dan. 3.17-18).

The motive is that the heroes will not worship any but the LORD. There is no indication whether or not they feared death. The heroes act in the knowledge that

---

44 The hiphil of the verb שׂכל can be used to instruct (Dan. 9.22; 1QS 9.19,20; 1QH 7.26). However, it could be objected to, as there is no clear object of the verb as in Daniel 9.22. Yet, the context of being a light to the nations suggests that the servant has a mission of giving understanding to the nations through his faithfulness to God in spite of suffering and death. Brownlee (1963):211 translates v.13: 'Behold, My Servant shall teach wisdom'.
45 Reventlow (1998):29.
46 Wheeler Robinson (1955):85; Isaiah 53.5 is the significant text in illustrating his understanding.
47 Goldingay (1987):284. What he calls 'situational midrash'.
48 Brownlee (1983):281-292; Klassen (1992):869 has observed hints of a shift from the biblical warrior God in segments of Judaism before Jesus' time. He notes also that LXX translates 'man of war' to 'one who destroys war (Ex. 15.3; Isa. 42.13; Judith 9.7 and 16.3). Yoder (1972):87 writes: 'The prophets remolded the holy war heritage in the use they made of it in recalling Israel to trust God'.

they might not be delivered. Death is preferable to apostasy.[49] The three heroes are warriors in a holy war. They are the righteous ones who are called upon to fight human wickedness. However, in this case it is not only a physical war but also a spiritual one.[50]

The narrative of the three heroes recounts a confrontation with the king played out in the public arena. The heroes are accused by members of the king's court of not obeying a decree issued by the king (v.12). The king is furious when he hears the report of the informers. The narrator establishes the scene for the contest between the Israelite heroes and the king. The noble spirits of the three men do not impress the king. Yet he offers a way out hoping for the heroes to confess their allegiance to him (v.15). The apostasy of the faithful is the great desire of the king. Through apostasy, the three would lose face in their own eyes and within their own community. On the other hand, readiness to die for their beliefs leads to greater group identity. The Weiners observe: 'One of the paradoxes of martyrdom is that the group is strengthened when individual members die as martyrs'.[51] This is understandable against the social theory of labelling and deviance in which it becomes an honour to have been rejected and condemned by the king of the powerful empire.[52] The confrontation between the king and the three men is a contest between prevailing truth and the martyr's conviction. In leading the three men to apostasy, the king would validate the accepted truth of the empire. If the three do not back down the king has to put the heroes to death. In putting them to death, he hopes similarly to establish the truth of the empire that the heroes have challenged by disobeying the king's decree. The outcome is that the three men are delivered. This results in Nebuchadnezzar's confession of the true God (v.28); in a decree making it a crime to speak against the LORD (v.29); and in the promotion of the three heroes (v.30). The three are martyr types but also holy warriors who are victorious against their enemy. Their weapons are not swords, horses and chariots. Rather their weapons are faithfulness and conviction.[53]

Continuing with the martyr theme in Daniel is the appearance of the מַשְׂכִּילִים (the wise ones sometimes referred to as the Maskilim) in Daniel 11.33:

> The wise among the people shall give understanding to many.

The Maskilim will fall and shall receive a little help and by their falling a cleansing will occur (v.35). Some suggest that v.35 may be the oldest interpretation of the suffering servant of Isaiah 40-55.[54] We observe above that the servant of Isaiah 40-

---

49 Goldingay (1987):74.
50 Brownlee (1983):285.
51 Weiner (1990):62.
52 Malina & Neyrey (1991):109.
53 Brownlee (1983):288.
54 Ginsberg (1953):400-404; Bruce (1955-56):176-190; North (1956):7, 9-10; Russell (1960):138-139; Brownlee (1964):211; Nickelsburg, (1972):24-25; Goldingay (1987):284, 303; Collins (1993):385; Leske (1998):160-161; contrary Williams (1975):112: even

55 is a witness who enlightens others and suffers because of his testimony. Similarly, Daniel depicts the wise ones as those who give understanding to many (v.33a). The similarities are particularly striking with Isaiah 53.11:

> he shall see the fruit of the travail of his soul and be satisfied; by his knowledge shall the righteous one, my servant, make many to be accounted righteous.

Also, the wise ones lead people to understanding (11.35; cf. 12.10):

> and some of those who are wise shall fall, to refine and to cleanse them and to make them white, until the time of the end, for it is yet for the time appointed.

Death has a cleansing effect in Daniel 11.35 (cf. 12.10). Who benefits from the death of the wise ones? Do the wise ones die for those who join themselves to them with empty words or is it for themselves? The similarities with Isaiah 40-55 might suggest that the wise ones suffer for others. Goldingay also agrees when he points out that the insincere adherents of v.34b are more plausible for those who are cleansed than the discerning of v.35a.[55]

Bruce observes: 'On these maskilim, as on the Isaianic Servant, the brunt of suffering falls on them because of their faithfulness to Israel's God'.[56] Ginsberg proposes that משכילים is an allusion to ישכיל in Isaiah 52.13.[57] משכילים is a derivative of שכל meaning 'to understand or to prosper'. The word implies one who instructs (Dan. 9.22).[58] Bruce suggests that not only the משכילים are modelled on the Isaianic servant but also the one like a son of man, who represents the 'saints of the Most High' in 7.13 and v.18.[59] It is not an obvious connection in terms of language. Yet there are similarities in theme: the saints, like the servant, are expected to suffer (7.25); similarly, the saints will be exalted (7.27). However, we

---

Williams is prepared to acknowledge that there are terminological parallels with Isaiah 53. His only problem is the absence of vicarious suffering being effective for others in Daniel. But this is not so, there is the same aspect in Daniel 11.35.

55 Goldingay (1987):280; also Nickelsburg (1972):24; contrary Williams; Collins (1993):386: Collins objects to the vicarious interpretation due to the fact that the משכילים have their effect on the רבים by instructing them and not by dying for them. However, the suffering servant of Isaiah 52.13-53.12 both instructs [ישכיל עבדי](52.13) and suffers for others (53.11), so also argued here do the *maskilim* in Daniel 11.35; Horsley (1987):63-64 discusses the *maskilim* as wise teachers who were being martyred for their faith. He writes: 'The motivation for active and steadfast resistance, besides an unshakeable attachment to the Torah, was the conviction that God was finally about to realize his historical purpose'. Horsley raises the possibility that the *maskilim* were committed to nonviolence, but as he acknowledges, there is not enough textual evidence to support this.

56 Bruce (1955-1956):176.

57 Also Nickelsburg (1972):24-25.

58 See Nickelsburg (1972):24.

59 Bruce (1955-1956):176 and (1960):65.

must note the contrast in that victory is not achieved by vicarious suffering in Daniel 7, which is what is so distinctive with the suffering servant of Daniel 11.35.

THE PIERCED ONE IN ZECHARIAH 12.10

Zechariah 12-14 is concerned with events leading to the establishment of God's universal kingdom. In this kingdom, many from the nations will confess the LORD and go on pilgrimage to Jerusalem (14.16; cf. Gen. 12.1-4; 22.18; 26.4; Pss. 2.10-11, 72.17; Isa. 2.2-4; Jer. 3.17, 4.2; Mic. 4.1-3; Zeph. 3.8-10; Zech. 14.16; *Ps. Sol.* 17.30-32 and vv.34-35). A theme associated with the events leading to the end is the pouring out of the spirit of compassion and supplication (12.10). In the last days, the spirit of compassion and supplication will be poured out upon God's chosen people. The spirit of compassion will lead the chosen people to see the one whom they pierced. There is uncertainty about the one they will see. Translators are hesitant about whether to accept the MT reading 'to me' or a conjectural correction of the text to 'to him'.[60] The result of 'seeing' is that they will lament as for a first-born child. Some scholars understand that the corrective reading 'to him' is to Jewish martyrs killed in war by the nations and that their death in the final battle is the price of Jerusalem's salvation.[61] Mitchell is probably right when he suggests that there is no one person in mind, 'but a considerable number of godly persons who have perished by violence'.[62] Zechariah 12.10 is an example of vicarious suffering that has redemptive power for the nation. To this extent, it is in line with Isaiah 52.13-53.12.

Peterson objects to the connection with Isaiah 52.13-53.12. He sees that there are two fundamental differences between Isaiah 52.13-53.12 and Zechariah 12.10. First, the servant in Isaiah 52.13-53.12 suffers from the LORD's intents. Second, the suffering has a vicarious effect on the people, whereas in Zechariah 12.10, people have killed the individual and the effect is one of lamentation.[63] Contrary to Peterson there are clear similarities with the fourth servant song of Isaiah. First, the servant of Isaiah was wounded (חלל). Although the verb for 'pierced' (דקר) in Zechariah is different from Isaiah the two verbs are found in synonymous parallelism in Jeremiah 51.4. Second, in Isaiah, those who caused him to suffer were shocked by their violence (52.15) and were accounted righteous because of their response (53.11). Such also is the sense of Zechariah 12.10. Those who pierced him also came to see their crimes as a result of receiving the spirit of compassion. This is stated in Zechariah 13.1:

---

60 NRSV translates the third singular while LXX and the Vulgate prefers the MT first person singular suffix as does NEB and NIV. In the latter, the pierced one is the speaker which is God. Therefore, death is not in the mind of the author which is implausible unless taken as metaphorical. See discussion in Redditt (1995):132-133.

61 Jones (1962):161; to some extent Mitchell (1912):331; contrary Petersen (1995):121; also against this would be the expectation of אליהם and not אלי, but the singular suffix can have a collective reference, see Waltke and O'Connor (1990):113.

62 Mitchell (1912):331.

63 Petersen (1995):121; Reventlow (1998):37.

On that day there shall be a fountain opened for the house of David and the inhabitants of Jerusalem to cleanse them from sin and uncleanness.

Not only are those who pierced the victim contrite, they are also able to cleanse their sins (cf. Isa. 52.15 and Ezek. 36.25).

SUFFERING WITNESSES IN THE PSALMS

The Psalms functioned liturgically within the temple reinforcing Israel's identity and history. The psalmists were often occupied with the suffering and oppression that Israel experienced. The author of Psalm 73 (and Ps. 49) engaged in the universal questions of innocent suffering and death. The psalmist seeks to persuade his community to remain faithful to its own traditions in spite of their apparently powerless and hopeless situation. Discussion of Psalm 73 will illustrate these points.

Psalm 73 declares that God is upright (v.1), yet God's faithful ones are suffering economic and material poverty (v.3). The psalmist is preoccupied with the problem of the prosperity of the wicked.[64] The innocent ones suffer violence and oppression at the hands of the powerful. The powerful are unjust and violent (vv.6-8). The unjust are able to deceive and oppress the poor. This suggests the possibility that apostasy among the people of Israel was a reality (v.10). Eaton comments that it was easy for the community to adhere to the teaching of the wealthy who speak against God. However, one who is loyal has to bear daily suffering and is naturally tempted to think his stand is in vain.[65] Being faithful in their witness sustains Israel's hope and obedience to tradition:

If I said, 'I will talk on in this way', I would have been untrue to the circle of your children (v.15).

The psalmist says that if he spoke like those Israelites who join the wicked he would betray the generation of God's children. What enables the psalmist to avoid renouncing his personal relationship with God? Weiser comments: 'the very moment when he is no longer able to see his God, he at least perceives the fellowship of the believers'.[66] If the witness denies God by praising and accepting the powerful, he betrays not only God, but also the children of God.[67] The psalmist includes words of encouragement to those who are faithful. There will be a destruction of the oppressor (vv.18-19). There is a suggestion of a heavenly bliss

---

64 Bauckham (1998):85.
65 Eaton (1967):185 also considers Isaiah 49.4, 50.6 and 53.4-5 which also have been observed in this chapter; Weiser (1962):510 suggests that 'the crowd eagerly listens to the fashionable spirit of the new age'; Anderson (1983):vol.2, 532 writes: 'Probably the wicked in their affluence appeared so impressive that even their evil seemed to be attractive'.
66 Weiser (1962):511.
67 Eaton (1967):185.

beyond earth (vv.23-26).[68] Weiser argues that there is no possibility that the poet sees his sufferings coming to an end in his own lifetime. Rather he hopes for the consummation of his communion with God after death.[69]

Similarly is the hope noticeable in Psalm 49.15. Here the poet reflects on the fact that the rich oppressors seem to have a happy lot (cf. Jer. 15.13-14; Wis. 2) yet he believes that God will ransom the soul from the power of Sheol (v.15; cf. 1QH 3.20). Anderson considers the possibility that the verse may allude to deliverance from present suffering but nevertheless concludes that this is an unlikely context. He points out that Sheol is the ultimate goal for both wicked and righteous. Therefore, deliverance is not seeing Sheol but being raised to life to enjoy fellowship with God.[70] Weiser comments that the poet expresses a confidence that at death God will take care of the righteous and will 'not abandon him to the power of the underworld'.[71]

Summary of Findings

Moses is faithful to God and suffered because he spoke God's word to Israel and Egypt. The testimony Moses gives is contrary to the values of the powerful nation and all that it represents: violence and oppression. There are some nonviolent aspects in the Moses narrative. Moses' central message is: 'Trust in God'. Moses himself discovers that liberation does not come through him killing the Egyptian guard (Ex. 2.14). It resulted in the process of liberation being delayed. Moses suffers with his people and for them. He bears the punishment they should have paid when he is unable to enter the Promised Land.

Jeremiah is opposed and oppressed because he gives his faithful testimony against oppression and violence. He hopes Israel will practise justice thus leading to the transformation of the nations from their violent ways. Jeremiah suffers the consequences of Israel's sin feeling their oppression as his own.

Ezekiel likewise proclaims God's message against the oppressor. Although the emphasis is much more on the religious crimes of Israel than, for example, in Amos, the message is still challenging the violent oppressors to repent. His message is that God wants transformation and not their destruction. His role as God's witness results in his suffering, and, like Moses and Jeremiah, he experiences Israel's sin as his own.

---

68 Anderson (1983):vol.2, 535 suggests that Psalm 73 represents a tentative venture to go beyond the current beliefs that the after life characterized a shadowy Sheol existence to the possibility of a heavenly bliss. Certainly in the case of Psalm 73 the connection is tentative but is significant in that there is a push towards understanding innocent suffering; also Rowley (1955):175; contrary Westermann (1989):141-142 who makes the unqualified assertion that there is no question of a bodily resurrection.

69 Weiser (1962):514; Rowley (1955):175.

70 Anderson (1983):vol.1, 379.

71 Weiser (1962):390; Rowley (1956):171; Caird (1980):245.

The servant of Isaiah 40-55, and particularly 52.13-53:12, witnesses about God to Israel and the nations. In doing so, he suffers. Through martyrdom, many are brought to God. In 52.13-53.12, ideas that only power and might can conquer are challenged. Rather, weakness and innocence triumph over evil by the transformation of the antagonist.

In Daniel 3 three young men witness to the LORD before the emperor in spite of the threat of death. The delivery of the three men from the furnace strengthens the group and falsifies the accepted state truth based on oppression and violence.[72] We find a more developed picture of suffering witness that brings about the transformation of the enemy. The witness is for the community of Israel and to the nations. In 3.28-30 we become aware of the story that the emperor of Babylon accepts the witness of the three men (cf. also 6.25-27).

In Psalm 73 there are parallels with the suffering servant of Isaiah. Even though there will be suffering and failure, his portion will be with God forever (73.26; cf. Isa. 53.12; 4 Macc. 18.3 and others). The idea of resurrection in the Psalms, especially Psalm 73, is associated with the question of why the innocent suffer. The righteous may expect to die for their beliefs but there is hope of life after death. The poet expresses a hope that the righteous will have an eternal relationship with God. Missing in the Psalm is the idea of vicarious suffering. The redemption of the innocent and powerless is a real hope in this encouraging text even for those powerless individuals who have died. It is not a martyrological narrative, but it presents key components that form a martyrological context. It may be influential to John, along with other texts, for his understanding of how the oppressor will be cast down and his hope to be eternally in the presence of God.

Conclusions

In the Old Testament God's witnesses:
1. Proclaim God's word to all opposed to God.
2. Suffer.
3. Are willing to die for their beliefs.
4. Take upon themselves another's suffering or death.
5. Will be justified by God.
6. Benefit their own people,
7. Benefit the nations.

These seven points are key ideas attached to faithful witnesses. It will be important to see to what extent these ideas reappear and develop in later Jewish thought as well as in Revelation. For Gandhi, many of the aspects above would be present in his thinking. There is in the above aspects the idea that nonviolence and weakness will transform the antagonist.

---

72 Nickelsburg (1972):55 and 95 writes that Daniel 3 and 6 are intended to inculcate steadfastness during the Antiochan persecution.

CHAPTER 8

Faithful Witnesses in
Later Tradition

I examined in the previous chapter traditions about faithful witnesses in the Old Testament. In doing so, I attempted to establish a literary context for understanding John. In this chapter I will explore faithful witnesses in later Jewish tradition. This tradition was in dialogue with Old Testament traditions in response to its own specific social situation. Again, in establishing this later literary context I am driven by the need to form more fully the context with which John was familiar and in dialogue with.

The Social Background to Later Jewish Tradition about Martyrdom and Witness

The development of martyrdom as a way of witness within Judaism is especially associated with the reign of Antiochus Epiphanes from 175 BCE. Three events stand out. (1) The ruthless and inept handling of Judea by Roman procurators leading up to 66 CE which marks the beginning of the rebellion of the Jews leading up to the destruction of the temple in Jerusalem. (2) The destruction of the temple in 70 CE. (3) The suppression of the Bar Kochba revolt in 132 CE. Without dispute, these events were significant for the rise of a Jewish martyrology. Martyrdom was a way of boosting morale and group identity against a powerful enemy who was determined to see Judaism fully accept the Hellenistic way.

Frend, however, rightly observes the importance also of the Old Testament for such a development: 'The early history of the Jews, as preserved in traditions enshrined in the earlier books of the Old Testament told of a long struggle against the odds, and an even greater one to maintain religious cohesion'.[1] John did not simply draw upon traditions resulting from the reign of Antiochus IV but also upon the Old Testament itself. John attempted to show that the issues his community faced had already been faced by faithful Israelites narrated in the Old Testament. Part of his concern was to strengthen the new Israel's distinctiveness. This was defined in part by the great figures of the Old Testament who had suffered under Egypt, Assyria, Babylon, Persia and Hellenistic empires. John had showed that Israelite rulers always sold out to the powerful nations because they did not trust God. Instead, they persecuted the faithful. As the Book of Daniel depicted the events and reign of Antiochus in continuity with the previous imperial rulers, it is

---

1 Frend (1965):31.

likely that John read Daniel 10-12 in continuity with the struggles with Egypt, Assyria and Babylon. John drew upon his tradition to present the new Israel, the church, in continuity with the situation of those who had suffered and died for their faith as related in the pages of the Old Testament. Just as it was the destiny of the Old Testament prophets to experience persecution, so it was also the lot of the prophetic witness of Jesus.[2]

In this period, the relationship between Judaism and Greco-Roman culture and beliefs was important. It will be helpful to consider briefly the climate and possible responses of Jews to that society as well as how relationships within the Jewish religion were affected. My selection of material for this section is restricted again to material that is at odds with the powerful empire. As we will see in the next short section, there were many responses to Greco-Roman culture and every response was influenced by that society. Hellenism influenced even the most ardent Jewish groups.

Adapting to the Ways of the World

Martin Hengel has shown that Jews, either from the Diaspora or Palestine, were by no means immune to Hellenization.[3] John Barclay offers three ways for establishing a greater appreciation of how a Jew might relate to Greco-Roman ideas. Such will help to assess the ways in which Jews were responding to the challenge of Hellenism.[4] This is important for understanding Revelation, in particular, Revelation's attitude towards both Rome and other Jewish groups. The first of Barclay's ways is *assimilation* which is the greatest threat to any ethnic group's distinctiveness - those who are assimilated would rightly be labelled, from their own group's perspective, 'deviant' – people who have abandoned their heritage. The second way is *acculturation*. This will be explored further to show the levels to which some Jewish literature had acculturated itself to the alien culture in language and education.[5] The acculturized group may consider themselves Jews, but others within Jewish tradition may withhold such an appellation, especially those who are strongly antagonistic to Greco-Roman ideas and way of life. The third way is *accommodation*. Barclay observes three levels of *accommodation*. (1) Submersion of Jewish cultural uniqueness. (2) Re-interpretation of Judaism preserving some uniqueness. (3) Antagonism to Greco-Roman culture.[6] Overall, it is erroneous to say, from a modern perspective, 'who is a Jew and who is a deviant?' A Jew might be at various stages of the above ways. Barclay writes: 'A Jew who was assimilated to the extent of attending a Greek school and visiting the Greek theatre might be

---

2 Trites (1977):160.
3 Hengel (1974); also a point made by Barclay (1996):82-88, 101.
4 Barclay (1996):92.
5 Barclay (1996):95.
6 Barclay (1996):97.

considered by some Jews as "apostate" but fully accepted as an observant Jew by others'.[7]

My concern here is to identify material close in time to John. Texts which can be categorized as antagonistic to Greco-Roman culture and whose ideas were popular and rooted in biblical traditions. This will facilitate greater understanding of the Jewish intellectual responses to Hellenism. It must be remembered that defining what was a faithful Jewish response also motivated such Jewish responses. Consequently, there was much altercation about who was and who was not a faithful Jew within the various synagogues of Palestine and the Diaspora.

Testimony through Suffering

The First Martyr Abel

The Old Testament does not present Abel as a faithful prophet. There is no hint that his death resulted from his faithful witness. Neither is there any element of vicarious suffering in the account of his death. Yet in the New Testament Abel is elevated to a martyr-prophet.[8] Jesus placed Abel at the beginning of the line of martyred righteous prophets (Mt. 23.35; Lk. 11.50-51). He described the Pharisees and scribes as the offspring of Cain who killed Abel (Mt. 23.34-35; cf. 1 Jn 3.12; Jude 11). Abel is presented as a faithful witness who acted in righteousness (Heb. 11.4). Abel's blood is compared to Jesus' blood shed on the cross (Heb. 12.24). This relates to the powerful impact it has for salvation. Such traditions are probably either a development of the New Testament writers and later Jewish tradition.[9]

Outside the New Testament, Abel was also understood as a martyr. In 4 Maccabees the father of the seven young martyrs read the account of Abel to his sons:

> He read to you about Abel slain by Cain, and Isaac who was offered as a burnt offering, and of Joseph in prison (4 Macc. 18.11).

The father draws upon Abel as a model of martyrdom. It seems likely that the status of Abel was elevated to that of a faithful witness to motivate those who were about to die for the testimony they gave.[10]

There is an interesting development of the Cain and Abel narrative in the Palestinian Targums. McNamara writes of the presentation of Abel in the Targums: 'we find Abel considered as a martyr who died for the point of doctrine denied by

---

7 Barclay (1995):118.
8 McNamara (1966):158; Vermes (1975):116; Pobee (1985):28.
9 McNamara (1966):157.
10 Hadas (1953):241.

Cain'.[11] The following targumic text is an important development of the Old
Testament story of Cain and Abel:

> Cain answered to Abel: 'Therefore your offering was accepted with delight, but my
> offering was not accepted with delight'. Abel answered: "The world was created by
> love and is governed according to the fruit of good deeds. Because the fruit of my
> deeds was better than yours and more prompt than yours, my offering was accepted
> with delight". Cain answered and said to Abel: 'There is no Judgement, and there is no
> other world, there is no gift of good reward for the just and no punishment for the
> wicked'. Abel answered and said to Cain: 'There is Judgement, there is a Judge, there
> is another world. There is the gift of good reward for the just and punishment for the
> wicked'. On account of these things they were quarrelling in the field and Cain arose
> against Abel his brother and drove a stone into his forehead. The Lord said to Cain:
> 'Where is Abel your brother?' He said: 'I know not. Am I my brother's keeper?' He
> said: 'What have you done? The voice of the blood(s) of your brother which was
> swallowed up by the ground cries before me from out of the earth. Now because you
> have killed him, you are cursed by the earth ...' (*Ps. Jon.* 4.8-11, tr. Vermes; cf.
> Josephus *Ant.* 1.52-56).

Abel witnesses to God's goodness before Cain leading McNamara to consider Abel
'a confessor of the faith'.[12] Cain denies that God acts with justice or love and claims
rather that he acts with no logic. The result is that Cain kills Abel.[13] Cain acts in this
way because he has no fear of retribution: 'There is no gift of good reward for the
just and no punishment for the wicked' (cf. Wis. 1.13; 2.1)[14]. Abel's blood calls out
for justice (*Ps. Jon.* 4.10; cf. *Jub.* 4.3). Cain is punished and God vindicates Abel's
testimony.

Abel was a prototype of the just teacher and martyr in the first century CE.[15] As
we have seen, there is evidence for this understanding of Abel in the New Testament
and 4 Maccabees. Josephus' account also elevates the status of Abel which again
suggests a development of the Abel figure early enough to suggest that the Targums
reveal first-century tradition:

> for Abel, the younger, was a lover of righteousness, and, believing that God was
> present at all his actions, he excelled in virtue (Josephus *Ant.* 1.52-53).

Abel believes in a God who is present in all things and who guides him in the way
of righteousness.

The New Testament corroborates Targum tradition to the first century. In
Matthew and Luke, Abel represents the first of a series of prophets - sent by God -

---

11 McNamara (1966):158 (not in Targum *Onkolos*).
12 McNamara (1966):157.
13 Isenberg (1970):435: the reason for the murder is the argument about reward and
punishment, a day of judgement, and the world to come.
14 Wisdom of Solomon will receive further discussion in this chapter.
15 Vermes (1975):116.

whose blood was shed by hostile groups (Mt. 23.35; Lk. 11.51).[16] It is also suggested that Jude had in mind Targum tradition.[17] Jesus' disciples, like Abel in the Targums and the prophets in the Old Testament, are portrayed proclaiming the unpopular teaching that judgement will come if there is not a transformation away from violence. In proclaiming this, like Cain and the prophets, they must be ready to suffer and die for such a message (Mt. 10.7-24). There will be judgement not only for those who kill, but also for those who are angry with their neighbours (Mt. 5.22). Jesus declares to his disciples that whoever rejects their message will be judged and punished (Mt. 10.15; 11.22). John the Baptist calls those who reject his message a 'brood of vipers' (Mt. 3.7-10). He challenges them, stating that they must bear better fruit. The offerings of the Pharisees were not pleasing just as Cain's offering was not acceptable. Jesus like John the Baptist warns the Pharisees of the judgement that will befall them. Possibly Matthew had in mind the type of death Cain experienced (*Jub.* 4.31-33). Cain is killed with the same weapon that he used to kill Abel (see below for quote). The Jewish leaders are like Cain (Mt. 23.35). Matthew presents these groups as having no belief in judgement or justice, which is why they are able to kill so easily. They have no understanding that their own violence will fall upon their own heads. Although Jewish leaders believed in the right punishment for the precise crime, they could not see their own crimes. They lived as if there was no such punishment. Like many leaders in the world, they lived by violence and vengeance.

In sum, in the Targum tradition, Abel acted in accordance with his beliefs. Those who heard this story in the synagogue would be encouraged to testify to the LORD. Abel was worthy of imitation, thus strengthening group morale and confidence in its cultural heritage.

What does Abel's death achieve?

> that upon you [the scribes and Pharisees] may come all the righteous blood shed on the earth, from the blood of Abel (Mt. 23.35; cf. Lk. 11.51).

> And to Jesus, the mediator of a new covenant, and to the sprinkled blood that speaks more graciously than the blood of Abel (Heb. 12.24).

The blood of Jesus speaks better things than the blood of Abel precisely because it cries from the ground for mercy, not retribution.[18] Instead of pleading for vengeance like the blood of Abel or that of the Maccabean martyrs, Jesus' blood

---

16 McKay (1996):84, 90:'Isaac and Abel call to mind the sacrifice of a beloved innocent'.

17 Bauckham (1990):79-80; also Grelot (1959):59-88; Isenberg (1970):433-444 argues that the tradition reflects anti-Sadducean polemic.

18 Caird (1984):85; Harrington (1993):94 suggests that Hebrews 12.24 challenges ideas of vengeance.

begs only for forgiveness and redemption.[19] This portrayal of Abel is illustrated in *Jubilees* in which the blood of Abel cries out from the ground to heaven making accusation against Cain (4.3). In chapter 4.31-32 the punishment is described:

> And he was killed by stones because he killed Abel with a stone.... Therefore it is ordained in the heavenly tablet: "With the weapons with which a man kills his fellow he shall be killed " (4.31-32).[20]

The punishment suggests the idea that those who live by violence will die by violence (cf. Rev. 13.10).[21] Clearly, God is in control, and the punishment is carried out in response to those who cry out for justice. Yet, for *Jubilees*, the idea that violence leads to violence is clearly in the mind of the author.

In both Genesis 4.10 and later developments of this text, justice is established. This involves revenge against Cain according to the law of the right punishment for the right crime. Consequently, Abel's testimony is justified and God is seen to act with justice. The idea of the blood of the martyrs calling on God to avenge their death can also be seen in Deuteronomy 32.43, 2 Kings 9.7 and Joel 3.21.[22] Also, Jesus teaches that the wicked in every generation, like Cain, should also expect the blood of their innocent victims to be the cause of their deaths (Mt. 23.35; Lk. 11.51). The blood of the martyrs cried for vengeance because such acts of bloodshed were in fact perpetrated against God himself (2 Macc. 8.3-4). Violence is directed against the very principles of mercy and compassion that are innermost to God's nature and creation. Violence cannot exist in God's creation. It destroys itself because that is the way of violence. In God's creation, there is only death for the violent ones because they live contrary to the principles upon which God made the world.

It is important to reflect on the nature of the love of God to which Abel testifies. It is not difficult to see that a tension could exist between justice and love (cf. *Gen. R.* 6:1, 3). Vermes adds that such a tension might lead 'Jewish theology into the trap of rigorous determinism'.[23] This is understandable if the emphasis is placed continually on God to act according to the rules that he has set. Vermes points out that God's love was believed to be more easily aroused than His justice.[24] This is illustrated in the slowness of God to act in destroying Cain. Moreover, whereas the

---

19 Brownlee (1983):290.

20 In a text from the fourth century CE, Paul meets Abel with some other known martyr figures (*Apocalypse of Paul* 51).

21 God sets enemy against enemy (2 Chr. 20.23). See also Psalm 7.16: 'Their mischief returns upon their own heads, and on their own heads their violence descends'. Schwager (2000):61-62 the wicked are punished by their deeds recoiling on themselves.

22 Also Downing (1963):183 suggests that 2 Maccabees 8.3 is a clear allusion to the story of Cain and Abel.

23 Vermes (1975):125.

24 His point is strengthened by texts from the Old Testament, for example: 'For his anger is but for a moment, and his favour is for a lifetime' (Ps. 30.5a).

wicked provoke God to justice, there can be seen the development of the idea that the righteous excite his love (cf. *Gen. R.* 33.3; 73.3). This ultimately leads to the idea that the righteous person can be a ransom for the wicked (Philo *De Sacrificiis Abelis et Cain* 121). Jesus' readiness to die has a transforming impact on those who oppose him. But in the case of Abel, the emphasis is more on vengeance (Heb. 12.24). This resembles the two aspects of martyrs within the nonviolent tradition. (1) Those who see their death bringing God's vengeance upon their enemy. (2) The innocent death that will bring about the transformation of the enemy. Even in this second type, there must be vengeance. In Hebrews 12.24 the vengeance theme although not emphasized, must still be present insofar as violence leads to violence (cf. *Jub.* 4). If the martyr's death does not have the transforming impact on them, they will die a violent death. The martyr can be said to be the cause of the death of their enemy. If they refuse the martyr's testimony, the testimony becomes their judgement (cf. Mt. 23.35; Lk. 11.51).

The Seven Faithful Men of Pseudo-Philo LAB 6 and 38

Chapter 38 of Pseudo Philo's *Liber Antiquitatum Biblicarum* is an expansion on Judges 10.3-6 which reports on the reign of the judge Jair. During his reign, Israel did not live according to the covenant (v.6). The story is considerably paraphrased in *LAB* 38. Jair forced the people by threat of death to sacrifice to Baal (v.1). However, seven faithful men were not willing to sacrifice to Baal for the sake of tradition (v.2). They used the same words of the faithful judge Deborah who stressed the importance of keeping God's law (v.3). Jair ordered his servants to execute them by having them torched. However, instead of the fire consuming the seven faithful men, the servants were burned. The same fire also consumed Jair when he drew near to see what had happened. Before his death, the angel of the LORD told Jair that he would die because he led his people away from the covenant of God. He is told that the seven men will be free and live (v.4) (The text bears similarities with *LAB* 6, Dan. 3, 6 and 2 Macc. 7).[25]

The focus of the text is on vengeance and the redemption of the seven men. There are no hints of immortality but simply the rescue from the furnace. The seven figures are parallel to the actual martyrs in 2 Maccabees 7. The author of *LAB* 38 is documenting a legend and not an event that was closely remembered. The author re-presents an ancient story influenced by Daniel 3 and 6 in order to encourage his community to stay firm against the onslaught of their enemies. It is also possible that the martyrdom of the seven brothers in 2 Maccabees 7 was in the mind of the author.

---

25 Murphy (1993):161.

The Faithful Isaac

Traditions that elevate the role of Isaac when Abraham bound him have been dated later than the New Testament.[26] But the argument is unpersuasive. Hayward has presented a firm rebuttal,[27] and Vermes has provided evidence from Qumran in 4Q225 for the early dating he had previously argued.[28]

Abraham was told to offer Isaac as a burnt offering upon a mountain in the land of Moriah (Gen. 22.2). The whole account is about God testing Abraham. The narrator points out regularly that Isaac was his only son. Isaac's only words in the narrative are to ask his father where is the lamb of burnt offering (v.8) suggesting that Abraham had not told Isaac that he was to be the sacrifice. Isaac speaks (v.7) and carries the wood (v.6). Abraham obeys God although God stops Abraham from sacrificing his son at the last minute. As a reward, God declares to Abraham that all the nations will be blessed because of his obedience (v.18).

Later Jewish literature, however, presents Isaac as a faithful witness. The following distinctive elements are of particular importance for understanding Isaac as a faithful witness.[29] (1) Isaac was informed of his role as a victim. (2) Isaac gave his consent and asked to be bound. (3) God would remember the binding of Isaac in favour of his descendants. (4) The Aqedah was associated with the site of the temple in Jewish tradition. (5) It was a source of inspiration and instruction. (6) It was associated with vicarious expiation. (7) Sacrifice was completed.

Sources relevant for this study are *Jubilees*, 4Q225, *Pseudo-Philo*, 4 Maccabees, Josephus, and the *Palestinian Targums*. [30]

Jubilees 17.15-18.19. This text develops Genesis 22 in a way reminiscent of Job 1. A conversation occurs between Prince Mastemah and God as to Abraham's faithfulness. This occurs on Nisan 12. Some link the offering with that of the Passover sacrifice on Nisan 12.[31] The evidence suggests a clear relationship between the Passover and the offering of Isaac. VanderKam strengthens the connection and argues that the Aqedah is intimately linked with the sequence of events that constituted the Exodus from Egypt.[32] The place of the offering of Isaac was on Mount Zion, the place of the temple (18.13). Jubilees possibly connected the

---

26 Davies and Chilton (1978):514-546. I will now refer to this tradition as the Aqedah (עֲקֵדָה) which is the Hebrew word 'to bind'.

27 Hayward (1981):127-150.

28 Vermes (1996):140-145; see VanderKam (1997):241-261 for a fuller treatment of 4Q225 and its relationship with Jubilees.

29 See Daly (1977):61; Swetnam (1981):76-80 and Vermes (1996):143-144.

30 Philo does not feature in this discussion. Barclay (1996):159 Philo was a Jew, but highly acculturated. Philo's discussion of Isaac is Alexandrian which placed great emphasis on inner disposition of the worshipper as being decisive for the validity of a sacrifice.

31 VanderKam (1997):260.

32 VanderKam (1997):260.

Aqedah with the daily temple sacrifices (*tamid*).[33] There is nothing in the text that would encourage Jews during difficult times.

4Q225. Isaac makes a speech to his father, unfortunately only the letter kaph (כ) is present in the manuscript (Frag. 2 col. II.4):

‫... כ אבזר אל יצחק אמר לו‬ – Isaac said to his father …

Vermes observes that there is enough space for another fifteen letters. The speech seems to resemble either *Genesis Rabbah* 6.7 or the Targum tradition which all begin with the letter kaph:[34]

‫ידי את כפות‬ 'bind my hands'.

Therefore, the proposed reading is that Isaac asks his father to bind his hands.[35] In II.8 we read:

‫כחש ימצא‬

The most likely subject of the verb ‫ימצא‬ is Isaac. The translation is: 'whether Isaac will be found weak'. Mastemah is keen to see if Isaac will be found weak. In Fragment II, line 10 Isaac is blessed and not Abraham as in Genesis 22.17. It can be concluded with certainty that 4Q225 heightens Isaac's role in the Aqedah and testifies to a pre-Christian dating for this aspect of the Aqedah.

LAB 18.5; 32.1-4 and 40.2. Isaac knows his father intends to offer him as the burnt-offering (32.2), and wholeheartedly agrees to be offered (32.3). Future peoples will be instructed and remember that the LORD has made the soul of a man worthy to be a sacrifice (32.3). Isaac is presented as one worthy of imitation. This is illustrated in the sacrifice of Jephthah's daughter when facing death. She draws upon Isaac's obedience to God for inspiration in facing her death (40.2).[36] The sacrifice was actually carried out (32.4).[37] Finally, Isaac's words to Abraham suggest that he

---

33 This is a position maintained by many scholars. Swetnam (1981):38 'In view of the author's etiological tendencies, this identification is probably to be regarded as a deliberate attempt to link the Temple sacrifices with the Akedah'. This was not a difficult link to make as the author of Jubilees would know of the placing of the temple on Mount Moriah (2 Chr. 3.1).
34 Vermes (1996):142.
35 Vermes (1996):142 all the Targums begin with the imperative: ‫ידי את כפות‬ 'bind my hands'.
36 Swetnam (1981):56 observes that the presentation of the Aqedah in Pseudo-Philo provided 'an example of the proper attitude in the face of death'.
37 Daly (1977):61. The Latin: '*et cum obtulisset pater filium in aram*'. *Obtulisset* is the pluperfect form of *offero* suggesting that the father had offered the son on the altar.

considered his death vicarious and an atonement for the sins of his people similar to that of the lamb of sacrifice (32.3).

4 Maccabees especially 7.14; 13.12; 16.20; 18.11.[38] This is a Jewish writing that at odds with Greco-Roman culture.[39] Yet the author was knowledgeable about the philosophies of the Hellenistic world, especially Stoic ideas (see 1.1, 16; 2.7, 22; 3.11; 6.38; 12.13, 19; 14.2, 6; 15.4, 10).[40] S.K. Williams argues that ideas regarding atonement and vicarious suffering in 4 Maccabees are to be found in Greek traditions, as such ideas are not easily found in the Old Testament.[41] As I have argued, there is sufficient material within the Old Testament to supply the author of 4 Maccabees with ideas for atonement and vicarious suffering.[42]

It seems unlikely that 4 Maccabees, which is concerned to maintain community spirit and with encouraging faithfulness to the Israelite tradition, would draw upon foreign ideas in the way Williams suggests. It rather focuses on examples of Israelite obedience from the past and more recent times. Reference is made frequently to the Jewish nation. The fathers of the nation are repeatedly recalled as the guardians of Israel's integrity. They will welcome the martyrs after death (5.37; 13.17; 18.23). Jews refuse to violate their ancestors (5.29) and cannot bear to be thought of as cowards or traitors (9.2). As a spur to courage, they bid one another to remember their origins (13.12) by addressing each other as 'Abrahamic offspring' (6.17, 22; 9.21; 18.1).[43] I suggest that the suffering servant of Isaiah 40-55 is an important text for 4 Maccabees.[44] The following similarities can be observed. (1) Eleazar and the seven sons experienced pain and suffering like the servant of Isaiah 40-55. (2) The fourth son has his tongue cut out (10.18). So, too, is the suffering servant dumb before his slayer (Isa. 53.7). (3) Although the sons are described as handsome (8.4), they are each described following their suffering as dissevered and deformed. They are clearly unrecognizable like the suffering servant (Isa. 52.13). (4) As with Eleazar and the seven sons there was no deceit on their mouths for they would not eat unclean food, so also the servant (53.9). (5) The Gentiles marvel (LXX: θαυμασάσονται) at the bravery of the sons (9.26; 17.16-17; 18.3). In Isaiah, they

---

38 Translation used is Anderson in Charlesworth.

39 Swetnam (1981):45; Barclay (1996):369; on p.371 Barclay writes: 'the philosophy of the treatise is present only to serve the interests of the author's Jewish commitments'.

40 Hadas (1953):116; Barclay (1996):369; however, Barclay points out that the book is not evidence of a text showing high acculturization.

41 Williams (1975):184-185; Croy (1998):87, 106.

42 Williams notes this to some extent, but he simply thinks that the author was more influenced by Greek ideas. He does not acknowledge the extent to which the Old Testament provides ideas of redemption from suffering. The author of 4 Maccabees draws upon Hebrew figures to encourage the faithful.

43 Barclay (1996):373-374.

44 There is debate as to the relationship between 2 Maccabees and 4 Maccabees. Many assume that 4 Maccabees draws upon 2 Maccabees for its atonement ideas. See O'Hagan (1974):107; Nickelsburg (1972):109. If this is the case, it is important to see the similarities between Isaiah 52.13-53.12 and 2 Maccabees 7, see Nickelsburg (1972):103-106.

marvelled (θαυμασάσονται) at him (LXX Isa. 52.14). The suffering servant received a portion with the great. The martyrs will receive a divine portion (4 Macc. 18.3). The certainty of the martyr's conviction makes its mark on the observers, and evokes admiration and emulation.[45] Dying for one's beliefs ensures the continuity of one's convictions and validates the truth claims of the culture. This is particularly relevant in terms of 4 Maccabees. Israelite truth claims are intellectually challenged. The faithful realized that dying would validate Jewish claims and in some strange way prove erroneous the claims of the enemy.[46]

In terms of the depiction of Isaac in 4 Maccabees, he is a model for Jewish martyrs (13.12) because of his willingness to die (16.20). An expiatory and intercessory role is given to Isaac (17.22; cf. 1.11; 6.29; 18.3-4). The expiatory function is not explicitly attributed directly to Isaac here or in any of the above texts. It is argued that because Isaac's blood was not spilt he could not be considered in the same light as those who were actually martyred.[47] Nevertheless, in 13.12, Isaac became as a sacrifice and is one of those intended in 17.22 and 18.3-4.[48] If Jews are exhorted to recall Isaac because of his readiness to die, it is unlikely that the author understood Isaac's act of obedience as inferior to that of the martyrs of the Maccabean revolt in that no atonement value was attributed to him.[49] Still, it could be objected that Abraham is used as an exemplary figure and he could not be considered a martyr. However, Abraham is not presented as ready to die, whereas Isaac is.

Josephus. Josephus sets out to defend the Aqedah in Gentile eyes as an act of faithfulness, and not a sacrifice to a morally reprehensible god. He was trained in Jewish exegesis and was proud of his expertise in Jewish learning (*Ant.* 20.263). He affirms the importance of learning Hebrew and Aramaic above that of Greek as well as the Law and the interpretation of Scripture (*Ant.* 20.264). He claims he would never forget his ancestral customs (*War* 6.107).[50]

Josephus presents Isaac as a twenty-five year old who was willing to die (*Ant.* 1.227-232). Josephus reports that Abraham informed Isaac that he was to be the sacrifice (*Ant.* 1.228-231). The place of the binding is the place of the temple. Therefore, the binding is linked to the various sacrifices carried out in the temple.

---

45 Weiner (1990):22.

46 For more detail of the sociology behind this see Weiner (1990):52-53.

47 Davies and Chilton (1978); Segal (1996):108; Swetnam (1981):48; contrary Daly (1977):57; O'Neill (1981):14.

48 Philo *On Abraham* 178 understood the sacrifice to have been completed.

49 O'Neill (1981):14 writes: 'If the seven brothers and their mother acted with the example of Isaac's sacrifice before their eyes, surely it is natural to assume that what they are said to have achieved by sacrifice is the same as what Isaac was assumed to have achieved by sacrifice...the whole passage is saturated with the image of Isaac's sacrifice'.

50 Barclay (1996):346-351 gives a good discussion of Josephus and his social context; see also Attridge (1984) for a summary of Josephus' works. Laqueur (1970):245-278 argues that Josephus' work is not representative of Jewish exegesis.

Such sacrifices removed wicked deeds (*Ant.* 1.226). Josephus, however, does not make the association with the temple explicit.[51] Josephus states rather that the sacrifice was to occur on 'that mountain upon which King David afterwards built the temple' (*Ant.* 1.226). Feldman points out that Josephus avoids theological issues and that is why he does not make associations with the temple sacrifice, not even the Passover. Rather, Josephus' concern was to provide an historical narrative.[52] Davies and Chilton add that Josephus develops the Aqedah as a response to the war against Rome and provides a proto-martyr figure for other Jews.[53] The Roman admiration for Jews who held out at Masada and who subsequently died may make this suggestion plausible (*War* 7.405). In other words, connecting the Aqedah with martyrdom would bring the admiration of Romans.

Targum Tradition. Most Targum developments of the Aqedah are detectable in the first century CE. All the Targums on Genesis 22 heighten Isaac's involvement in the binding. He cries out to Abraham:

> Bind me properly that I may not kick you and your offering be made unfit (*Neof.* 22.10).

Presumably, Isaac's concern to be bound is connected with his worry that he might move, the sacrificial knife would slip, and blemish the sacrificial victim thus making it unfit for sacrifice.

The actions of Isaac seem to have been understood as bringing about God's mercy on his people:

> You may remember on their behalf the binding of Isaac their father, and loose and forgive them their sins and deliver them from all distress (*Frag. Targ. Gen.* 22.14).[54]

In all Targumic traditions, the Aqedah is believed to have occurred on the mountain of the temple of the Lord (*Frag. Targum Gen.* 22.14). Vermes has argued that the daily sacrifice in the temple (*tamid*) was a memorial of Isaac's act.[55] It is to be observed in the Mishnah that Aqedah is a technical term for the way the lamb is tied before slaughter (*m. Tamid* 4.1). It is possible that with the destruction of the temple, the lamb was substituted with almsgiving or martyrdom, and both would remind God of the Aqedah.[56]

---

51 Daly (1977):58.
52 Feldman (1982):119.
53 Davies and Chilton (1978):521-522.
54 The significance of this text, especially 'loose' will be discussed in terms of Rev. 1.5 in a later chapter.
55 Vermes (1961):206-208.
56 A point that is supported by Davies and Chilton (1978).

Isaac: the Prototype Suffering Servant. The starting point for understanding the development of Genesis 22 haggadah is to look closely at the importance of Isaiah 52.13-53.12 as Vermes did in 1961.[57] Vicarious suffering for the sake of God was shown to run through the major strata of the canon from Moses to the prophets. Vindication would come through suffering. The Aqedah develops in response to the experience of religious persecution or challenge to their traditions. Rosenberg calls Isaac the 'prototype of the suffering servant'.[58] This is an apt description in view of the evidence. Pseudo-Philo, 4 Maccabees, 4Q225, Josephus, and the Targums all present Isaac as one who willingly suffered. Consequently, the nameless suffering servant of Isaiah 40-55 was the original exemplary figure. Vermes presented the following points: Isaac freely offered his life and it was accepted by God in favour of his descendants, so too the suffering servant; the servant is compared to a lamb brought to the slaughter. Isaac was also a holocaust lamb.[59]

The Faithful Moses

Jewish literature presents Moses as a prophet-martyr who was disbelieved, rejected, mocked, attacked and almost stoned.[60] The Babylonian Talmud develops the biblical material on Moses in the light of Isaiah 53:

> R. Simlah expounded: Why did Moses our teacher yearn to enter the land of Israel? Did he want to eat of its fruits or satisfy himself from its bounty? But thus spake Moses, "Many precepts were commanded to Israel which can only be fulfilled in the land of Israel. I wish to enter the land so that they may all be fulfilled by me". The Holy One, blessed be He, said to him, "Is it only to receive the reward [for obeying the commandments] that thou seekest? I ascribe it to thee as if thou didst perform them"; as it is said, Therefore will I divide him a portion with the great, and he shall divide the spoil with the strong; because he poured out his soul unto death, and was numbered with the transgressors, yet he bare the sins of many, and made intercession for the transgressor (*b. Sotah* 14a).[61]

---

57 A key text is *Targum Job* 3.18: 'Jacob, called the young one, and Abraham, called the old one, are there, and Isaac, the Servant of the LORD (עֶבֶד דֹּ יהוה) who was delivered from the bonds by his Master'. Vermes (1961):203; McNamara (1966):167; Segal (1996):105 is not convinced and believes that Vermes depends too much on *Palestinian Targum* tradition.
58 Rosenberg (1965):385.
59 Vermes (1961):202; see also Levenson (1993):201. It was a ram that was offered in Gen. 22 and not a lamb. This change has never been explained. Is it not possible that the choice of lamb was indeed influenced by the lamb of Isaiah 53.7?
60 Fischel (1946-47):275 lists primary texts. All texts are very late.
61 Quoted in Jeremias (1967a):854, and 873; Chavasse (1964):159-160; Fischel (1946-47):372-373 lists rabbinic texts supporting the belief that Moses had borne vicarious suffering.

The text explains why the suffering servant of Isaiah 53.12 was identified with Moses. It refers to Moses' offering of his life that Israel's sins may be forgiven (Ex. 32.32). Rabbinic tradition also says:

> Why did Moses die in the wilderness? In order that the wilderness generation should return and rise again through his merits.[62]

The texts elevate Moses' death to that of a sacrifice for the people. Does *b. Sotah* 14a express ideas which New Testament writers were familiar with in the first century? Scholars supporting a first-century CE date cannot provide a text earlier than the third century CE. Nevertheless, the presentation of Moses in the Old Testament as a suffering servant, and the later connection in *b. Sotah* 14a between Moses and the suffering servant of Isaiah 52.13-53.12, raises the possibility that Moses was understood as the suffering servant of Isaiah 52.13-53.12 in the first century CE. It is presumed that oppressed Jews looked back to Moses, the founder of their nation, for hope and inspiration. Moses after all led them out of slavery.[63] However, it is surprising that 4 Maccabees, an important text for understanding suffering and atonement, does not present Moses as an exemplary figure. This may suggest that the author did not perceive Moses as a martyr figure, like Isaac or Abel. This would urge us to be cautious in attributing too much significance to Moses in all later material. Yet Moses was a key figure to New Testament writers and is directly referred to more than any other Old Testament figure.

Jeremias writes regarding Moses in the New Testament: 'Acts paints a picture of the suffering messenger of God [i.e. Moses] who was misunderstood and rejected (7.17-44). The Moses of Hebrews (11.23-29) is one of the heroic models of faith'.[64] In spite of Jeremias' claims, in Acts few verses say anything about Moses' suffering and rejection (7.29, 35 and 39). There is no mention of Moses bearing the sins of the people, and no allusion to Exodus 32.32. Hebrews 11.24-27 offers Moses as an example of faith to be followed:

> By faith Moses, when he was grown up, refused to be called a son of the Pharaoh's daughter, choosing rather to share ill-treatment with the people of God than to enjoy the fleeting pleasures of sin. He considered abuse suffered for the Christ greater wealth than the treasures of Egypt, for he looked to the reward. By faith he left Egypt, not being afraid of the anger of the king; for he endured as seeing him who is invisible (Heb. 11.24-27).

---

62 Quoted in Jeremias (1967a):854.

63 Hafemann (1990) observes the figure of Moses in later tradition and points out the development of Moses as an authoritative figure for Jews.

64 Jeremias (1967a):865; D'Angelo (1979):17-64 uses the word martyr to depict the Moses of Hebrews 11.23-29.

Again, it is not possible to see the suffering servant of Isaiah 52.13-53.12 as underlying this text. There is a development in the aspect of suffering but no sense of Moses bearing the sins of the people.

Suffering Righteous in 1 Enoch

In *1 Enoch*, oppression of the righteous by sinners is a prime fact of life.[65] In some cases, this oppression has led to the death of the righteous (99.15; 100.7; 103.15). Such oppression will be punished. On the day of judgement the righteous will be vindicated (94.9; 96.8; 97.3, 5; 98.8, 10; 99.15; 100.4; 103.4; 103.7-8; 104.5). There is no presentation of a martyr in a public altercation with the ruler. The tradition is of an oppressor killing a righteous group. In the same way, the murdered righteous fired up their community with readiness to die just like the figures of the Old Testament.

The Maccabean Martyrs

In 1 Maccabees the king decrees that everyone should abandon his or her own laws and religion (1.42). The king's officers enforce the decree upon Mattathias and his sons. The officers are what might be termed 'wise persecutors'. They do not want martyrs on their hands. Rather apostasy is their aim. They seek the faithful to recant of their beliefs through seducing them by promising friendship with the king as well as much gold and silver (2.18). Mattathias refuses and slays the officer (2.25). On his death bed Mattathias reinforces to his sons the importance of keeping God's covenant even until death (2.50). He recounts the well-known narratives from their own culture about obedient men who were prepared to suffer and die:

> Now, my children, show zeal for the law, and give your lives for the covenant of our ancestors. Remember the deeds of the ancestors, which they did in their generations; and you will receive great honor and an everlasting name.

Dying for the covenant would result in their own names being immortalized within their tradition and their story being told to future believers to encourage them to be obedient to death. Redemption is not the motivating force that drives the martyrs to die. Zeal for God's law is the significant factor. Forsaking God's law is worse than death.

In 2 Maccabees 7 the faithfulness of seven brothers and their mother is told. We are told that they were commanded to eat unclean food and they refused. Van Henten sees in 2 Maccabees 7 parallels with philosophers (particularly Socrates).[66] I think it is unlikely that a Jewish author would draw from the very thing he condemns and despises, especially when sufficient material can be found from his own tradition.

---

65 Nickelsburg (1972):113.
66 Van Henten (1996):72.

2 Maccabees is not particularly concerned with the post-mortem rescue of the seven brothers put to death.[67] Rather the story anticipates God's vengeance on the enemies who put Jews to death. To this extent 2 Maccabees is completely grounded in the thought of the Old Testament. However, according to Downing, there is no concern for the post-mortem rescue of the martyr in the Old Testament and yet there is in 2 Maccabees 7.23.[68] This suggests a borrowing from Greco-Roman ideas. Yet the concern for vengeance and the post-mortem rescue of those put to death is seen clearly in Psalms 49.10-11, 14-16; 73.19, 24.[69] In these texts there is the yearning for the fall of the enemy and the rescue of the oppressed or murdered. There is much to commend the argument that the key early text for 2 Maccabees 7 is Isaiah 52.13-53.12.[70] I will explore the relationship between these two texts.

It is reported in verse 12 that the king marvelled (ἐκπλήσσεσθαι) at the young man's courage. The verb does not compare with LXX Isaiah 52.14. The author, although thoroughly trained in Greek thought, would equally be comfortable with the Hebrew language. He certainly sees the importance of the language of Israel (v.21). I suggest that v.12 was modelled on Isaiah MT 52.14 and not on the LXX. The verb ἐκπλήσσεσθαι corresponds chiefly with שׁמם (to be astonished) which is the verb that appears in Isaiah MT 52.14. This word describes the response of the kings and his officers who looked on in astonishment and shock. The fourth son looks for the reward of his faithfulness:

> It is good, being put to death by men, to look for hope from God to be raised up again by him (cf. vv.9, 11 and v.23).

The hope of resurrection in the Bible, although not a dominant theme, was present and allowed for the development of such ideas in later writers. The belief in a resurrection may have arisen when facing death for one's faith.[71] Martyrs are the innocent faithful ones who hope for redemption through their death.

In vv.37-38 the seventh son is an intercessor for his nation. God's wrath may be removed through suffering and death. Suffering is for the good of another. Martyrdom was a necessary chastening (παιδείας; cf. Isa. MT 53.5c: מוסר) necessary for reconciliation with God (vv.33, 37). Isaiah 40-55 provides the interpretative framework for the author. Vv.33 and 37 are influenced by Isaiah 53.5c for his use of παιδείας as a pre-requisite for putting the nation right with God.

---

67 Nickelsburg (1972):102.

68 Downing (1963):283. Hengel (1981):69 also observes that both 2 and 4 Maccabees contain numerous Palestinian traditions.

69 Nickelsburg's excellent and thorough treatment of resurrection, immortality and eternal life, does not consider Psalms 49 and 73. See also Psalm 16.10; see Bauckham's discussion of resurrection in the Old Testament (1998).

70 Nickelsburg (1972):103-109.

71 Russell (1960):146.

The synonymous parallelism in Isaiah 53.5c and v.5d makes clearer the sense of v.5c:

upon him was the punishment (מוּסָר) that made us whole, and by his bruises (וּבַחֲבֻרָתוֹ) we are healed.

Resulting from his beating is the healing of others. It is possible to establish 2 Maccabees 7 firmly within the biblical tradition regarding vicarious suffering and indeed the punishment of the persecutors.

Suffering in the Wisdom of Solomon 2-5

The writer of the Wisdom of Solomon was familiar with Isa. xl-lxvi needs no proof, and his descriptions of the sufferings of the righteous man in v.1-7 reads like a paraphrase of Isa. lii.15-liii.6 (North).[72]

In spite of North's confidence, there is some dispute regarding the stock of tradition from which the author of Wisdom of Solomon draws. My argument is rooted in the fact that the writer is at odds with the dominant power and is unlikely to appropriate from that which he despises, especially if his own traditions contain suitable material to choose from. Although the author is at home in Hellenistic thought, seen in his use of sophisticated vocabulary and rhetorical features,[73] the following discussion will show that the text is antagonistic to non-Jews and the Wisdom of Solomon employs Hellenistic learning not to integrate Judaism with the Hellenistic environment but to present a sophisticated attack upon it.[74]

The unrighteous are the wealthy ones who persecute the poor (2.7 and 2.10; cf. Pss. 49; 73). Nickelsburg suggests that the kings are the rich ones.[75] They deny the existence of a just God and the belief in a continuing existence after death (2.1).[76] They use up the creation's resources with no care for others, resulting in the oppression of the poor (2.6, 10; cf. Ezek. 34.18-19). The Wisdom of Solomon is an economic critique on the ruling powers. On the other hand, the righteous are those who admonish the unrighteous (2.12) and have knowledge of God (2.13, 16). They believe that God will punish the unrighteous (2.18) and test their patience and righteousness through the suffering they experience at the hands of the unrighteous (2.19). Chapter 3 develops the scene in which the righteous are said to believe and hope in immortality (3.4; cf. 2.23; 3.3):

---

72 North (1956):8.
73 Barclay (1996):183.
74 Barclay (1996):184.
75 Nickelsburg (1972):58.
76 In the *Palestinian Targums*, Abel supports a loving God who has made a creation with order, but not so Cain.

For though in the sight of others they were punished, their hope is full of immortality.

God vindicates those who were found righteous through suffering (3.5) and gives to them the authority to judge the nations (3.8). Those who pleased God were taken from the evil ones who sought to seduce them (3.10-11, 14). The wicked ones saw the obedience of God's faithful witnesses, but did not understand (3.15). They are punished:

> For they will see the end of the wise, and will not understand what the Lord purposed for them, and for what he kept them safe. The unrighteous will see, and will have contempt for them, but the Lord will laugh them to scorn. After this they will become dishonored corpses, and an outrage among the dead forever (4.17-18).

The righteous man stands before his oppressors on judgement day (5.1). The oppressor, when confronted by the ability of the righteous man to suffer for his faith, is troubled and amazed at his hope (5.2). The oppressor is repentant (5.3-4).

INFLUENCES ON THE TEXT

Reese provides a thorough study of the Hellenistic influence on the Wisdom of Solomon.[77] Possible influences on the writer may have been Stoic thought and stories regarding the unjust treatment of wise men in Greek literature, such as Socrates and Diogenes.[78] Lange suggested that the writing was influenced directly by Platonic thought.[79] My contention is that Isaiah 52.13-53.12 as well as Psalms 49 and 73 provide the conceptual background for chapters 2-5 of the Wisdom of Solomon.[80] The following conceptual parallels are found and have been observed above:[81]

Wis. 2.19-20/ /Isa. 53.7-9	Wis. 5.1bc/ /Isa. 52.14
Wis. 3.2-3/ /Isa. 53.7-10	Wis. 5.2/ /Isa. 52.15
Wis. 4.19/ /Isa. 52.15	Wis. 5.3-4/ /Isa. 53.3, 10
Wis. 5.1a/ /Isa. 52.14	Wis. 5.6 /Isa. 53.6

Of particular interest is the theme of immortality. The hero suffers because he believes that martyrdom will end in God raising and glorifying him (3.4). There is no need to read Greek ideas into this verse. The hope of a continued relationship

---

77 Reese (1970).

78 Reese (1970):112-113.

79 Lange (1936):293-302.

80 Suggs (1957); Nickelsburg (1972); Kolarick (1991); this is a position that not even Reese (1970):113 can deny when he writes that 'the Book of Isaiah serves as the basis for much of the author's speculation in Wis 3-5'. Barclay (1996) although he sees the book as culturally antagonistic to non-Jews, never discusses the possible influence of Isaiah 52.13-53.12 either in rejection or acceptance.

81 Parallels in Nickelsburg (1972):62.

with God after the death of the body is not as foreign to biblical tradition as those arguing for the influence of Greek suggest. The broad conceptual background behind the reward of the Lord for those who have been persecuted and martyred is the suffering servant of Isaiah 52.13-53.12.[82] However, it need not be confined to Isaiah 40-55. The Wisdom of Solomon is a conflation of concepts that may have originally been connected within the Old Testament. Schaberg, for example, has argued for the influence of Psalm 2 on the author of Wisdom 1-5.[83] The conceptual parallels (not lexicographical) are persuasive.[84] The wicked conspire against God and the righteous (Ps. 2.1-3//Wis. 2.10-20). Both texts are addressed to the rulers of the earth (Ps. 2.2//Wis. 1.1). God laughs scornfully at the unrighteous (Ps. 2.4//Wis. 4.18). In both texts, the righteous man is known as God's son (Ps. 2.7//Wis. 2.18). God will crush the unrighteous (Ps. 2.9//Wis. 4.19). There is the hope that the rulers of the earth will be wise (Ps. 2.10//Wis. 6.1, 9). Finally, there is the proclamation to the rulers to serve God in fear (Ps. 2.11//Wis. 6.21). Psalm 2 describes the hope that the people of Israel had in their king. They believed he would rule with justice and bring other nations to the LORD. The role of the king resembles that of the servant in Isaiah 40-55, although the context of hope has changed. In Isaiah 40-55 the servant of God will suffer. The hope that God will exalt his people through his servant and that the nations, too, will serve God is found in both Psalm 2 and Isaiah 52.13-53.12. I suggest also that Psalms 49 and 73 provided much of the framework for the Wisdom of Solomon. Psalm 73.12 presents the wealthy as untroubled. However, their end is predicted and there is a hint of immortality for the righteous. Also, Psalm 49.15 influences Wisdom 4.10, 14 (both echoing Gen. 5.24).

The argument that Wisdom 2-5 is firmly rooted in the Old Testament is compelling. Although the text is modelled on Greek literary convention,[85] the writer drew upon biblical tradition in difficult times to persuade his audience to remain faithful to tradition. Reese, however, opposes the biblical background and especially Suggs' thesis that Wisdom 2-5 was a midrash on Isaiah 52.13-53.12 simply on the grounds that Wisdom of Solomon was Greek in style.[86] However, as Mack and Murphy observe, this kind of scholarship is impoverished inasmuch as it 'has looked only for the system of Hellenistic-philosophical ideas'.[87] Rather, the text must be approached from a greater grasp of biblical theology. As Reese suggested, Jewish students are the audience and the writer wanted to show them the relation between their sacred history and the growth of the entire human race.[88] This may indeed be the case, which supports the view here that the writer was concerned with his Jewish audience and their possible apostasy. Wisdom 14.21 is a polemic against

---

82 Kolarick (1991):99.
83 Schaberg (1982):75-101.
84 Although there may be lexicographical parallels: Psalm 2.4 cf. Wisdom 4.18: 'the Lord will laugh them to scorn'.
85 Which Reese has shown (1970).
86 Reese (1970):113.
87 Mack and Murphy (1986):387.
88 Reese (1970):150.

idolatry.[89] The author attacks all engaged in the manufacture of objects of worship whether they work in wood (13.11-14.7) or clay (15.7-17) in a way that Isaiah 40-55 would be proud.[90] John Barclay rightly understands the text as antagonistic to Greco-Roman culture.[91] He believes it appropriates Greek learning 'not to integrate his Judaism with his environment but to construct all the more sophisticated an attack upon it!'[92] This concern is constant throughout the biblical corpus from Israel's settlement in Canaan up to the period of the Maccabees.

The Testament of Moses

The text exhorts the faithful to remain loyal under dangerous and difficult circumstances. Moses narrates Israelite history until the time of Antiochus Epiphanes (if the earlier date is accepted) and the readiness of Taxo and his sons to die rather than transgress the commandments (9). Moses is an exemplary figure who suffered many things (3.11). Israel is one who continually rebels against God (5.3). As promised, Israel will suffer if she does not keep God's covenant (Lev. 26; Deut. 28). God will use the hands of a cruel king to bring about such suffering (6.5-6).[93] Those who stay faithful to the covenant will be tortured and crucified until they blaspheme the covenant (8.1, 4).

Particularly relevant for this discussion are chapters 9-10: the recounting of Taxo and his seven sons who instead of blaspheming accepted martyrdom. In 9.1-7, many of the components of a narrative martyrdom are seen. The whole confrontation is staged as a public dispute in which the ruler challenges the faithful to renounce their faith. The faithful prefer death. Taxo urges his sons to seek death rather than deny their faith. The author believed that the blood of Taxo and his sons would be avenged before the Lord (9.7; cf. 10.2-3). The idols of the ruling nation would be destroyed (10.7). God's righteous people would be glorified and their place would be in heaven (10.9). They would see their enemies on the earth (v.10).

Nickelsburg suggests that the *Testament of Moses* is a rewriting of Deuteronomy 31-34. However, he suggests that the exaltation to the stars and the viewing of the enemies beneath it are new ideas to Deuteronomy 31-34.[94] This new material, argues Nickelsburg, is drawn from material related to but earlier than Daniel 12.1-3. Also of significance is Isaiah 52.13 in which the servant will be exalted. In Daniel 12.3 the *maskilim* will shine in the firmament as the stars shine forever. Their exaltation is connected with their suffering (11.34). As has been argued above, so is this the case with the suffering servant of Isaiah (50.6; 53.5, 7). Likewise, similarities can be detected with Taxo and his sons. The focus in the *Testament of*

---

89 Barclay (1996):187.
90 Barclay (1996):187.
91 Barclay (1996):183.
92 Barclay (1996):184.
93 Tromp (1993):202 points to Herod as the king mainly because of the 34 years he is said to reign (v.5) which coheres with Josephus *War* 1. 665; *Ant.* 17.191.
94 Nickelsburg (1972):29.

Moses is concerned with how God punishes his enemies as well as providing a positive vindication of Israel.

Taxo and his sons are eschatological martyrs insofar as their deaths are related to the coming of God's kingdom:

> Then his kingdom will appear throughout his whole creation. Then the devil will have an end. Yea, sorrow will be led away with him (10.1).

The eschaton will come because vengeance is provoked by the readiness of Taxo to die.[95] Taxo's martyrdom is a necessary link in God's scheme of suffering and salvation.[96]

Community Rule (1QS)

> They [the Council of the Community] shall preserve the faith in the Land with steadfastness and meekness and shall atone for sin by the practice of justice and by suffering the sorrows of affliction (1QS 8.3-4).

Suffering is associated with atonement. The council of the community, who are three priests and twelve men,[97] are said to be:

> witnesses to the truth at the Judgement, and shall be the elect of Goodwill who shall atone for the Land and pay to the wicked their reward (1QS 8.5).

Matthew Black proposed that these men fulfil the mission of the suffering servant of Isaiah 53.10, 12.[98] He writes: 'we have in these verses the developed theological conception of a community or group within a community identifying itself with the Isaianic Remnant and attributing to its sufferings a redemptive function'.[99] Atonement in 1QS is for the land of Israel that has been defiled (cf. Num. 35.33; Deut. 32.43).[100] The focus of this text is on vengeance that will fall upon the wicked. Suffering brings God's wrath.[101] Garnet argues that the atonement is to be effected by the punishment of the wicked. The land will no longer be polluted with the abominations of the wicked.[102] The suffering of the faithful will bring about the cleansing of the land through their suffering (cf. *T. Mos.* 9.1-7).

---

95 Licht (1961):97.
96 Licht (1961):99.
97 Sanders (1981):301 suggests that the subject is the community as a whole.
98 Black (1961):129; Bruce (1960):60; contrary Garnet (1976):65-66. He argues that the figures do not atone. He does not provide any discussion regarding line 5, and disputes the atoning value on the basis of his translation of lines 1-4.
99 Black (1961):129; see Bruce (1960):60.
100 Black (1961):129.
101 Brownlee (1983):290.
102 Garnet (1976):66.

The Hymns of Thanksgiving (1QH)[103]

The author of 1QH 9.6-8, 23-27 describes himself in language reminiscent of Isaiah 52.13-53.12. Lines 6-8 describe the desolation the servant has experienced and in lines 23-27 he speaks of the positive effects his suffering brings in words akin to the writer of Isaiah 53.5: 'And Thy wounds were for healing' (9.5) and 'with his stripes we are healed' (Isa. 53.5). The wounds that bring healing may be connected with the many being illuminated through the servant's suffering:

> In Thy glory did my light shine forth for a light out of darkness hast Thou caused to shine (9.27).

In 1QH 4.27:

> And through me Thou hast illumined the face of the Many (Vermes has the congregation).[104]

The text here has no interest in the conversion of the many according to Vermes' translation but just to the congregation and perhaps the conversion of Jews. In the Thanksgiving Psalms, the righteous suffer at the hand of the wicked. God also delivers them from their suffering and judges the wicked. The righteous receive wisdom and knowledge of God and will be raised to an everlasting height and enjoy communion with the angels:[105]

> Thou hast redeemed my soul from the Pit, and from the hell of Abaddon Thou hast raised me up to everlasting height (1QH 3.20).

Belief in the resurrection is evident among members of the Qumran community on the basis of this text. Josephus reported that the Essenes shared the belief in the immortality of the soul in the same way as the Greeks (*War* 2.154-155). He speaks, also, of life after death in terms of reincarnation (see *Ant.* 18.14 and *War* 2.163).[106] This is contrary to Hippolytus of Rome (about 170-236 CE) who reports that the Essenes acknowledge both that the flesh will rise again, and that it will be immortal (*Refutation of All Heresies* 9.27). VanderKam is right to doubt Josephus' account. He writes: 'This description has peculiar features, not least of which is that the Essenes, who otherwise are pictured as opposed to pagan teachings, are compared

---

103 Translations from Qumran are taken from Black (1961). I am indebted to Black's discussion here: 142-144.
104 Vermes (1995):202.
105 VanderKam (1994):63-64.
106 For example, Beall (1988):105 notes Josephus says that the Pharisees believed in reincarnation, the only kind of after life intelligible to pagans. Josephus writes: 'every soul is imperishable, but the soul of the good alone passes into another body, while the souls of the wicked suffer eternal punishment' (*War* 2.163).

with the Greeks'.[107] This agrees with the point I have argued throughout this book. A sectarian group antagonistic to the ruling nation would not share beliefs with the ruling nation. Indeed, those at Qumran had no need to do so. They had their own rich tradition to draw on and develop from. They were also isolated from the mainstream. Therefore, they would not have felt the same pressures to respond to Hellenistic culture in the same ways that their Jewish brothers and sisters felt who were living for example in Sepphoris. Also, Josephus' account at this point must be suspect as he writes to pagans to commend the Jewish tradition. Further, as Black points out, there is no evidence for such a belief among the Essenes in their literature.[108] The language in 1QH 3.20 resembles closely Psalm 49.15:

> But God will ransom my soul from the power of Sheol, for he will receive me (Ps. 49.15).

I have already argued that hope in the resurrection is apparent in psalms 49 and 73. The question of exactly what was meant by resurrection is a more difficult inquiry. There was no one understanding of resurrection in Judaism.[109] A consistent or sophisticated view of life after death should not be imposed on these ancient Jewish writers. All that can be said is that the poet believes and hopes for a continued relationship after death with God. Another text from Qumran has added to the data regarding belief in the after life and coheres with Hippolytus' account (see above). In the so called Messianic Apocalypse (4Q521):

> For he will heal the wounded, and revive the dead and bring good news to the poor (4Q521 line 12).[110]

SUMMARY

We find among Jewish writings the importance of suffering as a form of witness that brings about conversion and judgement. We find at Qumran the hope of the resurrection. In spite of their suffering, the faithful are encouraged to remember their heavenly hope.

The Testament of Levi[d] 4Q541

> He will atone for all sons of his generation and will be sent to all the sons of his [peo]ple. His word is like a word of heaven, and his teaching is according to the will of God. His eternal sun will shine, and his fire will spring forth to all the ends of the earth,

---

107 VanderKam (1994):79; Beall (1988):105.

108 Black (1961):138.

109 See Russell (1960):157-162, for summary of different understandings.

110 Tabor and Wise (1992):149-162; VanderKam (1994):81; Puech (1994):235-256; Vermes (1995):244 all are confident that the reviving of the dead indicates a belief in the bodily resurrection.

and will shine over darkness… They will utter many words against him and many
[…]s. They will invent stories about him, and will utter everything dishonourable
against him. Evil will overturn his generation …[111]

Little can be concluded regarding this fragment. Yet it is evidence regarding a key
figure who teaches and is rejected by the nations. A priestly figure is mentioned
who will atone for all the sons of his generation and all the sons of his people. This
figure has a mission to all peoples. It is worth remembering at this point that
although those living in Qumran were sectarian, there was found at Qumran,
Hebrew and Aramaic fragments of the Book of Tobit which contains a strong hope
that all nations will be converted (see Tobit 14.6):[112]

his eternal sun will shine, and his fire will spring forth to all the ends of the earth.[113]

Yet we are told that those whom he teaches will speak against him in the same way
that we have seen throughout the Old Testament and later Jewish literature.

Summary of Findings

Old Testament and later Jewish traditions suggest that the Jews expected to suffer
and die because of their faith in the LORD. Jews accommodated themselves to
varying degrees to the Greco-Roman culture. Yet the literature of particular interest
to my work is the type that was antagonistic to foreign influences. These texts
express continuity with the heroes of the past.

In this chapter, I examined Jewish literature from the third-century BCE to the
first century CE. This corpus of texts is diverse but they all express a high level of
loyalty to their tradition and an uncompromising attitude towards the foreign nations
and all those who are unfaithful to the God of Israel. I will briefly summarize my
findings.

The enemies of Israel's God are like Cain, and the righteous are like Abel. Abel
is an example of a faithful witness who is put to death as a result of his obedience to
God. Abel's death is understood as bringing about justice. He dies because he bears
witness to God who works with love and justice, and judges justly. Abel's death is
exemplary and to be imitated, God justifies him on principles of justice and love.
The importance of Hebrews 12.24 was observed in which the idea of the day of
vengeance is critiqued by principles of the compassion of Jesus.

Pseudo-Phlo *LAB* 6 and 38 depicts ancient figures in a conflict situation with the
authorities. The author depicts the faithful as prepared to die rather than deny their
faith. The situation is resolved, not by the conversion of the oppressor (as in Dan. 3
and 6), but with his death (6.17-18; 38.4).

---

111 Translation in Vermes (1995):305.
112 Puech (1994):243.
113 Language is reminiscent of Matthew 24.27 and Luke 17.24:

Isaac is presented as a suffering hero through whose death many will be blessed. Seven separate traditions of varying dates were observed: Jubilees, 4Q225, Pseudo-Philo, 4 Maccabees, Josephus and the Targums.

Moses may have been understood by some first-century writers as one who atoned for the sins of the people through being prepared to suffer or die, but there is no certainty. There is little evidence that Moses suffered a violent death. Still, both in the Old Testament and in later tradition, he was disbelieved, mocked, attacked and almost stoned. The presentation, therefore, of Moses as a special prophet is secure at an early stage of the tradition and there would be much material for later exegetes, as in *b. Sota* 14a (Num. 12.6-8; cf. Ex. 33.9-11).

The oppression of the righteous is a prime fact of life for the author of *1 Enoch*.[114] In some cases, oppression led to death (99.15; 100.7; 103. 15). Yet God will vindicate the righteous (94.9; 96.8; 97.3, 5; 98.8, 10; 99.15; 100.4; 104.5).

1 Maccabees presents the martyr worldview as significant to the Israelite mind. It is possible that a list of faithful heroes existed which would be cited almost liturgically, as seen in 1 Maccabees 2.51-68, to reinforce the worldview and maintain social discipline.[115] Mattathias is not martyred but he was prepared to die. Yet martyrdom was not the ideal to pursue. The death of the oppressor was their great hope. Martyrdom would come in the battlefields. 2 Maccabees 7 presents a classic martyr narrative. The martyrs are those who suffer for their own people, the punishment of the antagonists is hoped for.

The Wisdom of Solomon is at odds with Greco-Roman culture and ideas. It critiques abuse of the poor and all compromise and participation in idolatry. It hopes for the destruction of the wicked and the resurrection of those who have died as a result of their obedience to God.

The *Testament of Moses* points to the concern of Jewish writers to connect the writer's own situation with the history of Israel. Distinctive to such a history is the suffering that the nation has experienced arising from the breaking of the covenant, especially in the abuse of the poor. Even the faithful will suffer as a consequence of the nation's sin. In the text is a connection between martyrdom and salvation. Martyrdom is necessary because it will ensure the coming of God's kingdom and bring about the end of suffering for the people of Israel. It represents more the idea of God avenging the wicked rather than any act of faithfulness which might bring about the transformation of the wicked.

In 1QS 8.3-4 is a connection between suffering and atonement. Through suffering, atonement can be made for the land of Israel and for the faithful. Such suffering will also bring about God's vengeance upon the wicked.

1QH 9.6-8, 23-7 is reminiscent of the suffering figure tradition of Isaiah 53. The suffering of the faithful illuminates many. There is no vicarious suffering component. The text is evidence that resurrection was the hope of the Essenes.

---

114 Nickelsburg (1972):113.
115 See also Sirach 44.1-50.21, Wisdom 10, 4 Maccabees 16.20-24, 18.11-19 and Hebrews 11.

4Q541 is early evidence regarding a key figure who teaches the nations and is rejected. It would seem that the figure would be a blessing to many.

Conclusions

In the previous chapter seven key points were concluded. The Old Testament provides evidence of those who as God's faithful:
1. Proclaim God's word to all opposed to God.
2. Suffer as witnesses.
3. Show total willingness to die for their belief in the one true God of Israel.
4. Die or take upon themselves another's suffering or death.
5. Are ready to suffer and die for their beliefs. Such acts have a transforming impact on the antagonist as well as on their own community.
6. Will be redeemed as the oppressor is held accountable.
7. Are witnesses to the nations

In this chapter, I have observed that a considerable amount of Jewish literature is antagonistic to oppression and foreign powers. It is rooted in biblical traditions. The faithful expected to suffer and be rejected by their own people for speaking or acting in accordance to what they perceived to be God's will (points 1, 2, 3, 4). Some texts hope that through suffering God will vindicate his people by punishing the antagonist (point 6). Their suffering and readiness to die are acts of faithfulness and witness before the enemy. In suffering and martyrdom they did not appear as cowards before their own people. They suffer in the hope of keeping alive the traditions of their ancestors and strengthen those very traditions. Their hope is nationalistic and there is little evidence of any idea that their suffering transformed their enemies; rather they expected punishment (point 6). However, standing firm against the power and might of the empire is significant as dying strengthens the truth claims the martyr makes. Indeed, in 2 Maccabees 7.12 (cf. 4 Macc. 18.3) the king is said to marvel at the martyr's courage (point 5).

There is a change of emphasis between the Old Testament and Jewish developments. Particularly pertinent is the move towards the idea of the act of martyrdom prompting God to avenge the martyr. Martyrdom prompts God to punish the enemy and not to transform them. However, this latter component is not totally missing; the transforming effect is present and it is not beyond the realms of possibility that the enemy may indeed be so impressed by the witness to God that a transformation may occur. Such belief may be even found at Qumran.

In this current chapter, I have put together a broad literary context for understanding Revelation. These texts, which form my literary basis, do not have all things in common. I have examined them not as isolated texts but texts that belong to each other. Each text is a development of an earlier text in the way that Revelation will also be seen to be. Such texts all belong to one tradition developing in different ways their sacred traditions from the particular social setting unique to them. Before considering the Book of Revelation it is necessary to examine in the next chapter the particular social setting that was unique to the writer of the Book of Revelation and his community.

CHAPTER 9

Domitian's Reign

Introduction

I attempted in chapter 8 to establish the literary context that was influential for John. I reinforced how important it is to be aware of this context as it provides the traditions from which John drew and, therefore, is the key to understanding John's intentions in writing. The literary traditions are formative for the believer and the community responding to their particular social and political situations. Correspondingly, these situations have significance for the reading of the traditions. It is therefore paramount that John's particular social situation be fully examined.

John does not simply respond to his individual circumstances. He responds rather to the way he reads and defines his situation in terms of what he expects from it.[1] My work rejects any idea that thought occurs in isolation from the social context. I will endeavour to draw the line from the thought of the thinker to the social world.[2] Interpretation, development, and readjustment of a person's ideology will occur when facing new situations. Groups adapt to protect and develop their community so that they may achieve their goals and assert their interests within the social context of conflict.[3]

Most scholars agree that Revelation was written in the latter period of Domitian's reign, as documented by Irenaeus writing about a century later: 'It was seen ... almost in my own lifetime, at the end of Domitian's reign (*Adv. Haer.* 5.30.3).[4] The main argument against this dating is the paucity of evidence for a widespread persecution in this period. Some argue that Revelation assumes a persecution against the churches and must be dated during a period when there was such a major persecution. I will demonstrate that there is nothing in Domitian's reign that militates against the dating of Revelation to the period suggested by Irenaeus.

---

1 Malina (1983):21-22 uses a symbolic interactionist model to express this phenomenon in which human behaviour is organized around meanings inherited in the tradition.

2 Berger (1986):129.

3 Malina (1983):20.

4 The majority of scholars support this dating; Yarbro Collins (1981):33-45 provides a defence; contrary Bell (1979):93-102; Robinson (1976):221-253, especially 232-233. Margaret Barker (2000):76 argues for more than one date: 'The final form of the Book of Revelation may date from the reign of Domitian, when it was translated in Greek and first made known to the churches. The Book of Revelation is a collection of prophecies and their interpretation, with the oldest material pre-Christian and all the rest clearly antedating the separation of Judaism and Christianity'.

Reliability of Sources about Domitian

The question of the historical Domitian is debated due to the dubious historicity of the sources concerning his life.[5] The general opinion has been to accept that Domitian was a tyrant, and that this affected all around him including the provinces. Along with this goes the acceptance of the historicity of some kind of persecution against churches under Domitian. However, this consensus can no longer be accepted uncritically due to the work of L.L. Thompson and Jones who both argue that Domitian was not a tyrant because there is no evidence for a persecution under Domitian.[6] The starting point for this discussion is Suetonius's biographical work on *The Twelve Caesars*.

How reliable is Suetonius?

Certain criteria should be observed in assessing Suetonius' reliability.[7] Suetonius was born about 70 CE, eleven years before Domitian came to the throne, and he wrote sometime after Domitian's reign. Therefore, Suetonius would have been in his twenties when Domitian was assassinated in 96 CE. Baldwin confirms that Suetonius 'lived through whereof he writes; thus he is as much or as little to be believed as Pliny, Plutarch, Tacitus, Martial or Juvenal'.[8] Thompson wishes to reconstruct Domitian's reign on the basis of particular writers who wrote during that period. Surely it does not necessarily follow however that someone writing during the period should be more reliable.[9] Rather, it is likely that they had more constraints placed upon them.[10] Kennedy suggests, for example, that Quintilian, writing during Domitian's reign retired early because Domitian was exerting too much pressure on him to write eulogies.[11] Suetonius writing later is as reliable as any other source for Domitian.

---

5 Thompson (1990):97 provides a useful summary of the source material for his life.

6 Thompson (1990); Jones (1996); as well as these scholars, earlier scholars were also sceptical about a persecution during Domitian's reign. Henderson (1927):45 admits that there might have been a persecution, but if there was, it was very short lived; Merrill (1945):154-164 there was no persecution; also Krodel (1989):35-39; Wall (1991):10-12.

7 Most classical historians accept the reliability of Suetonius: Ektor (1980):317-326; Baldwin (1983); Wallace-Hadrill (1983); Grant (1970, 79 and 94); Carradice (1993) to name but a few. L.L.Thompson is one of a few who question it.

8 Baldwin (1983):296.

9 Thompson (1990):103. Review of Thompson see Strand (1991).

10 Wells (1984):180.

11 Kennedy (1969):26.

*Is there evidence for both negative and positive presentations of Domitian? Does
Suetonius avoid giving his own opinion on events regarding Domitian's reign?*

Suetonius gathers together information both for and against the respective
Caesars.[12] This is illustrated well in terms of Domitian:

> Some of Domitian's campaigns were unprovoked, others necessary (*Dom.* 6).

Domitian 6 challenges Thompson's understanding that Suetonius speaks with a
negative voice regarding Domitian's military successes. The impartial nature of
Suetonius is clear, unlike those writing during Domitian's reign, who, Thompson
notes, sing the praises of his military successes and upon whom Thompson so
depends.[13] Baldwin writes:

> Tacitus and Pliny, followed by Dio, retail indignant accusations of sham wars and fake
> triumphs. The grinding of axes in both Tacitus and Pliny is so loud as to be self-
> evident. There is none of this nonsense in Suetonius . . . A far cry from the rabid
> sarcasms of Pliny and Tacitus. Suetonius is echoing the favourable and often forgotten
> tributes to Domitianic military exploits.[14]

Some argue that Suetonius wrote to portray Domitian badly in order to please his
emperor Trajan.[15] This argument is difficult to sustain for Suetonius often writes
positively of Domitian, as well as negatively (as with the other Caesars). For
example, Suetonius tells us that Domitian restored a great many buildings that were
gutted (*Dom.* 5). He made a number of social innovations that could be seen to
benefit society (*Dom.* 7). Suetonius reports that during Domitian's reign, the
honesty among provincial governors and city magistrates had never before been
seen (*Dom.* 8.2). This is hardly a way to portray someone badly. Suetonius suggests
that the situation in Domitian's time was better than in Trajan's regarding the
handling of administration. The argument that Suetonius wrote to portray Domitian
negatively for the purpose of heightening Trajan cannot easily be sustained. In
chapter 9 Suetonius writes:

> While still young, Domitian hated the idea of bloodshed . . . and drafted an edict
> forbidding the sacrifice of oxen. No one thought of him as in the least greedy or mean
> either before, or some years after, his accession - in fact, he gave conspicuous signs of
> self-restraint and even of generosity, treating all his friends with great consideration . . .
> (*Dom.* 9).

---

12 Grant (1989):8; Jones (1996):xiv-xv.
13 Thompson (1990):103.
14 Baldwin (1983):299.
15 Thompson (1990):114; Yarbro Collins (1984b):72.

Is there a tendency to avoid building up the characteristics of Domitian into a coherent picture?

Suetonius avoids building up his characters into coherent pictures.[16] I will examine this in terms of Domitian. Suetonius writes of the deterioration in Domitian's character:

> His leniency and self-restraint were not, however, destined to continue long, and the cruel streak in him became apparent (*Dom.* 10).

This needs to be compared with *Dom.* 3:

> At the beginning of his reign Domitian would spend hours alone every day doing nothing but catch flies and stabbing them with a needle-sharp pen.

Suetonius does not attempt to harmonize his account of Domitian to present a coherent picture of his character. The presentation of a man who hates bloodshed, yet is prepared to carry out wars does not tally. Today we are aware of the subjective nature of journalism and the writing of history. So often the writer in control of an account feels the need to fill in the gaps and produce a more consistent picture of events for that is what the reader expects. However, the most accurate accounts of events in life are not necessarily coherent, since people are neither always consistent nor always coherent. This must be kept in mind in reconstructing the nature of Domitian's life.

Domitian 3 comments on the reasons for Domitian's decline:

> it was lack of funds that made him greedy, and fear of assassination that made him cruel.

It is not easy to talk about the early, noble, Domitian and the later, tyrannical Domitian. Seeds of tyranny are sown from an early age, and the most noble can become the most tyrannical. This is especially the case with a leader of an empire whose aims were once noble yet deteriorated with continual failure leading ultimately to despotism. Suetonius does not blame the emperor. If anything, there may be hints of compassion in his account. Domitian tried hard but continual failure led to a decline in his psychological state. This decline is given an historical base by some scholars in the uprising of Saturninus. Kennedy writes:

> At the beginning of AD 89, he [Domitian] had an experience from which he never totally recovered: a dangerous revolt by Saturninus, who was in command of the army

---

16 Grant (1989):8.

in Germany. The revolt was put down, but it aroused in the emperor feelings of
suspicion and insecurity which lasted until his assassination in 96.[17]

Concluding Remarks

Suetonius lived and worked in Rome and was aware of the various intrigues during
the reign of Domitian and on one occasion, provided his own eyewitness account of
an incident during Domitian's reign (*Dom.* 12). Domitian is portrayed both
negatively and positively. It is clear that Suetonius avoids giving his own opinion on
the events. In view of this, we should conclude that Suetonius is a reliable source for
understanding Domitian's reign.

Domitian and the Provinces

The pressures of leading an empire resulted in great extremes in Domitian's
behaviour. Suetonius suggests that he set out to achieve good, but even in the early
days, he appeared to show tendencies to melancholy and paranoia. Increasing
pressure from those who thought they could do a better job, and a lack of money,
caused Domitian to drift towards despotism. However, his clever handling of many
events never deserted him, even in his attempts to put down usurpers or perceived
usurpers to his throne.

Domitian was an able man who restored many important buildings (*Dom.* 5). He
took measures to deal with the high price of grain (*Dom.* 7),[18] and against the
planting of vines in Italy (*Dom.* 7). *Domitian 7* illustrates that Domitian was aware
of what was happening and was prepared to issue edicts for the benefit of his
citizens. The fact that he did not impose them may be read positively inasmuch as
he had the good sense to leave well alone.[19]

In *Domitian* 8 Suetonius reports that Domitian was conscientious in dispensing
justice. 8.2 points to Domitian's administrative skill:

> [Domitian] kept such a tight hold on the city magistrates and provincial governors that
> the general standard of honesty and justice rose to an unprecedented high level - you
> need only observe how many such personages have been charged with every kind of
> corruption since his time (*Dom.* 8.2).[20]

---

17 Kennedy (1969):26; also, Carson (1990):30; for the revolt of Saturninus see Dio Cassius's
RH 65.2,2,1.

18 Thompson (1990):165.

19 For further discussion see Court (1979):59-60; Wells (1984):181-182; Thompson
(1990):165; Sweet (1979):140; Kraybill (1996):147-148.

20 This text illustrates the points Thompson makes in his discussion of Domitian and the
Provinces (64-167); also Bell (1979).

There is little reason to question the accuracy of Suetonius's praise.[21] The main function of the governor was to control the army rather than the administration of justice or the supervision of tax collections. However, Jones believes that this was not the case during Domitian's reign. He writes:

> in view of Domitian's fondness for the minutiae of administration coupled with his suspicious nature, it would not be surprising if both imperial and local administrators were comparatively honest (or rather if they avoided blatant dishonesty), the former from fear of detection, the latter through hope of promotion as well.[22]

Jones argues his point also on the basis that many innovations occurred in the provinces during Domitian's reign, including building projects and changes in the way that the provinces were organized. He observes incidents that reveal Domitian autocratically instructing the procurator of Syria. Jones suggests that Domitian was involved in the issuing of a decree in 85 that prevented local officials of Acmonia in Phrygia from embezzling the endowments of wealthy provincials to their native city. Pleket observes that according to Pliny, after Domitian's death the provincial governors started extorting money from the provincials (2.11, 12; 3.9; 4.9; 5.20; 6.5, 13; 7.6, 10). Pleket comments that this could never have happened during Domitian's reign.[23] Starr suggested that: 'one root of Domitian's difficulties with the Senate was his effort to check senatorial abuses in the provinces'.[24]

Evidence of Unrest in Asia Minor

In nearly every major city of the Roman Empire, there were incidents of ordinary members of the community picking up cobbles, broken tiles, and rocks to throw at the rich, especially in times of hunger.[25] It is also significant that the emperor gave priority to Rome and its needs. In a time of famine, for example, Rome's needs would come first.[26] This would surely exacerbate the feelings of the poor towards the aristocracy of Rome. According to the forty-sixth discourse of Dio Chrysostom there was a riot in north-western Asia Minor. The cause of this riot was connected

---

21 This has been challenged. See Jones (1992):109.

22 Wells (1984):145; Jones (1992):110; Swete (1922):xciii; Caird (1984):22-23 observes that the governor in the provinces was entrusted with full powers which enabled him to make his own rules and assess his own penalties. On the evidence of Trajan's reply to Pliny's letter about the Christians (Pliny, *Ep*, x.97), the only restriction on the governor was that he could not initiate procedure, there must be an accuser; Price (1984):2, and 43-44 realizes the limitations of the Roman governor and states that in many cases the cities continued to organize themselves (2).

23 Pleket (1961):301.

24 Starr (1982):75; Wells (1984):18: 'the people of the empire had much to thank him for, even though the Senate feared him and hated him'; see Rogers (1984):71.

25 MacMullen (1974):66.

26 Garnsey & Saller (1987):99.

with an increase in the price of grain.[27] This incident is usually dated to the latter part of Vespasian's reign, but it does show the tensions that prevailed in Asia Minor. Domitian would be only too aware of the potential for violence and this awareness may have led to his concern regarding the failure of the grain harvest. Such circumspection was wise. He knew the potential for mob violence and resentment against Rome and its representatives. This circumspection may account for the provincial praise of Domitian in the Jewish *Sibylline Oracles* 12.124-142.[28] This text is dated around 235 CE. It is difficult to establish why a Jew would praise Domitian at such a late date unless there was a tradition that he aided the provinces, which is corroborated by Suetonius in *Domitian* 8. There is evidence of unrest, which supports the view that there was poverty among the provinces. However, it might be argued that Domitian would do his best to control the situation to avoid economic instability. In so doing, he would maintain *pax Romana*.

Evidence of Persecution

I will consider the ancient sources that may provide clues as to whether Domitian persecuted churches in the provinces. Evidence for a persecution has been detected in 1 Clement, Suetonius, Dio Cassius, and Pliny's letter to Trajan.[29]

Suetonius: The Jewish Tax

praeter ceteros Iudaicus fiscus acerbissime actus est; ad quem deferebantur qui vel improfessi Iudaicam viverent vitam vel dissimulata origine imposita genti tributa non pependissent (*Dom.* 12.2).

Apart from the other (treasuries), the Jewish tax was administered severely; to those who had been accused/indicted (*deferebantur*) either (*vel*) of not professing Judaism but living a Jewish life, or (*vel*), their origins being dissembled, did not pay (*non pependissent*) the tax (*tributa*) imposed upon the nation (*genti*) (my translation).

This tantalizing text tells us how Domitian extended the Jewish tax to two groups who had not previously been thought liable to it (*Dom.* 12.1). Scholars have shown much interest in questions regarding the identities of these groups. It has also been a conundrum as to whether Domitian extended the tax to make money - or was it a fee Jews paid to be exempt from imperial cult activities - or both? I will appraise whether the events referred to in this text would impinge upon church members living in Asia Minor.

---

27 Yarbro Collins (1984b):96.
28 Thompson (1990):137; Kraybill (1996):35.
29 Swete (1922):lxxviii-xciii; Beckwith (1919):204; Caird (1984):20.

The tax imposed upon the nation refers to Vespasian's imposition of the tax which occurred before Domitian's reign.[30] According to Dio this tax was imposed only on practising Jews during Vespasian's reign.[31] Wallace suggests after his careful study of Egyptian documents that Vespasian taxed women, slaves and children.[32] He considers that those who publicly confessed and lived a Jewish life would be liable to the tax. According to Josephus, Vespasian made all Jews, wherever they lived, liable to the tax. The money from the tax would also be paid to the Capitoline temple (*War* 7.218). Dio suggests that the tax Josephus and Suetonius mention also was an exemption fee:

> From this time forth it was ordered that Jews who continued to observe their ancestral customs should pay an annual tribute of two denarii to Jupitor Capitolinus (*RH.* 65.7.2).[33]

DOMITIAN'S ADMINISTRATION OF THE TAX

It is assumed that Suetonius' account in *Domitian* 12.2 supports the view that the tax, imposed originally by Vespasian, was extended by Domitian to those not previously liable.[34] An inscription from the period of Nerva indicates that Nerva took the following measures: 'FISCI IUDAICI CALUMNIA SUBLATA'.[35] According to this, Nerva removed (*sublata*) the false accusation (*calumnia*) of being liable to the Jewish tax. It seems that Domitian's reforming policy, to gather taxes from groups not previously liable, had given rise to false accusations against those who really were not liable to the tax, or were liable on the slenderest and most technical grounds. Goodman outlines a context that makes it understandable how some might be considered Jews when they technically were not:

> Gentiles in Rome had taken up Jewish practices without considering themselves, or being considered, Jews: the sabbath was widely observed, avoidance of certain meats would implicate vegetarians such as Pythagoreans, many gentiles might attend synagogues out of curiosity, even circumcision could be endured for non-Jewish reasons.[36]

The tax established by Vespasian became a serious issue under Domitian, whereas before it had been collected with little vigour. Now, Domitian demanded it be collected with more rigour. This understanding is verified in the way those who were ordered to collect the tax ruthlessly inspected a ninety-year old man to see

---

30 Thompson (1982):332; Barclay (1996):310.
31 Dio Cassius *RH*. 66.7.2.
32 Wallace (1938):170-171; Jones (1996):103; Barclay (1996):76-78.
33 Smallwood (1956):3; Barclay (1996):76.
34 Smallwood (1956):4; Williams (1990), argues that it is simply a clamp down on those who are evading it.
35 'the false accusation of the Jewish tax removed'.
36 Goodman (1989):41.

whether he was circumcised (*Dom.* 12.2). Thompson rightly sees the tax extension as fitting with Domitian's reputation as a careful administrator: 'his policy of rigor merely fits with Domitian's general administrative principles of rationality and consistency'.[37]

Suetonius mentions two groups who did not pay Vespasian's Jewish tax. 1) *improfessi Iudaicam viverent vitam* (those who did not profess Judaism but lived the Jewish life). 2) *dissimulata origine* (those who concealed their Jewishness). The text does not suggest that the groups were intentionally evading paying the tax through their *improfessi* and *dissimulata*. Rather, because of their *improfessi* and *dissimulata*, they were not liable to the tax and, therefore, did not pay it.[38] The groups were probably a source of discussion. This resulted in them being accused (*deferebantur*) of *improfessi* and *dissimulata*. They may have been seen to be doing so in order to avoid paying the tax. This rigorous reform in the law implies that Domitian reformed the tax to embrace groups whom he and many others felt should be paying it.[39]

First Group (*improfessi Iudaicam viverent vitam*)

The *improfessi Iudaicam viverent vitam* are those who did not publicly profess Judaism, yet lived a Jewish life. By living the life of a Jew, they practised some aspects of Judaism. Prominent aspects would be the keeping of the sabbath, food laws, reading of the scriptures, synagogue attendance and monotheistic belief. There were many in Asia Minor who did, and they would, therefore, have been prominent to the pagans of Asia Minor. Suetonius distinguishes them as they that *improfessi Iudaicam* (did not profess Judaism). There are two possible understandings of this. 1) They did not make a public spectacle of being Jewish. Therefore, they were technically not Jews in the eyes of the authorities. 2) They had not become fully fledged Jews by being circumcised. Presumably, this meant that they were not signed up members of a synagogue.

The next stage is to test these two understandings and see how they explain how they lived the Jewish life. If they were Jews and they wanted to keep their 'Jewishness' a secret, it is clear that in doing so they sought by not publicly professing Judaism to evade paying the tax. They concealed the fact that they did not eat pork, did not participate in the imperial cult, and kept the sabbath. Yet it is hard to foresee a setting in which such individuals would be able to conceal their Jewishness. Many Jews fitted well into society and adopted pagan customs, including the use of Greek names. This suggests that Jews may not have been so distinguishable.[40] Clearly by their practices they were separate from the rest of Gentile society. It is hard to see how Jews could conceal their Jewishness. The only

---

37 Thompson (1990):134.
38 So supporting Smallwood against Williams.
39 To this extent my position aligns with Williams inasmuch as the tax is a clamp down on those who are evading it. But they are evading it legally, and so the base of the tax needed to be extended to make them liable (so Smallwood).
40 Trebilco (1991):35, 174.

possibility is that they met secretly in each other's houses, and bought kosher from secret butchers or were vegetarian for the sake of practicality. However, there remained the sabbath and Jewish religious festivals that could not be celebrated without being observed. Consequently, identifying the *improfessi Iudaicam viverent vitam* as those living the Jewish life, but who had not made a full commitment to Judaism seems the most plausible reading.[41]

If this is the case, a test case can be established to show how, in the eyes of the authorities, not making a public confession of Judaism was connected with not paying. The groups and individuals, in the eyes of the authorities, were seen as those who lived the Jewish life. Yet in order to avoid paying the tax they refused circumcision (*improfessi*) which meant that they would not fall into that category of needing to notify the authorities that they were Jews. The authorities felt themselves cheated on a technicality in the law which allowed them only to tax fully signed up, synagogue attending, practising Jews. Nevertheless, there are other reasons for not being circumcised. Circumcision was abhorrent to Gentiles. Some objected to being circumcised on theological grounds because they did not believe in synagogue Judaism. This fits the Gentile church members. It could be argued that church and synagogue members were separate groups in the eyes of the Romans by the end of the first century. This is unlikely as both were clearly seen as of the same stock.[42] The reasons for people not being circumcised were irrelevant to the authorities; they were simply seen as a group who had escaped the tax on a technicality in the wording of the law. This is supported by Dio (*RH.* 65.7.2 see above for quote). Dio states that paying the tax exempted the payee from participation in emperor-cult activities. Paying the Jewish tax was a sign of loyalty and subjugation to Rome and its gods. Barclay comments that the tax was a public humiliation as well as an increasing financial burden.[43] He points out that Josephus carefully omits to mention that the money from the tax was used for the temple of Jupiter. This would suggest that Josephus was aware how humiliating this would be, and therefore failed to mention where the money went.[44] Consequently, some were neither paying the tax, nor participating in the emperor-cult. Domitian, with his suspicious nature and administrative acumen, would not allow this to continue. In extending the wording of the law to embrace this group, he would solve the problem of needing to deal with a large number of people who were opting out of the emperor-cult without paying the fee of exemption. This would satisfy the populace who would be quick to inform (*deferebantur*) against such groups. This understanding avoids the problem

---

41 So Smallwood (1956):1-13; Barclay (1996):311; Thompson (1982):329-342 rejects the idea that Gentiles who had taken up Jewish practices were in the mind of Suetonius. Ethnic apostate Jews were in mind.

42 Lieu (1996):12 'Pagan writers who still confused the two religions may have been representative of some popular perception even among adherents of the two religions'.

43 Barclay (1996):310; Smallwood (1956):3 comments that in effect Jews purchased the right to worship the LORD by subscription to Jupiter. See also Oakman (1993):13.

44 Barclay (1996):76. However, Josephus does report that the tax was paid to the Capitoline temple (*War* 7.218). This would not suggest that Josephus was embarrassed.

of why anyone would evade paying the tax if it allowed him or her freedom to practise his or her religion.

Also, it allows for the abuses to which the Nerva inscription testifies. Goodman noted that many Gentiles kept personal rules with regards to diet and occasional synagogue attendance, and yet had no wish to be identified as Jews.[45] Such people would be vulnerable to the new reforms. Although many from this group would participate in the emperor-cult, they now perhaps found themselves vulnerable on a technicality in the law. This was indeed an abuse. Today's law on child abuse may serve to illustrate the point. Government agencies are rightly concerned to develop laws to detect any abuses committed against children. Such agencies have to investigate all reported incidences of child abuse and are empowered to act even to the extent of placing a child in care. Even though this can lead to cases in which false accusations are made, the parents and guardians must still suffer the stigma of being accused, and possibly would have their child taken away. Most would agree that this is an abuse of a good policy.[46] In much the same way, Domitian's policy became open to abuse.

The Second Group: concealed their origins (*dissimulata origine*)

The setting was that of Jews not registering as Jews when those who acted as informers felt they should. They were Jews by birth and yet had not registered to pay the Jewish tax.[47] The *dissimulata*, therefore, would be parallel with the *improfessi* (see above). Such actions were seen as ways of not registering or avoiding paying the tax. This explains the case of the ninety-year old reported by Suetonius (*Dom.* 12.2). The man had not registered as a Jew and was thus humiliated by the inspection that followed Domitian's reform.

Three groups are understood to have been concealing their Jewish origins. 1) Practising Jews trying to evade payment as an understandable protest against supporting a pagan cult. 2) Apostates. 3) Jewish Christians who did not consider themselves members of the synagogue and did not register for the Jewish tax. Jewish Christians were, also, apostates in the eyes of the synagogue and were considered apostate Jews by pagan writers in the second century.[48] We can distinguish two groups of apostates. One group consisted of Jews who willingly participated in the emperor-cult and a second group who did not participate in activities connected with the emperor-cult, i.e. Jewish Christians. These groups need further consideration.

---

45 Goodman (1989):41.

46 Bredin (1998):160-164; Thompson (1982):200 also agrees insofar as he states that Nerva rejects the Domitian interpretation of Vespasian's original decree by declaring that apostate Jews were not required to pay. However, where we disagree is that Thompson argues that Domitian intentionally extended the tax to embrace apostate Jews.

47 Barclay (1996):77 writes that 'tax collectors perhaps relied on lists of members supplied by the synagogues'. This may be the case, but with the extension it should be assumed that people were liable who were not on the synagogue list, such as gentile Christians.

48 Origen *Contra Celsus* 2.4, see also Wilken (1984):113.

Jewish apostates who were not Christian had no reason to avoid participating in the life of a pagan culture. Why then impose the tax on them if they participated in the emperor cult? Goodman observes that the policy of Rome was to accept the right of ethnic Jews like other people to assimilate into the Roman community so long as they gave up their peculiar customs.[49] Domitian's tax reforms regarding apostates breaks with this policy. It is difficult to appreciate why Domitian imposed the tax on this group. Goodman suggests that Nerva reformed Domitian's tax in order to remove such apostate Jews from liability. Such reform he writes 'might be considered by Nerva as a means to court popularity in the city of Rome'.[50] It is possible that Domitian's zeal for the imperial cult led him to glean money from as many as possible. Suetonius also reports that Domitian's new building programmes and increased army pay had exhausted his resources (*Dom.* 12).[51] Carradice writes: 'Possibly because of a growing awareness of impending financial difficulties he perhaps now began the rigorous enforcement and collection of taxes, including the Jewish tax'.[52] Still it seems unlikely that Domitian had this group in mind. There have been two observed motives underlying the reform of the Jewish tax. Firstly, to make those pay who were not participating in the emperor-cult. Secondly, to raise money to build up a depleted treasury. It is difficult to see why anyone would accuse an apostate of not making public their origins in order to avoid paying the tax, when there was no reason why they should pay the tax. It is more likely that the authorities would encourage apostasy. The synagogue might indict an apostate out of vengeance.[53] This would fit with the Nerva inscription and accounts for the incident of the inspection of a ninety-year old reported by Suetonius.

The main group that Domitian may have had in mind were circumcised, ethnic Jews who did not participate in the cult. Their accusers saw them as not being honest about their Judaism, those who dissembled information that should be revealed to the authorities. They were ethnic Jews, but they had no sympathies with synagogue Judaism, yet still they did not take part in the cult. Another group were Jews who simply refused to pay the tax because the money was paid towards the rebuilding of the temple of Jupiter and, consequently, they did not register as liable for the tax when they were liable. This group concealed their origins so as not to pay the tax. In concealing such origins, they did not attend the local synagogue and were not seen as signed up members. Two groups would conceal their origins.

Firstly, Jewish Christians would be liable to Domitian's reform of the tax. They were Jews by birth and all had been circumcised. They also lived a Jewish life but without being members of the synagogue. This group did not identify with the synagogue. They did not wish to identify with them by paying a tax peculiar to them. Further, they did not participate in the emperor-cult by supporting it with their

---

49 Goodman (1989):41; this is opposed to Thompson (1982).
50 Goodman (1989):41.
51 See discussion in Carradice (1983):165; Jones (1992):74.
52 Carradice (1983):165.
53 Goodman (1989):41; Barclay (1996):77.

money. Goodman comments that the: 'Roman definition of a Jew depended on his or her public declaration of Judaism and acceptance of the burden of the consequent tax'.[54] Jewish Christians were not declaring synagogue Judaism and therefore avoided the tax. This would change with the reforms.

Secondly, there were Jews who refused to pay the tax on grounds of conscience. They would be liable to the reformed tax. A circumcised Jew could intentionally evade paying the pre-reformed tax by not registering. There were Gentiles and synagogue Jews who were unhappy about this and informed against them for not registering. The authorities did not ask questions as to why people were *improfessi* or *dissimulata*. They simply reformed the system to make more people register and pay. In fact, as Hemer notes, Domitian was not fussy about theological distinctions and categories.[55] He was concerned to make all pay who should pay. The opportunity to pay the tax was a great opportunity for some to show loyalty to Rome. It was, however, not so good for those who refused to pay on grounds of conscience. Their sentiments and attitudes towards Rome were now conspicuous if they continued to avoid paying the tax.

CONCLUSION

Domitian widened the Jewish tax to embrace groups and individuals who were not previously considered liable. The reformed Jewish tax impinged on Jews, and those resembling Jews or identified with Jews, everywhere, including Asia Minor. Suetonius does not say that the reformed tax is being evaded. Rather, that there are those, in the eyes of the authorities, who evaded the Jewish tax as established under Vespasian on a technicality in the wording of the law. They were seen as intentionally avoiding paying the tax. There was public unease with these groups which resulted in them being indicted (*deferebantur*). Many who wished not to participate in the emperor-cult would view Domitian's extension favourably. Domitian's administration was in the position to have them tried for not participating in the emperor-cult. Domitian gave such groups a chance to show their loyalty by paying a tax independently of belonging to the synagogue. Domitian needed money and demanding payment from more people would satisfy this necessity.[56] Domitian's policy was effective in dealing with the potentially volatile situation insofar as it separated the loyal from the disloyal. Many were willing to pay the tax, but others would not. Domitian had in mind those who were ethnic Jews who did not participate in the emperor-cult. It may be surmised that the system may have been abused by tax paying Jews, who informed against apostate Jews out of vengeance. The most probable groups were Jewish Christians and rebel Jews (further discussion of the Jewish tax and its significance to Revelation will be discussed in chapter 10).

---

54 Goodman (1989):44; Barclay (1996):77. Both suggest that the tax served to define identity more easily.
55 Hemer (1986):8.
56 Carradice (1983):165.

Further Evidence of Persecution

Melito, bishop of Sardis about 170 CE, observes that:

> Nero and Domitian, also of all [emperors], persuaded by certain malignant persons, desired to bring our doctrine into ill repute; and since their day, by an unreasonable custom, lying information about the Christians has come to be prevalent (*apud* Eusebius *HE*. IV.26.9; translations of Eusebius is from S.E. Parker).

It is possible that this text originates from oral tradition relating to the persecution of church members during Domitian's reign. Church members suffered at the hands of informers. Melito believed, rightly or wrongly, synagogue members were instrumental in making accusations against church members. This is argued on the basis that Melito had no love of Jews and had blamed them for the death of Jesus (*PH*. 73-81). Melito had good sources for his claims that Domitian persecuted Christians. His account is knowledgeable of details regarding informers that could even be related to the Jewish tax.

Tertullian writes:

> Domitian almost equalled Nero in cruelty, but because he had common-sense, he soon stopped what he begun and recalled those he had exiled (*apud* Eusebius *HE*. 3.20).

Tertullian writing a century after the events he describes plays down the persecution under Domitian although saying that the emperor exiled those who were considered a threat. This is further corroborated by Dio who recounts the fate of Domitilla who was exiled to Pandateria (*RH*. 67.14). The common sense of Domitian is seen in not instigating a pogrom against church members. More likely Domitian carried out *ad hoc* acts against individuals and small groups throughout his reign. Tertullian records that Domitian recalled those who had been banished. This suggests that Tertullian had some example in mind that would indicate the use of a written or oral source. The church historian, Hegesippus, in the second century narrates something similar when remarking that Domitian ordered that a previously established persecution against Christians should cease when he concluded after investigating certain Christians that they were 'as simpletons' (*apud* Eusebius *HE* 3.20). This bolsters the picture of Domitian as one who sought out those who were political threats to his reign and were in positions to stir up ordinary people.[57] Here he lets the simpletons go. Unfortunately, the historicity of Hegesippus's account is dubious. It seems doubtful that Domitian himself would question a few church leaders from

---

57 Barnard (1963-64):254, 'The account falls into line with what we know, from Roman sources, of the character of the Emperor. Christians no more than others would escape if Domitian thought they were a threat to his position. But it is unlikely . . . that he would have instituted a wholesale persecution of Christians simply because of their faith'. Barnard's comments are fair; however, one needs to take care in separating religion from politics. For the first-century person, the two were interconnected and new sects would be viewed suspiciously; see Kraybill (1996):50-52.

Palestine. It is questionable also that he would be foolish enough to think that only members of the elite would be a threat to him. He would know too well that the economically deprived also would be a threat, for they had nothing to lose.[58]

Clement of Rome

> Owing, dear brethren, to the sudden and successive calamitous events which have happened to ourselves, we feel we have been somewhat tardy in turning our attention to the points which you consulted us (*1 Clem.* 1.1; tr. R. Robertson and F. Crombie).

The *First Epistle of Clement* to the Corinthians deals with problems that the Corinthian Christians were experiencing. The letter is contemporary with Domitian. Troubles in Rome caused a delay in the sending of the epistle to Corinth. The text expresses one of two possibilities. The 'sudden and successive calamitous events' could refer to a persecution.[59] Yet they could also refer to a delay due to internal problems within the church of Rome. It is difficult to see that a letter offering advice about the internal problems to the Corinthian church would begin by referring to its own internal problems. It would be like a marriage guidance counsellor arriving late to a session with a couple and excusing herself on the grounds that she had just had an irreparable row with her husband. In chapter 7 Clement of Rome refers to the suffering they all share because of the faithful witness to God they give. The suffering that the Church was experiencing in Rome was connected with specific policies of Domitian.

Pliny the Younger

Pliny's letter to Trajan about 112 CE recognizes that church members suffered under Domitian:

> Others, whose names were given to me by an informer, first admitted the charge and then denied it; they said that they had ceased to be Christians two or more years previously, and some of them even twenty years ago (*Ep.* 96).

The letter implies that there had in the past been occasional, though not necessarily frequent, instances of church members being taken to court on criminal charges.[60] What is significant is that Pliny informs Trajan that there were those who had abandoned their faith twenty years before, i.e. in 92 CE. This may reveal the policies of Domitian as the cause of the investigations. Yet there can be no certainty. There may only have been a local outbreak of persecution in Bithynia at that time.

---

58 See Bauckham (1990):90-91.
59 This is the argument preferred by Barnard (1963-64):255-256.
60 Caird (1984):20.

The fact that Pliny had no precedent for what to do with church members might indicate that there was no persecution of Christians.[61]

Domitian and the Imperial Cult

> 'Lord and God' [*dominus et deus*] became his regular title in writing and conversation. Images dedicated to Domitian in the Capitol had to be of either gold or silver, and of a certain weight (Suetonius *Dom.* 13).

As this text suggests, aspects of the imperial cult were endorsed and encouraged by Domitian. However, Thompson, as we have seen, challenges by and large the historicity of Suetonius's account.[62] He points to the lack of inscriptions, coins, and medallions to verify the above text. He also observes that Domitian is not referred to as *dominus et deus* in the important writings of Statius and Quintilian. This is surprising as Domitian commissioned both to write and would expect full titles and gratitude to be given.

There can be no disagreement with Thompson's observation regarding the title *dominus et deus* being absent on coins. Janzen, however, points out the 'message is clearly communicated in other ways'.[63] Carradice carefully observes about 211 coin types relating to Domitian's reign. On the basis of his observations Carradice concludes:

> Not only does Domitian himself appear on an unprecedented quantity of designs, but the deities which appear most commonly also had in contemporary legend the most intimate associations with him. Domitian even appears on one reverse type holding a divine attribute (the thunderbolt of Jupiter) and the regular use of the aegis on the obverse portrait adds to the impression that the coinage was being employed to project an ideological message related to the Emperor's aspirations to divinity.[64]

Carradice also observes Domitian's unusual 'Neronian' hairstyle which possibly relates to the promotion of self-apotheosis, like Nero.[65] A brief observation of the data will show clearly that Carradice's conclusion is well supported.

During Domitian's reign several unprecedented developments in coinage issues occurred which led to an understanding of an emperor who aspired towards divinity.[66] The 'present' divinity of Domitian's family is reflected on those issues where his wife, Domitia, was presented as the mother of the divine Caesar. These issues refer to the son they had lost as an infant. Janzen comments that this is a new development insofar as they reveal that Domitian had his son consecrated while he

---

61 See Downing (1988) and in a later chapter of this book.
62 Thompson (1990):105.
63 Janzen (1994):655-656.
64 Carradice (1983):148.
65 Carradice (1993):170.
66 Janzen (1994):645; Kraybill (1996):63.

was alive. The son is pictured as a baby Jupiter seated on a globe with arms outstretched surrounded by seven stars. Astrological representations such as the globe and stars were common on coinage, but the appearance of an infant is not common. The consensus regarding the message of the coin is that the globe was representative of world dominion and power, while stars communicate the divine nature of the figure they surround.[67] It is, therefore, reasonable to conclude, with Janzen, that this particular coin portrays a son of a god, and Domitian is clearly the father of god.[68] Similarly, and more forcefully, this deified status of Domitian can be seen on the 'Minerva with *fulmen*' type coins. In some cases, Domitian holds the *fulmen* himself thus seizing for himself a divine attribute - the thunderbolt. It is interesting to note the chronology of minting. Janzen points out that it is in 85-86 CE that Jupiter and Domitian share the *fulmen*. However, in the years 87-96 Domitian alone held the *fulmen*, thus leading to the conclusion that Domitian became increasingly hungry for power and deification in the latter years thus supporting the evidence of Suetonius that Domitian became a tyrant in the latter period.[69] Carradice suggests that 'we might see Domitian himself as Jupiter on earth, holding the thunderbolt'.[70]

Although the coinage supports the view that Domitian extended his status in the imperial cult, there is no evidence in the writings of Statius or Quintilian that the designation *dominus et deus* was used of Domitian. On the contrary, Statius reports that Domitian rejected the title of *dominus* when acclaimed so at a banquet (*Silvae* I, vi, 82-83). However, Scott, commenting on *Silvae* I, vi, 82-83, observes that this moderation was of short duration.[71] Moreover, it fits the evidence of Suetonius, so far observed, inasmuch as Suetonius portrays the early Domitian as moderate, but that this was short lived. A brief assessment of Statius's and Quintilian's work will confirm this.

Statius refers obsequiously to Domitian's sacred frame, hallowed feet, and celestial eyes. He depicts Domitian as one like Jove (*Silvae* V, i, 37-38). He writes that Domitian:

reclines among the stars with Jupiter and receives the immortal wine from the hand of Trojan Ganymede (*Silvae* IV, ii, 10-12).[72]

Scott points out that the designation *Dominus* itself is used in the description of a banquet in the royal palace. Statius refers to it as *dominica mensa* (the table of the

---

67 Janzen (1994):646.

68 Janzen (1994):647.

69 Janzen (1994):648; Carradice (1983):144.

70 Carradice (1993):172, Martial and Statius (contemporaries of Domitian) repeatedly refer to Domitian as Jove and Thunderer, 172.

71 Scott (1933):249.

72 Note that this coheres with the above coin evidence of Domitian with the thunderbolt.

Lord) (*Silvae* IV, ii, 6).[73] Elsewhere Statius refers to the *numen* (godhead) of Domitian:

Hail, offspring and sire of mighty deities, whose godhead (*numen*) I heard from afar! (*Silvae* I, i, 75).

Similarly in his introduction to Book Four which he addresses to his friend:

I believe that no work of mine has opened without an invocation of the godhead of our mighty prince [Domitian].

In the same vein, Statius speaks of the divinity of Domitian quite unambiguously:

Lo! A god (*deus*) is he, at Jove's command he rules for him the happy world.

Statius reports that the goddess Minerva wove for Domitian a robe with her own hand (*Silvae* IV, i, 21-22). The implication is that Minerva was understood as the mother of Domitian and Domitian as a son of god.

In sum, the evidence about Domitian gathered from Statius does not support Thompson's argument. On the contrary, it indicates the opposite conclusion. Even if Statius were a flatterer,[74] he would not have been so excessive if Domitian had been a more moderate man. There is further evidence that coheres with Statius.

We encounter a more sober style than that of Statius in the writings of Quintilian. He, on the whole, never names or sings the praises of the emperors.[75] There are, however, exceptions in the case of Domitian. Quintilian knew that Domitian lived in the shadow of his father, Vespasian, and his brother, Titus. Domitian did not take part in the wars in which his father and brother had been involved. He justified this absence saying that he voluntarily chose to withdraw into a life of writing (Tacitus *Histories* IV, 86). Quintilian breaks his usual custom and states that what Domitian said was true. In saying this, Quintilian refutes those who thought him a coward. This would suggest that Domitian was sensitive about this accusation. Quintilian and others felt compelled to praise Domitian's poetry, thus corroborating Domitian's account.[76] Kennedy suggests that this reference in the restrained Quintilian suggests that Domitian was very touchy on the subject, and that there was some danger that an informer might accuse Quintilian of slighting the emperor.[77] Kennedy also comments that Quintilian's early retirement was linked with a

---

73 Scott (1933):250.

74 Jones (1992):108: 'The best that an emperor could expect after death was to be declared a divus, never a deus'. Domitian was in fact attributed with this name. Jones argues that it was due to Statius being a flatterer. But Suetonius reports that Domitian encouraged the use of the title and Statius provides an example of it being in part attributed to Domitian. *Deus* occurs elsewhere in *Silvae* I, i, 61-2; V, i, 37-38. See also Dio Cassius *RH* 67.13.3-4.

75 Slater (1998):236-237 also notes the significance of Quintilian.

76 *Valerius Flaccus* 1.12; Silus *Italicus* 111, 620; Statius *Achilleid* 1, 15-16.

77 Kennedy (1966):110.

deteriorating situation beginning with Saturninus' revolt in 89 CE. In other words, Quintilian was shrewd and saw 90 CE as an excellent time to retire. Kennedy may be right about this text. Yet it is also possible that Quintilian is just telling the truth. However, given what we know about Domitian and his tendency to like flattery, Quintilian probably defended Domitian for the sake of safety.

The Impact of the Imperial Cult in Asia Minor

they revere him [Augustus] with temples and sacrifices over islands and continents, organised in cities and provinces, matching the greatness of his virtue and repaying his benefactions towards them (Nicholaus of Damascus).[78]

The imperial cult was popular among the populace in Asia Minor.[79] The nature of the cult was to give honour to Caesar. Price quotes (above) Nicolaus of Damascus's biography of the emperor Augustus as providing a view of the imperial cult. Price observes that the forms of practice of the cult varied from place to place.[80] It was expressed through public celebrations, festivals, and special imperial festivals where the imperial priests representing the people offered sacrifices.

Imperial temples and sanctuaries were extremely common in over sixty cities in Asia Minor and dedicated to the imperial cult. The emperor received statues in special rooms off the main square of half-a-dozen cities and buildings.[81] Images of the emperor are seen even in a less significant city like Laertes where archaeological work has uncovered seven imperial statue bases. I will now look at the evidence regarding the imperial cult in the seven cities of Asia Minor to which Revelation was sent.

The imperial cult in *Ephesus* became particularly prominent in Domitian's reign.[82] It was graced with four imperial temples, an Antonine altar, and an imperial portico. Four gymnasia were associated with the emperor. Some Imperial statues were found in public buildings and in the streets.[83] Something of the atmosphere of the city can be sensed from its civic centre where imperial temples and sanctuaries can be found. Within the upper square is a double temple of Roma and Julias Caesar along with statues of Augustus and his wife Livia, a temple of Augustus, and a temple of Domitian.[84] Friesen believes that the buildings are distinctive and unique

---

78 Quoted in Price (1984):1; other literary references to the cult: Philo *Legatio* 149-151, and Lucian *Apologia* 13.
79 Price (1984) provides a thorough study of this subject.
80 Price (1984):3.
81 Price (1984):135.
82 Friesen (1993):41-49; Kraybill (1996):27.
83 Price (1984):137; Friesen (1993):41-49; Kraybill (1996):64 comments that the huge statue found at Ephesus is the very 'image of the beast' condemned by John.
84 Price (1984):139, also 197-198: Price suggests that the dedication of the temple to Domitian and his deified relatives prompted the author of Revelation to write. See also Court

to Asia Minor suggesting real zeal for the cult in Asia Minor.[85] A temple in *Smyrna* was dedicated to Tiberius (Tacitus, *Ann.* 4.15). Within is a cult statue of Tiberius in a toga, perhaps with a veiled head (the official dress of the Roman emperor). The veiled head might imply that the emperor was depicted as a priest.[86] This should not be surprising as the gods often had their own priesthoods.[87] *Pergamum* was considered the capital of Roman Asia. It was also a great religious centre that had a separate temple for the worship of Rome and the emperor.[88] Augustus in 29 BCE permitted the erection of temples to Roma and himself at *Pergamum*. The provincial temple at *Pergamum* is portrayed on many coins of the city.[89] Thyatira is infrequently referred to in ancient literature and remains of the city reveals few signs of its past. These two factors make it difficult to reconstruct the importance of this city. In spite of this, Hemer ventures to conclude that 'its religion and organisation point to a quest for a syncretistic reconciliation of diverse elements in its population'.[90] The city served an important function in the Roman road system, for it lay on the road from *Pergamum* to *Laodicea*. It would therefore have been a busy cosmopolitan city. It was also known as a strong manufacturing town. Its industries were indebted to the imperial cult, for example, dyeing, garment making, and brass working (cf. Acts 16.14).[91] Much is known of *Sardis* and its enthusiasm for the cult. For example, in commemoration of the coming of age of Gaius Caesar, the city decreed a festival and the consecration of a cult statue of Gaius Caesar in Augustus's temple.[92] *Philadelphia* existed in fear of earthquakes. Some writers refer to the generosity of the emperor in providing relief after the great earthquake of 17 CE.[93] It is known from the coinage that under Vespasian the city took the imperial epithet 'Flavia' and this continued until Domitian's death. Finally, in *Laodicea* lies a temple dedicated to Domitian thus strengthening the connection between city and cult.

(1994):100. Interestingly, Price (1984):178 suggests that the temple of Domitian at Ephesus was rededicated to Vespasian after Domitian's memory was discredited.

85 Friesen (1993):73; Kraybill (1996):28.

86 Price (1984):185.

87 Price (1984):185.

88 Harris (1979):21.

89 Hemer (1986):84; Kraybill (1996):60.

90 Hemer (1986):127.

91 Hemer (1980):121 comments that the city was remarkable for the number of its temples and religious festivals.

92 Price (1984):66, for a detailed list of the evidence see 259-260.

93 Dio Cassius *RH* 57.17.8; *Strabo* 13.4.8.

Impact of the Imperial Cult on the Churches

It is likely that the imperial cult troubled church members.[94] Tertullian records how a Christian was rebuked in a dream because his slaves had put wreaths on his gates at the sudden announcement of public rejoicings concerning the emperor (*de Idol* 13-16). There is little evidence reporting any imperial sacrifice. Price comments that the major part of the evidence comes from inscribed descriptions of and prescriptions for the sacrifices.[95] Price writes that sacrifices were made on a variety of occasions, public and private, by individuals or by the representatives of city or province. The burning of incense, on altars, or the killing of an animal, normally a bull, were the standard offerings at public festivals. There is evidence to suggest that such sacrifices were made before an imperial statue or temple.[96] Price observes two main categories of sacrifices, namely, sacrifices to the emperor and sacrifices on behalf of the emperor.[97] Most of the evidence points to the latter sacrifice being the most common. However, there is support of sacrifices being offered to the emperor.[98] Price points out that church members were unable to make any sacrifice due to that fact that the sacrifice of Christ upon the cross had in principle ruled out the efficacy of any other sacrifices.[99] Moreover, to sacrifice to the emperor or Roman gods would be to imply that the emperor was a god, that Rome was supreme, and this was unacceptable. The refusal of church members to offer sacrifice on behalf of the emperor was a sign of disrespect and treason.

Sweet objects to the significance of the emperor cult: 'Domitian did affect divinity; Domitian indeed required to be addressed as "Lord and God". But in actual practice the emperor cult . . . was the preserve of the local aristocracy; the average provincial had no direct part'.[100] However, Price sees the involvement of all classes. He writes that the involvement of the whole community was expressed by the regulation that householders should sacrifice on altars outside their houses as the procession passed.[101] The processions were aspects of the cult and often a bull was sacrificed at the end of the procession.[102] It is the expectation that all were required to offer sacrifices. Omitting to do this would cause problems for church members.

Finally, the cult tested the loyalty of those suspected of disloyalty to the emperor. Such a test did not discriminate on the basis of class. All classes of people would be tested through showing their loyalty to the cult. We rely for our knowledge on Pliny's letter enquiring of Trajan what was to be done with Christians. Church members had to renounce their loyalty to Jesus. They were to repeat a formula of

---

94 Price (1984):123. Interestingly he comments that Christian resistance to the cult consisted in passive resistance.
95 Price (1984):208.
96 Price (1984):208-209.
97 Price (1984):209.
98 Price (1984):216.
99 Price (1984):221; Slater (1998):245.
100 Sweet (1979):25-26.
101 Price (1984):112; see Heliodorus *Aethiopica* X 3.
102 Price (1984):111.

invocation to the Roman state gods, and to make offerings of wine and incense to the statue of Trajan, which Pliny reports was brought into the room along with the other images of the gods (*Ep.* 96).

In view of this, it seems likely that all ranks of people participated in the imperial cult. During the period of Domitian's reign, when there was an expansion of the cult, a shrewd observer of political change, such as John, would have been quick to observe the consequences of such developments for the churches. This would have played a significant part on John's thinking as he composed Revelation.

Summary and Conclusions

Domitian was an able administrator. He was aware of the affairs of the empire and was a force to be reckoned with in the provinces. John's community existed within an environment that showed great fervour for the imperial cult. The provinces were willing to express their loyalty to the emperor through worshipping Roman gods and honouring the Caesar.[103]

Domitian's expansion of the imperial cult was related to his need to control and rule. The opposition of church members to any aspect of giving homage to the emperor was dangerous. Pagans and many synagogue members alerted the respective authorities to treasonable behaviour. The deification of the emperor is symptomatic of what is fundamentally wrong with Roman rule, that is, that it claims absolute power. Consequently, the nature of Revelation was political and anti-Domitian, rather than concerned with offended religious sensibilities

The evidence does not suggest a full-scale persecution hypothesis; neither does it support a view that Domitian himself instigated persecution against church members. Domitian was an influential man who knew much that went on in the provinces and would be keen to make sure that suspect groups were dealt with. His influence would impinge upon the governors who would feel pressure to maintain economic and social order. In addition, they would also feel the need to implement Domitian's policies conscientiously, for example, in terms of the imperial cult and paying of the Jewish tax. It would be up to the governors to make sure that such things were done and stability maintained. Christian safety depended on getting on well with their neighbours and authorities. Their existence could be said to be precarious, and certainly if a particularly hostile attitude was adopted towards Rome, it should be expected that suffering would follow. It seems from the above reconstruction that synagogue and church members could do well during Domitian's reign as long as they provided evidence of some compromise towards the cults of gods.

Overall, the rule of Rome was based: (a) on its power and ability to crush any who posed a threat to it through violence; (b) on the principles of gaining wealth. Its policy of *pax Romana* was not a peaceful principle but one that allowed peace

---

103 Kraybill (1996):60-62 suggests the imperial cult was celebrated as an expression of gratitude, a sign of loyalty.

simply for the wealthy to become more wealthy and provide enough for the ordinary citizens so that their disenchantment would not explode into full revolutionary action; (c) on a successful propaganda that convinced ordinary people that Roman rule was divinely ordained and a good thing. It was a rule that invited synagogue and church members to throw their lot in with Rome's ways so that they might become wealthy.

Like all superpowers throughout history, dominion was based on the principles of power and might. There was no place for love and compassion. It was a world far from the one that God intended and one that the prophets of the Old Testament challenged.

CHAPTER 10

The Way of the World
and the Way of Revelation

A preaching that says nothing about the sinful environment in which the gospel is reflected upon is not the gospel. Oscar Romero

Introduction

In the last chapter I attempted to establish what kind of man and emperor Domitian was and how his reign impinged on life in the provinces. Domitian represents the way of the world. My concern in this chapter is the way of Revelation and the particular issues that John faced and took to his meditations on his sacred texts. Of all the New Testament texts Revelation is the most critical of Rome. Oakman sees Revelation as the most exquisite and finely tuned critique of all ancient literature.[1] In this final chapter of Part Two I will consider Revelation as a piece of subversive writing in its first-century context. I will draw upon previous chapters of this book to help understand Revelation as a text in the tradition of subversive literature like the Old Testament prophets and in the light of what we know about the late first century CE. Ultimately, the way and message of Revelation is not the way of the world but the way of God. More precisely, it is the way of love and compassion.

Revelation's Depiction of the World

John's worldview is uncompromising and opposed to Rome and all who support it. The author's experiences of hostility and suspicion in part fuelled the writing of Revelation. Domitian's reign encouraged and invited such hostility. People and groups do not hate and react against a government unless there is reason.

Compromise with the world is idolatry for John. John describes the crimes of humanity, which include the works of their hands as well as the worshipping of demons, idols of gold, silver, bronze, stone, and wood (Rev. 9.20). John calls those associated with Rome cowards, faithless, polluted, murderers, fornicators, sorcerers, idolaters and liars (Rev. 21.8, 22.15). John's essential message is that there is one God, and no one else is to be worshipped. As Oakman writes: 'Fundamental to an appreciation of John's theology is the identification of his concern for God's

---

1 Oakman (1993):15.

honor'.[2] However, this religious message is politically and economically rooted. Bauckham writes:

> Not to submit to Roman power, not to glorify its violence and its profits, required a perspective alternative to the Roman ideology which permeated public life. For John and those who shared his prophetic insight, it was the Christian vision of the incomparable God, exalted above all worldly power, which relativised Roman power and exposed Rome's pretensions to divinity as a dangerous delusion.[3]

Faithful witness means testimony through dissociation from Rome's evil leading possibly to martyrdom. Religious aspects are very important for John but cannot be separated from the political and economic issues that he faced. Like the Old Testament prophets, Revelation understands the political and economic abuses as rooted in a world that refuses and ignores God and his message.[4] It is a world based on the principles of violence and power, which rejects God and the principles upon which he created the world. Its rulers and those who compromise with it delude themselves in the idea that their reign is immortal.[5]

Persecutor and Martyr

The clearest examples of John coming to terms with the everyday possibility of being a victim are seen in Revelation 6.9, 7.14, 12.11, 13.15, 16.6, 17.6, 18.24, and 20.4.[6] It is unimportant whether John is or is not referring to those who have been killed within his own community. If some of the texts refer to previous martyrs, they serve John's purposes in providing suitable models of exemplary behaviour in presenting the superpowers as standing against God.

In Revelation 13.15 and 20.4, those who will and have been killed because they would not worship or offer sacrifices to the image or statue may have actually refused to worship images of Domitian. Price suggests: 'the establishment of the provincial cult of Domitian at Ephesus, with its colossal statue, is what lies behind the depiction in Revelation 13'.[7] Central to Revelation is the message of encouragement and response to questions that the faithful in the communities were asking. In 6.9 the cry of how long will it be before righteousness is victorious is the cry of a suffering community. In 7.14 martyrdom will result in victory. In 12.11 there is the development of the idea that through martyrdom victory will be gained. Those who shed the blood of the saints will drink the cup of their own violence (16.6). The woman who is arrayed in luxurious attire (17.6) represents the city of Rome (17.18) who is drunk on the blood of the martyrs (cf. 16.6). Her demise is

---

2 Oakman (1993):12.
3 Bauckham (1993b):39.
4 Gandhi believed that central to violence was a lack of belief in God.
5 Oakman (1993):12.
6 Parkes (1934):87.
7 Price (1984):197-198.

portrayed in 17.16. In 18.24 after a careful attack on the economic system of Rome and the consequences of its policies, it is reported that the blood of the saints was found there. The hope of victory is clear. John believes that the martyrs will be given justice (20.4).[8]

The Synagogue of Satan (Revelation 2.9-10)

It is important to recognise . . . an intra-Jewish dispute. This is not the Gentile church claiming to supersede Judaism, but a rift like that between the temple establishment and the Qumran community (1QH 2.22) (Bauckham).[9]

Bauckham here reminds us that the relationship between the synagogue and the church was hostile and we must be aware of this relationship as we approach Revelation. In this section I hope to show that the synagogue of Satan accusation in Revelation 2.9 reflects an internal dispute between two Jewish groups, i.e. the synagogue and the church. I will demonstrate that the dispute is connected with how Jews should relate to Rome during the reign of Domitian. I propose that the dispute resulted in each group denying the other, with the honoured title of 'Jew'[10] resulting in the church being considered politically suspect before the Roman administration (Rev. 2.10).

Dispute in Revelation 2.9-10

I know your affliction and your poverty, even though you are rich. I know the slander on the part of those who say that they are Jews and are not, but are a synagogue of Satan. Do not fear what you are about to suffer. Beware, the devil is about to throw some of you into prison so that you may be tested, and for ten days you will have affliction. Be faithful until death, and I will give you the crown of life (Rev. 2.9-10).

The church at Smyrna is poor and in tribulation. Yet it is rich because of its affliction and poverty. Jesus who is 'The First and the Last' knows not only of their poverty and affliction, but of the slander uttered by those who say that they are the true Jews (2.8). The synagogue's blasphemy leads John to retort that they are not Jews but a synagogue of Satan. The context for this is the synagogue's accusation that church members are not Jews. This fits the etymology of the word Satan: 'one who accuses falsely' (Job 1-2; Zech. 3). It also corresponds with 'blasphemy' that indicates 'slander' as the NRSV has translated (Mt. 12.31, 15.19; Mk. 15.29; Rom.

---

8 This translation and interpretation of 20.4 will be discussed in more detail later.

9 Bauckham (1993b):124.

10 The question as to who is a Jew is also reflected in Romans 2.28-29; see discussion in Ladd (1978):44 and Aune (1997):162, who compares the dispute in Revelation 2.9 with Romans.

3.8; 1 Cor. 10.30; Eph. 4.31; Col. 3.8; 1 Tim. 6.4; 1 Pet. 4.4; Jude 9).[11] Therefore, underlying the word is a charge made against the church.[12] In sum, Revelation 2.9 is understandable in the context of the synagogue accusing the church of not being Jews.[13]

The synagogue's accusation heightened the church's expectation of trouble in which the faithful would be thrown into prison by the devil (2.10). The ancient serpent is also the devil and Satan (Rev. 12.9 and 20.2). These three signify the forces of opposition to God represented in the contemporary political power that is Rome.[14] Rome is the beast, the devil and Satan. The synagogue of Satan reflects not only a synagogue that accuses falsely, but also a synagogue in collusion with Rome. This idea of collusion and compromise fits with Kraybill's understanding of the use of Satan: 'a way of highlighting commercial or political relationships some Jews had with Rome'.[15] The setting is then that of the synagogue informing Roman officials that the churches are not synagogues of Jews. Because only Rome had the power to incarcerate, this act of the synagogue had consequences for the church.[16]

In conclusion, the accusation that the synagogue is of Satan is a rebuttal to allegations that the synagogue made against the church that the church was not Jewish. The synagogue informed Rome that members of the church were not Jews. This led to a heightened sense of danger for the churches. The church argued that the synagogue informers were hand in hand with Rome and, thus, no longer worthy of the name "Jew". As Satan is Rome, the synagogue is of Rome. In sum, in 2.9-10 two groups have differing attitudes towards Rome, and those who compromise with Rome cannot be considered faithful to the God of Israel according to John.

I believe it is possible to be more precise about the underlying Domitianic policies that allowed Jews to inform against the church.

Revelation and Domitian's Reform of the Jewish Tax

There was a debate among Jews on how they should live and work in a non-Jewish milieu. Varying degrees of compromise and failure to compromise are evident among Jews in Hellenistic times. This was also the case for the church.[17] There is evidence in the New Testament for a more compromising attitude towards Rome (see Rom. 13; 1 Pet. 2.13-17; 1 Tim. 2.1-2) than we would find in Revelation.

An empire defeats a nation when it seizes its particular tax which is used to maintain the people's sacred traditions, and then uses it for its own sacred

---

11 See Aune (1997):162.
12 So Sweet (1979):85; Ladd (1978):43 also observes the 'slander' aspect; Harrington (1993):58 who compares Romans 9.8 as to who are the true heirs.
13 This should not argue against Christians also being in mind, those who were more in line with the synagogue, see Knight (1999):44-45.
14 Bauckham (1993a):187.
15 Kraybill (1996):170.
16 Yarbro Collins (1979):17.
17 Kraybill (1996):168.

traditions.[18] This happened to the Jewish people when the tax was used to rebuild the Capitoline temple to Jupiter in Rome. Oakman thinks that the Jewish tax is alluded to in Revelation 13.3, the wound on one of Rome's seven hills (the Capitol) that had been healed.[19] In this section I will consider again the Jewish tax, and looking this time at what it might have meant to John.

Domitian's reformation of the tax legitimated the churches and exempted them from participation in the cult as long as they paid the tax. Previously, they had not paid because they were not eligible. Therefore, in the eyes of many Gentile and Jewish followers of Christ, the extension would be welcomed. The social setting had not deteriorated for the church because of specific policies introduced by Domitian. Rather, it had improved, and as Thompson suggests, Domitian was a benevolent emperor towards synagogue and church.[20] Those who did not compromise and pay the tax would face prosecution and prison. The church at Smyrna was uncompromising and refused to pay the tax. The synagogue accused them of not being Jews because they did not pay the specifically Jewish tax. However, the church said that they were true Jews because they refused to pay the tax.[21]

The church at Smyrna was economically poor in an economically rich city and was experiencing or about to experience affliction (θλῖψις). This suggests that the synagogue had informed the authorities about the failure of the churches to pay the tax. This points to a dispute between church and synagogue. It is likely that the synagogue would make accusations to the authorities that the church members were not Jews because they did not pay the tax. This is why the church felt that prison was a possibility. Not paying the tax exposed them as showing contempt for the emperor and not compromising in spite of policies that allowed them to compromise. Both uncompromising synagogue and church members were placed in a difficult situation. The synagogue and pagans would be quick to pick up on this and expose such an uncompromising group for not paying the tax. This again fits the setting of Revelation 2.9. The synagogue accused the church faithful of not paying the tax. John interpreted this as the synagogue saying that church members are not Jews and for John this was blasphemous. John counters this blasphemy by stating that church members were Jews and in fact the synagogue was not a synagogue of God but of Satan. This suggests that John believed the synagogue to be hand in hand with Rome. John therefore believed that the synagogue was the property of Satan. Through not paying the tax, church members would be thrown into gaol (2.10). Hemer suggest that 'the tax placed the Jewish communities in a position of peculiar power *vis-à-vis* Christians. By disowning a Christian and informing against him, he might deprive him of his possible recourse to toleration at

18 Oakman (1993):17.

19 Oakman (1993):17. Hills are not part of the depiction in Revelation 13 although a possibility, on the basis of Revelation 17.9-10 as the seven mountains are seven heads and also seven kings. Nero is in mind here.

20 Thompson (1990):172.

21 Similarly Justin argues against Trypho that the church is the true spiritual Israel (*Dialogues with Trypho* 11.15).

a price, and render him liable to the emperor-cult'.[22] However, the evidence suggests more that the churches during Domitian's reign were considered liable to the tax and refused it so as not to compromise with Rome. The evidence, however, that I looked at in the previous chapter suggests that many synagogue members would inform against church members for not paying it. Jews were not *religio licita* (a permitted religion). Romans rather responded to the needs of the moment according to the prevailing political situation.[23] Many Jews were worried that rights could be revoked at any point if Domitian and the governors thought them a danger in society.[24] There is evidence that compromise was an issue for many Jews and Christians. Issues such as to what extent did believers accommodate themselves to foreign powers and yet remain loyal to their traditions were conundrums to many. Revelation's message, however, was uncompromising to the way of the world.

Compromising and Uncompromising Attitudes

Extreme poverty, however, was a factor, and the consequences of such poverty, as many economically poor people know, can be described as a tribulation in which individuals and groups are divested of power.[25] The church in contrast saw the synagogue in collusion with Rome, suggesting that the setting was right for a debate on the correct attitude towards Rome and its policies. During the early Roman imperial era, Jewish merchants reached the far corners of the Roman Empire selling wine, spices, perfumes and perhaps textiles.[26] There is evidence that provincial Jews co-operated closely with the Roman government in administrative affairs.[27] Rabbinic tradition holds that Johanan ben Zakkai spent forty years in trade (*Sifre* 357.14). Tamari comments that 'Judaism never had any religious or ethical objections to buying and selling goods for profit'.[28] However, it cannot be assumed that all synagogue members were doing well and all church members were doing badly. Revelation's first readers, as we know from the seven messages to the churches in Revelation 2-3, were by no means all poor and persecuted like the Christians at Smyrna. Many were affluent, self-satisfied and compromising.[29] There was potential for a Jew or Christian to improve on their financial situation. The first-century Roman satirist Petronius Arbiter, writing before Domitian, recounts the deeds of Trimalchio, a slave in Asia Minor, who through wheeling and dealing

---

22 Hemer (1986):8; see also DeSilva (1992):279.

23 Trebilco (1991):8. See also Applebaum (1976b):420-463.

24 Philo, *Leg.* 44.353 writes that, under Gaius, Jewish rights were sometimes revoked; Jews were also expelled from Rome under Tiberius (Josephus *Ant.* 18.83-84; Tacitus *Ann.* 2.85; Suetonius *Tib.* 36).

25 Aune (1997):161 emphasizes the literal poverty.

26 Kraybill (1996):186.

27 Kraybill (1996):188.

28 Tamari (1987):65-66 quoted from Kraybill (1996):186.

29 Bauckham (1993a):377.

becomes a very rich man. Asia Minor had a flourishing economy.[30] Oakman comments that during Domitian's reign there was great prosperity, but there was also an unequal spread in the distribution of this wealth.[31] Given this situation the churches were urged not to compromise in any way with the Roman system. Revelation would also be against wheeling and dealing that was needed to make money. It can be seen, therefore, that the question of wealth gained from involvement with Rome was an issue in a dispute between synagogue and church.

Uncompromising Christians found it difficult to make a living in a pagan environment.[32] The writer to the Hebrews also acknowledges the poverty that goes with faith (Heb. 10.34). This led to even greater separation between synagogue and church. Goodman points out that there is much evidence that the early church set out to convert members of the synagogue and that the synagogue was hostile to proselytizing or at least ambivalent.[33] The desire to proselytize is connected with an uncompromising attitude to Rome and society as a whole. This attitude is most clearly seen in Revelation 18 in which a verbal attack on Rome is made and the evident manifestations of her rule listed (vv. 11-13). It is likely that Jewish merchants who did business with Rome were considered as those who compromise with Rome (Rev. 18.15). The word for merchant used in Revelation 18 (ἔμπορος) is the one used for the Jewish merchants in Philo (*Flaccus* 57). It is not suggested that Revelation has only synagogue merchants in mind in 18.15, rather, all who compromise with Rome. Still, the evidence suggests that many both in the synagogue and in the church were among the merchants.

Pliny's trial of Christians in 112 CE suggests that the church could be in a vulnerable position before Rome, not for being Christian, but for being opposed to Rome. Downing points out that there are really no accounts of the trials of Christians for being Christians before 112 CE and thus the Jewish tax had not resulted in arrests or trials.[34] Surely if Christians were being arrested or put on trial over the last twenty or so years, Pliny would not have needed to write to the emperor Trajan asking him for advice, he would have found precedents for his situation in the archives. Moreover, Pliny acknowledges that he is not even sure whether being a Christian is punishable, or if only the crimes associated with being a Christian were to be punished; he writes:

> I am not at all sure whether it is the name of Christian which is punishable, even if innocent of crime, or rather the crimes associated with the name (*Ep.* 96).

---

30 Kraybill (1996):109-110.
31 Oakman (1993):213.
32 Aune (1997):161; see also Charles (1920):vol. 1, 56; Caird (1984):35; Roloff (1993):48.
33 Goodman (1992):70 and (1994); contrary Feldman (1993) and Borgen (1996):45-69 who does not acknowledge Goodman's arguments.
34 Downing (1988):118.

Before Trajan's reign, being a Christian was not punishable; however, anti-social behaviour would have been. Law abiding Christians would be left in peace, but not troublemakers.[35]

In sum, the situation was opportune for a dispute between the synagogue and the church regarding who truly was a Jew. Moreover, Revelation reveals an attitude that could lead to punishment for being anti-social, for example, its attitude towards wealth, and its desire to stand firm against the Roman system.

Evidence for an Internal Conflict

> During all those years Satan shall be unleashed against Israel, as He spoke by the hand of Isaiah . . . saying: *terror and the pit and the snare are upon you, O inhabitant of the land* . . . Interpreted, these are the three nets of Satan with which Levi son of Jacob said that he catches Israel by setting them up as three kinds of righteousness. The first is fornication, the second is riches, and the third is profanation of the temple (CD 4.14-20).

The Qumran community harshly criticized other Jews.[36] There are parallels between the accusations that the synagogue was of Satan with similar accusations we read from Qumran.[37] The Damascus Document illustrates this point. The three nets, especially the one regarding riches, closely resemble the argument being made about the synagogue being rich. An issue involved in this dispute was the pernicious nature of wealth that would result in alienation from God. The agent of this alienation is Satan. The Qumran text suggests that Israel belongs to Satan. It might also be interesting to consider this text in the light of the view of some Qumran scholars who suggest that the Damascus Document was not intended for the group living at Qumran but for others who adopted similar beliefs and practices and yet had not exiled themselves to Qumran. Their main argument for this is based on where the Damascus Document mentions 'camps' (7.6), 'the camp' (10.23), 'the assembly of the towns of Israel' (12.19) and 'the assembly of the camps' (12.23).

Similarly, Qumran calls a gathering of Jews 'a gathering of Belial' (1QH 2.22).[38] The word for 'gathering' could be rendered 'synagogue'. Belial is used as a proper name for Satan in the Damascus Document and the War Scroll. Thus, the gathering of Jews is a synagogue of Satan.

In sum, there is evidence not only for disputes between Jewish groups, but, also, that compromise with Satan was part of the accusation, an accusation that perceived wealth as an attribute and sign of belonging to Satan.

---

35 Slater (1998):249.
36 Borgen (1996):282.
37 Beale (1999):241.
38 Bauckham (1993b):124; Beale (1999):241.

Conclusion

An intra-Jewish dispute underlies Revelation 2.9-10. It is like a rift that existed between the temple establishment and the Qumran community (1QH2.22). The synagogue's blasphemy that they were Jews and not the church is connected with the church's uncompromising attitude towards Rome. It seems that the synagogue was concerned to distance itself from the church inasmuch as it attached great importance to maintaining good relations with Rome. Domitian's policy on the tax was crucial as it gave the church its own right of exemption from participating in the imperial cult. However, a refusal to pay would be seen as the church's confession that they are not 'Jews', but troublemakers. Consequently, Domitian's tax led to the synagogue declaring both to the Roman authorities and to the church itself that 'we are Jews'. Revelation 2.9 is a response in which John protests that 'you are not, but are a synagogue of Satan'. Ultimately it could result in church members being detained (Rev. 2.10). This would be welcomed by the synagogue, and would lead synagogue members to think twice about joining the church. Moreover, it helped draw a distinction between synagogue and church in the eyes of Rome. However, from Revelation's perspective, to pay the tax would be to participate in the cult. In the same way as 1QH2.22, Revelation reacts against Jews who compromise with Rome. Consequently, the synagogue would be of Satan and not God's chosen.

Prisoner on Patmos

John, your brother who shares with you in Jesus the persecution and the kingdom and the patient endurance, was on the island called Patmos because of the word of God and the testimony of Jesus (1.9).

Was John a prisoner on Patmos for his loyalty to the life of Jesus? Beasley-Murray points out that John is probably not living on the island at the time of writing. John writes ἐγενόμην ἐν τῇ νήσῳ - I was on the Island (1.9).[39] He argues that John was banished in order to avoid the possibility of more disturbance, and presumably released when it seemed appropriate to the authorities. However, it is odd that John would have been released; surely, he would always have been a threat. It is wrongly assumed that Patmos was used for the imprisonment of political offenders (Tacitus *Ann.* iii. 68, iv. 30, xv. 71, Juvenal *Sat.* I. 73, vi. 563 f., x. 170, and Pliny *NH.* iv. 12. 23).[40] None of the evidence mentions Patmos as a custodial island. Pliny mentions Patmos, but he does not say it is a place of detention. Tacitus and Juvenal mention some islands, namely Gyarus, Donusa and Seriphos, islands that are within the vicinity of Patmos, which may indicate that Patmos served a similar function. In

---

39 Beasley-Murray (1983):64; Aune (1997):77. How is ἐγενόμην (I was) to be accounted for? Beasley-Murray overestimates the significance of the aorist insisting it is more precise than it need be. Aune sees the aorist having an ordinary narrative use that does not imply that John is no longer on Patmos.

40 Charles (1920):vol.1, 21.

spite of this, Charles believes the syntax supports John being imprisoned.[41] He argues that the preposition ἕνεκα should be expected if John was on Patmos to receive the revelation rather than being in prison. However, ἕνεκα and διὰ are hardly distinguishable in meaning when accompanied with the accusative and both could indicate that he was on the island. διὰ (on account of) could indicate that he was on the island either as a punishment, or to receive the revelation.[42] In Revelation 6.9 and 20.4 it is clear that 'witness to Jesus' is the cause of suffering and punishment.[43] In view of the prevalence of persecution and suffering being connected with faithful testimony, and John's own sense of suffering (1.9), it seems more likely that John was on Patmos as a punishment.

In sum, it is probable that John resides as a prisoner on Patmos. His way of life was deemed threatening and disturbing to the *pax Romana*. Like Gandhi, John spent many years in prison contemplating the way of the world and the way of the true follower of Jesus.

Religion, Economics and Politics

As a subversive text, it is important to consider more precisely what Revelation was attacking. Revelation is not a text directed only against the imperial cult and the ruler cult.[44] The evidence points to a more complex picture in which the safety and well-being of church members was dependent on being on good terms with their neighbours. Domitian astutely created a system that used and rewarded those who were loyal to him. At the heart of Revelation's critique were economics and politics. Embracing both is the imperial cult, which we have seen, in the previous chapter to be strong in Asia Minor. Revelation attacked Rome on a number of levels. Overall, it challenged a system that promised peace and well being under the guise of wealth and power. Obedience to Rome promised security to the obedient.

Revelation and the Imperial Cult

Roman power was ultimately represented in the figure of the emperor, and central to the maintenance of the power relationship was the imperial cult. Religion, politics and economics, however, were all intertwined within this. The resistance of church members to any expression of homage to the emperor would be dangerous and the pagans and many synagogue members would soon alert the respective authorities to such treasonable behaviour. The deification of the emperor was symptomatic of what was fundamentally wrong with Roman rule, that is, it claimed absolute power. Consequently, the nature of Revelation was political and opposed to Domitian, rather than concerned with offended religious sensibilities. If so, John, like the Old

---

41 See Charles (1920):vol.1, 20 for discussion.

42 Blass and Debrunner δ222.

43 Beasley-Murray (1983):64. Note also 7.15, 12.11. Swete (1922):11-12 emphasizes that John sees himself as a fellow sufferer with the churches.

44 Bauckham (1993a):338-384; Wengst (1987):118-135 and Kraybill (1996).

Testament prophets, confronts political and socio-economic abuses. Beckwith, however, places the emphasis on the fact that Domitian arrogated to himself an inherent religious character.[45] Beckwith perhaps underestimates the general political sense that Revelation has. If society puts its trust in its power and wealth it becomes a worshiper of its own works, an idolater and rejecter of God. Therefore, for Revelation, the economic and political abuses and inequality with the violent consequences stem from rejecting God. As Oakman has pointed out, crucial to John's theology is the concern for God's honour. He writes: 'The Roman imperial cult demands such honor for Caesar'.[46] Political and economic policies on earth offend God's honour.

CRITIQUE IN CHAPTERS 13, 17 AND 18

> the critique in chapter 13 is primarily political, the critique in chapters 17-18 primarily economic, but in both cases also deeply religious (R. Bauckham).[47]

In Revelation 13 John sees a beast ascend from the sea (v.1). Most agree that the beast expresses the military and political power of the Roman Emperors. The destruction of Jerusalem would still be present in John's mind, and still is the source of oppression. The ten diadems upon the horns represent royalty (v.1).[48] The seven heads indicate seven Caesars. The 'blasphemous name' alludes to the title applied to the emperors increasingly through the first century, and which culminated in the desire of Domitian to be addressed as *Dominus et Deus*.[49] One of the beast's heads had been mortally wounded (v.3). It is widely agreed that this head is Nero.[50] The beast that recovers alludes to the restoration of the empire under the Flavians.[51] It made war on the saints, and conquered them; it blasphemed God; it is all-powerful and rules over every tribe, people, tongue, and nation, and they worship it. The second beast, like a lamb, makes the earth and the inhabitants worship the first beast (v.11). This perhaps points to the imperial priests who perpetuated Rome's dominance in the provinces by promoting the imperial cult. Sweet suggests that this alludes to those in the church who were arguing for the divine authority of the

---

45 Beckwith (1919):201.

46 Oakman (1993):12.

47 Bauckham (1994):36; Provan (1996):88 argues against Bauckham that the sin of Revelation18 is not economic, but religious, yet the two for Bauckham are intimately connected.

48 See Stevenson (1995):257-272 for a discussion of the crowns' significance.

49 Beasley-Murray (1983):209.

50 Beasley-Murray (1983):210; Bauckham (1993b):37 and most commentators.

51 Bauckham (1993b):37. It is also interesting to note that Domitian was likened to Nero, and is the only emperor portrayed having a Nero type haircut! See *Sibylline Oracles* 5.93-110, 214-227 in Charlesworth for the return of Nero and discussion in Bauckham (1993a):423-431 contrary Corsini (1983):230-234.

state.[52] This makes sense of the beast portrayed as a lamb (13.11), i.e. the enemies to the church belonged to the beast but presented themselves as followers of Christ. They persuaded members of the church, probably members of their own community, perhaps even from the synagogue, to accept Roman rule. Compromise was the greatest danger to synagogue and church. It is suggested that John intended the parallel as a christological parody. The first beast (Rev. 13) parodies Christ, the dragon (Rev. 12) parodies his father, and the second beast (13.11) parodies the Holy Spirit (or prophets inspired by the Holy Spirit). This parody shows that John saw certain features of the Roman Empire as constituting a divine and messianic claim that rivalled Christ's.[53] The parody is developed in such a way as to show that Christ is the conqueror and not the emperor. Also, there is the possibility that John intended a clear parallel between the death and resurrection of Jesus and the death and resurrection of the beast. There is a hint of the economic exploitation of those who would not conform to the worship of the beast (v.17).

In chapter 13 Rome is a seductress of the faithful. Moreover, Rome is a violent, oppressive, and idolatrous representative of Satan through its emperors, its armies and its propaganda machine. There may be hints of an internal debate within the church and against the synagogue members who urged compromise with Rome. Ultimately, John urges a response of nonviolence (13.10) in his critique of the political values of the world.

In Revelation 17-18 John attacks the economic values of the world. The harlot is the city of Rome who rides upon the military powers of its army in Revelation 17. Jesus the Lamb is given the title 'Lord of lords and King of kings' in conscious opposition to Domitian's imperial pretensions (17.1).[54] Rome is wealthy and dressed in expensive items (18.16). This wealth was exploited from other nations. The list of goods arraying Rome was brought to Rome by the great network of trade throughout her empire (18.16).[55] Rome's subjects gave far more to her than she gave to them.[56] Perhaps the shortage of grain in Revelation 6.6 results from this economic policy.[57] It is likely that Revelation had in mind those synagogue and church members who compromised with Rome and informed against church members to the authorities. Similarly, John addresses his own community in 18.4 when he writes: 'Come out of her, my people, lest you share in her plagues'. This fits with the nature of John's message to Sardis and Laodicea.[58] It is also likely that

---

52 Sweet (1979):214-215.

53 Morris (1979):171; Sweet (1979):216; Bauckham (1993a):441; Harrington (1993):144.

54 Sweet (1979):25.

55 Wengst (1987):122; Bauckham (1993a):346; Kraybill (1996):103-104.

56 Bauckham (1993a):346; also Wengst (1987):122 'whereas Rome and its vassals live in abundance, like those who do business with them, and make profits, famine prevails in the province'.

57 Hemer (1986):45; Wengst (1987):122; Kraybill (1996):147-148; Beale (1998):381; Observe also that part of what John attacks is theft that suggests the plunder of a nation's resources (9.21).

58 Yarbro Collins (1984b):88-89.

John would refuse to pay the tax as part of his nonviolent resistance against Rome (see above discussion on Revelation 2.9-10). This was connected with his refusal to engage in any way with supporting the military machine, the building of ruler cult temples, or the buying of special privileges. Such a response is indeed reminiscent of Gandhi's non-cooperation policy. Non-cooperation meant suffering for John (see Rev. 13.17). Similarly, Gandhi wrote: 'Nonviolent non-cooperation means renunciation of the benefits of a system'.[59]

THE MERCHANDISE IN REVELATION 18.12-13

> The merchandise in question was generally seen as a feature of the newly conspicuous wealth and extravagance of the rich families of Rome in the period of the early empire (R. Bauckham).[60]

> The list of articles of trade might stand for a sketch of the commerce of Rome, but when examined it is evidently no more than a selection from the tabernacle and temple specifications (W. Schoff).[61]

I will now consider in some detail the merchandise listed in Revelation 18.12-13. Bauckham points out that the items in vv.12-13 are the wealth that rich citizens of Rome gained from the provinces. This wealth was spent on conspicuous luxuries leading ultimately to discontent among the lower classes.[62] The inhabitants of Asia Minor were struggling to purchase the basic foodstuffs.[63] John's critique could be aimed at any ruling military might throughout history, however corrupt and tyrannical. As I have argued above, the culture and tradition are important in the way someone interprets their social setting. There is evidence which suggests that during Domitian's reign there was a particularly good opportunity for trade and making money. Yet it will be argued below that underlying Revelation 18 is John's perception of Rome as one who is like the previous representatives of Satan who plundered the innocent but will in turn be plundered following the traditions of the prophets we looked at earlier in chapter 5.

Opinions differ regarding the motivations, functions and intentions behind Revelation 18.[64] The central motivation underlying chapter 18 is John's hatred of Rome as a plundering nation. In chapter 5 I considered the traditions of plunder that

---

59 Quoted in Jesudasan (1984):75.
60 Bauckham (1993a):352. See also Wengst (1987):124-125.
61 Schoff (1920):99.
62 Bauckham (1993a):363.
63 Hemer (1986):158-159 discusses this in more detail.
64 For a brief summary see Yarbro Collins (1980):185-187. Recent important publications include Bauckham (1993b):338-383 in which he pays particular attention to the list of cargo and argues that chapter 18 is an economic critique of Rome. Provan (1996) rejects Bauckham's work and argues that there is no particular setting being addressed, and emphasizes the importance of the Hebrew background to the text.

previous foreign nations and Israel seized from less powerful nations. This earlier chapter will be important for this section as I consider Revelation as a text that is critical of plunder and violence. In other words, John's attitude arises from his reflection and appropriation of tradition, as well as Rome's abuse of power. To this extent, I want also to consider the items not as merchandise particular to Roman trade as Bauckham does, but items that are evident in the Old Testament and in later Jewish literature which reflects to some extent Schoff's understanding.

John encouraged his community in its policy of non-cooperation against Rome and its allies. In doing this, John presents Rome, in Revelation 17-18, in particular, as one who will fall like the previous foreign nations.[65] The distinctive contribution I hope to make is to show that the merchandise in Revelation 18.12-13 are items Rome plundered from the nations like the previous foreign nations also plundered. My proposal draws much from the insight of W. Schoff's unacknowledged study in 1920 on commerce in the Bible. In the above quote Schoff links the list of merchandise in Revelation 18.12-13 with the items from which a nation establishes their sacred traditions.[66] Indeed, he sees the items in Revelation 18.12-13 as those that were plundered and the very material that sustained the imperial cult of Rome (cf. Rev. 17.3-5).[67]

I will not argue that all the items must be understood only in terms of the temple to the extent that Schoff does. However, I do agree the background to these items must be seen in the Old Testament. Yet my discussion will not negate the view that many of the items were connected with what Rome imported as Bauckham argues.

Plunderer and Plundered: the Way of the World

Mounce writes of Babylon:

> The introduction of this symbolic reference without explanation assumes that the readers would understand the allusion. The ancient Mesopotamian city of Babylon had become the political and religious capital of a world empire, renowned for its luxury and moral corruption. Above all it was the great enemy of the people of God. For the early church the city of Rome was a contemporary Babylon.[68]

The historical Babylon was, indeed, a morally corrupt capital within the Old Testament. It was, therefore, the perfect symbol for John in depicting the superpower of his day. It was hedonistic, morally corrupt, idolatrous, and a plunderer. My study of the Old Testament and Jewish literature in chapter 5

---

65 See chapter 5 of this book.
66 Schoff (1920):45.
67 Schoff (1920):97; cf. Josephus *War* 7.5.7 (or 7.158-162):observes how the vessels of the plundered Jerusalem temple were used by Vespasian in the temple of peace: 'he also laid up therein, as ensigns of his glory, those golden vessels and instruments that were taken out of the Jerusalem temple'(tr. Whiston).
68 Mounce (1977):273; Kraybill (1996):149-152 discusses the parallels between Rome and Ancient Babylon.

provides the interpretative framework for comprehending John's motives and intentions for chapter 18. My argument is that the language in chapter 18 could have been used of any of the cities and nations at their most powerful, a time when they exploited the poor. However, John was also motivated by his own reflections upon the particular oppressive outworking of Roman rule as discussed in chapter 9.[69] John writes of Babylon the wanton plunderer:

> As she glorified herself and lived luxuriously, so give her a like measure of torment and grief - ὅσα ἐδόξασεν αὐτὴν καὶ ἐστρηνίασεν, τοσοῦτον δότε αὐτῇ βασανισμὸν καὶ πένθος (18.7; cf. Isa. 47.8-9).

Babylon as a consequence of glorifying herself and playing the wanton, caused much suffering. The Greek word ἐστρηνίασεν describes the action of one who 'flaunted her power'. The word is related to insolent luxury (Nah. 3.4). The Greek translation Symmachus of Isaiah 61.6 translates the Hebrew אכל (to consume) with the same Greek word John uses i.e. ἐστρηνίασεν. Isaiah describes how Israel will consume the wealth of the nations. Babylon will experience the same tortures that she caused for others (see Lev. 24.17-22; cf. Rom. 1.24-32 for the idea of punishment by means of one's own sin).

> Since in her heart she says: 'A queen I sit, I am no widow, mourning I shall never see', so shall her plagues come in a single day (18.7b-8a).

Rome's rule has led to death and mourning; the very things that the superpower boasts she will not experience (18.7). Rome has consumed the nations. John comments that Rome's wealth will be plundered (ἀπώλετο v.14; ἠρημώθη vv.16, 19) experiencing what she has done to others (cf. v.7). The Greek words suggest utter loss and destruction. The Hebrew חרב underlies ἀπώλετο in v.14 and points to destruction of a nation that has sinned (cf. Josh. 23.16). חרב underlies ἠρημώθη in 18.16, 19 indicating plunder (cognate Arab *haraba* actually means 'to plunder'). Significantly, it occurs in the oracle against Babylon (Jer. 50.21, 27; cf. Ezek. 26.12). Plunder is associated with holy war and the loss of wealth through military invasion. There is no clear military invasion envisaged here and therefore it may be argued that plunder is not a key theme in Revelation 18. However, the importing of goods by a superpower is plundering and means loss for others. It was Rome's insatiable appetite for wealth that caused much suffering as Ezekiel reports that Tyre was filled with violence because of the abundance of her trade (Rev. 18.6; Ezek. 28.16). In the same way, Rome's wealth would be taken (vv.14, 17, 19). John describes Rome in language resonant in Old Testament tradition (Rev. 18.16; cf. Jer. 4.30; 10.4; Ezek. 16.8-14; 23.40; Hos. 2.13; 1QM and 6 Ezra 15.46). Bedecked in expensive items is common in the Old Testament, especially of the harlot Jerusalem.

---

69 In many ways it might be said that I take a middle way between Bauckham (1993a):377 who argues for the particularity of Asia Minor here, and Provan (1996) and Buchanan (1993a):489 who argue that there is nothing particular about Asia Minor.

Babylon is depicted as so rich that it was Eden like (Ezek. 28.13). It is described as the 'great city' in Revelation 18:

> they will stand far off, in fear of her torment, and say, "Alas, alas, the *great city*, Babylon, the *mighty city*! For in one hour your judgment has come" (18.10).

> Alas, alas, the *great city*, clothed in fine linen, in purple and scarlet, adorned with gold, with jewels, and with pearls! (18.16).

> What city was like the *great city*? (18.18).

> And they threw dust on their heads, as they wept and mourned, crying out, "Alas, alas, the *great city*, where all who had ships at sea grew rich by her wealth! For in one hour she has been laid waste" (18.19).

> With such violence Babylon the *great city* will be thrown down, and will be found no more (18.21).

Babylon is ἡ πόλις ἡ μεγάλη (the great city). The phrase 'that great city' occurs for the first time in the Old Testament in Genesis 10.12. 'Great' is used of the cities built by Nimrod (Gen. 10.6-14). This is significant in that the cities of Japheth and Shem are not called 'great'. I suggest that 'great city' must be understood in the light of Genesis 10.6-14 and as a pejorative term which is used for those that set themselves up as mighty and wealthy, thus rejecting God. The second occurrence in the Old Testament is in Joshua 10.1-2:

> Now it came to pass when Adoni-Zedek king of Jerusalem heard how Joshua had taken Ai and had utterly destroyed it -- as he had done to Jericho and its king, so he had done to Ai and its king -- and how the inhabitants of Gibeon had made peace with Israel and were among them, that they feared greatly, because Gibeon was a great city, like one of the royal cities, and because it was greater than Ai, and all its men were mighty' (New King James).

Gibeon was inhabited by Hivites (Josh. 9.7). The Hivites were descended from Canaan (Gen. 10.17), the uncle of Nimrod. They are related to those who were cursed by Noah (Gen. 9.25). The expression 'great city' occurs in the context of the fall of the great city which in spite of all its power, it would fall.

We find in Jeremiah 22.8 the only occurrence of Jerusalem described as 'the great city':

> And many nations will pass by this city; and everyone will say to his neighbor, 'Why has the LORD done so to this great city?'

The phrase is spoken by the nations with regards to the fall of the city which failed to keep its covenant with God and plundered its own people (Jer. 22.13-14). Jerusalem is now like a foreign nation to Jeremiah, it is like the cities built by Ham and his descendants. Jerusalem now puts its trust in the way of the nations.

Nineveh, again connected with the family of the cursed Canaan, is described in Jonah as 'the great city' (1.2, 3.2, 4.11). In 3.3 we meet the unusual expression, עִיר גְּדֹלָה לֵאלֹהִים usually translated 'superlatively great city'. The phrase expresses the idea of a city belonging to god.[70] Nineveh is described as both great and as one that was inhabited by those who did not know their right hand from the left. It may be possible to see some significance in these texts. All occurrences of 'great city' are connected with wickedness. There may be some irony here; greatness may indeed not be so great. I put forward that John was aware of the phrase 'great city' and its connection with wickedness and arrogance. In this case, the expression 'great city' alludes to ironic claims to being like God or as God.[71] Consequently, any city that was in opposition to God would be intended by this phrase. The great city is not the city where there will be peace, John is very careful to call this the 'holy city' (Rev. 11.2; 21.2, 10, 16; 22.19) that has 'the glory of God and a radiance like a very rare jewel' (Rev. 21.11). John's opposition to Rome is that, like the other superpowers, she claimed to be as God, that is 'great', she is wealthy and plunders the innocent, but will fall.

> Fallen, fallen is Babylon the great! (18.2).

> and the voice of bridegroom and bride shall be heard in thee no more; for thy merchants were the great men of the earth, and all nations were deceived by thy sorcery. And in her was found the blood of prophets and of saints, and of all who have been slain on earth (18.23-24).

The grim picture of a superpower's fall includes also the absence of song and music. This alludes to the fall of Tyre (18.22; cf. Isa. 24.8; Jer. 25.10; 33.11; Ezek. 26.13). John tells us that Babylon deceived the nations by sorcery and murder (18.23-4). The practice of the black arts was common in John's world as it was during the time of Babylon. John wrote ὅτι ἐν τῇ φαρμακείᾳ σου ἐπλανήθησαν πάντα τὰ ἔθνη - and all nations were deceived by your sorcery (v.23). In the Old Testament, sorcery was synonymous with wickedness and foreignness (Deut. 18.9; *1 En.* 65.6).[72] Nahum suggests that through sorcery a ruling nation can beguile people through trade (Nah.

---

70 NEB has 'vast city' expressing the size of the city. Sasson (1990);228-230 discusses this phrase. One translation he allows for is 'a large city to the gods' (p.228). Luther believes the expression refers to God's love for Nineveh (quoted in Sasson 229).

71 John is aware of the irony in the phrase 'great city'. It could mean 'great' in the sense of exalted and successful, possibly a common phrase of the city of an empire, but it could mean arrogant and haughty used of someone who claims to be and lives as if God.

72 Esler (1994):139.

3.4). Nahum also placed sorcery beside wealth and harlotry.[73] In other words, Babylon seduced the nations to feel that ultimate security rested in wealth and luxury'.[74] Accusing an outsider of sorcery was often motivated by the need to strengthen community boundaries. Esler makes an interesting point: 'Rome is not, in fact, a source of any great difficulty for the Christian communities of Asia at this time. Rather it [sorcery] functions in the cycle of myth created in the work as a scapegoat for problems which are largely internal to the seven congregations'.[75] In other words, John blames internal misfortune on sorcery outside his own community. This sounds similar to that which Girard believes Jesus challenged. Yet central to John in accusing Babylon of sorcery is his need to depict Rome as one who had beguiled the nations by wealth and this is what Rome did. Rome was deceiving the members of the church who themselves had become deceivers. Moreover, by it Rome increased her profit and those who could fulfill her desires. Surely John had in mind Ezekiel 13.18 for his understanding of a sorcerer, one who deceived and disposed people of their own culture and religion all for her own profit (see above discussion relating to Assyria in chapter 5).

Babylon the sorcerer is also Babylon the murderer. Babylon murdered the prophets, saints and all who had been slain upon the earth (cf. 6 Ezra 15.52-53). The blood cries from the ground for vengeance (cf. Gen. 4.10; Job 14.18; Ezek. 24.7; 6 Ezra 15.7-8; 2 Macc. 8.3; *1 En.* 9.3-5). Jerusalem was known to have murdered the prophets. Indeed, this was a phrase used of Jerusalem (Jer. 2.30). John presents all the murdered upon earth as slaughtered by Babylon, the ruling empire. Such could not be attributed to Jerusalem.[76] But this wanton city would fall and there would be those who stood and mourned her destruction:

Ezekiel 27	Revelation 18
Mariners and all the pilots stand on the shore and wail aloud over you and cry bitterly (v.29).	Kings of the earth weep and wail over her when they see the smoke of her burning (v.9); they will stand far off, in fear of her torment...[77](v.10)
They cast dust on their heads . . . and they weep over you in bitterness (v.30).	And the merchants of the earth weep and mourn over her (v.11)
They raise lamentation: 'Who was destroyed like Tyre in the midst of the seas . . . you satisfied many peoples with your abundant wealth and merchandise . . .' (v.32)	Shipmasters and seafaring men, sailors...threw dust on their heads as they wept (v.17).
	What city was like the great city . . Alas, alas, for the great city where all who had ships grew rich by her wealth (v.18).

---

73 Beale (1998):922.
74 Ladd (1978):243.
75 Esler (1994):145.
76 Barker (2000):270 argues that it refers to Jerusalem.
77 Appears also in 16.14; 17.2, 14, 18; 19.19; 21.24.

John identifies six groups who lament the demise of the ruling nation (vv.9, 11, 17). They will suffer because of the loss of a good buyer for their goods listed in vv.12-13. There are similarities in language and theme with Ezekiel 27. Tyre enriched the kings of the earth in the same way that John reports Rome did (27.33). However, the kings of the earth in Revelation 18.9-11 may be a conflation of ideas from especially Psalm 2.2 and Deuteronomy 28.25 and indeed this may be an example of John correcting one text by another. The psalmist says in Psalm 2.2:

> The kings of the earth set themselves, and the rulers take counsel together, against the LORD and his anointed.

The Hebrew 'to set themselves' is יִתְיַצְּבוּ often translated by the LXX into the Greek ἵστημι which John uses in 18.10. John appropriated the traditions of the kings of the earth standing against God to correct the tradition in which it is said no one can stand against God or God's people (Deut. 7.24, 9.2, 11.25; Josh. 1.5; Job 41.10). Thus, John places the kings of the earth standing (ἑστηκότες)[78] far from where God is present, i.e. punishing Rome, because of fear that they will suffer the punishment of Rome (v.10). In other words, as Psalm 2.2 presents the kings of the earth standing against God, John rather presents them standing far away from God and his punishment. In Deuteronomy 28.25 Israel is warned that if she does not keep God's covenant she will become a horror to the kingdoms of the earth. This may also have influenced the aspect of standing far away. The kings of the earth in Revelation 18.9-11 are in horror of Babylon.

John was familiar with merchants and sailors who traded on the sea. Ephesus and other Aegean parts were regular trade points. However, it is not easy to account for v.23: 'your merchants were the magnates of the earth'. Traders and merchants were not considered among the magnates.[79] However, John develops his attack on Rome alluding to Isaiah's oracle against Tyre:

> Who has planned this against Tyre, the bestower of crowns, whose merchants were princes, whose traders were the honored of the earth? (Isa. 23.8).

This is the only connection between the 'magnates' and 'merchants' in the Old Testament. Rome had grown in luxurious material wealth to such an extent that the merchants themselves had become very rich or so they claimed in John's eyes.[80] As has been pointed out, wealth is not bad for John if it is combined with having the right attitude and knowing from where the wealth comes. However, this was not so with the merchants. Babylon's sin did not consist in the fact of her wealth, but in the

---

78 ἑστηκότες is in the perfect tense (v.10) whereas when used of the merchant in v. 15, the verb is used in the future. It may be chosen to emphasize the past and present aspect of what they are doing.
79 Swete (1922):240.
80 Bauckham (1993a):373.

overweening pride and self-exaltation induced by her wealth.[81] Indeed, Ezekiel made the connection between pride and wealth explicit:

> By your great wisdom in trade you have increased your wealth, and your heart has become proud in your wealth (Ezek. 28.5; cf. Jer. 9.23-24).

List of Merchandise

> cargo of gold, silver, jewels and pearls, fine linen, purple, silk and scarlet, all kinds of scented wood, all articles of ivory, all articles of costly wood, bronze, iron and marble, cinnamon, spice, incense, myrrh, frankincense, wine, oil, fine flour and wheat, cattle and sheep, horses and chariots, and slaves, that is, human souls (vv.11-12).

I demonstrated in chapter 5 that these items are prominent in the Old Testament. The longest list of merchandise appears in Ezekiel 27.12-25a. Eichrodt believes this list is secondary material added to an original funeral lament composed by a Jew with an intimate acquaintance with Phoenician trade.[82] Ezekiel 27.12-25a reveals a detailed knowledge of what Tyre imports. However, the nature of trade does not change greatly. Many of the items in Ezekiel 27.12-25a are present in Revelation 18 and the other items can be seen elsewhere in the Old Testament and Jewish literature as items that were traded and seized by the ruling nations from defeated nations. I agree with Schoff that the items were chosen because of their previous appearance in the Old Testament and due to their association with the tabernacle, temple, palace, and priestly spoil.[83]

Bauckham has attempted to show that the merchandise would have been exported to Rome.[84] Provan has disputed Bauckham's claims arguing that the items must be understood intertextually against their biblical background and that the list is not intended to have specific external reference to Rome in terms of economic critique.[85] I believe it is unnecessary to separate John from his own social particularity and to claim that John is not motivated by the need to provide an economic critique of Rome. Provan's criticism of Bauckham does not take into account why John would choose to emphasize the 'merchant theme' if Rome was not known as a great trading nation. Moreover, John could have easily structured his criticism against Babylon on lines resembling Jeremiah's attack on Babylon, thus making no mention of the trade theme (Jer. 50-51). Yet Provan is right when he

---

81 Ladd (1978):243.

82 Eichrodt (1970):387.

83 Schoff (1920):69-70.

84 Bauckham (1993a):338-383; he has been followed by Kraybill (1996), Beale (1999):910 and Knight (1999):121. However, it is interesting to note that Schoff (1920):103 when comparing the list in Revelation18 with the lists of the commerce of Rome in Pliny and Periplus, was left in no doubt that Revelation18.12-13 is not a specific list relevant to Rome, so also Provan (1996).

85 Provan (1996):87; also Schoff (1920); Buchanan (1993) and Moyise (1995):74.

quotes Thompson that John's perceived crisis with Rome is primarily connected with John's own perspective on Roman society.[86] However, the perspective is often testified in social reality; John reviled an abuse of power manifested in items imported to Rome. Provan argues for the Old Testament background, yet he does not provide a thorough study of the items against their Hebrew background. Provan observes that if John's list was firmly based on knowledge of the particularity of Roman imports, he could have chosen more obvious items than cattle, sheep and wheat.[87] Indeed, supporting Provan, even gold, according to Pliny the Elder, comes 'scarcely tenth' in the list of valuables and silver 'almost as low as twentieth' (Pliny, *NH.* 36.204).[88] Yet gold and silver were prominent items of the rich and ruling nations in the Old Testament thus again supporting Provan. Provan suggests that if Bauckham's interpretation is correct then would John not be expected to have included exotic foodstuffs on his list? Provan points out that only thirteen of John's twenty-eight items occur in Pliny's list of costly products.[89] Provan and Schoff, however, overestimate the differences between Revelation 18.12-13 and Pliny's list. John, like the prophets, is an acute observer of society and John knew items that were being shipped out of Ephesus to Rome and he was aware of particular incidences of suffering that such imports created.

It is unnecessary to over emphasize that John included every item in reference to a particular situation. The Old Testament influenced some of the items.[90] This will be seen specifically in terms of horses and sheep. However, Bauckham writes: 'The first century was the period in which Roman aristocracy had acquired large sheep and cattle ranches (*latifundia*) both in Italy and, by conquest and confiscation, in the provinces'.[91] He notes that such ranches were being filled with improved breeds (the *Epirote*) from Greece, for which he cites Strabo and Varro for his evidence. However, his point is not in harmony with Garnsey and Saller, who point out that there is no definition or technical discussion which records actually what a *latifundium* is. They point out that it is highly improbable that there were many large ranchers specializing in animal husbandry. Varro had 800 of his own sheep, but he fails to cite another, which to Garnsey and Saller suggests pastoralism was practised on a modest scale.[92] Even if Bauckham is right and the importing of improved breeds was more common than Garnsey and Saller suggest, how aware of this breed of cattle would John be? According to Strabo such breeds were imported from Greece and not Asia Minor (*Strabo* 7.7.5, 12). John was based in Asia Minor

---

86 Provan (1996):97.

87 Provan (1996):86.

88 A point that Knight (1999):121 fails to mention when he writes: 'Gold is an obvious luxury'.

89 Provan (1996):86.

90 Beale (1998):909 points out that the items not in Ezekiel 27 'reflect the actual products of trade at John's time'. Interestingly, Moyise (1995):74 is more sceptical about this when he writes that 'it is unclear how he would know such a thing'.

91 Bauckham (1993a):364; Knight (1999):122.

92 Garnsey and Saller (1996):68.

and it is highly unlikely that he was aware of even a large import of special breeds of cattle to the *latifondisti* in Italy, and he certainly would not be aware of the import of small quantities. Therefore, it is probable that the Old Testament inspired John's inclusion of sheep and cattle, as I will argue below. John perceived that his own particular setting resembled that of Tyre's trade that resulted in suffering (Ezek. 28.16) and Assyria and Babylon (see Nah. 3).

My contribution to this discussion is that the merchandise was the opulent booty with which Rome constructed her consecrated places. In the same way Egypt, Jerusalem, Assyria, Tyre, Babylon, Persia, and Greece established their own sacred places with plunder (see chapter 5). In addition, they were symbols of her importance, and independence, by which she showed that all were subject to her. This is specifically done through the imperial cult and Rome's obvious consumption of merchandise. However, the items in Revelation 18 are rooted in the Old Testament and Jewish literature as well as Roman trade. They create a link between Rome and former ruling nations through showing the similar attitudes towards wealth and the consequences of those attitudes. Bauckham argues that knowledge of trade in the first-century Roman Empire was primary to the inclusion of the items on the list. I argue that John presents Rome as a large importer of goods, wares that John saw in the light of possessions plundered throughout the Old Testament. I will now look at the items and their position in the Old Testament and Jewish literature.

Gold, silver, jewels and pearls[93]

Gold, silver and jewels are precious things and were associated with the temple and plunder (Ex. 3.22; 25.1-9). Pearls were expensive items (Pliny *NH*. 9.106) and belong with other precious items: gold, silver, and jewels. They were connected, as with the other precious things, with a nation's religious identity. Israel will receive back her plundered pearls and her walls will be built with precious stones (Isa. 54.12; *Tg. Ps. Jon on Isa.* 54.12 has 'timbers in pearls'). My argument is not that God will actually build the New Jerusalem with pearls or precious stones, but that these express the restoration of Jerusalem in splendour. The New Jerusalem of Revelation has twelve gates made from pearls (21.21) and is contrasted with the beast (17.4). Rome is clothed with jewels and pearls (18.16). The idea of Rome being clothed in jewels and pearls means that her sacred buildings, temples and festivals were decorated with such sumptuousness. The Old Testament tells us that Israel bedecked herself in expensive stones to participate in Baal festivals (Hos. 2.13; cf. Jer. 4.30). This contrast suggests that what once belonged to Jerusalem now belongs to Rome. Tyre also is bedecked in expensive items from which the temple was made (Ezek. 27.1-9). The acquiring of pearls also according to Pliny resulted in suffering.[94] Pliny acknowledges how Lollia Paulina, the consort of Gaius 'obtained [pearls] with spoils from the provinces' (*NH*. 9.117). Precious things were seen as

---

93 See Ezekiel 16.8-15; Haggai 2.7; Daniel 11.38, 43; *1 Enoch* 94.6-7 for mention of these items.
94 Bauckham (1993a):353-354.

important items of spoil in war (2 Chr. 20.25). Merchants and sailors profited and increased in number because of Rome's love of pearls.

Fine linen, purple, silk, scarlet

All these items are expensive (Jer. 10.9). Linen was especially connected with plunder. In an acted parable, Jeremiah bought a linen waistcloth to wear, and then hid it by the Euphrates (Jer. 13.1-7). When Jeremiah returned he found it spoiled. The importance of the linen is not that it was expensive, but it was the most intimate. Its destruction symbolized to what extent Judah had been humbled. John depicts Rome as possessing in abundance even items of clothing.

Silk was a costly product according to Pliny (*NH*. 36.204). All these items were used for clothing and Israel took as booty (2 Chr. 20.25). Silk appears only in Revelation 18 in the New Testament. In the Old Testament silk is the clothing of Jerusalem (Ezek. 16.10, 13; cf. Rev. 18.16):

Ezekiel 16.10	**Revelation 18.16**
I clothed you also with embroidered cloth and shod you with leather, I swathed you in fine linen and covered you with silk. And I decked you with ornaments, and put bracelets on your arms... Thus, you were decked with gold and silver; and your raiment was of fine linen, and silk, and embroidered cloth.	Alas, alas, for the great city, that was clothed in fine linen, in purple and scarlet, bedecked with gold, with jewels, and with pearls.

These items had belonged to Jerusalem who no longer possessed them due to her disobedience but Rome did have them.[95] There may also be a connection with the items from which the veil of the temple and the attire of the high priest was made.[96] The Exodus narrative depicts the making of the tabernacle from goods plundered from Egypt (see chapter 5). Josephus mentions the temple veil (*Ant.* 5.5.4 or 5.212-213) that has its origins in Exodus 26.9 (cf. 2 Chr. 3.14). The LORD has given (cf. Hos. 2.8) and can take away (Ezek. 16.39). Whether or not it is taken away depends on whether the covenant is kept (Lev. 26; Deut. 28; Jer. 9.23-24). When this is taken as booty, a nation suffers its ultimate defeat as Jerusalem did in 70 CE. Antiochus

---

95 Provan suggest that the Hebrew literary antecedents would more likely lead to identifying Jerusalem. There is much to commend this position, especially in terms of the literary antecedents. I think the literary antecedents are indeed present, but that such traditions were applied to a new ruling power.

96 Chilton (1987):456; Barker (1991):106.

Epiphanes in 169 BCE also took the temple veil among his spoils (1 Macc. 1.21-22).[97] Further, the Jerusalem connection leads to John's depiction of Rome 'clothed in fine linen, in purple and scarlet, bedecked with gold, with jewels, and with pearls' (18.16-17), the very things with which Jerusalem had herself been bedecked and which Rome had plundered from Jerusalem.[98]

Parts of the sanctuary were made from scarlet (see Josephus in his description of the inner temple; also Ex. 26.31). Scarlet was also part of the veil and the high priest's outfit (Ex. 28.33). It is associated with comfort and luxury (2 Sam. 1.24). God will remove it from the haughty daughters of Zion. It is plundered by Babylon who seeks her life:

> And you, O desolate one, what do you mean that you dress in scarlet (Jer. 4.30).

Jesus is dressed in a scarlet robe and mocked as being the king of the Jews because of his appearance. This suggests that scarlet was associated with royalty (Mt. 27.28). There may also be a connection with the attire of conquering soldiers, thus emphasizing again marauding and plundering armies (Nah. 2.3).

Building Items: Citrus wood, Ivory, Costly items of Wood, Bronze, Iron and Marble
πᾶν ξύλον θύϊνον is wood of the tree θυία, a sweet scented African tree belonging to the Cypress family which includes cedars, cypresses, citrus and thujas.[99] Solomon's temple was built from cedar (1 Kgs 5.6-10) and the second temple (Ezra 3.7) and the chariots were built from cedar (Song 3.9). Wood of any kind is seen as the prize of a conqueror (Lam. 5.4):

> We must pay for the water we drink, the wood must be bought, it is also said that boys stagger under loads of wood (Lam. 5.13; cf. Ezek. 39.10).

Marble is a major feature of the temple (*War* 5.190; 1 Chr. 29.2). Marble also was plundered when the temple was destroyed. Marble was important to Rome and was imported especially from Asia. In a letter to Trajan, Pliny the Younger points out that the transportation of marble across land was very expensive and demanded much labour (*Ep.*10.41.2). Moreover, Pliny the Elder treats the private use of marble as an absurd and indefensible luxury (*NH*. 36.2-8, 48-51, 110, 125). This highlights the suffering caused by Rome's craving for marble.

Cinnamon, spice, incense, myrrh and frankincense
Although cinnamon is not mentioned in the list of merchandise in Ezekiel 27, it is associated with cassia in Ezekiel 27.19 (cf. Ps. 45.8). Cinnamon was used as sacred

---

97 Barker (1991):107.
98 Bauckham (1993b):355. Silk was the extravagant dress of Roman soldiers (Josephus *War* 7.126).
99 Johnson (1973):102.

anointing oil for use in the tent of meeting and the ark of the testimony. The anointing oil was made from myrrh, incense and cinnamon (Ex. 30.23). These three along with frankincense allude to the anointing oil. Cinnamon was imported to Jerusalem for its regular temple service.[100] The conquering Davidic king will be robed in garments fragrant with myrrh, aloes and cassia (Ps. 45.8). Pliny says that cinnamon is one of the most expensive items on earth and was used in religious ceremony including funerals (*NH.* 12.93; cf. Jer. 34.5).[101]

John's ἄμωνον (spice) does not appear in LXX Ezekiel 27.22, but ἡδύσμος (cooking spices) is present. Esler argues that John replaced Ezekiel's cooking spices in order to emphasize the use of spice for incense.[102] ἡδύσμος appears as mint in Matthew 23.23 and Luke 11.42 thus supporting Esler's point. However, Ezekiel refers to something 'sweet smelling' and not necessarily cooking spices. It appears as a spice used for incense in LXX Exodus 30.34, as an ingredient from which incense was made (cf. LXX Lev. 4.7, and 16.12). It appears as a luxury in the part of King Ahasuerus' court wherein the girls would be purified with it for six months (Esth. 2.12). Spices probably went under different names according to the time and it is possible that John is simply applying his own familiar term for spices in his list, thus indicating that he was aware of the particular spice of his time. Spices were used in Jewish and Roman festivals and provided much money to the exporters, especially north India. 1 Kings 10.10 reports that Sheba came to Jerusalem bearing spices. The destruction of a nation's sacred places meant a nation being dispossessed of their spices or the need for them.

Wine, oil, fine flour and wheat[103]

σεμίδαλιν appears only in Revelation 18.13 in the New Testament. It means fine wheaten flour. Pliny reports that it was ground from the inner kernels of the wheat thus making it expensive (*NH.* 18.21). It figures very much in the Levitical sacrifices (Lev. 2). Abraham fed God himself when he appeared at Mamre with fine flour (Gen. 18.6). Provan argues that the food items are not items of extravagance and luxury.[104] However, food is a central item of plunder and a nation can be kept low with its absence or shortage (2 Kgs 7; Jer. 12.10; Ezek. 16.19; *1 En.* 96.5). In Ezekiel 16.19 Israel is depicted similarly to Babylon in Revelation 18. She is plentiful in expensive clothing (Ezek. 16.10); jewellery (v.12); in gold, silver, fine linen, fine flour, honey and oil (v.13); and fine flour (v.19). With these items she played the harlot as Babylon does in Revelation 18. However, such items will be plundered (vv.38-44). Isaiah reflects this when he looks to the fulfilment of God's promises:

---

100 Applebaum (1976a):674.
101 Kraybill (1996):105.
102 Esler (1991):20 kindly gave me a copy of an unpublished paper on the list..
103 Schoff (1920):101 observes how these items are connected with the temple.
104 Provan (1996):86.

I will not again give your *grain* to be food for your enemies, and foreigners shall not
drink your *wine* for which you have laboured (Isa. 62.8; cf. Isa. 65.22).

For Jeremiah the restoration of grain, wine and oil are crucial for happiness:

and they shall be radiant over the goodness of the LORD, over the grain, the wine, and
the oil and over the young of the flock and the herd (Jer. 31.12).[105]

Thus, those who had 'fine wheat' were in John's eyes the plunderers who did not
work for their bread. This is illustrated in a letter from an unidentifiable emperor to
the Ephesians:

first the imperial city should have a bounteous supply of wheat…and then the other
cities may also receive provision in plenty.[106]

Rome supplied free wheat for its poor. This involved importing, and many from the
provinces would have resented this.[107] Whether or not this was a fair policy due to
the very large population in Rome, it certainly was perceived as unfair among some
provincials, for example, John.[108] Especially, when they consumed the best wheat.
Wheat also appears in Revelation 6.6 in which the prices of wheat were very high.
Sweet suggests Domitian's edict in 92 CE is alluded to in which soil only fit for
vines was used to grow wheat and barley, therefore the policy would have been
disastrous.[109] However, more likely is the Old Testament background of plunder.
Ezekiel reports the words of the LORD to Israel about a time of suffering and
plunder:

behold I will break the staff of bread in Jerusalem; they shall eat bread by the weight
and with fearfulness; and they shall drink water by measure and in dismay (Ezek.
4.16).

Leviticus 26 reports the importance of obeying God, but a refusal will result in a
shortage of daily needs caused by the invasion of their enemy (26.25-26).

Cattle, sheep, horses, chariots, slaves
The ownership of cattle and, indeed, sheep, signify the economic situation the
owner occupies (Gen. 12.16; 20.14; 24.35; 26.14). The dominating theme associated

---

105 Wine itself may have not been a luxury item, but it is likely that the author of Revelation
has in mind expensive wine which was a luxury in the same way that the author of the
Wisdom of Solomon castigates not only those who want expensive ointments but also
expensive wine (2.7).
106 See Garnsey and Saller (1996):99.
107 Garnsey and Saller (1987):86.
108 Finley (1985):198, adds that Rome was a huge importer of grain.
109 Sweet (1979):140.

with cattle is that of plunder. King Jehoshaphat plundered many cattle (2 Chr. 20.25; cf. Deut. 2.35; 3.7; 28.18; Isa. 13.20; Ezek. 38.12-13; and elsewhere). In describing the fall of Judah Jeremiah shows that the absence of cattle is a reason to lament (Jer. 9.10). In looking to the time of restoration, Jeremiah depicts the return of the people of God who will be rejoicing over the young flock and the herd (Jer. 31.12; 33.12). The important stipulation in Deuteronomy 28 regarding the rewards and punishment includes cattle. If the Israelites obey, there will be an increase of cattle (Deut. 28.4, 11; see also Isa. 13.20).

In sum, although not a commodity of wealth to Pliny, the Old Testament saw cattle and sheep as a status symbol of affluence. Thus the inclusion of cattle and sheep in Revelation 18 highlights the power of one who possesses many sheep and cattle.

John's chariots do not figure in Pliny's list of expensive items and occur nowhere else in the New Testament or LXX. Liddell and Scott describe them as a 'wagon' from the Latin *raeda* that suggests a 'four-wheeled travelling-carriage'. John did not choose the word to highlight war chariots, he would have used ἅρμα (war-chariot Liddell and Scott; cf. Rev. 9.9). In the Old Testament, possession of wagons and chariots suggests power and wealth. According to Ikeda: 'fine chariots and horses were among the items most sought by all the princes of the ancient Near East and were among the most desirable gifts to be expected'.[110] He points out that they displayed the princes' glory and status in processions and ceremonies, not for the battleground.[111] This would certainly be the case with Solomon who was not a man of war. 1 Samuel 8.11 points out that chariots were looked upon as symbols of the worldly splendour of a king. Connected with this, chariots and horses need people to operate them. The possession of horses and chariots is connected with the possession of slaves and the plunder that comes when one has a powerful king. 1 Kings 10.26 emphasizes the might of Solomon over the kings of the earth with reference to fourteen hundred chariots and twelve thousand horsemen as well as gold and silver. Jeremiah tells Judah that if she listens to the LORD she will be great, and a sign of this is the presence of kings riding in chariots and on horses (Jer. 17.24-25). In addition to highlighting the glory of a king, chariots and horses were associated with plunder (1 Chr. 18.4). However, the reference is to war chariots. John is more concerned to highlight the power, glory and wealth of Rome gained as plunder from other nations. In this case, Rome would be the recipient of gifts from defeated nations as well as the trade that their merchants were bringing. John may have had in mind:

> there you [Jerusalem court official] shall die, and there shall be your splendid chariots (Isa. 22.18).[112]

---

110 Ikeda (1982):221.
111 Ikeda (1982):221.
112 Kaïser (1980):150 suggests the 'you' is the 'Jerusalem court official'.

Bauckham's observations reinforce and particularize John's setting when he points out that ῥεδῶν (chariots) could be silver-plated and gilt chariots (see Pliny *NH.* 33.140 and *Martial* 3.62).[113] The word indicates a form of transport for the wealthy. John probably knew of the chariots and horses of Rome and compared them with the days of Solomon

Summary and Conclusions

Domitian's reign brought problems to a community that saw itself as heirs to the hope of Israel and witnesses in the tradition of the prophets. Compromise with Rome was a real fear for John. John saw Rome's rule as violent like the nations before. Yet Domitian's shrewd reign offered an easy option to compromise, and many from the synagogues and churches were tempted to do so. John attacked Rome through the universal language of his tradition.[114] He presented Rome like the previous exploitative nations. These included the leaders of Jerusalem who had persecuted and killed their own people. Rome beguiled the nations by her wealth, plundered the nations, and murdered peoples. John announces war on Rome and anticipates victory.

John foresees a future when Rome's wealth will be taken and God will establish his community in wealth and prosperity. This is prefigured in the Lamb in Revelation 5.12 who has already received prosperity. Rome will no longer consume the world's resources. The New Jerusalem will be the centre to which the kings of the earth bring their glory (Rev. 21.24).

John critiques the ideals of power and violence. John hopes for a break in the spiral of violence, and that aggression will cease and the peaceful Kingdom of God be established as depicted in the New Jerusalem.

The response and attitude of Revelation to its environment is not unlike Gandhi's.

1. Non-co-operation.
2. It understands violence as a spiral that increases in every generation. Humanity is dominated by an ungodly power that seeks total power and immortality for itself.
3. There is a holy war against violence. Victory will not be through weapons of war, but in its obedience to God and godly weapons of nonviolence: love and forgiveness. The war is also a religious one in which the way of the world is an assault on the very principles for which God created it.

This brings Part Two to a close. The broad horizons that influenced John have been established. In this chapter I have attempted to demonstrate how John responded to the challenge of Domitian's reign in the light of his sacred traditions.

---

113 Bauckham (1993a):365.
114 To this extent there is agreement with Provan.

In the next part, I will assess the evidence about Jesus and endeavour to show that Jesus was a revolutionary of peace who stood firm against the powers of violence and aggression and sought to transform people from it. This will mean an examination of key titles and descriptions of Jesus. In particular, those texts that appear to show Jesus as a warmonger will be considered.

PART THREE

A Nonviolent Christology in the Book of Revelation

I will consider Jesus as he is presented in the Book of Revelation using previous background material to help understand John's understanding of Jesus. I will examine the key descriptions and titles used of Jesus and ask to what extent Jesus can be described as a revolutionary of peace in the way I have defined the phrase in Part One.

CHAPTER 11

Jesus the Faithful Witness

In Part Two, I considered faithful witness themes in the Old Testament as well as in later Jewish developments of the Old Testament. These provide a broad context from which John drew for his presentation of Jesus as a faithful witness. In this chapter I will examine the more exact phrase 'faithful witness' along with the antecedents to it in the Old Testament.

Faithful Witness in the Old Testament

'Witness' occurs some sixty-seven times in the Old Testament. It most commonly refers to the role of the witness in the courtroom of one who has firsthand knowledge of an event or testifies on the basis of a report of another (Lev. 5.1). Israel was viewed as God's witness (Isa. 43.9, 10; 44.8, 9), although the ultimate witness is God (1 Sam.12.5; Job 16.19; Jer. 29.3; 42.5; Mal. 3.5). Those who transgress God's covenant could be put to death only on the evidence of two witnesses (Deut. 17.6; cf. Rev. 11). However, in Isaiah 40-55 only one witness is needed, namely, God's servant. For example, the witness is known as the servant (Isa. 44.1; cf. 44.8); only Israel is needed as a witness to establish the truth - that God is one - against the nations' attacks on God's honour.

God's anointed is like a faithful witness in the skies (Ps. 89.37b). There are various possibilities as to the originally intended identity of the 'witness' in Psalm 89. Eaton suggests the Davidic kings themselves make a perpetual witness.[1] Those immersed in the literature and temple liturgy of the Bible might have conflated the text with Isaiah 55.4 in which the witness describes God's servant (see further discussion below).[2]

Israel is also the faithful witness. In a controversy between the LORD and the false gods, God is represented by Israel and the world by the pagan nations (Isa. 50-55).[3] Israel is to be a light to the nations (Isa. 42.6-7; cf. 43.10, 12; 44.8). The peoples are gathered together (41.1) and judgement will follow (41.11). Judgement is the justice which will proceed from the testimony that God's witness gives (42.1, 4). The witness/servant is portrayed as one who is an example of suffering patience (42.1-4). In the context of the courtroom God gives his enemies an opportunity to present their case through their witnesses (43.9-10). However, when they have no

---

1 Eaton (1967):221; Bauckham (1993b):73; Beale (1999):191-192.
2 Bauckham (1993b):73.
3 Trites (1977):45.

case, God's witnesses are charged to declare the truth so that justice might follow. Suffering is a consequence of the faithful testimony that the servant gives (Isa. 50.4-9; 52.13-53.12). Although the servant is not called a 'witness', the servant functions similarly to the servant in the preceding songs. The language is of the law court (50.8-9) and the servant is one who argues the case of God (50.4) and suffers as a result of the word of God that he must speak (50.6-7).

Israel is described as God's servant in a way that compares her role to God's witness (41.9 and 43.10, 12).[4] Von Rad writes: 'when Deutero-Isaiah describes Israel as a "witness" for the nations (Isa. 43.10; 44.8; 55.4), he is not thinking of sending out messengers to them [the nations]. In the prophet's mind Israel is thought of rather as a sign of which the Gentiles are to become aware'.[5] Von Rad plays down the idea of a missionary being sent to proclaim a message. However, the witness is more than just a sign. Trites writes: 'It is the task of the witness not only to attest the facts but also to convince the opposite side of the truth of them'.[6] Caird comments that the most important aim of the witness 'was not to convince judge and jury, but to convince the adversary, so that he would withdraw his own case and acknowledge defeat'.[7] In other words, God's witnesses hope that people will deny the beast and then turn to God.

Faithful Witness in the New Testament

Lampe suggests that, although influenced by the Old Testament, the Christian understanding of faithful witness is distinctive. He sees suffering and death, in the Old Testament, resulting from a defensive aspect, whereas in the Christian's case it was not merely a matter of passive resistance, but of active testifying to the gospel. He writes: 'The Christian was essentially a missionary, and martyrdom was for him the most supreme and most effective mode of evangelism'.[8] Similarly, von Campenhausen argues that martyrdom can only be spoken of where the suffering is expressly related to the idea of witness bearing, and not to loyalty to the Law, as in the Old Testament.[9] Hengel writes that there is no superhuman transfiguration of the martyr because it is completely alien to the Old Testament.[10]

However, in my examination of the Old Testament in Part Two, I showed that the Christian developments of witness activity are present in the Old Testament, especially in the prophets. John advocates that faithful witnesses should be active in

---

4 Trites (1977):39-40, 47; further, Job functions as witness in taking God's side (1.21; 2.10; 42.8) and is described as 'my servant' (1.8; 2.3; 42.7,8).

5 Von Rad (1975): vol.2, 249.

6 Trites (1977):46; Bauckham (1993b):105 a witness is one who seeks to win people from lies and illusion to the truth. He points out the double-edge to witness: 'witness which is rejected becomes evidence against those who reject it'.

7 Caird (1980):158.

8 Lampe (1981):118.

9 Von Campenhausen (1964):3.

10 Hengel (1981):7.

proclaiming the gospel until death to the nations hoping that they, too, will come to accept Jesus' testimony as truth. Therefore, a faithful witness is a middleman of God before the nations.[11] The Old Testament is influential upon John both in providing examples of heroes within the tradition, but also heroes who were active in witnessing to the nations. The Old Testament does not simply contain traditions that are introspective and concerned simply with social control through advocating separation from the world. Within the Old Testament are the seeds of an ideology in which God's servants, through their faithfulness, aim to bring about a transformation of their enemy to live according to the principles God established. They are God's middlemen to the world.

Witness in The Book of Acts

In the New Testament, ὁ μάρτυς 'witness' occurs especially in the forensic sense (Mt. 18.16; 26.65; Mk. 14.63 and elsewhere). The risen Jesus commissions his disciples to be 'my witnesses' in Jerusalem and to the ends of the earth (Acts 1.8; cf. 22.15). The role of Jesus' followers is to testify to the world the truth that they have received from God. Truth is the resurrection of Jesus to which a witness must testify (1.22; cf. 2.32; 3.15; 5.32). Jesus' followers are witnesses to the whole life of Jesus and all that he did including his death (10.39; cf. 1 Pet. 5.1). For Luke, these are not only those who are eyewitnesses to Jesus' ministry, but also those to whom God has given the gift of being a witness. According to Acts, Paul sees his role as servant and witness even though he had not been with Jesus from the beginning (26.16). Marshall sees the influence of Isaiah 42.6-7 on Acts 26.18, in which the servant is to be a light to the nations.[12] Luke is also influenced by the forensic use of 'witness' in Acts 6.13. Stephen is set up as the complement of Jesus who, like Jesus, is challenged on the same charges by false witnesses (Acts 7.58).[13] The fate of Stephen is that of a martyr as with Jesus. His martyrdom is intimately connected with his role as witness. Luke shows the correlation between Stephen's witness and his death (Acts 22.20).[14]

---

11 O'Hagan (1974):94.

12 Marshall (1980):396.

13 Blaiklock (1977):78 makes this connection quoting Rackham: 'Like Jesus, Stephen was accused of blasphemy, and by false witnesses; even the charge ran in almost the same words, "destroy the temple"'.

14 Trites (1977):66-67 points out that witness here is beginning to be used in the sense of 'martyr'; cf. Marshall (1980):357.

Witness in Revelation

Revelation 1.2, 5

John who bore witness to the 'testimony of Jesus' (1.2).

Jesus Christ the faithful witness, the firstborn of the dead (1.5).

Faithful witness is influenced by Psalm 89.37b in which the unending witness of the moon is compared to the unending reign of David's seed.[15] John probably links together Psalm 89.37b and Isaiah 55.4 (see also discussion above).[16] The king establishes God's justice which is central to the role of God's chosen (Ps. 45.4,7; 72.1-2,4,12; 110.6). John is concerned to depict Jesus as a 'witness' in the forensic sense. As a 'witness' he seeks to establish justice similarly to the Davidic king. John has not necessarily in mind church members standing trial before the court; rather, he may have in mind Jesus' trials before the Sanhedrin and Pilate. Moreover, the law-court language is metaphorical. The law-court for the Israelites was the only context in which they experienced a systematic quest for truth.[17] In Revelation, the conflict is between the beast who tempts and seduces the world, and God's witnesses who defend God and seek the transformation of those who have been seduced by the beast. The witness can accept and embrace the accusations of their opponent as a way of reinforcing their truth claims. One such response is to die rather than deny God.

'Faithful witness' describes Jesus (1.5; cf. 3.14) and Antipas in 2.13 (cf. 11.3 and 17.6 in which only 'witness' is used). Trites detects a five stage diachronic development whereby μάρτυς (witness) became synonymous with 'martyr'.[18] He observes that witness originally belongs in the court of law with no expectation of death. In its final stage such an idea of witness disappears and it refers only to martyrdom. Certainly μάρτυς undergoes a change in meaning from the forensic sense in Isaiah 40-55 to the martyr understanding in the *Martyrdom of Polycarp*. Trites' application of a five stage diachronic development of μάρτυς is, however, unnecessary. Isaiah 40-55, for example, shows that suffering and death resulted from the testimony that a witness might give. Brownlee rightly observes that: 'the association of עד (witness) with the suffering servant perhaps prepared the way for the early use of ὁ μάρτυς in the sense of martyr'.[19] I have shown that suffering and death may be a consequence of delivering a testimony. Therefore, 'witness' and 'suffering' are related at a much earlier stage than Trites allows.

---

15 Beale (1999):190.
16 Sweet (1979):65; Schüssler Fiorenza (1972):199-200; Beale (1999):192.
17 Caird (1980):158.
18 Trites (1973):72-73 for the list of categories.
19 Brownlee (1957):208.

'Faithful witness' is placed beside 'firstborn from the dead' thus John establishes a relationship between witness and death. John is called a servant of God because he testified to the 'word of God' and the 'testimony of Jesus' (v.2). 'Testimony of Jesus' can be the witness *to* Jesus that John gives. This means that John teaches and witnesses about Jesus' death, rather than the testimony which Jesus gives.[20] However, the testimony Jesus *gives* before the world is expressed in his life and death. Therefore, John testifies to the testimony Jesus gave in his life, death and resurrection. Thus, an understanding of the Christology of Revelation must take into account Jesus as a witness who dies as a result of the lived and spoken testimony that he gave.[21]

The 'testimony of Jesus' is that which a witness gives. It is a distinguishing characteristic which all who follow Christ have in common, that is the testimony of Jesus (19.10). On five occasions 'testimony' is related with Jesus (1.2 [Christ is added]; 1.9; 12.17; 19.10 [twice]; 20.4). The word group is used repeatedly in conjunction with the deaths of Christians.[22] It is often associated with death resulting from giving witness to God (6.9; 11.7; 12.11, 17; 20.4). On three occasions, it means the testimony given by the witness (6.9; 11.7; 12.11) and in 6.9 and 11.7 the witnesses have been martyred because of their testimony.

Jesus, like Israel in Isaiah 43, is called to give testimony on God's behalf.[23] There is something of the prophet understood in the title 'witness' as well as the 'suffering servant'.[24] As we have already seen, the prophet came to be understood as a martyr by the first century CE; moreover, the prophet/servant/witness of Isaiah 53 suffered as a consequence of his testimony.[25] Thus, the phrase 'testimony of Jesus' suggests a testimony Jesus gave to others, the verbal witness of Jesus, summed up at his trial and his obedience to his Father, in his life especially in Gethsemane and on the cross.[26] His witness before Pilate was a known tradition in the early church (1 Tim. 6.13). Jesus' death resulted from his testimony, therefore, establishes a link between death and witness.

Jesus' refusal to play the power games of his oppressor is critical to testimony. His testimony is to accept the condemned condition. He embraces his suffering and rejection and in this way stands firm before his condemners. J.H. Yoder comments that:

---

20 Holtz (1962):56.

21 Sweet (1981):104 the testimony given is both the verbal witness to his father summed up at his trial, and his obedience on the cross.

22 Beale (1999):190.

23 Reddish (1982):128 unpublished dissertation.

24 Dehandschutter (1980):287.

25 Comblin (1965):160 suggested that the originality of Revelation is to have introduced the idea of martyrdom, as in 4 Maccabees, into a theology of witness. Comblin does not make enough of the connection between witness and servant and thus does not recognize the importance, as testified in Jewish literature like 4 Maccabees, that Deutero-Isaiah synthesizes the idea of death following from witness.

26 Ladd (1978):23; Sweet (1981):104; Bauckham (1993b):72.

suffering is not a tool to make people come around, nor a good in itself. But the kind of faithfulness that is willing to accept defeat rather than complicity with evil is, by virtue of its conformity with what happens to God when he works among us, aligned with the ultimate triumph of the Lamb.[27]

There is something of this in Jesus' sending out of his disciples as sheep among wolves (Mt. 10.16). Neil and Travis observe that too often followers of Christ 'when faced by "wolves" adopt the tactics of the wolves - to play the power game, or to rely on the security of schemes and organizations. Too easily we forget that we are sent out as sheep by one who himself "was led like a sheep to the slaughter" (Isa. 53.7)'.[28] The essential witness is not to be like the wolves but to persuade them by unconditional love. The ultimate expression of this witness is inevitably to die rather than apostatize. Therefore, martyr and witness are closely linked.

Revelation 1.9

John tells the churches that the reason for him being on Patmos was because of the 'word of God' and the 'testimony of Jesus' (cf. 6.9). John is one who pursued a lifestyle, modelled on Jesus, that was in harmony with the suffering servant/witness of Isaiah and elsewhere.

Revelation 2.13

Antipas my witness, my faithful one, who was killed among you.

Antipas is held up as an example of one who died because he held fast to the name of Jesus. John has Jesus describe Antipas as 'my witness, my faithful one'. Antipas is a witness to Jesus and this means that he is a witness to God as was Jesus. The witness Jesus gave to God inspires the faithful to bear witness to the witness Jesus gave, for the testimony of Jesus is the spirit of prophecy (19.10; cf. 22.9).[29] The message of Jesus is the essence of prophetic proclamation.[30] Jesus is associated with the tradition of prophets and servants of God, yet is the most supreme example. Just as it was the destiny of the Old Testament prophets to experience persecution, suffering and death for the sake of their message, so it is also the lot of the prophetic witnesses of Jesus.[31] Jesus has become the message in the same way that those who die for a cause can become immortalized within the message, they, too, become the message. Antipas stays faithful to God's promises through standing firm to the message that Jesus testified, that is to keep God's commandments (12.17). Antipas

---

27 Yoder (1994):238.
28 Neil and Travis (1981):74.
29 Sweet (1981):104; Comblin (1965):156.
30 Bauckham (1993a):161: the witness Jesus bore is the content of Spirit-inspired prophecy.
31 Trites (1977):160.

is a prophet of the New Covenant with Jesus as the Lord. Although Antipas was not numbered among the distinct group of prophets (11.18; 16.6 and 18.24),[32] Sweet points out: 'potentially all the Lord's people were prophets - if they were true to their baptismal vocation - and all were called to the same witness as their Lord, and the same result'.[33]

Revelation 6.9 -10

When he opened the fifth seal, I saw under the altar the souls of those who had been slain for the word of God and for the witness they had borne. They cried out with a loud voice, 'O Sovereign Lord, holy and true, how long before thou will judge and avenge our blood on those who dwell upon the earth?'

With the opening of the fifth seal John sees under the altar those slain for the word of God and the witness they had borne (the Greek has 'the testimony *which they had*'). It is not stated that the testimony *which they had* was the testimony of Jesus. Yet this is often assumed in that the testimony, which the faithful had, is that of Jesus. Still, the text does not say this. We must assign some significance to this. John is referring to those faithful witnesses to God's word who have died because of the testimony *they had*. The identity of the souls is not made explicit. Beale suggests that the souls are those who have recently died for their witness to Jesus.[34] However, it is more likely that John has in mind a broader category of innocent people who have been murdered for their testimony, which accounts for John's omission of Jesus with 'testimony'. John deliberately omits 'Jesus' and has only 'witness' as the Old Testament prophets had not the witness of Jesus. Caird believes also that John meant to include the martyrs of the Old Testament, for the cry "How Long?" had echoed down centuries of oppression.[35] Also in Psalm 79, God's servants and holy ones are murdered, their bodies are treated dishonorably (vv.2-3; cf. the death of the two witness) and they cry out: 'How Long, O Lord?' The Psalmist looks for vengeance (vv.10, 12).

THE BLOOD OF THE INNOCENT CRIES FOR VENGEANCE FROM THE ALTAR

The connection with the altar emphasizes the Jewish idea that justice will be given to the innocent, the place where God will meet his people. The witnesses have been slain. As with Christ, those following him will have their defeat turned into victory.[36] If the altar is the bronze altar of burnt-offering, atonement may be

---

32 Dehandschutter (1980):287; Bauckham (1993a):161 comments that it was not only prophets who prophesied, but clearly in 11.10 'prophecy and witness seem to be equated'.
33 Sweet (1981):105; also Bauckham (1993a):161.
34 Beale (1998):388; Sweet (1979):142, those under the altar are those slaughtered by Nero.
35 Caird (1984):84. See Psalms. 7.3; 13.1; 35.17; 74.9; 79.5; 80.4; 89.46; 90.13; 94.3; Isaiah. 6.11; Jeremiah. 47.6; Habbakuk.1.2; Zechariah. 1.12.
36 Beale (1998):389.

associated with those other than Jesus (Lev. 4). This certainly can be seen in Jewish texts in the first century as we have seen with 2 and 4 Maccabees. Hengel, however, writes that Jewish martyrdom differs from Christian martyrdom: 'In early Christianity, the whole expiatory power is connected in the sacrificial death of Jesus'.[37] This has led others to suggest the golden altar of incense in the *debir* (holy of holies).[38] This it is thought avoids the idea of another sacrifice insofar as atonement for people is not the function of the golden altar. Yet there might be ideas of atonement associated with this altar (Ex. 30.10; Lev. 16.17-18).[39] It is more likely that the bronze altar is intended as the blood was poured at the base of it (Lev. 4.7, 25).

Therefore, can the witnesses of Jesus also conquer because of their witness and death? In Revelation 12.11 it is the blood of Jesus and the testimony the witnesses gave that led to their victory. Part of their witness is their suffering and death. Vermes has argued that in first-century thought the blood of the binding of Isaac was understood as atoning for the Jewish nation. There is no evidence to establish certainty as Vermes' case rests on later rabbinic material. However, Revelation 6.9 may provide such evidence.

The idea of the blood of the innocent crying out from the ground for vengeance was common in some parts of Jewish tradition. Vermes points to the Rabbinic *haggadah* on Psalm 102.21 which links the blood crying out with Isaac's Aqedah in the *tannaitic midrash*:

> Through the merits of Isaac, who offered himself upon the altar, the Holy One, blessed be He, shall raise the dead. For it is written (Ps. 102.21): "From heaven the Lord looked upon the earth to hear the groaning of the captive, to deliver the children of death".[40]

Although this is too late to be considered significant on its own, it explains the presence of the altar in Revelation 6.9 in a way that brings to mind sacrifice and prayer. In Revelation 6.9, the groaning of the martyrs is heard and they will be raised as a consequence of the merits of Jesus' sacrifice. The altar alludes to the

---

37 Hengel (1989):267-268.

38 See Ladd (1972):102-103; Mounce (1977):157 thinks it is the altar of burnt offering, but the question does not really matter, they are blended together. No reason is given. Bauckham (1993a):269 thinks it is the incense altar, the one altar in the heavenly sanctuary; Beale (1999):391 argues for the golden altar arguing that atonement was associated with this altar. However, in observing Leviticus 4.7 what he omits to point out is that the blood is placed on the horns of the Golden altar and not on the base of the altar.

39 Leviticus 16.18 is usually associated with the bronze altar (cf. Lev. 16.11-12); however, the altar in v.18 was taken by *b. Yoma* 58b as the golden altar and so atonement would be associated with this altar. See Barker (1991):41.

40 *Tannaitic Midrash* is quoted by Vermes (1961):207 as PRK (i.e. *Pesikta de Rab Kahana*), *Piska* 32, f.200b. Text is very late, dated by Musaph-Andriesse (1981):57 between 500 and 640 CE.

temple sacrifices, which in rabbinic writings were intended as a memorial of Isaac's self-oblation.[41] In this text, the sacrifice of Jesus is remembered.

Revelation 11.3-13

The church, symbolized in the two witnesses, must stand firm before its oppressor. They expect to die and so follow Jesus. In death, resulting from their testimony, the figures are redeemed in the resurrection. Religion depends upon the credibility of the banners it puts in the hands of its members as they stand before death.[42] John has them. Death will result in the resurrection of life and in the continuance of the community of believers.

The role of the two witnesses is to prophesy (v.3). The reason for the 'two' may be accounted for by the remembrance of two recent historical figures.[43] It is more likely they represent the faithful witnessing church (11.4; cf. 1.20) and the 'two' emphasizes the forensic background in which two witnesses are needed for a testimony to stand in court. The background remains rooted in Jewish tradition in which the church is in continuity with the ancient prophets of Israel. God's holy ones are those whose bodies are left unburied (Ps. 79.3b). Although the two witnesses allude to Moses and Elijah (11.8),[44] Jesus is the supreme model and those who witness should expect the same fate.

The testimony the two witnesses give is not the testimony of Jesus, but it is their own (11.7; cf. 12.11). This emphasizes the importance of their actions and words. Jesus' testimony is their testimony that results in death. It is important, however, to observe that the death is not itself part of the witness. Death follows from their testimony. Yet, they are exalted before their oppressor (11.11) in a way similar to the way the suffering servant (Isa. 52.13-53.12) is exalted (Isa. 52.15).[45]

Revelation 12.11

And they have conquered him by the blood of the Lamb and by the word of their testimony, for they loved not their lives unto death.

---

41 Vermes (1961):209.

42 Berger (1990):51.

43 See discussion in Ford (1975):177-178 of the various suggested possibilities and thorough footnote number 293 in Beale (1999):573. Possibilities include: Paul and Peter; two Jewish high priests martyred in 68 CE (Josephus *War* 4.314-318); and others.

44 Bauckham (1993a):85 notes the reason for using Moses and Elijah: 'Both are prophets. As prophets who both confronted the world of pagan idolatry they set a precedent for the church's prophetic witness to the world'.

45 Nickelsburg (1972):24 pointed out that the servant of Isaiah 52.13-53.12 is exalted before the kings and nations.

The saints have conquered through the blood of the Lamb and by the word of their testimony (see discussion on 6.9 for the conquering through the blood of the Lamb). There is a third aspect that may be connected with 'conquering':

for (καὶ) they loved not their lives unto death.

Their testimony is their faithfulness. Such faithfulness is expressed in their lives through not compromising and fighting their condemners on their own terms. The RSV translates καὶ 'for' linking the above phrase directly in relationship with 'the word of their testimony'. Καὶ can be translated 'since' or 'because' and this changes the meaning:

and they conquered him by the blood of the Lamb and by the word of their testimony *since* they did not cling to life in the face of death. [46]

They fight not with the weapons of the challenger. They accept their fate at the hands of the challenger, but without compromising. Their testimony relied upon their readiness to die, hence the translation 'since'. They conquer because they did not compromise. They persevered in their testimony to Christ, despite persecution. The mark of genuine Christian conquerors is that they love their Lord more than their own earthly welfare.[47] Their readiness to stand firm before their persecutors reminds God of the faithfulness of Jesus (see discussion on 6.9), which explains why their conquering is dependent on the blood of the Lamb.

Revelation 12.17

This verse depicts the ancient mythical struggle between good and evil. The oppressor or accuser is the ancient serpent who is enraged against God's chosen people. God's people are those who keep God's commandments and have the testimony of Jesus. Persecution and death are associated with the way they live; keeping God's commandments is to bear witness to Jesus.

Revelation 17.6

And I saw the woman, drunk with the blood of the saints and the blood of the martyrs.

The blood of two groups is mentioned: 'the blood of the saints' (τῶν ἁγίων) and the 'blood of the martyrs' (τῶν μαρτύρων). The RSV translates τῶν μαρτύρων as

---

46 For the causal use see Genesis 24.56. See also Aune (1997):cxciv. Aune makes the point that the causal usage is not strictly Semitic as it is found in other Greek literature.
47 Beale (1999):665.

'martyrs' rather than 'witnesses'.[48] 'Martyr' is an unnecessary translation as the 'saints' are murdered as well as the witnesses. Both are martyrs in the English sense of the word. 'Witnesses' convey the sense of the Greek more than 'martyrs'.

The 'saints' are prominent in Revelation (5.8; 8.3-4; 11.18; 13.7; 13.10; 14.12; 16.6; 18.24; 19.8; 20.9). John is aware of the Hebrew background to the 'saints'. In the Old Testament, Psalm 79 is a cry to God regarding the servants and saints who have been murdered by the Gentiles. Two groups are in synonymous parallelism in v.2: the servants and the saints. Both are depicted as food for the birds of the air and beasts of the earth, their blood is poured out, and they are left unburied. This resembles the presentation of God's faithful in Revelation. God's servants in Psalm 79.2 are both prophets and witnesses (Rev. 11.18; 16.6; 18.24). John also connects the two groups: witness and saint to the extent that they are considered the same.[49] In this way, the blood of the saints is the blood of the witnesses of Jesus. In addition, Psalm 116.15 adds to the usage of 'saints'. The RSV translates: 'precious in the sight of the LORD is the death of his saints'. The saints have been murdered. Also, the 'saints' in Daniel 7.25 are the 'saints' who will be defeated, but they will be redeemed (v.26). John used 'saint' because of its associations with innocent death.

Revelation 20.4

Καὶ εἶδον θρόνους καὶ ἐκάθισαν ἐπ' αὐτοὺς καὶ κρίμα ἐδόθη αὐτοῖς, καὶ τὰς ψυχὰς τῶν πεπελεκισμένων διὰ τὴν μαρτυρίαν Ἰησοῦ καὶ διὰ τὸν λόγον τοῦ θεοῦ - Then I saw thrones, and those seated on them were given authority to judge. I also saw the souls of those who had been beheaded for their testimony to Jesus and for the word of God.

It seems that two groups are mentioned: those seated on thrones and those who have been beheaded. There is no obvious group said to be seated on the throne. I propose that John is using καὶ to explain the group who have been given authority to judge.[50] I suggest the following translation assuming the Hebrew background:

Then I saw thrones and seated upon them were the souls who had been beheaded on account of the testimony of Jesus and the word of God; they were so seated because justice had been given in favour of them.

There is a difficulty in understanding those on the throne having become judges. It is unlikely that judgement is given to the faithful as judgement has already been

---

48 Trites (1973):73 and 78-79 locates witness here in the third stage of semantic development in which death is regarded as part of the witness. It is misleading to apply such categories, as Trites' 'third stage' can be identified in Isaiah 40-55.

49 Beale (1999):860.

50 Caird (1980):118 lists six uses of the Hebrew word *waw*; Waltke and O'Connor (1990):652-653; Sweet (1979):288 also takes καὶ as 'that is'. See also discussion of the use καὶ in Beale (1999):974-976.

passed (19; 20.1-3); moreover, Jesus is the judge (19.11-17) and not the faithful.[51] Another possibility will be suggested.[52]

Daniel 7.9, 21-22, 26, influences John. In Daniel 7, God's chosen ones, described as one like a son of man, and the beast prevails over them (v.21). However, a time is seen when judgement will be given in favour of the chosen (v.22),[53] and the oppressor will be judged in the court by those seated upon thrones (v.9), and the beast's dominion will be taken away (v.26). In Matthew 19.28 the Greek is unambiguous and judgement is given to the twelve apostles but the Greek is not so in Revelation 20.4 (cf. 1 Cor. 4.8; 6.2; Eph. 2.6). In Revelation 20.4 those who die for the witness that they give will be exalted and their testimony will be vindicated by God in the divine court in the judgement that will be given in their favour. God is the judge (Isa. 30.18). It is better to read αὐτοῖς in 20.4 'in favour of them.[54] Therefore, judgement was given in favour of them or on behalf of them. Moreover, it is likely that κρίμα (justice) is used in an unfavourable sense in respect of the enemy.[55] For example, κρίμα is used of the condemnation of the harlot (17.1). God establishes κρίμα in favour of the faithful against the false accuser (18.20).[56] The Greek associates the judgement with God's chosen: τό κρίμα ὑμῶν (your justice). This agrees with 20.4 in which κρίμα is given to the chosen. Yet this does not suggest that they are judges. Rather, κρίμα is the 'sentence passed'.

Summary of Findings

Faithful witnesses are servants of God who suffer and die as a result of delivering God's message. The testimony they proclaim and live is embraced in Jesus' life and death, particularly before his oppressors. Antipas follows the example of Jesus and dies. 'Faithful witness' connects Jesus with the past figures who suffered and died for the testimony that they gave. John reminded his readers that compromise was not the way of faithfulness. He remembers Antipas' act in order to remind them of a recent believer who would rather die than compromise. Readiness to die for one's beliefs is a powerful testimony before the oppressor. The prayer for vengeance from the altar (6.9) may allude to the Aqedah tradition; the sacrifice of the faithful reminds God of the willing sacrifice that Jesus made, leading to the redemption of those in bondage to the way of the beast. In 6.9 those who have been martyred like Jesus, died because of the testimony that they gave. The testimony is the testimony of Jesus, which he gave before his accusers in his silence, and readiness to die.

---

51 Note the unnecessary translation given by NRSV in which 'authority to judge' is supplied.
52 Beale (1999):997; Krodel (1989):333; similarly Aune (1998):1085: 'It is possible that the major purpose of depicting the enthroned figures in Revelation 20.4 is to emphasize their exaltation'.
53 Goldingay (1987):146 writes that judgement is given on behalf of the saints.
54 See Blass and Debrunner (δ188); Aune (1997):clxxvi notes the use of this dative in 13.14, also note 2.5, 16; Beale (1999):997 also reads the text in this way.
55 According to Arndt and Gingrich, p. 451, κρίμα usually appears in this way.
56 Sweet (1979):275. See also Caird (1984):229.

Gandhi writes of Jesus' atonement: 'Jesus atoned for the sins of those who accepted his teachings by being an infallible example to them. But the example was worth nothing to those who never troubled to change their lives'.[57] Jesus is the unique example and model. He inspires his people to make his testimony their testimony and that they should expect martyrdom (11.1-14). A faithful witness and a holy life lead to an innocent death (17.6). The reference to the 'saints' alludes to the 'saints' of the Psalms and the saints in Daniel 7. They so inspired John as they were put to death because of their faithfulness. The saints are the witnesses of Jesus (17.6). Justice will be given in favour of his witnesses against the false witnesses (20.4; cf. 18.20). Those who reject the witness of the saints bring punishment upon themselves. This denial is emphasized in the grisly outcome of God's witnesses, i.e. to be beheaded. They accept their lot and refuse to participate in the power games of their violent persecutor. The whole situation is presented using the law-court metaphor where the witnesses are depicted as seated on thrones of judgement, but this expresses their exalted state rather than their status as judges.

Conclusions

Jesus is remembered as a faithful witness to the world in his teachings, actions and death. In his life and death, Jesus sought the transformation of the world from the values of the beast. His faithful witness was not to play the power games of the beast and his followers. Witness brought to mind the suffering servant who chose the way of weakness to transform the way of the beast. His testimony becomes a judgement upon those who refuse to listen to it.

Jesus the faithful witness inspired Gandhi in his testifying to the ways of truth, which it is clear in both traditions, are nonviolent. Change from the values of violence and oppression occurs when God's witnesses cease to fight such values on their own terms. A witness is one who fights and desires victory, the antagonist must be confronted, and his way of life must be challenged.

---

57 Quoted in Jesudasan (1984):74.

CHAPTER 12

Jesus the Pierced Servant

Introduction

In the last chapter I examined the depiction of Jesus as a 'faithful witness' and how this connected with faithful witnesses in Israel's past. Faithful witnesses should expect to suffer as a consequence of giving their testimony. In this chapter I will consider Jesus as the 'pierced one'. Suffering is clearly associated with this description. This depiction is used for God's faithful in the Old Testament (Zech. 12.10). Jesus is described as a suffering faithful servant in a way that alludes to the faithful in Israel's past. John makes subtle us of this Old Testament depiction I will consider what this contributes to our understanding of Jesus in the Book of Revelation.

Exegesis

Revelation 1.7	Zechariah 12.10
Behold, he is coming with the clouds, and every eye will see him, every one who pierced him; and all tribes of the earth will wail on account of him.	And I will pour out on the house of David and the inhabitants of Jerusalem a spirit of compassion and supplication, so that, when they look on him whom they have pierced, they shall mourn for him, as one mourns for an only child, and weep bitterly over him, as one weeps over a firstborn.

The influence of Daniel 7.13 on Revelation 1.7 is seen in the 'coming with clouds'. It is clearly an allusion to the arrival of the son of man. The clouds function to emphasize the exalted status of Jesus. 'Cloud' in Hebrew thought is associated with divine presence (Ex.13.21; 16.10; cf. Mt.17.5; Acts.1.9).[1]

Those who see *the pierced figure* are the ones who pierced him, yet it is every nation that laments on account of him (Rev. 1.7). The verb ἐκκεντέω 'to pierce' appears in the New Testament in John 19.37 as well as Revelation 1.7. In both John and Revelation Jesus is compared to the figure in Zechariah 12.10.[2]

---

1 Mounce (1977):72.
2 Caird (1984):18; Sweet (1981):111-112 & (1979):112; Bauckham (1993a):319-322; Aune (1997):56; Beale (1999):196-199.

Zechariah 12.10 presents a suffering figure like the servant of Isaiah 53. Those who caused the suffering express regret at the suffering they caused. In Zechariah, mourning is that of penitential grief, which is followed by divine pardon, cleansing, and restoration.[3] Caird believes John is true to this context of Zechariah. In Revelation 1.7 the mourners will one day express regret for the suffering they have caused the pierced figure.[4]   Ladd, however, believes John alters the context of Zechariah 12.10. He observes that the crucified one has become the object of their sorrow; i.e., they are grieving because they have crucified him. This would mean that men will be convicted for the evil of their terrible crime, and in repentance will seek God's forgiveness. Yet there is in the Book of Revelation no indication of the repentance of the wicked.[5] Sweet objects to Ladd's interpretation as it has no respect for the context of Zechariah and John shows a sharp awareness of context, especially with Daniel and Zechariah, and so it is in 1.7 with the pierced figure.[6] Generally, Revelation is concerned with repentance and not judgement (1.7; 5.13; 9.20-21; 10.11; 11.13-15; 14.6-7; 15.4; 16.9, 11; 21.3, 5, 23-26; 22.2).[7]

John interprets Zechariah 12.10 messianically.   Jesus is the pierced messianic figure. Those who mistreat the messiah servant will come to see their deeds as evil (cf. Isa. 53.11). Isaiah 52.13-53.12 may have influenced Zechariah 12.10. It is possible that John made the connection between Zechariah 12.10 and Isaiah 52.13-53.12. The suffering servant is for John not only the figure of Isaiah 52.13-53.12 but also the one pierced by the nations. John depicts Jesus as an exalted martyr figure who willingly accepts death, and those who pierced him will come to acknowledge the truth of Jesus' testimony; not simply because of his spoken testimony, but because he was willing to die for what he believed in. Those who pierced him will mourn for him. Here, the impact of the martyrdom is seen.

The mourning is a result of the pouring out of the spirit of 'compassion' and 'supplication' (Zech.12.10). The Hebrew word in Zechariah 12.10 for 'supplication' can suggest the mercy of the victor for the vanquished (Josh. 11.20). It is interesting to note the conclusions of some sociologists who deduce from their observations that the martyr can shame the oppressor.[8] Feeling shame can relate to the mercy that the oppressor feels for the oppressed. Those who have pierced the figure show shame at what they have done. In so doing the action of martyrdom is beneficial to the oppressor. In Zechariah 12.10, the figures show respect and this makes living together possible. John is influenced by the wider context of Zechariah 12-14 which

---

3 Caird (1984):18.
4 Caird (1984):18; also Sweet (1979):62 and (1981):101, 112; Beale (1999):197.
5 Ladd (1978):28-29.
6 Sweet (1979):63; Beale (1999):197. It can be argued that allusions to the Old Testament by John are contradictory to their original Old Testament context. However, where this occurs, Beale has shown that there is a precise pattern to this usage, what he calls 'an inverted or ironic use' (1999):94.
7 Caird (1984):18; also Sweet (1979):62 and (1981):101, 112; Beale (1999):197; Harrington (1993):231-232 lists the key texts which show Revelation's concern for repentance.
8 Weiners (1990):22.

is concerned with the establishment of God's universal kingdom in which many from the nations will confess the LORD: this is the concern of the witness (especially 14.2, 8, 11). Sweet has observed that in Revelation the victory of witness brings about conversion and healing, as opposed to the hardening effect of the retributive plagues. This interpretation is supported by appeal to its structure and use of scripture, particularly Zechariah 12-14 (cf. Isa. 53.11).[9]

Although John has not altered the context of Zechariah 12.10, it is obvious that John has broadened the group who repent. It is not just the lost house of Israel, but all tribes and nations repent. Bauckham discusses the development here in terms of the influence of the promise to Abraham in Genesis 12.3, 22.18, 26.4 and 28.14. The early Jewish and Christian exegetical interest in Genesis 22 is important to my consideration of the book of Revelation and it seems quite plausible that John has alluded to it in 1.7, although the wider conceptual framework for broadening the groups who can be saved would be seen elsewhere, especially in Isaiah 40-55. Yet it is likely that there is an intertextual relationship between the promises made to Abraham and the more universal theology of Isaiah 40-55.

Conclusion

Jesus is a suffering witness/servant who is martyred. His death leads to sorrow among those who oppressed him. Willingness to die would have associations with the Lamb of Isaiah 53.7 and Isaac in Genesis 22 as both are connected with martyrdom. In the use of this description for Jesus, John is emphasizing Jesus as a suffering figure, one who does not play the power games of the beast's followers. This coheres with the depiction of Jesus as a faithful witness who testifies to the antagonists in weakness and not violent power. Such a portrayal relates closely to Gandhi's vision of the effectiveness of *satyagraha*. Parekh writes: 'The *satyagrahi's* love and moral nobility disarmed his opponent, weakened his feelings of anger and hatred, and mobilized his higher nature'.[10]

In the next chapter I will consider Jesus as one like the son of man and trace the continuity with the pierced one and the faithful witness.

---

9 Sweet (1981):101.
10 Parekh (1997):56.

CHAPTER 13

Jesus the Son of Man

Introduction

In the last chapter I considered the description of Jesus as the pierced one of Zechariah 12.10. This figure suffers, and through his suffering he brings his oppressors to their senses. This figure is a suffering servant who cares not for his life. Jesus is the son of man of Daniel 7, which I have examined in Part Two. In this chapter, I will consider this description and John's understanding of it as he uses it to describe Jesus.

It has been observed that one like a son of man in Daniel 7.13 represents the *maskilim* of Daniel 11.35, and both could be associated with the suffering servant/witness of Isaiah 53. The presentation of Jesus in Revelation as a son of man, or more precisely as *a humanlike figure*, will be assessed as to what extent this connects with witness and martyrdom and thereby associates Jesus with the suffering witness/servant of God and the pierced one.

Revelation 1.12-16

Then I turned to see the voice that was speaking to me, and on turning I saw seven golden lampstands, and in the midst of the lampstands one like a son of man, clothed with a long robe and with a golden girdle round his breast; his head and his hair were white as white wool, white as snow; his eyes were like a flame of fire, his feet were like burnished bronze, refined as in a furnace, and his voice was like the sound of many waters; in his right hand he held seven stars, from his mouth issued a sharp two-edged sword, and his face was like the sun shining in full strength (RSV translation).

One like a Son of Man

Jesus is 'one like a son of man'. This is better expressed by a 'humanlike figure'. It is not a title as the NRSV has it: the Son of Man (1.12-16). The phrase 'like a son of man' is not a christological title.[1] Rather, John is referring to the figure of Daniel 7.13 who receives dominion, glory and kingship from God. The 'humanlike figure'

---

1 Swete (1922):15; Lindars (1983):159; Harrington (1993):51; Bauckham (1993a):295 and (1993b):97-98; Charles (1920):27 the figure is like an angel; Beale (1999):209 sees the figure as a priest on the basis of the lampstands as they are temple items.

and those identified with the figure are afflicted (Dan.7.21). The figure of Isaiah 52.13-53.12 and the figure in Daniel 7 are related by their suffering.[2] Beale suggests that the 'humanlike figure' in Revelation 1.13-16 relates to suffering reinforcing the connection with the Lamb.[3] Further, Jesus is 'a pierced one' and 'the faithful witness' again the descriptions relate to suffering. Yet scholars believe that judgement is given to the figure in Daniel as they also believe in the case of Revelation.[4] Yet judgement is not given to the 'humanlike figure' in Daniel 7.[5] The key text for those who understand judgement to have been given is Daniel 7.22: 'then judgement was given to the holy ones'. However, this need not be translated as 'to the saints', but rather, 'in favour of or on behalf of the saints'.[6] The beast defeats God's people, yet justice will be given in favour of them.

As we have seen in Part Two, the son of man of Daniel 7.13 may allude to the *maskilim* in Daniel 11.35 and 12.3. The figure is a witness of God who seeks to win the nations away from the beast's dominion. Such a witness wishes to receive them into the universal kingdom, which the son of man has received from God, in which all will obey God's laws (cf. Rev. 5.10).[7]

The Clothing of the Son of Man

Revelation 1.13	**Daniel 10.5**	**Ezekiel 9.2**
clothed with a long robe and with a golden girdle round his breast	I looked up and saw a man clothed in linen, with a belt of gold from Uphaz around his waist	Among them was a man clothed in linen, with a writing-case at his side. They went in and stood beside the bronze altar

The figure in Revelation 1.13 is clothed with a long robe and with a golden sash across his chest. Beale suggests that the garments of the high priest are in the mind of John.[8] The following are the holy garments of the high priest (Ex. 28.4 cf. Lev.

---

2 Goldingay (1987):170-171.

3 Beale (1999):356.

4 See especially Comblin (1965):55 in which he writes that the mission of the Son of man is to execute the judgement of God.

5 Bauckham (1993a):97 points this out. Rowland sees a judge figure here, but he cannot cite evidence other than 19.11 which is not the Son of Man. Bauckham (1993a):295 suggests persuasively that John uses the exact phrase of Daniel 7.13-14 because that figure is not a judge. The Son of Man in the Similitudes would be a judge.

6 Goldingay (1987):146 ודינא יהב לקדישי the preposition before the holy ones can be translated 'in favour of'.

7 Bauckham (1993b):97.

8 Beale (1999):209; contrary Morris (1979):53: 'though priests did wear the girdle higher than others, in their case it was a woven sash and not 176 golden clasp, which was rather the mark of royalty'.

16.4 and Wis. 18.24): breastpiece, an ephod, a robe, a chequered tunic, a turban, and a sash. If John presents Jesus as the high priest, it is not obvious why, of the six important items of clothing, John only includes two: the long robe and sash.

Like John, Daniel sees a man dressed in linen and a golden girdle around his loins (MT: מתן and LXX: ὀσφυν (10.5). There is also a figure in Ezekiel 9.2 who has something around his loins (MT: מתן, LXX: ὀσφύος). It is uncertain what is placed around this figure's waist. The Hebrew has קסת around his waist. קסת appears only here and its meaning is unclear although the translations have 'writing-case'. However, LXX Ezekiel 9.2 reads:

καὶ εἷς ἀνὴρ ἐν μέσῳ αὐτῶν ἐνδεδυκὼς ποδήρη καὶ ζώνη σαπφείρου ἐπὶ τῆς ὀσφύος αὐτοῦ καὶ εἰσήλθοσαν καὶ ἔστησαν ἐχόμενοι τοῦ θυσιαστηρίου τοῦ χαλκοῦ - and there was one man in the midst of them clothed with a long robe down to the feet, and a sapphire girdle was on his loins: and they came in and stood near the brazen altar (Tr. Brenton).

LXX Ezekiel 9.2 compares well with Revelation 1.13 except that Revelation translates מתן as μαστοῖς (breast). The original meaning underlying קסת is not clear but John has opted for LXX. Yet John draws upon Daniel MT 10.5 for the detail that the girdle is golden and not sapphire as in LXX Ezekiel 9.2. The 'long robe' in Revelation is not present in Daniel 10.5 (either LXX, Theodotion or MT).[9] It is also important to observe the figure in LXX Ezekiel 9.2 who is wearing a long robe. John has drawn upon LXX Ezekiel 9.2 for the long robe that the son of man is dressed in.

In sum, while it is not possible to conclude that Daniel 10.5 influenced John, it is possible that LXX Ezekiel 9.2 underlies John's usage, yet he probably drew upon both.[10] It is important to see why John drew upon these two traditions.

The Influence of Ezekiel 9.2 and Daniel 10.5

The figure in Ezekiel 9.2, who stands besides the bronze altar, puts the divine mark on the righteous so that they will not be punished (9.4-5). The whole action reminds us of the events of the Passover in Egypt. Some are to be protected by a mark of preservation (Ex. 12.7, 13, 22-23, 27; cf. Ezek. 9.4, 6). Just as the Lord 'passed through' Egypt (Ex. 12.23), so the LORD's emissaries in Ezekiel 9.4-5 pass through Jerusalem.[11] This should echo as we read Revelation in which the mark serves the same function for the servants/witnesses of God (7.2-3; 14.1; cf. Ezek. 9.4-5 and Ex. 12.7). The mark in Exodus 12.7 was the blood of the lamb over the door. Jesus is introduced as a Lamb in Revelation 5.6, one who has lived a life of obedience until death, and provided them with an example which becomes their mark and which results in their victory. The 'mark' in Revelation is a metaphor for belonging to God; to belong to God is to keep his commandments, give his testimony and do

---

9 LXX Daniel 10.5: ἐνδεδυμένος βύσσινα; MT: לבוש בדים.
10 Beale (1999):210.
11 Brownlee (1986):144.

good works and in so doing win over the followers of the beast for God. John read Ezekiel 9.4-5 alongside Exodus 12.7. Jesus is compared to the figure of Ezekiel 9.4-5 through whose actions people are saved. Moreover, the faithfulness of God's servants reminds God of Jesus' faithfulness, which is the mark of Jesus; indeed, it is the name of Jesus (Rev. 14.1). Their faithfulness will be their protection.[12]

In sum, the two items of clothing are related to LXX Ezekiel 9.2 and Daniel 10.5. The mission of the one like a human figure is to save the righteous. The 'mark' Jesus places upon them is similar to that of the blood of the Lamb, which could be related to the Aqedah. The mark on the faithful is the name of Jesus, a mark that separates them from the beast. The 'mark' expresses the way they live. Their good works will remind God on the day of judgement that they carry the mark of Jesus.

Exalted Figure (1.14-16)

His feet were like burnished bronze, refined as in a furnace.

Sweet suggests this alludes to the furnace in Daniel 3.6 in which the three faithful servants would rather die than worship Nebuchadnezzar.[13] Sweet's proposal links with John's presentation of Jesus as one who has conquered through suffering and connects with the Hebrew idea that suffering will strengthen the sufferer (especially Ps. 66.10-12). John fears that members of the church will worship the image of the beast (13.5). This detail reminds his audience that John would rather die than disobey God. Similarly, this reminds them of the three figures in Daniel 3.18 who declare before Nebuchadnezzar 'we will not worship the golden statue that you have set up'.

His head and his hair were white as white wool, white as snow.

God, the Ancient of Days (Dan. 7.9) has hair like pure wool and his clothes were white as snow. The author of *1 Enoch* describe the hair of the Messianic Son of Man in the same way:

His head was white like wool (*1 En.* 46.1).

This clearly belongs within the tradition of Daniel 7.9, but in *1 Enoch* the Son of Man is identified as a judge figure. It seems unlikely that John is presenting Jesus as a judge figure as he is only seen as a judge in Revelation 19.11. It is interesting to observe *1 Enoch* 106.10:

the hair of his head is whiter than white wool.

---

12 It is interesting to compare this idea with Revelation 11.1-2 in which the holy of holies will not be trampled on symbolizing the spiritual protection that the faithful will experience.
13 Sweet (1979):72; Beale (1999):210.

The figure that is described in this way is unlike a human being (*1 En.* 106.10). However, the figure is a human being, Noah, born of woman, a righteous person, upon who rests the hope of God's people (*1 En.* 106.16-18). He will be a remnant of the righteous, i.e. those who belong to him, who will be saved from the sin and oppression (*1 En.* 106.18). The figure is a righteous person amidst sin and oppression. However, a greater time of oppression is predicted (*1 En.* 106.19). John, influenced by this tradition, presents Jesus as faithful to his church. They are a righteous remnant amidst sin and oppression.

The description also conveys such notions as respect, honor, wisdom and high social status.[14] Such notions are seen in the figure of Noah (note also Jacob in the Jewish writing *Joseph and Aseneth* 22.7).

In his right hand he held seven stars.

Janzen suggests that Roman imperial coinage provides the key to understanding this description.[15] However, the number seven has important symbolic value in Jewish tradition and it symbolizes completeness. In addressing seven churches, John indicates that his message is addressed to specific churches as representative of all churches.[16] The stars are described as the angels of the seven churches (v.20). The angels are the spiritual counterparts of earthly realities. John depicts Jesus' relationship with the whole church, which is one of protection and encouragement.

From his mouth came a sharp two-edged sword (cf. 2.12, 16).

Isaiah, like John, describes a faithful servant who has a mouth like a sharp sword (49.2). Such a sword symbolizes the irresistible power of divine judgement.[17] God's faithful witness seeks to win people from lies and illusion. The setting for Isaiah is the court and not the battlefields, although the court is a type of battlefield but with different weapons. The witness is to be a light to the nations that God's salvation would reach to the ends of the earth (Isa. 49.6; cf. Acts 1.8). The mouth like a sharp sword is the symbol of the prophet, whose utterance has a cutting edge to it, because he speaks the word of God.[18] The sword is like the witness, which Jesus gave to win nations to God from the beast.[19] However, the sword is said to slay them (Rev. 19.15). Yet it is the rejection of the witness that leads to their destruction (cf. Jn

---

14 Aune (1997):94.

15 Janzen (1994): 651.

16 Bauckham (1993b):16. The seven stars here must be seen in the wider context of the book rather than particularizing and applying numismatics upon the text.

17 Mounce (1977):80. Discussion of the significance of the 'sword' will be discussed in more detail when examining the rider on the horse in Revelation 19.11-16.

18 Caird (1984):245.

19 Bauckham (1993b):105; cf. Harrington (1995):66; contrary Ford (1975):314; Yarbro Collins (1979):135.

12.48; *1 En.* 10.9; 4 Ezra 13). To this extent it is the testimony that destroys the enemy. Revelation highlights this by using the sword as the testimony. However, the testimony is love and forgiveness. Gandhi similarly used sword:

> The sword of *satyagraha* is love, and the unshakeable firmness that comes from it (11-59).

Conclusion

Jesus the humanlike figure is a suffering servant who gives his witness faithfully. Justice will be given in favour of him. The clothing points to him as one who stands in the midst of suffering as God's faithful witness. The association of mouth and sword emphasizes his witness to God's love. His verbal testimony and actions reveal his unconditional love that leads the antagonist either to transformation or to death. There is nothing in Revelation 1.13-16 that contradicts the previous presentations of Jesus as faithful witness and the pierced one.

In the next chapter, I will continue to test the extent to which Jesus is depicted as a suffering figure with the description of Jesus as a slain Lamb.

CHAPTER 14

Jesus as a Lamb

I have considered Jesus as the faithful witness, the pierced one and a humanlike figure. In this chapter, I will look at Jesus as a Lamb. Jesus is described as a slain Lamb twenty-eight times in various contexts in Revelation. Understanding this image is significant for discerning John's christology and establishing to what extent this christology can be considered nonviolent.

The Use of Imagery

For Engnell the purpose of using imagery is not aesthetic but practical inasmuch as the intention is to argue and persuade. This is done by making use of stereotyped phrases and figures, which often approach a kind of literary cliché. In this way, the speaker demonstrates his knowledge and 'wisdom', the most important proof of his familiarity with the tradition.[1] Bauckham writes: 'They [images] do not create a purely self-contained aesthetic world with no reference outside itself, but intend to relate to the world in which the readers live in order to reform and redirect the readers' response to that world'.[2] Beale sees the symbolic language functioning 'to encourage and exhort the audience'.[3] This is seen especially in terms of the Book of Revelation 'to motivate the readers not to compromise with the world but to align their thoughts and behaviour with the God-centred standards of the new creation'.[4] These observations will provide guidelines for this chapter.

Sacrificial Lamb or Military Figure?

The Lamb in the Book of Revelation has been linked variously to the Passover Lamb in Exodus, the slain Lamb of Isaiah 53.7, and the Lamb warrior leader of the *Animal Apocalypse* in *1 Enoch*.[5] There are those who oppose a sacrificial understanding of the Lamb based on Exodus or Isaiah 53.7. They point out that if a sacrifice were intended, sin would be that which the Lamb removes.[6] The Greek

---

1 Engnell (1970):244.
2 Bauckham (1993b):20.
3 Beale (1999):69.
4 Beale (1999):69.
5 Sacrificial image: for example, Ladd (1978):85-86; Sweet (1979):124; Bauckham (1993b):71; military image: Charles (1920): vol. 1, 141; Ford (1975):86.
6 Ford (1975):91.

word used for 'slain' is σφαζω and it is argued suggests being killed in battle. If a sacrificial death was intended the Greek word to sacrifice, θύω, would be more appropriate for Revelation 5.6;[7] martyrdom provides the background to the Lamb image[8] and the Lamb is a military conquering figure.[9] I will consider these arguments point by point.

Sin

To him who loves us and freed us from our sins by his blood (1.5).

and made us to be a kingdom, priests serving his God and Father, to him be glory and dominion forever and ever (1.6).

Jesus removed sin (1.5). Those who argue against a sacrificial death, point out that sin is not present in Revelation 5.9. Yet John says that the Lamb freed people for God and made them priests serving God (1.6). Although sin is not present in Revelation 5.6, surely being freed from bondage is John's understanding of what the Lamb's death achieves. Revelation's understanding of sin is rooted in the Old Testament in which sin is servitude from which humanity cannot be freed except by a miraculous intervention of God.[10] For John, sin is bondage to the beast and those who follow it. One in sin is one who does not live according to the principles of love and compassion - the aspects of God's nonviolent nature and creation. The Lamb exemplifies these principles.

Murdered or Sacrificed?

The Greek word John used for 'slain' (σφαζω) can mean both 'to murder' and 'to sacrifice', but, on the whole, sacrificial slaying is conveyed (Gen. 22.10; Ex. 12.6; Ezek. 6.20; Lev. 1.5, 11; 4.24; 9.8; Num. 19.3). Also, **θύω** need not indicate a sacrificial death (Jn 10.10; Acts 10.13; 11.7). It is difficult to understand Revelation 7.14 other than as sacrifice. Those who have been saved wash their robes in the blood of the Lamb.

---

7 Ford (1975):90; Laws (1988):52-68.

8 Ford (1975):90-91.

9 Dodd (1963):232; Beasley-Murray (1983):125.

10 Lyonnet and Sabourin (1970):9. See Galatians 3.13 and 4.5 in which Jesus' death has resulted in being redeemed (ἀγοράζω) from the curse of the law. In fact ἁμαρτία is rare in Galatians (only three times), but this does not prevent scholars supposing a sacrificial understanding of death. 1 Corinthians 6.20 and 7.23 present a similar understanding to Revelation in which Jesus has bought humanity from slavery.

Martyrdom and Sacrifice

It is not necessary to say that if the Lamb is a martyred figure, then it cannot be a sacrifice. There is a strong connection between the use of sacrificial metaphor and the notion that martyrdom could be viewed as a means of purification for the sins of the people (2 Macc. 7.38; 4 Macc. 6.29).[11] The placing, also, of the martyrs under the altar of burnt offering (6.9) suggests a correlation between sacrifice and martyrdom.

Lamb as a Military Leader.

It is difficult to find evidence of a Lamb as a military leader.[12] It is suggested that Moses and Aaron are Lambs (*1 En.* 89.16, 18). The Aramaic has אמר (lamb), but the Ethiopic has *bag* (sheep). Hillyer points to the Greek version of *1 Enoch* 89.45 which has ἀρνην.[13] However, why does John have ἀρνίον? The most important text that scholars depend on is *1 Enoch* 90.37-38.[14] But this depends on an emendation to the text, which is disputed.[15] Moreover, the animal does not have horns. Dodd points to *1 Enoch* 90.6-16 in which Lambs are portrayed as having horns (especially v.9). Nevertheless, it is not the lambs that have the horns, it is from one of the sheep that the great horn sprouts. The great leaders are not Lambs but rams or sheep. The *Testament of Joseph* 19.8, which is considered a later Christian interpolation, indicates such an understanding of a warrior Lamb.[16] However, there are strong arguments for a Jewish author made by O'Neill for this text.[17] He with Koch points also to the Lamb in Pharaoh's dream who outweighed all of Egypt (see *Pseudo-Jonathan Targum* Ex.1.15).[18] However, even if as O'Neill claims: 'Jews before Jesus Christ looked for a Messiah who would be called the Lamb of God',[19] it does not argue that Revelation is presenting Jesus in such a light. In fact, it is probable

---

11 Aune (1997):373.

12 Bauckham (1993a):183: 'There is no substantial evidence that the Lamb was already established as a symbol of the messianic conqueror in pre-Christian Judaism'; Aune (1997):368. *Testament of Joseph* 19.8 is the only evidence comparing the Messiah to a Lamb which may well be a popular Jewish view, see O'Neill (1979):2-30.

13 Hillyer (1967):229.

14 Dodd (1953):232; Lohmeyer (1927):51-52 does not even acknowledge the textual problem.

15 Knibb (1978):216; full discussion see Lindars (1976).

16 Note also Testament of Benjamin 3.8 in which the Lamb of God appears but will be betrayed. This is probably a Christian interpolation based on John 1.29, 36, see Aune (1997):369; O'Neill (1979):7 thinks it is unlikely that this is a Christian interpolation on the grounds that a Christian would not refer to Joseph as a Messiah.

17 O'Neill (1979):2-30.

18 Koch (1966):79-93; O'Neill (1979):9. Aune (1997):370-371 dates this tradition to the eleventh century and is influenced by the tradition that Moses was the servant of God thus making the connection between טליא meaning both 'Lamb' and 'servant'.

19 O'Neill (1979):27.

that the tradition is Jewish rather than Christian, as there is little to support that Jesus or anyone else thought Jesus was a military messiah. Jesus is a slain Lamb. So if there is a tradition in Jewish thought of a Lamb as a military leader, this does not suggest a Lamb is used to present Jesus as a military leader. Rather, Jesus is the antithesis of the Jewish military leader.[20] However, more plausible is Beale's observations which suggest that an aspect of retributive irony may be at work, even among the Jewish thinkers who were anti-military. The *Testament of Joseph* 19.8 may fit the same tradition as 4 Ezra 13. The presentation of a Lamb trampling his enemies under his feet is ironic. Beale writes of John's use of irony: 'ironic use is to mock the enemy's proud attempt to overcome God and his people and to underscore the fitting justice of the punishment'.[21]

It has been argued that Lamb should be translated 'ram' because the animal has seven horns.[22] 'Horn' denotes physical might and power. Those who defy God do so by lifting their horns (Ps. 75.4-5). God exalts the horns of the righteous (Ps. 75.10; cf. Ps. 92.10). The exalting of the Davidic king is associated with a sprouting horn (Ps. 132.17; cf. 89.17). God is called 'the horn of my salvation' (2 Sam. 22.3). It is not surprising that Jesus the Lamb is presented with seven horns, as one whom God has given victory; horns indicates the power of salvation.[23] There is no need to associate the Lamb with a conquering ram on these grounds. Even if ram is accepted, the presentation of the ram as slain hardly supports a conquering reading of the text. Still the juxtaposition of the Lamb with the Lion of the tribe of Judah suggests a ram image. However, this is not the case. This will be looked at in detail later.

Summary

There is little to distract from a sacrificial association with the Lamb image. Lamb is not an obvious or understandable symbol for a military leader. There is little precedent for such an understanding, and it does not fit the context in which John has used the Lamb. However, John may well have been appropriating military expectations in showing Jesus as conquering, but not with military weapons. To this

---

20 Sweet (1979):124 thinks there was an expectation of Lamb military figure, but John takes the other view.

21 Beale (1999):95.

22 Beale (1999):351, while accepting the importance of the sacrificial background (otherwise he would not suggest ram as an adequate translation), tentatively suggests that *1 Enoch* 90 and *Testament of Joseph* 19 provide the background to the 'horns'.

23 It may be argued that a Lamb with seven horns is not a coherent picture and only a ram has horns. How many rams have seven horns? The significance of the seven must be seen in the Old Testament in which it is the number of fullness or totality; see Bauckham (1993a):16, 26-27, 40, 67, 109; contrary Yarbro Collins (1984a):1276-1279 who argues that seven suggests order rather than totality; so also Corsini (1983):42-44.

extent the proposal that underlying the Lamb are both military and sacrificial metaphors is acceptable.[24]

Revelation 5.5-6

Then one of the elders said to me, 'Do not weep. See, the Lion of the tribe of Judah, the Root of David, has conquered, so that he can open the scroll and its seven seals.' Then I saw between the throne and the four living creatures and among the elders a Lamb standing as if it had been slaughtered, having seven horns and seven eyes, which are the seven spirits of God sent out into all the earth.

The death of Jesus is the death of the greater Isaac, God's own Son, who truly died and rose again to act as Intercessor before God.[25]

In this section I propose that the Lamb is understandable in the context of martyrdom and witness ideas. Moreover, that John had in mind traditions relating to Isaac when using Lamb imagery, especially in Revelation 5.6.[26] In addition, and related to this, is the question of the author's motive for appropriating this tradition. I suggest that the author felt the need to respond to a debate between church and synagogue. As we know, imagery functioned rhetorically in the Old Testament in order to persuade. In the same way, John uses the image of the Lamb as he addresses the debate with the synagogue.

Jesus the Slain Lamb.

The Greek for Lamb in Revelation is ἀρνίον. The more common expression of Lamb is ἀμνός. Both Greek words are associated with similar Hebrew words for Lamb. Hillyer suggests that John uses ἀρνίον to emphasize that Jesus is not just a sacrificial Lamb, if he were, John would have used ἀμνός.[27] I am not convinced by this argument. There is no indication that ἀρνίον cannot mean the sacrificial Lamb. In fact, the term is used for a sacrificial victim in LXX Jeremiah 11.19:

ἐγὼ δὲ ὡς ἀρνίον ἄκακον ἀγόμενον τοῦ θύεσθαι - But I as an innocent lamb led to the slaughter (tr. Brenton)

The Lamb is Jesus who is, also, the 'faithful witness', 'the pierced one' and 'a humanlike figure'. Lamb appears in the Old Testament as the Passover Lamb whose

---

24 Aune (1997):368.

25 Wood (1967-1968):587-588.

26 This has been argued by Bredin in (1996b):26-43 with some changes.

27 Hillyer (1967):229; Beale (1999):354 suggests that 'if the diminutive nuance still held, it intensified the contrast between the powerful lion image of the Old Testament prophecy and the fulfilment through the little, apparently powerless Lamb'.

blood has an apotropaic effect in Exodus 12.13. Lamb is used metaphorically to describe the faithful, suffering servants of God in Isaiah 53.7. There is also the burnt-offering Lamb which in later Jewish developments of the binding of Isaac narrated in Genesis 22 is Isaac. We have seen that all three traditions were probably linked. Many scholars are convinced that the Passover Lamb or the Lamb of Isaiah 53.7 or both underlie Revelation 5 although it has only tentatively been suggested that Jewish developments of Genesis 22 are of any importance.[28]

The Lamb conquered and redeemed, by its blood, many from all tribes, tongues, people and nations and made them a kingdom and priests, and they will rule the earth (vv.9-10; cf. 12.11). One more occurrence of the redemptive role that Jesus plays is seen in another hymn to Jesus in Revelation 1.5:

Τῷ ἀγαπῶντι ἡμᾶς καὶ λύσαντι ἡμᾶς ἐκ τῶν ἁμαρτιῶν ἡμῶν ἐν τῷ αἵματι αὐτοῦ, 6 καὶ ἐποίησεν ἡμᾶς βασιλείαν, ἱερεῖς τῷ θεῷ καὶ πατρὶ αὐτοῦ - to him who loves us and freed us from our sins by his blood, and made us to be a kingdom, priests serving his God and Father

The similarities with Revelation 5.9-10 are clear:

ἐσφάγης καὶ ἠγόρασας τῷ θεῷ ἐν τῷ αἵματί σου ἐκ πάσης φυλῆς καὶ γλώσσης καὶ λαοῦ καὶ ἔθνους καὶ ἐποίησας αὐτοὺς τῷ θεῷ ἡμῶν βασιλείαν καὶ ἱερεῖς - for you were slaughtered and by your blood you ransomed for God saints from every tribe and language and people and nation; you have made them to be a kingdom and priests serving our God.

The syntax and changes between these texts can be accounted for by change of setting. Only here in the New Testament is λύω used of release from sin. John uses λύω in its more usual sense and, therefore, knows its literal meaning (see 5.2, 20.3, 7). How can we account for this use in 1.5b? An Aramaic marginal reading of the Targum *Neofiti on Genesis* 22 may provide a clue:[29]

Now I pray for mercy before You, O Lord God, that when the children of Isaac come to a time of distress, You may remember on their behalf the binding of Isaac their father, and loose (ושרי) and forgive (ושבק) them their sins and deliver them from all distress (*Frag. Tg. 22.14*)

The Aramaic word שׁרי (to loose) is not used in Aramaic texts in the Old Testament for the forgiving of sins.[30] The marginal *Neofiti Targum* reading heightens Isaac's

---

28 Farrer (1964):94; Spiegel (1967):85; Dahl (1974):138 rightly mentions Revelation 5 as 'reminiscent of the Akedah' but unfortunately never makes the allusion explicit; Ford (1975):91 misses the connection between sacrifice and martyrdom; Daly (1977):73.

29 I am indebted to Carnegie (1982):250 who originally suggested that a Targum tradition on Genesis 22 underlies this.

30 See Brown-Driver-Briggs δ8281.

action. This makes a link between Revelation 1.5 and the Targum possible.[31] John is concerned with the distress that his community will experience if they are faithful to the testimony of Jesus and this tradition expressed in the Targum would recommend itself to John, but with the emphasis now being on Jesus.

As has been seen, Isaac was considered a sacrificial Lamb in Jewish exegesis. Similarly, Jesus is a sacrificial Lamb. Both Isaac and Jesus were believed to have released people from sin. Isaac was understood as a proto-martyr. Likewise, John presents Jesus. Given the prominence of such traditions in the first century CE, it is quite possible that John has linked three traditions together: Isaac, Passover Lamb and the suffering servant of Isaiah 52.1-53.12. All have three things in common: 1) Isaiah 40-55 draws heavily upon Exodus traditions in which a new Exodus is presented;[32] 2) Deutero-Isaiah's universalism is reflected in Genesis 22.18; 3) all contain a slain Lamb. Revelation has much in common with all three. Isaac expected his father to offer up a שׂה (Lamb) in Genesis 22.7-8. Abraham intends to slay (שׁחט) his son Isaac in Genesis 22.10. The Passover Lamb in Hebrew is the same word as the Lamb in Isaiah 53.7 and Exodus 12. Moreover, the Hebrew verb 'to slaughter' is שׁחט. The suffering servant is compared to שׂה (Lamb) in Isaiah 53.7. The word for slaughter is not שׁחט but טבח in Isaiah 53.7. But still the similarities provide excellent material for the use of the Jewish exegetical technique *gezērâ šāwâ* (connecting similar words).

Yet in Revelation 5.5 John depicts Jesus as the Lion of the tribe of Judah, the Root of David, who has conquered. Lion is a militant Messianic title.[33] This would seem to oppose the argument I am making that Jesus is a nonviolent martyr. Indeed, Jesus now seems to be a military figure. This image would support those who want to translate 'Lamb' as 'Ram'. However, the juxtaposition of Lamb and lion may be intentional. Caird writes: 'Wherever the Old Testament speaks of the victory of the Messiah or the overthrow of the enemies of God, we are to remember that the gospel recognizes no other way of achieving these ends than the way of the Cross'.[34] However, Moyise asks why military David language is used in the rest of the Book of Revelation and not reinterpreted with the Lamb?[35] Moyise looks to the work of Richard Bauckham who observes John's tendency to juxtapose contrasting

---

31 Carnegie (1982):247, 249. This particular Targum is very old.

32 Comblin (1965):29: 'Le retour d'Israël est annoncé comme un nouvel Exode plus brillant que le premier'. Comblin was in no doubt that a strong link existed between the Passover Lamb and the Lamb of Isaiah 53.7. This may well have been the original intention, but there is no way of being certain.

33 Caird (1984):74. See Genesis 49.9; Isaiah 11.1-10; Sirach 47.22 and Revelation 22.16. The Lion image in reflected in Genesis 49.9 which as Bauckham (1993a):180-181 has observed was important for Jewish messianic hopes at the time of John. In 1QSb 5.29=1Q28b the Messiah is addressed: 'you shall be as a lion; and you shall not lie down until you have devoured the prey which naught shall deliver'. The image is drawn from Numbers 23.24; Micah 5.8 as well as Genesis 49.9.

34 Caird (1984):75; Sweet (1979):125-127; 150-151; Beale (1999):353.

35 Moyise (1995):133. For more detailed discussion see (2001): 181-194.

images in order to address a precise situation of debate. He argues that John, in using lion and root of David, did so because they embodied the idea of victory through destructive power.[36] Bauckham does not wish to silence the military language as it has something important to say.[37] Bauckham writes that in using Lamb 'John forges a symbol of conquest by sacrificial death'.[38] John forces a reinterpretation.[39] Moyise puts it well: 'The power of John's work is not that he replaces military imagery with Christian imagery but that he forces an interaction between them'.[40] Similarly, in Revelation 7 we see the juxtaposition of the remnant 144000, particularly resonant in Zionistic ideas that only a few from the Jews will be saved, with a huge inclusive number from every tribe, nation, people and tongue (7.9). Such a debate as to whether those from the house of Israel will be saved or those from among the Gentiles was common in the first century. John may even be responding to those in his own community as well as to those in the synagogue.[41]

Use of the Aqedah for anti-Synagogue Purposes in Asia Minor

In Asia Minor there was hostility between synagogue and church. By the time of the mid-late second century CE, the situation had deteriorated. It is in this climate that Melito's works were composed, one of which is directed against the synagogue. In his *Paschal Homily* synagogue members are blamed for the suffering and death of Jesus, similarly they are accused of stubbornness and an inability to understand the figure that they had put to death in Jerusalem. Central to this work is the desire to show the superiority of the church. The church demonstrated that Christianity had superseded Judaism through its interpretation of tradition over that of the synagogue's interpretation. Wilken proposes that Melito appropriates the Aqedah tradition in order to respond to criticisms made by synagogue members.[42] Wilken's argument is that the binding of Isaac, for the synagogue, was considered a symbol both of God's faithfulness to his people and his continuing love for them.[43]

---

36 Bauckham (1993a):182; Moyise (1995):133-135.

37 Bauckham (1993a) 229-230; Moyise (1995):134.

38 Bauckham (1993a):183.

39 Moyise (1995): 134.

40 Moyise (1995): 137.

41 Bauckham (1993a):180 sees this contrast in Revelation 7.4-8 see also Revelation 21.9-10; Sweet (1979):147 when he observes that John is here responding to slanders that all can be saved and not only the house of Israel; cf. Bredin (1996b):95-111 argues that such a debate underlies also Matthew's development and incorporation of language. Such a juxtaposition is seen in terms of the women in the genealogy, and the response of Jesus to his disciples in contrasting their views regarding the Canaanite women (Mt. 15.21-28).

42 Wilken (1984):53-69; Lieu (1996):226; contrary Hayward (1990):303-306.

43 Wilken (1984):53-69; Lieu (1996):225; Kraabel (1971):84 does not mention the fragments in discussion of the hostile attitude of Melito towards the Jews.

However, Melito contends that the binding of Isaac had no such meaning and could not be used to comfort and support the Jews.[44] In *fragmentary* 9 Melito retorts:

ἀλλὰ Χριστός ἔπαθεν· Ἰσαάκ δὲ οὐκ ἔπαθεν – but Christ suffered, but Isaac did not suffer

Wilken suggests that Melito wishes to emphasize that Isaac did not die but that Jesus did. The Aqedah was understood in Judaism as a sacrificial offering and it became the basis for God's mercy towards Israel. However, that the offering was not completed caused certain difficulties.[45] This seems a logical argument to make from observation of Genesis 22, and one that Melito and, it is argued here, John made use of. However, Hayward counters that Melito does not state that Jesus' blood was shed. Melito states that Jesus suffered (ἔπαθεν).[46] Lieu observes from a selection of texts that πάσχειν can suggest death and so can be understood this way in Melito.[47] Melito continues his argument in *fragmentary* 10 staying closer to the sense of Genesis 22. He demonstrates that the ram was sacrificed and redeemed Isaac. Wilken comments that Isaac seems to become a type of the redeemed.[48] In *fragmentary* 11 Jesus is called the Lamb like the ram (ἀμνὸς ὡς [ὁ] κριὸς), so Jesus the Lamb in *fragmentary* 11 is compared to the ram in *fragmentary* 10 who redeems humanity by his sacrifice: 'Christ not Isaac' was his battle cry.

Conclusion

The likelihood of an Aqedah influence on the composition of Revelation 5.6-9 is strong. John in 5.6-9 formulates an antithetical contrast between Jesus (the true proto-martyr, represented in the Lamb imagery who was sacrificed and whose martyrdom has atonement value) and Isaac (who did not die). As Wood points out: 'The death of Jesus is the death of the greater Isaac, God's own Son, who truly died and rose again to act as Intercessor before God'.[49] The Lamb functions, then, as an image which elevates Jesus above Isaac. Jesus is portrayed as the exemplary martyr, the true and faithful witness to God, the one whom the church must look to and emulate if they, too, are to be conquerors.

The situations which John addresses and the importance and priority biblical traditions play against the life setting are important to my argument. These cohere well with the points Engnell makes. John is motivated in his use of imagery by the need to argue for Jesus and to persuade his community that they must continue to be

---

44 Wilken (1976):64-69.
45 Wilken (1976):65; Hayward is not convinced (1990):304: 'Melito does not remark that Christ's blood was shed whereas Isaac's was not'. The Greek, πάσχω, does not suggest death but it does indicate suffering until death.
46 Hayward (1990):304.
47 Lieu (1996):226; used of dying in Herodian 1, 17, 7; see Arndt and Gingrich, p.639.
48 Wilken (1976):66.
49 Wood (1967-1968):587-588.

faithful to Jesus and not be persuaded by the synagogue or any other representatives of Satan.

Other Occurrences of Lamb in Revelation

Bauckham understands the work of Christ around three motifs: messianic war, new Exodus, and witness/martyr.[50] He does not recognize the third category to be important for the understanding the work of the Lamb. The Lamb is not named a 'witness'; there is no mention of a 'testimony of the Lamb'. Yet 'witness' is connected with Jesus' death; his testimony leads to his crucifixion and his death to victory. John presents Jesus as a faithful witness who stands against his enemy and is ready to die; it would seem odd to use an image that does not develop such themes. So witness is important for understanding the Lamb. The following themes are suggested to assist understanding the Lamb in Revelation: Lamb is a redeemer; Lamb is a martyr/witness figure; Lamb is a conquering leader; wrath of the Lamb; Lamb in relation to his church; Lamb as a pastor.[51]

Redeemer

We have already considered this theme in our consideration of Revelation 5. In addition, the multitudes from every nation acknowledge that salvation belongs to God and to the Lamb (7.10). The multitudes are saved by washing their clothes in the blood of the Lamb (7.14; cf. 12.11). Along with Revelation 5 these are the other occurrences of victory being linked with sacrifice, thus cohering with the Lamb in chapter 5.

Conquering Leader

> Then I looked, and there was the Lamb, standing on Mount Zion! And with him were one hundred forty-four thousand who had his name and his Father's name written on their foreheads (14.1).

> It is these who have not defiled themselves with women, for they are virgins; these follow the Lamb wherever he goes. They have been redeemed from humankind as first fruits for God and the Lamb (14.4),

---

50 Bauckham (1993b):71-72.

51 The fifth and sixth categories must surely be related as the Lamb's relationship with the church was that of a pastor.

they will also drink the wine of God's wrath, poured unmixed into the cup of his anger, and they will be tormented with fire and sulfur in the presence of the holy angels and in the presence of the Lamb (14.10).

and the Lamb will conquer them, for he is Lord of lords and King of kings (17.14).

Jesus is a military hero in Revelation 14.1. His followers are chaste (14.4). Chilton understands 'chastity' as a symbolic reference to the requirement of sexual abstinence by soldier-priests during holy war (cf. Ex. 19.15; Lev. 15.16; Deut. 20.7; 23.10-11; 1 Sam. 21.4-5; 2 Sam. 11.8-11 cf. Deut. 23.9-14; 1QM 7).[52] However, these texts do not suggest that the soldiers are priests. What is in mind is the chastity of soldiers. The enemies of God will be tortured before the Lamb (14.10). War is made on the Lamb but he conquers because he is Lord of lords and King of kings (17.14). How does this fit together with a sacrificial/martyr reading of chapter 5, and the pierced one?

Bauckham commenting on 14.4 suggests that following the Lamb implies faithfulness as far as death, since the Lamb was led to the slaughter (Isa. 53.7; Rev. 5.6).[53] Therefore, in Revelation 14 John draws upon holy warfare tradition, except that his soldiers do not hold swords. They fight against Satan and his representatives with weapons of love and forgiveness. Their ultimate sword is their witness to truth until death.[54] Every occurrence of the sword of the saints refers to the witness of the potential martyr or to God's word, not to a literal sword (1.16; 2.12; 2.16; 19.15; 19.21). The other occurrence of the literal sword warns against its use (13.10).[55] The idea of martyrs being an army is not a surprising depiction. Gandhi also talked about his followers being pure and disciplined. There was nothing passive about nonviolence as he wrote about 'soldiers of peace' (1-366). Moreover, the 144000 in Revelation 7 surely includes not only men, but also women and children.[56] As Gandhi pointed out, the only real weapon for the masses, including women and children, was nonviolence (11-41). Similarly, in chapter 14 Jesus' followers are truthful and their witness to truth would gain them victory (14.5). Moreover, chastity is not necessarily applied literally, but metaphorically for purity: Harrington believes the 144000 are contrasted with the followers of the beast because they have refused to worship the beast and have remained faithful to the Lamb. In not giving themselves to the cult of the beast they have kept their virginity.[57] In addition, Philo uses 'virgin' to express detachment from earthly concerns (*On the Cherubim* 49-50).[58] The mention of gender in v.4 might suggest that only men form the 144000,

---

52 Chilton (1990):356; see also Bauckham (1993a):229-232.
53 Bauckham (1993a):231.
54 Compare Ephesians' use of the warfare metaphor in 6.10-17.
55 In 6.4 the sword results in devastation; cf. 6.8.
56 So Harrington (1995):62: 'the 144000 represent all the redeemed, women and men'.
57 Harrington (1993):147.
58 Sweet (1979):223; Schüssler Fiorenza (1991):88; Beale (1999):741.

but as Sweet writes: 'The maleness is simply part of the military metaphor; they represent the whole church'.[59] The Lamb in chapter 17.14 is the conquering Lord of lords and King of kings. Beale suggests the background to the title in Revelation 17.14 is Daniel 2.37, 47; 3.2; 4.37 (LXX 34).[60] Nebuchadnezzar is called 'King of kings' (2.37). Nebuchadnezzar acknowledges that only God is King (2.47; cf. 4.37). His kingship is a gift from God, but it will be taken from him. The King becomes powerless as a tree trunk (4.25-26). Daniel tells Nebuchadnezzar that to be a King he must practise righteousness and show mercy to the oppressed (4.27). In 4.37 (LXX 34) the king is restored when he is humble and confesses the LORD. John has recycled this title alluding to Nebuchadnezzar and its context. This recycling is directed by a well defined, specific ideology in order to establish Jesus' righteousness based on the values of justice and obedience to God. Jesus lived obediently to God thus resisting the world of injustice. Through obedience he is victor over the powers of violence and oppression; he is the true King because he is the direct opposite of oppressing leaders who are not kings because they are oppressors. This is another example of the juxtaposition of two apparently opposing types, i.e. Lamb with King of kings. John uses the militaristic King of kings and insists that it is used in a non-military sense. However, as Moyise points out, John does not wish to silence ideas associated with military imagery.[61] Ideas associated with King of kings are that of victory, and Christians look for victory, but not with military weapons but through faithfulness and witness.[62]

Therefore, violence is not present in chapters 14 or 17. John depicts an army of obedient faithful witnesses who refuse to play Rome's power games. The weapons of the faithful are their witness before their enemy. Truth is nonviolence and it is the only way to God and the establishment of the kingdom of God. The way of Jesus was his way to the Father, the means to establish the kingdom of God.[63] The victory of Christ and the saints is the victory of the cross, which is won not by killing others but by undergoing voluntary death.[64] The image of the Lamb redefines violent imagery in terms of self-suffering through which victory is gained.

The Wrath of the Lamb (6.12-17)

When he opened the sixth seal, I looked, and there came a great earthquake; the sun became black as sackcloth, the full moon became like blood, and the stars of the sky

---

59 Sweet (1979):222; Schüssler Fiorenza (1991):88.
60 Beale (1985):618-619.
61 Moyise (1995): 134.
62 Bauckham (1993a): 223.
63 Jesudasan (1984):130.
64 Hanson (1957):166; Klassen (1966):306: 'victory comes not by engaging in armed battle but by refusing to love one's life so much that one resists martyrdom and through consistent patterning of one's life upon the Lamb's sacrifice'; cf. Harrington (1995):59: 'they have won by suffering death, not by inflicting hurt'.

fell to the earth as the fig tree drops its winter fruit when shaken by a gale. The sky vanished like a scroll rolling itself up, and every mountain and island was removed from its place. Then the kings of the earth and the magnates and the generals and the rich and the powerful, and everyone, slave and free, hid in the caves and among the rocks of the mountains, calling to the mountains and rocks, "Fall on us and hide us from the face of the one seated on the throne and from the wrath of the Lamb; for the great day of their wrath has come, and who is able to stand?

The first four seal openings derive from the Old Testament and not any particular social event or events (Isa. 2.19; 13.10; 34.2-4; 24.19-31; 50.3; Jer. 4.24; Ezek. 38.19; Joel 2.31; cf. *T. Mos.* 10.4-5). The first four seals, described in Revelation 6.1-8, represent evils that are not directly caused by the will of God.[65] They reveal to us the self-defeating character of sin.[66] The scene does not depict a malevolent God or Lamb who seeks to destroy a particular group. It is the result of human history (cf. 4 Ezra 13.38). John hopes that all will be saved (15.5-19.21). The rebellion of humankind in the end only provides the occasion for a greater unfolding of God's majesty (see Ps. 76.10).[67] As the four seals are opened, riders appear and are summoned by one of the four living creatures (6.1-7). The first, second and fourth rider are given the power of destruction from one of the four living creatures. Similarly, the four angels are said to have the power of destruction over earth and sea (7.1-2). Rowland writes: 'Revelation seems to portray death and destruction as in some sense coming from God'.[68] Hanson suggests that Revelation 6 describes various judgements that are a result of rejecting God including the sufferings of the faithful in the churches.[69] More precisely, Jesus has been rejected and disaster ensues because they have not listened to his testimony. Likewise, Paul writes of God giving the wicked up to their lusts and impurity (Rom. 1.24, 28). Rowland writes: 'In Rev. 6.4 the second horseman removes peace from the earth, so that people slay one another: here is the consequences of the strife, envy and covetousness that Paul has spoken in Rom. 1.28'.[70] Revelation acknowledges that God is in control of the destruction that occurs. At the same time for John, humankind in some sense brings upon itself destruction through its violence and rejection of God's will. Its rebellion against God brings the disaster that God allows, thus bringing about a repentant heart. The Psalmist puts it well: 'surely the wrath of men shall praise thee' (Ps. 76.10a).

---

65 Rissi (1964):413-418; Morris (1979):102; Caird (1984):81; Sweet (1979):137; Wink (1992):298; Harrington (1993):91; Beale (1999):377; contrary Ladd (1978):98 sees the white horse as Christ; Chilton (1990):186 points out that the white horse is Christ. Beale (1999):376 finds it odd that Christ might open a seal that contains a vision in which he is also the subject.
66 Morris (1979):102.
67 Eaton (1967):193.
68 Rowland (1993):83.
69 Hanson (1957):170; cf. Caird (1984):91; Sweet (1979):144.
70 Rowland (1993):87.

When the fifth seal is opened, John sees the martyrs pray for vengeance on those who murder (6.10). Throughout Revelation is contained the hope that, as a result of estrangement from God, people will repent through the tragedies of history (Rev. 9.20-21; 11.13b).[71] Sweet writes that 'the answer to the prayer comes not in the punishment of individual enemies but in the "judgement of the great harlot" who deceives the nations (17.1-19.2), and the coming of a new order, symbolized by the Bride'.[72] Ultimately, the great harlot is the source of violence and oppression.

In vv.12-17 John describes the scene when the sixth seal is opened. There is a great earthquake (6.12). John portrays a world that is not at one with its creator's intentions (cf. Isa. 2.20-21). No one benefits from the disaster that results from a society based on violence (cf. *1 En.* 10.9; 4 Ezra 13.9, 10, 31 and v.38). Yarbro Collins describes the scene in Revelation 6.12-17 as one of devastation to those who were wealthy and powerful.[73] Yet the number of categories of people in the vision suggests that it is not just the wealthy and powerful who are in mind. Numbered with the wealthy and powerful are also slaves (6.15; cf. 19.18). Harrington rightly observes that: 'All classes of society will be terror-stricken by the cosmic portents'.[74] What people most fear is the wrath of the Lamb (6.17).

The earthquake described in Revelation 6.12 heralds the coming of God in judgement (see Isa. 13.13; 24.18-20; 34.4; Jer. 51.29; Ezek. 38.20; Nah. 1.5).[75] It is not a picture of destruction. Rather, the earthquake accompanies the appearance of God as Judge'.[76] The people are not fearful of the earthquake. They are terrified of what the earthquake heralds: an appearance of God and the day of judgement. The earthquake is a recurring symbol of the dissolution of the godless world at God's self-manifestation.[77] John portrays the people in terror before the 'wrath of the Lamb' and not the devastation resulting from the earthquake.

The 'wrath of the Lamb' in Revelation 6.17 and 'wrath' in the Old Testament and within Pauline literature has been considered either as 'affective' i.e. the personal attitude of God and the Lamb towards sinners, or 'effective' i.e. impersonal and in no way an activity of God, but the calculable effect of certain behaviour.[78] Wrath is a holy war word associated with the purging of evil and the establishment of justice. Wrath belongs to God and describes something of God's essence. Yet in describing God, people fall short of expressing their full understanding. I believe

---

71 Klassen (1966):304; Bauckham (1993b):86-87.

72 Sweet (1979):141.

73 Yarbro Collins (1979):49.

74 Harrington (1993):96; Beale (1999):400.

75 Bauckham (1993a):202; Sweet (1979):145.

76 Bauckham (1993a):208.

77 Sweet (1979):145.

78 'Affective': Chilton (1990):198; Yarbro Collins (1979):48-49 argues that it is the response to the cries of the martyrs for vengeance. 'Effective': Dodd (1954):23-24; Hanson (1957):170; Hillyer (1967):234; Mounce (1977):162; Caird (1984):91; Sweet (1979):144; Harrington (1993):96.

that 'wrath' is better understood within the *effective category* when viewed against the fuller context of Revelation.

The juxtaposition of 'Lamb' and 'wrath' may, at first sight, appear incomprehensible, as was the combination of Lion and Lamb in Revelation 5.5-6. John reinterprets 'wrath' by placing it alongside the most non-militaristic image, Lamb.[79] Wrath no longer depicts a military, conquering God on the battlefield; God is not one who slays with a sword. Suffering love is the essence of wrath, and therefore suffering love is that which brings about God's judgement and kingdom.[80] The cross marks the judgement of the world. Proceeding from the cross is a new revolutionary paradigm in which power and strength are exposed as inadequate. However, as we have seen, it is not just the 'mighty' in Revelation 6.15 who are defeated, but 'servants' too. The desire to be hidden from 'the wrath of the Lamb' expresses a person's unwillingness to hear the message of the cross. This message challenges and judges all that a person's life has previously been based upon. As the poet of Proverbs 28 shows, many are the wicked that flee (Prov. 28.1). This world order is defeated. The person who says 'yes' to the cross embraces a position that is in antithesis to the world. This results in suffering and martyrdom. It is this challenge of the cross that the powerful and powerless have to face, saying 'yes' or 'no' to the values of the world (6.15). Therefore, the theophany that is heralded by the earthquake creates terrible fear among people. Their lives of violence and oppression are judged and repentance is needed. In this way, the vision of the sixth seal points to the Last Judgement.[81] Therefore, the sequence in 19.11-20.15 should be seen as expanding the vision seen in 6.12-17.

But in Revelation 19.17-21, there are those who do not repent; those in 19.18 remind the reader of those in 6.15 who have chosen their fate and rejected truth by hiding 'in the caves and among the rocks of the mountains'. The grisly language of 19.17-21 belongs within the Hebrew idiom regarding the outcome of those who live such lives (cf. Ezek. 39.17-24; see also Mt. 24.28; Lk. 17.37). The outcome is grim as the remaining wicked have hardened their hearts and committed even more violent acts; John expresses how he sees their end. It may be that the writer of Psalm 79.2-3 (cf. Isa. 49.26) also influenced John. The Psalmist laments that the servants of the LORD have become food for the birds and beasts and are left unburied as the heathen defile Jerusalem. For John, those who reject God will also become food for the birds (19.17-18).

Summary

John reinterprets his tradition in the light of the life and witness of Jesus. Jesus is not presented here as a vindictive, vengeful figure. He is one who suffered the violence

---

79 This does not mean that 'wrath' is replaced by 'Lamb'. John preserves the paradox thus affirming the sense conveyed by 'wrath' which is judgement and victory. See Moyise (1995): 134 who preserves the paradox that is seen in the juxtaposition between two opposites.
80 Sweet (1979):146 observes that the wrath of the Lamb is not the cosmic disasters.
81 Bauckham (1993a):209.

of the world and was rejected because he represented truth. John presents humanity in the light of its rejection of Jesus in mythological, holy war imagery, i.e. the crises and chaos that beleaguer individuals, societies and the world when truth and justice are rejected. In facing these crises, the point of decision is reached, either to face the message of truth or to engage in the results of violence which are described in *1 Enoch* 10.9, 4 Ezra 13 and elsewhere.

The Lamb and His Church

Let us rejoice and exult and give him the glory, for the marriage of the Lamb has come, and his bride has made herself ready; to her it has been granted to be clothed with fine linen, bright and pure -- for the fine linen is the righteous deeds of the saints (19.7).

Then one of the seven angels who had the seven bowls full of the seven last plagues came and said to me, "Come, I will show you the bride, the wife of the Lamb". And in the spirit he carried me away to a great, high mountain and showed me the holy city Jerusalem coming down out of heaven from God (21.9).

The bride in 19.7 is arrayed for the wedding and she is called the New Jerusalem in 21.9. The Bride is the church seen from the perspective of the parousia.[82] The New Jerusalem is the hope of the faithful witnesses – a peaceable kingdom. The New Jerusalem is established on the basis of their righteous deeds, which involved holding to the testimony (19.10).[83] The clothing expresses their justice (19.8) but also alludes to the clothing of the priests. Presumably, the city is a kingdom of priests (1.9; 5.10). Jesus as the Lamb emphasizes the sacrifice he makes for others (cf. Eph. 5.25b). As a husband Jesus has provided an example of what it means to be God's servant showing his bride the way to be holy (cf. Eph. 5.27). In addition, the marriage imagery affirms that the Lamb and the New Jerusalem are one (cf. Eph. 5.29). This coheres with the Lamb in that he is the temple and light of the new city (21.22-23). The idea of feast in Revelation 19.9 harmonizes with the idea of a banquet as an image of the Kingdom of God as seen in Matthew 22.1-14 and parallels.

In sum, the Lamb is one with the Kingdom of peace - the New Jerusalem. The Kingdom is the righteous works of his followers. The feast represents the glorious time and place that will result from people living in peace. It will be a time when there is great wealth for all, in contrast to the wealth of Babylon, which we have seen in Revelation 18 and which disappears.

---

82 Bauckham (1993a):167; Miller (1998):301.
83 Beale (1999):934.

Lamb as Pastor

for the Lamb at the center of the throne will be their shepherd, and he will guide them to springs of the water of life, and God will wipe away every tear from their eyes (7.17).

Then the Lord GOD will wipe away the tears from all faces, and the disgrace of his people he will take away from all the earth, for the LORD has spoken (Isa. 25.8).

for he who has pity on them will lead them, and by springs of water will guide them (Isa. 49.10).

Jesus is the shepherd of the new chosen people. He is not the shepherd of the rich oppressor who is called Death in Psalm 49.14. These chosen people come from all nations and are not the exclusive tribes of Israel. Isaiah 25.8 and 49.10 have influenced John's writing of 7.17.[84] The idea of shepherding, however, is too common a tradition to suggest that one particular text or texts are in mind (see also Ps. 23 and Ezek. 34.23). Ezekiel 34.23 may also be in John's mind:[85]

And I will set up over them one shepherd, my servant David, and he shall feed them and be their shepherd.

Jesus is the LORD's shepherd, an attribute of the expected Davidic king. However, 'shepherd' is not only used of a king or the LORD. Zechariah records the idea of a prophet being a shepherd of the LORD:

Thus said the LORD my God: "Become shepherd of the flock doomed to slaughter" (Zech. 11.4)

John may have compared the oppressions that people suffered in Zechariah 11.5 with the sufferings of the churches as well as embracing the hope of Zechariah 11.6 in which justice will be established. John is presenting Jesus in his prophetic role when he depicts Jesus as shepherd of his people. Jesus like the prophet says and does God's word and suffers the consequences of doing so. Larkin suggests that the prophet figure in Zechariah 11.4 is compared with Moses; Moses is the *type* of a good prophet.[86] Moses is 'shepherd of the flock' in Isaiah 63.11, and leads God's people out of Egypt in Isaiah 63.12. The people detested the prophets as they detested Moses (Zech. 11.8), and God gave them up to themselves. They perished because they rejected God's witness. The testimony to truth is that which results in their destruction. So also Jesus is compared to Moses and is a shepherd figure.

---

84 Fekkes (19994):171.
85 Beale (1999):442 observes this.
86 Larkin (1994):115-116.

Jesus, like the LORD, cares for and feeds his sheep (Rev. 7.17; cf. Isa. 49.10). Jesus has led the chosen witnesses out of slavery and oppression (Rev. 12.14; 15.2-5; 21.2, 12-13; cf. Isa. 49.18). The people Jesus shepherds are from all nations (7.9). Revelation relies on the tradition in Isaiah 49.6 linking the tribes of Israel with the nations. John is aware of this, making the link himself (7.4-8 and vv.9-17) using tradition to critique those who reject the idea that salvation is for all.[87] Jesus will be a shepherd to the New Israel. The 144,000 are reinterpreted in the light of the nations. The influence of Isaiah 49 with its new exodus imagery on Revelation 7.17 supports a connection with Moses. A further text in support of the Moses connection is 15.3. Moses is explicitly named. The reworking of the song of Moses is in line with the most universalistic strain in the Old Testament hope: the expectation that all the nations will come to acknowledge the God of Israel and worship him. There is a shift of emphasis in the new exodus. God delivers his people not by judging their enemies, but by bringing the nations to acknowledge the true God.[88] The song of Moses becomes the song of the Lamb. Both are servants of God. The Lamb is the new Moses who leads to a new exodus in which it is hoped that all peoples turn to the true God.

The wiping away of every tear (7.17c also 21.4) remembers the promise in Isaiah 25.8. Jesus is the LORD's messenger of comfort to those who are afraid of living a life opposed to the values of the world. The Lamb is a shepherd figure who is followed wherever he goes (14.4 and 7.17). This following implies their faithfulness until death, since the Lamb was led to the slaughter (Isa. 53.7; Rev. 5.6).[89] In 7.17b the Lamb 'will guide them to springs of living water' (cf. Rev. 21.6). The followers are guided by one whom was himself led to the slaughter. The background underlying the 'springs of living water' may be in Psalm 36.8-9 in which it is said that with God is 'the fountain of life'. The Lamb guides his followers to be with God that they might dwell in the fountain of life.

In sum, the Lamb is the messianic suffering servant who will nurture his people. In choosing his Lamb image John has also in mind the witness figures in Isaiah 40-55 and Moses the rejected shepherd; similarly, there is the prophet figure in Zechariah 11-12 who also is modelled on suffering ideas attached to leaders. Jesus is a shepherd who has suffered but now leads as the LORD's representative (Rev. 7.17).

Conclusions

Imagery echoes the rhetorical purposes of persuasion and argument in terms of internal debate among groups who share similar cultural-linguistic traditions. The

---

87 View presented by Kraft (1974):131; Ford (1975):126-128; Fekkes (1994):173-174 finds this suggestion attractive but unconvincing on the basis of an understanding of the significance of the 144000.

88 Bauckham (1993b):101.

89 Bauckham (1993a):231; Sweet (1979):223 observes the double meaning of ὑπάγῃ which is often used in John's Gospel of Jesus' death (cf. 13.36-38).

language of the Old Testament imagery is taken up and read and heard in the new context. 1) Lamb highlights the sacrificial nature of Jesus' life and death and draws comparisons between Jesus, Isaac, and the suffering servant of Isaiah 53. Perhaps the Passover Lamb, if atonement ideas were attached to that particular Lamb in the first century, is also in the mind of John. 2) Lamb links with the witness/martyr tradition that fits with the purpose of John's work of encouraging his community to be faithful to death. 3) John depicts the church in relationship with the Lamb, the new Israel that will conquer through sacrifice. 4) John critiques the Jewish military expectation of a messiah by using the Lamb image.

John chose his image not on the basis of his knowledge of Lambs, but in terms of their function in the Old Testament. Lamb in no way is an adequate metaphor for an active revolutionary or a martyr. However, Lamb was attached to previous suffering figures in the Old Testament, not military or warrior types. John has woven this imagery into holy warfare imagery resulting in a text that utilizes the holy war tradition that seeks justice, in such a way that the idea of advocating hatred was transformed into the hope of the transformation of the sinner. This construction of imagery hates compromise with deception, but seeks transformation on the basis of truth.

CHAPTER 15

The Rider on the White Horse

He is worthy precisely as the slain Lamb, as the crucified One. Like Paul and Mark, John, too, in his manner, proposes a *theologia crucis*. W. Harrington[1]

The gutters of the city are running with blood, there are flecks of blood in the loaves of bread, blood feeds the roots of the apple trees where stinking dead men hang among the apples. A.S. Byatt [2]

Jesus is a faithful witness, a humanlike victim of the beast, a pierced figure of Zechariah 12.10, and a sacrificial Lamb. Now I will consider the imagery in Revelation 19.11-16 where it appears at first sight that Jesus is more akin to a Hollywood action hero rather than a suffering servant. The rider is reminiscent of the Davidic king. He rides upon his warhorse to establish justice in Psalm 45.4 and slays his enemy beneath him as the LORD also slays his enemy in Isaiah 63.1-6. John Sweet asks the important question: 'can John be simply echoing the Old Testament? Can Christ finally conquer in the manner of the beast?'[3] How can Jesus be both the Lamb and the rider?

Review

It is argued that Christ slays his enemies and their blood is upon his clothes.[4] This cannot be reconciled easily with the way of fighting previously attributed to Jesus. Is John contradicting his previous presentation of Jesus as a suffering Lamb? Corsini considers the image of the rider warrior a cruel vision that has helped to make Revelation into a message about a future ferocious revenge.[5]

Bauckham and Hart emphasize that the image of the rider gives 'imaginative expression to the hope that God must finally remove evil from this world before it can be a new creation'.[6] The image does not describe 'what will happen at the end of history, it is simply an imaginative expression'.[7] They urge that 'people perish

---

1 Harrington (1993):87-88.
2 Byatt *Babel Tower* (1992):30.
3 Sweet (1979):232.
4 Kiddle (1940):384; Beckwith (1919):733; Holtz (1962):172; Mounce (1977):345; Müller (1984):237; Fekkes (1994):198; Aune (1998):1057 to name but a few.
5 Corsini (1983):352.
6 Bauckham and Hart (1999):140.
7 Bauckham and Hart (1999):140.

because they have thrown in their lot with the beast',[8] that is the historical reality and reflects the idea of the spiral of escalating violence.[9] Bauckham and Hart, commenting on the images of condemnation in Revelation, emphasize that they are 'not literal depictions, they depict the unimaginable horror of rejection by God'.[10] They point out that it is important to avoid understanding the image in a way that is inconsistent with what we know of God and God's purpose in Christ.[11] Therefore, the rider or the images of punishment must be interpreted in the light of God's love and compassion. Bauckham and Hart's point is helpful in emphasizing that the image is not literal but an expression of ideas and that the imagery must be interpreted in the light of love and compassion. The vision of the rider expresses hope that evil will come to an end. Yet we are still left with the image of a warrior rider crushing his enemies. Surely, even though the language of the rider is imaginative, it still depicts Jesus as covered in the blood of his enemies. This hardly develops John's depiction of Jesus conquering through death.

There is of course the scholarly tendency to see the blood on the garments as Jesus' blood.[12] This interpretation points out that the blood has been shed before the battle begins. This alludes to Jesus' blood in death and is the reason no actual battle takes place here. Although this interpretation fits more with a Lamb christology and the argument I am making, it remains that the rider smites the nations (v.15a). He appears to trample upon their bodies and their blood is upon his garments (v.15b). This is a particularly brutal depiction and resonates with an Old Testament messianic figure that rides forth victoriously for the cause of truth, as in Psalm 45.4. He represents God as he tramples his enemy in anger with their blood upon his garments as in Isaiah 63.3.

My examination has found the works of G.B. Caird, J. Sweet and W. Harrington helpful. They emphasize a rebirth of tradition in this text. Also useful are Beale's observations regarding John's inversion or ironic use of the Old Testament.[13] W. Harrington argues that Divine Warrior as representing Jesus' role for the world is transformed by the dominant suffering Lamb image.[14] He writes of Jesus in Revelation: 'He is worthy precisely as the slain Lamb, as the crucified One. Like Paul and Mark, John, too, in his manner, proposes a *theologia crucis*'.[15]

I propose that John has transformed certain expectations of a military Messiah, popular among some, in the light of his meditations on Jesus' teaching, life and death. Jesus never taught that he was a military messiah, and his way of battle

---

8 Bauckham and Hart (1999):141.

9 Bauckham (1993b):52.

10 Bauckham and Hart (1999):146.

11 Bauckham and Hart (1999):147.

12 Rissi (1972):24; Morris (1979):231; Caird (1984):242-243; Sweet (1979):283; Bauckham (1993a):106; Harrington (1993):192; Grimsrud (2000):63.

13 Beale (1999):94-96.

14 Harrington (1993).

15 Harrington (1993):87-88.

cannot be compared to a trampling of his enemies and neither was his martyrdom intended to prompt God to take revenge on his account. I will argue that John responds to some in the synagogue who claimed that the Messiah would not suffer, thereby challenging claims that Jesus was the Messiah. John appropriates a sequence of ideas gleaned from his tradition and rebirths the imagery in a way whereby martyrdom transforms holy war. John even mocks the way of war that some seek. John was not the only Jew who did this. There are two interesting examples in Jewish literature where military imagery is transformed and a nonviolent God is portrayed.

Nonviolence in 4 Ezra 13 and *1 Enoch* 10

Examination of these texts will set Revelation 19.11-17 in a wider literary context in which humans condemn themselves by rejecting the witness of God's witnesses.

> After this I looked and saw that all who had gathered together against him, to wage war with him, were filled with fear, and yet they dared to fight. When he saw the onrush of the approaching multitude, he neither lifted his hand nor held a spear or any weapon of war; but I saw only how he sent forth from his mouth something like a stream of fire, and from his lips a flaming breath, and from his tongue he shot forth a storm of sparks. All these were mingled together, the stream of fire and the flaming breath and the great storm, and fell on the onrushing multitude that was prepared to fight, and burned up all of them, so that suddenly nothing was seen of the innumerable multitude but only the dust of ashes and the smell of smoke. When I saw it, I was amazed. After this I saw the same man come down from the mountain and call to himself another multitude that was peaceable (4 Ezra 13.8).

> and [the son] will reproach them to their face with their evil thoughts and the torments with which they are to be tortured (which were symbolized by the flames), and will destroy them without effort by means of the law (which was symbolized by the fire)(13.38).

Bauckham understands 4 Ezra 13 in part as a polemic against apocalyptic militarism; victory will not be achieved by military means.[16] The rider, like the mythological figure in 4 Ezra 13, when faced with violence does not fight back with the weapons of war (v.9; cf. Isa. 2.4; Mic. 4.3-4). The figure destroys the violent with his flaming breath, sparks and tempests (13.10, 38; cf. Isa. 11.4). Judgement proceeds from his mouth against those who reject the truth.[17] It is the witness against them, which lays before them their evil thoughts as we read in 13.38. The 'flame' links with the description of the eyes of the rider: 'eyes like flames of fire' (13.38; Rev. 19.12) which belong to the one who 'searches minds and hearts' (Rev.

---

16 Bauckham (1993a):219-220.

17 B. Longenecker (1995):79 notes the similarity in ideas between *Psalm of Solomon*. 17.33-35 and 4 Ezra 13: 'The man needs no weapons or instruments to carry out his defeat of those who oppose him'.

2.23) and condemn sinners with their own thoughts (cf. *Ps. Sol.* 17.25). Those who are condemned are violent whereas the chosen are for 'peace' (4 Ezra 13.12). It is violence that devastates sinners (v.31; cf.12.27-28; 15.15, 35; also Zech. 8.10; Rev. 13.10).[18] Their evil thoughts and torments will be the cause of the torture which is like a flame, and their destruction will be the law, which is like a fire (v.38). Although a 'word' is not said to be the cause of the enemy's demise as in Revelation 19.15, 'word' is connected with the law (Ex. 34.28; Deut. 4.13; 10.4).

> Send them [the wicked] one against the other that they may destroy each other in battle (*1 En.* 10.9) (Tr. R.H. Charles)

In *1 Enoch* 10 the message is about the destruction of the wicked (vv.1-2). The source of evil is represented in the fallen angel, Azazel, who is bound in the desert under the rocks that the earth may no longer be corrupted (v.4). The Lord sends Gabriel against the wicked (v.9) that the wicked may rise against each other that they may be destroyed in the fight (cf. v.12 and Zech. 8.10). The unrighteous are the violent ones who live by no law and oppress the righteous (v.17). In order to establish a just society, described as peaceful (vv.17-22), the violent ones must be excluded as otherwise the new order would not be peaceful. However, it is their violence that brings their destruction.

From these texts, we can see that the God of Israel was in charge and established justice. He punished the wicked. However, there is not a single statement about a direct violent act of God. Humans attack one another violently. In the same way it will be seen to be the case with the warrior rider in Revelation 19.11-17.

The War of the Rider

> Then I saw heaven opened, and there was a white horse! Its rider is called Faithful and True, and in righteousness he judges and makes war (19.11).

In John's Gospel, Jesus states that he is not a judge (12.47). It is the testimony that he gives that will be their judge. Those who are not for truth reject the way of peace and justice. God seeks the transformation of the sinner; on the other hand, there is destruction through the sinner's own violence and rejection of his word (cf. *1 En.* 10.9; 4 Ezra 13). Therefore, Jesus is the source of condemnation insofar as those who reject his witness condemn themselves. Not only is this so in John's Gospel it is also the case in Revelation.

---

18 Jeremiah teaches that 'your apostasies will convict you' (Jer. 2.19). Apostasy is to compromise with the values contrary to God's law. It is their own actions which convict them and bring about their destruction.

Jesus judges in righteousness. It is important not to read 'righteousness' uncritically from a modern perspective, i.e. as stern and unforgiving.[19] Righteousness (δικαιοσύνη) is the opposite of violence in Psalm 58.1-2. The rulers instead of judging in righteousness (v.1) deal out violence (v.2). Righteousness is associated with steadfast love, peace and faithfulness in Psalms 85.11, 89.14 and 103.17. Isaiah states that 'the effect of righteousness will be peace' (Isa. 32.17). The LXX translator of Genesis often felt the need to use righeousness (δικαιοσύνη) to express his understanding of the Hebrew חסד which means steadfast love and such associated ideas (Gen. 19.19; 20.13; 24.27; 24.29; 32.11; also Ex. 15.13; Isa. 63.7). A better translation of the Greek of Revelation 19.11:

> and in steadfast love he judges and makes war.

Jesus judges and acts with steadfast love. He does not act with violence like the rulers in Psalm 58.1-2. If Jesus and his followers' testimony of steadfast love is rejected, then steadfast love will be rejected, and they will persist in their violence which will become their judgement. Gandhi, for example, resisted his opponents not in violence but by steadfast love with no anger towards them. It was always Gandhi's hope that in facing his enemy in this way, steadfast love would transform the enemy. Similarly, Jesus faces his enemy in steadfast love and not with the sword.[20] Jesus presents a new paradigm and validates the truth claims he has made through his readiness to die rather than abandon his obedience to steadfast love. Followers should so imitate Jesus as John tells us they did (v.14). His followers are imitators and this is what it means to be 'in Christ'. Victory for the followers depends on their faithfulness in imitating the way of Jesus (cf. Rev. 12.11).[21]

John also tells us that Jesus, the warrior rider, makes war (πολεμεῖ) against his enemy. Fighting with weapons of war is not, however, the meaning intended by John (2.16; cf. 19.11c). Michael and his angels fought against the dragon and his angels (12.7). This resulted in the dragon and his angels being cast out of heaven (12.9). The dragon fought against the woman in anger (12.17). The worshippers of the beast boast 'who can fight against the beast?' (13.4). The followers of the beast make war with the Lamb in 17.14. It is observed that on each occasion violence is associated with the verb 'to make war' except 2.16 and 19.11 which are in antithesis to the others (cf. 12.17; 13.4; 17.14).[22] Yet Michael and his angels fought and conquered. Still, the dragon and his angels are not killed, but dwell away from the

---

19 For a thorough study on the Hebrew basis of righteousness see Quell and Shrenk in *TDNT* II.174-225; also Onesti and Brauch (1993):827-837.

20 This also may explain the Q saying [Mt. 10.34-35//Lk. 12.51-52]: 'not peace but a sword'. Jesus' witness will bring about division because the time of decision is forced upon people. If they choose violence there will be increased violence. See Black (1984):287-294.

21 Swartley (2000):237-238.

22 Klassen (1966):305 discusses also the significance of 'to make war' drawing similar conclusions.

peaceful kingdom. Revelation 12.7 represents in heaven what is happening on earth, and in this case, the defeat of the enemy is by nonviolence (12.11).[23] John contrasts the way in which Jesus stands out against the enemy, not with weapons of war but because he is himself 'Faithful' and 'True', the very antithesis of war and killing.

Jesus fights in truth, but only because he does so in his faithfulness to God and not through killing. John alludes to Isaiah 11.4 regarding the judging and fighting in righteousness.[24] There are other parallels (Ex. 15.13; Pss. 9.4; 67.5; 72.2; 96.13). The king judges in righteousness (Ps. 72.2a). He crushes the oppressor (72.4b). The king rides forth for 'truth' (Ps. 45.4). He loves righteousness and hates wickedness (45.7). Jesus is the Messianic king who will rule and judge in righteousness bringing to an end the reign of the unrighteous (cf. Isa. 11.4-9; Ps. 72.2). Envisaged is the time when all war and enmity will vanish (cf. Isa. 11.6-9). Similarly, the rider will rule the New Jerusalem in justice and peace.

The Rider as a Priest and his Name

on his head are many diadems; and he has a name inscribed that no one knows but himself (19.12).

The obvious allusion seems to be connected with the vestments of the priest as described by the author of Exodus:

and you shall set the turban on his head, and put the holy diadem on the turban (Ex. 29.6)

They made the rosette of the holy diadem of pure gold, and wrote on it an inscription, like the engraving of a signet, 'Holy to the LORD' (Ex. 39.30; cf. 28.36).

The wearing of the many diadems is an intended contrast between the seven diadems of the dragon and the ten diadems of the monster on the one hand, and the many diadems of the rider on the other (cf. 12.3; 13.1).[25] Priests will also wear a diadem on their heads (Ex. 29.6). In Exodus 39.30 again we are told that the priest will wear a diadem of pure gold on his head. What is interesting for our purpose of understanding the rider is the connection between the diadem and the inscription with the name 'Holy to the LORD'. Surely John alludes to this text. John states that no one knows the name that is inscribed. In Revelation 2.3, 2.13 and 3.8 the faithful are those who are steadfast to the name of Jesus. In 2.17 the faithful will receive a new name that only they know. In 3.12 the faithful receive the name of God and the name of Jesus. In 6.8 we encounter another rider whose name is 'Death'. The 144000 faithful will have the name, which Jesus has, and the name of God written

---

23 Hanson (1957):167.
24 Fekkes (1994):223-224.
25 Caird (1984):241.

on their foreheads (14.1). In 19.13b we are told that the name is 'The Word of God'. Jesus is given the name 'King of kings and Lord of lords' inscribed on his robe and thigh (19.16).

'Name' is clearly important to John and the name of the faithful and Jesus should be contrasted with the name written on the forehead of Babylon who is called a 'mother of whores' (17.6) and the rider who is named 'Death'. John states that Jesus' followers will be called priests (1.6). All will therefore receive the name that only they know. The Name had great power and was the bond of creation. Evil angels tried to learn it from Michael to gain power over the creation because it was the key to heaven and earth (*1 En.* 69.14-21).[26] This tradition may account for the name being only known to those whom it is revealed. It was the reward of the faithful, their guarantee of victory over the forces of evil. The promise of being a nation of priests is found in Exodus 19.6. It is in Exodus also that God reveals his name (3.14).[27] Moses is told that this had not previously been revealed (Ex. 6.2). The name of God and of Jesus is revealed to the new Israel in Revelation. John alludes to Exodus and the revealing of the name and the exodus from slavery to the beast. This is what John means when he says that the name is known only to the faithful. Only those who are priests receive this name. Holtz stressed the connection between 'name' and 'being' of a person.[28] The Name expresses the many aspects of the way God acts and the way God acts is connected with his being which is compassionate and forgiving. Jesus is called the Word of God (19.13b). This phrase occurs five times in Revelation (1.2, 9; 6.9; 19.13b; 20.4). Only in 19.13b is the phrase translated as a title: 'The Word of God'. The background to this phrase is in Wisdom 18.15-16. The word to which Jesus bore testimony in his life and death is now recognized to be indistinguishable from the person of the witness.[29] Jesus is equivalent to the task he has achieved. The word of God is the testimony of Jesus. Now his testimony will become the judgement on those who reject it. This does not suggest a military warrior, but a warrior who has carried out his war against idolatry and violence in his obedience to God by testifying to the word of God.

The Rod of Iron and the Sword of the Word (v.15)

The only 'iron bar' God needs to reduce the rebellious nations to submission is the Cross of his Son and the martyrdom of his saints (Caird).[30]

Jesus tends or rules (ποιμαίνω) his sheep (Rev. 2.27, 7.17 and 19.15). He has in mind MT Psalm 2.8. The Hebrew word underlying the Greek ποιμαίνω 'to tend' or

---

26 Beckwith (1919):732; Barker (2000):307; Carrell (1997):213.

27 Barker (2000):307 discusses the name and the rider as the high priest.

28 Holtz (1971):174.

29 Caird (1984):244; Rissi (1972):25.

30 Caird (1984):245.

'to rule' is רעה which, depending on how it is vocalized, can mean either 'to crush' רעע or 'to shepherd'. MT assumes 'to crush' רעע but LXX has 'to shepherd' assuming the Hebrew verb רעה suggesting there was some dispute over the pointing.[31] John may be playing ironically on this double meaning in Psalm 2.8.[32] John suggests one who cares for his sheep (7.17; cf. Isa. 49.10), but in Revelation 2.27 and 19.15 Jesus is depicted as one who deals sternly with his sheep (cf. Ps. 2.9). This double use is probably intentional. Jesus seeks the transformation of sinners and will lead them to springs of living water (7.17). However, as Jesus leads his flock to living waters, those he leads can reject the truth. So Jesus the shepherd exposes their sins and the consequences of an unrepentant heart. Those who do not see the violence of their lives ultimately in the cross and the murder of the saints will suffer the consequence of their lives.[33] John may allude to Psalm 49.10: 'Death shall be their shepherd'. Schwager comments that the loving acts of faithfulness 'work like a judgement upon the world because it makes humans confront themselves in the deepest recesses of their hearts'.[34] In sum, the rod of iron is the witness that brings humans to the springs of living water but also is a rod that brings death (Ps. 2.9).

In parallel with the rod of iron is the sword of the word:

> From his mouth comes a sharp sword with which to strike down the nations.

God's servant/witness has a mouth like a sharp sword (cf. Isa. 49.2) and is a light to the nations (Isa. 49.6). Some understand a sword that kills as in Wisdom 18.15-16:[35]

> your all-powerful word leaped from heaven, from the royal throne, into the midst of the land that was doomed, a stern warrior carrying the sharp sword of your authentic command, and stood and filled all things with death, and touched heaven while standing on the earth.

The imagery of the sword in Wisdom 18.15-16 is controlled by the witness theme. The sword is the word that judges. There is judgement in Revelation 19.11-17, but the judgement of one who rejects the witness of the faithful. The word of God is alive and communicated through his witnesses. It is sharper than the sword as it confronts each person and nation with the truth of their violent and oppressing lives. The author of Hebrews knows this to be true when he writes that 'the word of God is

---

31 LXX has ποιμανεῖς αὐτοὺς ἐν ῥάβδῳ σιδηρᾷ - you shall rule/shepherd them with a rod of iron.
32 Beale (1999):267.
33 An important insight of Girard.
34 Schwager (2000):219.
35 Yarbro Collins (1979):135; Caird (1984):244 and Sweet (1979):283; Barker (1996):136 connects Wisdom 18.15 with the witness theme of Isaiah 49.2.

living and active, sharper than any two-edged sword' (Heb. 4.12).[36] With the word
of God, or metaphorically with the sword issuing from the mouth, hidden resentment
against God and secret violence are both unmasked.[37]

It is important to remember that the 'sword' is in parallel with the 'rod of iron'.
Therefore, as the 'sword' is associated with the 'word', so also the 'iron rod' is
associated with the word. In *Psalm of Solomon* 17.24 and v.27, the 'rod of iron' is
associated with 'word of his mouth' as in Revelation 19.15 (also Rev. 2.6).[38]
According to this psalm, sinners will be condemned by the thoughts of their hearts
(17.24-25). Yet the messianic figure of this psalm is compassionate (*Ps. Sol.* 17.32)
and will not rule by war and fear (*Ps. Sol.* 17.33b). He will have compassion on all
nations who stand before him (*Ps. Sol.* 17.34b).[39] He does not strike the earth with
the sword, but with the word of his mouth (*Ps. Sol.* 7.35a; cf. Isa. 11.4). The poet
writes of this messianic figure in words reminiscent of Old Testament traditions we
have looked at in Part Two trusting in God to deliver Israel from their enemy and
not to trust in the ways of the nations:

> he will not rely on horse and rider and bow (17.33).

In sum, the sword is also the iron bar. It is to those who ignore the testimony a
sword that kills, and a shepherd's crook to those who respond (cf. Ps. 23.4).[40]
Central to the judgement and punishment of the wicked is the principle of the
punishment matching the sin (*jus talionis*). Judgement is the time for the destroying
of the destroyers (Rev. 11.18) as they will die with the weapons with which they
have murdered (16.6; 18.6; 22.18-19; cf. Wis. 11.16). John sees the consequences of
the eschatological *jus talionis* as their destruction because of their violence.[41] Jesus
taught:

> For nation will rise against nation, and kingdom against kingdom (Mark 13.8).

God's representative, the rider, is associated with righteousness, truth and
faithfulness, the antithesis of violence. Consequently, violence cannot remain in his
creation. Therefore, God's word will be the ultimate cause of their destruction.
Violence cannot exist in God's completed creation as the ruling principle is 'peace'.
Yet how does this fit with the most violent picture of Jesus as one who tramples the
wine press?

---

36 Caird (1984):244.
37 Schwager (2000):219.
38 To this extent Caird (1984):245 probably pushes the significance of the sword as replacing
the rod in Revelation 19.15 too far.
39 That is those who reverently stand before God or the Messiah.
40 Sweet (1979):96.
41 Bauckham (1993b):52.

Trampling the Wine Press

He will tread the wine press of the fury of the wrath of God the almighty (Rev. 19.15b).

He who treads the wine press of the fury of the wrath of God the Almighty is none other that the Lamb that has come, not to slaughter but to be slaughtered (Schwager).[42]

Although Schwager is confident in this declaration, it is by no means clear how Jesus can be the slaughtered Lamb who tramples the wine press. So far, in my study, I have attempted to explain some of the warlike imagery in the light of Old Testament tradition. Now I will examine the trampling of the wine press in both Revelation 14.17-20 and 19.15 as they seem to be related. I will consider the influence particularly of Joel 3.13 and Isaiah 63.1-6 on John. I believe also in the importance of a military messianic tradition based on Isaiah 63.1-6 represented in *Palestinian Targum (PT) on Genesis* 49.11. I will argue that traditions existed in Jewish circles about a bloody, violent Messiah that necessitated a response from John. John drew upon the same text as the Targumist but argued for a nonviolent messiah.

How beautiful is the King Messiah who is to arise from among those of the house of Judah! He girds his loins and goes out to wage war on those that hate him, and slays kings with their rulers, making the mountains red with the blood of their slain and making the hills white with the fat of their warriors and his vestments are soaked in blood. He is like the presser of grapes (*Palestinian Targum on Genesis* 49.11).[43]

This text expresses a very old pre-Christian tradition that is quite in accord with the expectations of the warlike Messiah who, as we know from Josephus and other sources, was awaited by the Jews in the New Testament period (see *War* 6.312-313; Tacitus *Hist.* 513; Suetonius *Vesp.* 4).[44] The Targumist links the Hebrew of Genesis 49.11 and Isaiah 63.1-6. A warrior Messiah is expected to crush his enemies while soaking his garments in their blood (cf. Isa. 63.2-3). The Targumist's translation of Genesis 49.11 shows the extent to which Isaiah 63.1-6 was of interest among Jewish exegetes near to the time of John. Therefore it is not surprising that Revelation 19.11-16 especially v.15 draws upon Isaiah 63.1-6, however, with a difference.

Reinterpreting Joel 3.13 and Isaiah 63.1-6

The wine press imagery in Revelation 19.15 cannot be separated from Revelation 14.14-20. The one who tramples the wine press in 14.20 is the rider in 19.15.[45] The prophet Joel writes:

---

42 Schwager (2000):219.
43 Translated by McNamara (1966):232.
44 McNamara (1966):233.
45 Bauckham (1993b):97.

Put in the sickle, for the harvest is ripe. Go in, tread, for the wine press is full. The vats overflow, for their wickedness is great (Joel 3.13).

John writes:

Use your sharp sickle and gather the clusters of the vine of the earth, for its grapes are ripe (Rev. 14.18).

Like Joel, John has the gathering of the grapes at the right time (Rev. 14.18). The LORD's Chosen will trample the wine press because it is full. Yet for John the reason for gathering is because the grapes are ready (Rev. 14.18), whereas in Joel the vats overflow with great wickedness. John has preferred the readiness for trampling the wine press to being full of great wickedness. Jesus and his followers were not examples of a military success story and Jesus is not the military warrior of the above targum on Genesis 49.11. John understands the vats to be overflowing not with the enemy, but with the oppressor's victims. John tells us in Revelation 6.11 that the time of judgement is connected with the time when the number of murderers is complete. It is when this occurs that Babylon will fall. Caird writes:

John's object in this paragraph, then, has been to persuade the prospective martyrs that the world-wide carnage, in which their lives are to be forfeit, will not be simply the vindictive work of Babylon; it will also be the gracious work of the Son of Man, sending out his angels to reap a great harvest of souls, and incidentally to prepare the intoxicating cup that prove the ruin of the mother of harlots.[46]

In Revelation 19.15 the vats overflow with the murderous consequences of the wicked life, yet not with the murderers themselves. The victims will be gathered to God's wine press and there prepared so that the enemy may consume its victim's blood. It will be a time of redemption for the slaughtered. John reflects upon Isaiah 63.1-6 to aid his depiction of the time of judgement.

"Who is this that comes from Edom, from Bozrah in garments stained crimson? Who is this so splendidly robed, marching in his great might?" "It is I, announcing vindication, mighty to save." 2 "Why are your robes red, and your garments like theirs who tread the wine press?" 3 "I have trodden the wine press alone, and from the peoples no one was with me; I trod them in my anger and trampled them in my wrath; their juice spattered on my garments, and stained all my robes. 4 For the day of vengeance was in my heart, and the year for my redeeming work had come. 5 I looked, but there was no helper; I stared, but there was no one to sustain me; so my own arm brought me victory, and my wrath sustained me. 6 I trampled down peoples in my anger, I crushed them in my wrath, and I poured out their lifeblood on the earth" (Isa. 63.1).

In this text John looks to the mighty LORD to come and establish his justice (v.1). His garments are red with the blood of his enemies (vv.2-3). In Isaiah 63.6a the

---

46 Caird (1984):193; Sweet (1979):232; Harrington (1993):194.

LORD tramples the peoples thus preparing the wine that must be drunk although NRSV does not express the Hebrew - אשכרם בחמתי - I made them drunk in my wrath. The New Kings James version is closer to the Hebrew and the author's original idea as this is the more difficult reading:

> I have trodden down the peoples in My anger, Made them drunk in My fury.

Treading the wine press prepares the wine that is the judgement, the poison of their violence that Babylon will drink.[47] The process of 'treading' is preparatory and not the final result. This is suggested to John by Isaiah 63.6b:

אשכרם בחמתי - I made them drunk in my wrath

John reflects on Isaiah 63.6c in which God poured out their lifeblood on the earth. For John the lifeblood was the lifeblood of the victims of violence and not the wicked. When the blood reaches the earth, their lifeblood cries for justice. This blood forms the contents of the 'wine press of the fury of the wrath of God', which is how John describes the winepress that the rider treads (19.15).[48] Although Isaiah 63.6b does not state that Babylon will be drunk on its own blood, John so read it in the light of Isaiah 49.26b which says that the oppressors will drink their own blood and become drunk on it as if drinking wine.[49] Babylon's blood is the blood of its victims. Such blood is the mark of their violence.[50] Spilt blood pulsates through the body of an oppressor. It is metaphorically their own blood as such blood is the very essence of their being – that of killing. John depicts:

> And I saw that the woman was drunk with the blood of the saints and the blood of the witnesses to Jesus (Rev. 17.6)

The woman, Babylon, is depicted as one who lives off the blood of the innocent. The Roman Empire, also, was built and maintained by violence and oppression like the original Babylon. The psalmist speaks of sinners as thirsty for blood (Ps. 26.9). Further, the LORD prepares the foaming wine which the wicked of the earth will consume until there is nothing left (Ps. 75.8). The author of Proverbs 4.17 sees sinners drinking the wine of violence. The author used 'wine' as a metaphor for the

---

47 Caird (1984):246.

48 Caird (1984):192; points out that vineyard is always used of God's chosen (Hos. 10.1; Isa. 5.1-7; Jer. 2.21; Ezek. 17.1-8; Ps. 80.8-13). Caird (1980):155 comments that Isaiah compares Israel with a vineyard in that it expresses the idea that God has planted and taken care of his vineyard.

49 Harrington (1993):194 notes the importance of Isaiah 49.26.

50 Harrington (1993):194 draws upon Isaiah 49.26 for the idea that the enemies will drink their own blood.

blood that the violent shed.[51] John would also know the words of the prophet Jeremiah:

> King Nebuchadnezzar of Babylon has devoured me, he has crushed me; he has made me an empty vessel, he has swallowed me like a monster; he has filled his belly with my delicacies, he has spewed me out (Jer. 51.34).

The innocent victims' blood becomes Babylon's blood; she drinks it and is sustained by her continued violence. The author of Numbers 23.24 depicts the violent as 'drunk on the blood of the slain'.[52] The destructive Babylon also led astray the nations by causing the nations to drink the blood of her fury and fornication - τοῦ οἴνου τοῦ θυμοῦ τῆς πορνείας – the wine of her impure passion (Rev. 14.8; 16.6a).[53] In the Old Testament, Babylon's wine renders the nations powerless (Jer. 51.7; cf. Isa. 49.26; 63.6; Ps. 75.8).

Therefore, the wine is the blood of its victims. Those who drink Babylon's wine are the supporters of Babylon in her violence. The 'wine of her impure passion' is also 'the wine of God's fury'. Babylon's own blood is in mind – the wine of her impure passion - the martyrs' blood that she has become drunk on (Rev. 16.6; 17.6).[54] This may account for 'fury' and 'wrath' to describe the wine press: 'the winepress of the fury of the wrath of God' (19.15). 'Fury' and 'wrath' suggest that the blood is Babylon's fury (14.8). Babylon's blood, and the wrath of God refer to the fact that 'winepress of fury' has become the 'winepress of the wrath of God'. This compares well with Isaiah 63.6a and 63.6b, connecting Babylon's own blood that it drinks with God's wrath.[55]

Yet Revelation 19.15 says nothing about drinking wine. Rather it is about the crushing of grapes. Charles observes: 'The two ideas of the winepress (14.19) and the cup of the wrath (14.10) are here (i.e. in 19.15) combined, and mean that from the wine press trodden by Christ flows the wine of the wrath of God, of which his

---

51 In Proverbs 4.17 the oppressor is sustained by violence. He cannot sleep unless he has acted violently (v.16), thus he would perish without being violent to someone. V.17 develops this, eating is vital to life, the oppressor survives by the food of wickedness and wine of violence.

52 Barbé (1983):10. Barbé suggests that the oppressor devours the enemy's flesh in order to absorb the enemy's valor and courage.

53 16.6a could be read as the blood being given to the saints and prophets to drink. Most read it as the enemy drinking the blood which they have shed: Mounce (1977):295; Morris (1979):194-195.

54 Caird (1984):202-203 writes: 'when the ocean of blood which the worshippers of the monster have shed contaminates their own water supply, so that Babylon staggers to her appointed doom, drunk with the blood of saints and prophets; Sweet (1979):255 suggests 17.6 refers to the slaughter by Nero.

55 To hide from God's wrath is to refuse to hear the message of the cross which is a decision to live a life of violence and oppression.

enemies are to be made to drink'.[56] It is possible that the eschatological banquet in Revelation 19.17-18 is linked insofar as the wine that is prepared for Babylon to drink, her own blood - the blood of her violence, is essentially the violence that will come upon Babylon. She will drink the cup of her own wrath; she will be destroyed similarly to the way she destroyed. This also links with Isaiah 49.26a. Here the oppressors will eat their own flesh and drink their own blood; in Revelation 19.17-18, the birds will consume the bodies of the oppressor, which alludes to Ezekiel 39.17-19:

> 17 As for you, mortal, thus says the Lord GOD: Speak to the birds of every kind and to all the wild animals: Assemble and come, gather from all around to the sacrificial feast that I am preparing for you, a great sacrificial feast on the mountains of Israel, and you shall eat flesh and drink blood. 18 You shall eat the flesh of the mighty, and drink the blood of the princes of the earth-- of rams, of lambs, and of goats, of bulls, all of them fatlings of Bashan. 19 You shall eat fat until you are filled, and drink blood until you are drunk, at the sacrificial feast that I am preparing for you.

The violent will consume the violent and there will be enough even for the birds in mid-heaven. John draws upon Ezekiel 39.17-19 but clearly rejects the idea of Israel consuming the blood of its enemies at God's behest.

The White Horse

Jesus treads the wine press while riding a white horse (19.11). In Isaiah 63.1-6 the LORD tramples the wine press with his feet without the aid of a horse. This added detail of the white horse in Revelation 19.11 has not drawn much discussion from scholars, but surely it is a significant addition to the imagery with a precise purpose. Caird states that 'the white horse is the symbol of victory'.[57] I suggest that John drew upon Psalm 45.4 for his horse imagery, in which the Davidic king rides forth for justice and truth.[58] The horse is a military figure. The poet of the *Psalms of Solomon*, however, proclaimed that the faithful should not put their trust in such figures:

> he will not rely on horse and rider and bow, nor will he collect gold and silver for war
> (*Ps. Sol.* 17.33)

As a horse would not be used to tread a wine press, John has placed Jesus on a horse that resonates with the expectation of some Jews for the Davidic king (Ps. 45.4), but in such a way that the picture is implausible. John is intentionally subverting the idea of a warrior on a warhorse through the irony of a horse treading grapes. A white

---

56 Charles (1920):137; Caird (1984):246.
57 Caird (1984):240.
58 Contrary Carrell (1997):206 who suggests that the background to the horse addition lies within angelology and that the image is of an angelic horseman.

horse also appears in Revelation 6.2. The rider on this horse is not Jesus but one who is committed to violent overthrow with his bow. John uses the white horse in Revelation 19.11 also to contrast Jesus with the rider in 6.2. Jesus is not one who rides out to conquer through violence but by his word. Sweet believes that 'white' is the colour of heaven',[59] but this hardly fits with the horse image in Revelation 6.2 who, as Harrington points out, represents war and its attendant evils – the war, strife, famine and pestilence.[60] John may be alluding to Psalm 20.7 in which the Psalmist contrasts those who trust in chariots and horses and those who trust in the LORD. The whole idea of a military warrior is mocked.[61] This may be an example of John inverting the expectation of a warrior in a way that the *Psalm of Solomon* 17.33 did not.[62]

Blood on the Garments of the Rider (19.13, cf. Isa. 63.2; PT. Gen. 49.11)

And as the slain men fall, the Priests shall trumpet from afar; they shall not approach the slain lest they be defiled with unclean blood. For they are holy, and they shall not profane the anointing of their priesthood with the blood of nations of vanity (1QM 9.5-9).

The blood marks the rider's attire because the wine press has been trodden. The blood that is on the LORD in Isaiah 63.3 is Babylon's blood. For John, this blood is also the blood of Jesus and the saints, the blood Babylon shed. The blood on Jesus' garments is therefore his own blood for he suffered and was murdered. Jesus' blood is 'the wine of her impure fury' which Babylon drinks (17.6; cf. Isa. 49.26).[63] It is argued that there is no connection between the blood on the garments and the treading of the wine press simply on the grounds of logical sequence, i.e. that Jesus has the blood on his garments before the treading. Such an approach suffers from over-literalism presenting events in their logical sequence is not a major concern for John.[64] Jesus treads the wine press because he is the prototype martyr who has made known the way to victory. It seems therefore that the blood is not only his own blood, but also Babylon's blood as such blood sustains Babylon. Yet Jesus does not trample his enemies underfoot, covered in their blood. Given John's expectation that the chosen will be priests to God (1.6), and that Jesus is therefore a priest as we

---

59 Sweet (1979) 282.

60 Harrington (1993):91.

61 Note contrast with the expectation of a humble King in Zechariah 9.9 riding on an ass; not the act of a military King.

62 For discussion of inverted uses of the Old Testament see Beale (1999):94-96.

63 There is some dispute regarding βεβαμμένον 'to dip'.

64 The blood as his enemies: Beckwith (1919):733; Kiddle (1941):384; Holtz (1962):172; Mounce (1977):345; Müller (1984):237; Fekkes (1994):198; Aune (1998):1057; contrary Rissi (1972):24; Morris (1979):231; Caird (1984):242-243; Sweet (1979):283; Bauckham (1993a):106; Harrington (1993):192.

know from his appearance in Revelation 19.12, such a person would not be contaminated with the blood of his enemies as the War Scroll quoted above suggests.

Summary and Conclusions

John develops his own traditions in conflict with those who attack his understanding of Jesus. John's work subverts and mocks certain readings and interpretation of the tradition to which he is an heir in presenting Jesus as a nonviolent, faithful witness whose message is for all nations. It is my suggestion that John appropriated the tradition from the synagogue, possibly even some church members, that the Messiah would be a Davidic, military conquering hero,[65] and for rhetorical purposes rebirthed the tradition. Jesus was not a military leader and from the earliest traditions regarding Jesus' teaching, he appears to have taught love and forgiveness. Therefore, John's presentation of a rider with the blood of his enemies on his garments is incongruous with one who was nailed on the cross, a death which, for Jews, rendered the executed person unworthy of being a messiah (Deut. 21.23). John engages with his conventions, and flouts them. Such was Jesus' life that it leads to a new engagement with his cultural system. There were those who were opposed to the teaching of Jesus and who sought to subvert his followers. Jesus was not necessarily the expected Messiah type, as Revelation 19.11-16 might represent, or even the king of the Royal Psalms. It is inconceivable to make sense of Revelation 19.11-16 in the obvious way in terms of Jesus. He was in no way a warrior and from the earliest traditions about Jesus there is nothing to suggest that he was seen in any way other than that of a suffering, martyr figure. Therefore, John responds to certain interpretations and expectations regarding the Messiah in Jewish tradition; those which subverted Jesus' teachings and John's and his readers' understanding as a result of erroneous assumptions. John does this by reinterpreting the rider in the light of the Lamb. It is the Lamb image that alerts the modern reader to the subtle meanings inherent in 19.11-16. Throughout the Book of Revelation the emphasis has been on the suffering that God's chosen must undergo. Therefore, those trodden can be only those who must suffer in order for victory to be achieved. It is inconceivable that John could suddenly abandon his controlling ideology of suffering to achieve victory. Jesus tramples the grapes because he prepares for God's kingdom, which means the end of the beast's reign. It is also his and the

---

65. There is ample evidence that a Davidic king would trample down his enemies in the Old Testament. *Palestinian Targum Genesis* 49.11 and the *Testament of Joseph* 19.8 suggest such an understanding. Maybe John attacks such. However, as Klassen (1992):869 has shown, the idea of a military victory was not necessarily an expectation of all Jews. There is some evidence that there was an anti-military group among Jews. This has been shown in which martyrdom was a preferred action rather than killing among some Jews. However, nonviolence can have different motives which are not always Gandhian. See Yoder for discussion of other Jewish approaches to their enemy.

martyrs' blood that will bring about the end of the beast's reign. The followers of the beast will become drunk on their blood, the blood of their oppression. Therefore, it is indeed Jesus' own blood marking his garments as well as the blood of all the saints.

It would appear therefore that there is nothing in this text to contradict the previous presentations of Jesus. Jesus the rider, like the faithful witness, pierced one, humanlike figure, and the Lamb, is a prophet against the principles of power and violence. He exemplifies a nonviolent revolutionary in the tradition of Gandhi, that is, one who seeks through love to transform the enemy. His witness and death reveal to the world's oppressors that if they continue in their violence, they will bring about their own death by violence. The vision of the rider is not about the martyr getting his revenge, but is a vision showing that the violent will drink their own punishment. Their acts of violence and greed are their own punishment. Yet Jesus and his followers have died by violence although they have not lived violently, there still is the belief that by their faithfulness they will be with God eternally and that the violent cut themselves off from God and thus stand outside the New Jerusalem (Rev. 21.27).

CONCLUSION

I smell myself daily and the smell disgusts me. I have had enough blood. The gutters of the city are running with blood, there are flecks of blood in the loaves of bread, blood feeds the roots of the apple trees where stinking dead men hang among the apples. You may not believe me now, but a killer by trade who has had enough of blood is a good founding member for a community based on kindness and freedom as yours is to be. *A. S. Byatt 'Babel Tower', 30.*

Revelation offers a different way of perceiving the world which leads people to resist and to challenge the effects of the dominant ideology. *R. Bauckham 'Theology of the Book of Revelation' 159.*

All God's Children

Violence and power are the dominating values of our society. The easy way in which bloodshed is justified as a lawful way of maintaining justice seems to make the two inseparable. Politicians claim that 'force must be met by force'. Hollywood films rejoice in evil being met by the violent force of the conquering hero. Such violence is 'redemptive violence' a violence that has dominated the history of humankind.[1] The beginning of the twenty-first century does not encourage us to hope that peaceful ways of resolving conflict can be found. The destruction of the twin towers on September 11 is engraved on the human mind, as is the vengeance America took upon its enemies. So it is not surprising that the figure of Jesus in the Book of Revelation is interpreted as one who seeks vengeance against his or her enemies.[2]

The novelist and literary critic A.S. Byatt describes the fictional character Colonel Grim - the trained killer. The so-called peaceful cry out against him: 'we should put him to the sword for the suffering of our families and our friends; we should cement our social bonds with his foul blood'. But Grim bearing the mark of Cain says: 'Cain was marked so that the children of Adam should not harm him'. He continues: 'You owe it to me to see how I can live peaceably'. Grim utters the teaching of the Book of Revelation. Grim experiences the truth behind violence in society. He beholds the world as grim, like his name, as the blood of the murdered flows through its veins just as the blood of the murdered nourished Babylon. Unlike Colonel Grim, few grow weary of blood. Hardly any are like Grim who has grown weary of violence, as he smells blood on his garments and the blood that runs through the gutters of the city. Only a minority smells the blood and sees that like Revelation's Babylon, the world is fed by blood, the blood of victims whose suffering sustains privilege and power. A small number of people equate trade and the market economy with violence, but most live lives obtuse to the cruelty in which they participate. Violence is glamorized on television sets and the many are careless and ignorant about involvement in destroying less powerful nations and strangely forgetful about the poverty and abuses nearer home. Grim, the killer by trade, knows violence first-hand. He knows too well the blood of his victims that he smells. This figure Revelation hopes to convert, as all are God's children. Grim says: 'I can tell you much of the nature of control, and terror, and control of terror, which you do not think you need to know. But it is what all men need to know…' The Old Testament prophets knew too well violence and control. Because of this, their message was

---

1 Wink (1984):17-31.
2 See Wainwright's history of interpretation of Revelation (1993). Interpretation is dominated by redemptive violent readings.

more powerful. John, too, knows the history of plunder. The Book of Revelation speaks to the powerful as much as to the poor and oppressed.[3] Central to Revelation is the hope that the violent, like Grim, can be transformed and make a significant contribution to establishing a peaceful society. Is it not the case that on Peace marches the most poignant sight are the war veterans who have fought and killed for their country and through it seen the horror of their violence?

Change comes through showing the violent where violence leads. The peaceful revolutionaries must expose the nature of sin in the world. They are not to be like the community to which Grim wishes to belong. This community ironically desires to form a social bond with his blood as Abel's blood cries for Cain's life. William Blake in his final etching in 1822 called 'The Ghost of Abel' depicts the victim Abel crying out: 'Of Blood O Earth Cover not thou the Blood of Abel'.[4] The LORD asks what Abel desires and he cries out: 'Life for Life! Life for Life!'[5] To which the LORD replies: 'He who shall take Cains life must also Die O Abel'.[6] Blake describes how Abel persists in his desire for vengeance as he 'sinks down into the Grave...'[7] Blake powerfully depicts that from this Grave 'arises Satan Armed in glittering scales with a Crown & a Spear' like an all American Hollywood hero.[8] This Abel through his desire for vengeance becomes the instrument of Satan, a source of violence. Satan says to God: 'Thou shalt be Sacrificed to Me thy God on Calvary'.[9] Such violence is seen as belonging to Satan who deceives humanity into thinking that peace can only be established when vengeance is done. Yet Blake shows clearly that what Satan wants is the death of God. Blake describes how God agrees and in doing so tells Satan: 'Thou Thyself go to Eternal Death'. This Eternal Death is described as 'Self Annihilation'. Through the death of the innocent Son of God, the world beholds the true nature of violence as light shines in the darkness. It is a world which seeks scapegoats to establish peace by putting the innocent to death. Instead of heeding the LORD's word that none shall kill Cain, rather humanity rejects this. Unfortunately, Cain's actions do not teach us anything. The sons of Cain, like Grim, should be the foundation of a community based on forgiveness and freedom. They have seen blood polluting our waters and earth. We should not make a scapegoat of them labelling them an affliction on humanity - people who are violent whom we must be rid of. Samuel Taylor Coleridge wrote in 1798 'The Wanderings of Cain' in which Coleridge reflects on the lot of Cain after he murdered Abel.[10] Unlike Byatt's Colonel Grim, Coleridge's Cain is devoid of hope. He says: 'Abel, my brother, I would lament for thee, but that spirit within me is withered, and burnt up with extreme agony' (170). Cain's crime is more than he can bear. There is

---

3 Bauckham (1993b):161.
4 *William Blake The Complete Poems*:865.
5 *William Blake The Complete Poems*:865.
6 *William Blake The Complete Poems*:865.
7 *William Blake The Complete Poems*:866.
8 *William Blake The Complete Poems*:866.
9 *William Blake The Complete Poems*:867.
10 In *Samuel Taylor Coleridge Poems* edited by John Beer 130-134.

no greater punishment for him. Cain says: 'how can I be afflicted more than I already am?' Cain's sin is his punishment.

The Christian tradition is rooted in Jewish tradition which teaches that the believer should trust in the LORD. Yet it is a compromising tradition that has its roots in the soil of respectability and human achievement. If it is nonviolent, it is so because it proclaims inaction and some otherworldly personal piety. It willingly has commissions on a multitude of issues but does not teach and act as the Book of Revelation urges. It does not even glimpse the world as Revelation does and even corrupts its message unknowingly. The church does not resist and challenge the effects of the dominant ideology as Jesus and Revelation do. Is it not the case that the church can only be truly the body of Christ when in Bauckham's words it is a witness to the truth? True witness is the worship of the true God and in our society it 'is the power of resistance to the deification of military and political power (the beast) and economic prosperity (Babylon)'.[11]

As readers of the biblical text, we seek to be open to the message as revelation from God. I have aimed to get back to John's world and understand his work as his reflections on Jesus and the cross. If we are open to the radical message of the Book of Revelation, we may become like Grim and taste and smell the stench of the blood of the innocent that the world consumes insatiably. We will identify both with Abel and Cain. We seek justice like Abel, but we know that the justice is Cain's sin. We are all both Abel and Cain. We seek vengeance and others seek vengeance against us. This is the *way of the world*. To resist the dominant ideology is to see that Jesus and many others are innocent people put to death. As Girard has observed too well in his mimetic theory, the dominant ideology, what he calls the classic myth, is to sacrifice the innocent to establish peace, but a short-lived peace. As with the Israelite suffering servant of Isaiah 52.12-53.13, the Christian church and the Jewish synagogues must bear witness to expose the sin of murder.

Reflections on Studies of Revelation and this Study

I am indebted to the labours of those involved in various areas of scholarship. Methodologically, conflict theory and intertextuality are important for the way I have examined the texts. My underlying presupposition of research has been to understand John as one who builds upon his tradition in the challenging setting of an all powerful Rome and against those who reject or compromise Jesus within his own tradition. The importance of an internal Jewish debate is a key for understanding Revelation, as is the insight that the use of metaphor takes its starting point in the conflict between interpreters of the same tradition. In terms of exegesis, I considered Revelation 2.9 as linked to a debate over the extent to which one should compromise with Rome. The depiction of Jesus as a Lamb is again linked to debate, this time over the claims about Jesus being a suffering messiah and a reaction against the expectation of a Messiah being a military leader. In the vision of Jesus as a Rider,

---

11 Bauckham (1993b):160.

the setting is once more motivated by John's need to defend the way of Jesus against those who looked for a military messianic leader.

In terms of exploring to what extent Revelation's understanding of Jesus compares with the Jesus of the gospels, I hope that my argument has taken further the debate regarding Jesus as a Revolutionary leader of Peace. In developing this exploration, Gandhi's thinking about nonviolence was applied heuristically to the exegesis. In doing so 'nonviolence' has been precisely established. Nonviolence from this Gandhian perspective was used in comparing and contrasting various aspects of nonviolence and understandings of martyrdom within Jewish tradition in order to reach a point at which a conclusion can be reached as to what extent the Jesus of Revelation can be compared to Gandhi's Revolutionary of Peace.

My hope is that I have developed the idea of Revelation and its portrayal of Jesus in the light of those scholars who have emphasized that Jesus and his witnesses testified to the world through love and who sought the conversion of the world from the way of the beast.

Points of Comparison between the Jesus of Revelation and Gandhi's Revolutionary of Peace

I will conclude finally in the form of points as to the extent to which Revelation's Jesus compares with Gandhi's revolutionary of peace:

1. Jesus as a revolutionary is an overwhelming picture gained from my study. The Jesus of Revelation was in opposition to the values of the world such as power, oppression and violence.

2. His life was as a 'faithful witness' in the cosmic law court against the world of violence, greed and aggrandizement. Jesus' testimony was of word, action and death, all of which set him against the values of the world represented in the form of idolaters, murders, and liars (see Rev. 9.20; 21.8; 22.15) in order to persuade them to turn from their idolatry. Jesus is a faithful witness inasmuch as it is hoped that humankind, as a whole, can be released from its bondage to the values of the world. All suffering and death are brought about in the recurring spiral of violence and revenge. There is no sense that John saw Jesus as one outside of this punishment. All suffer the consequences of violence and oppression, the strong and the weak. Jesus suffers and dies at the hands of such values. Jesus is not, because of his suffering and death, one who stands in a position of power outside of suffering and punishment. He is not a typical revolutionary who projects evil on to someone else who must be eradicated, as for example Hitler did with the Jews, or the Marxists with the bourgeoisie. Jesus is one who stands for all humankind, having experienced the consequences of its sin in his violent death. Instead of seeing it as despicable, he assumes the suffering of the other and thus changes their condition by forgiveness and acceptance.

3. In worldly terms, Jesus is a failure. He cannot be considered a powerful leader such as the Roman Emperor. Rather, Jesus is like a sacrificial Lamb, the very antithesis to power and might as the world sees it. Jesus is a deviant, rejected by

the world. He refuses to abandon his testimony and chooses his place in society as an outsider. Indeed, in doing so he becomes victorious in that he does not give in and in his death he demonstrates his faithfulness to God. Gandhi also was in many ways rejected and his policy of love and compassion resulted in his assassination.

4. Violence is the essence of maintaining a society of greed and oppression. Therefore, violent revolution is a contradiction in terms insofar as 'revolution' seeks fundamental change or reversal of conditions. Pursuing violent means to change the dominant ideology is to embrace that very ideology which the so-called revolutionary seeks to eradicate. A 'true' revolutionary is, therefore, nonviolent, the very antithesis of the ideology dominant in the world. Therefore, intrinsic to revolution is the belief that the transformation of violence can occur. Jesus is the exemplar of this way.

5. Revelation urges non-cooperation with the world. Revelation in no way breaks with the teaching of Jesus. Jesus exemplifies in his whole way of life the principle of non-cooperation with the antagonist. To accept death rather than play the power games of the antagonist is the ultimate expression of non-cooperation.

6. Jesus in Revelation is an exalted figure. His life was based on the principles of nonviolence and that compares with Gandhi's understanding that the attainment of perfection is achieved only when a life is based on the principles of nonviolence, especially in the offering of one's life for another.

7. Revelation depicts Jesus in battle with the forces of violence. Victory is sought. As with Gandhi, this is a war only to the extent that it is a contest between nonviolence and violence. But still a war. Revelation portrays Jesus as conquering through nonviolence expressed in suffering, witness and non-cooperation.

In sum, there is little ground for seeing the Jesus of Revelation as a corruption of the gospel's Jesus. The Jesus of Revelation is a Revolutionary of Peace comparable with the tradition of Gandhi's revolutionary of peace and the text itself is an able example of the ideology of peaceful revolution.

Bibliography

Alison, J., *Raising Abel: The Recovery of the Eschatological Imagination* (New York: Crossroad, 1996).

Allen, G., *Intertextuality: The New Critical Idiom* (London/New York: Routledge, 2000).

Anderson, A.A., *Psalms 1-72* (New Century Bible. London: Marshall, Morgan & Scott, 1983).

—, *Psalms 73-150* (New Century Bible. London: Marshall, Morgan & Scott, 1983).

Applebaum, S., 'Economic Life in Palestine', in S. Safrai and M. Stern (eds.), *The Jewish People in the First Century*, II, (Compendia Rerum Judaicarum ad Novum Testamentum. Assen: van Gorcum, 1976a), 631-700.

—, 'The Legal Status of the Jewish Communities in the Diaspora', in S. Safrai and M. Stern (eds.), *The Jewish People in the First Century*, I, (Compendia Rerum Judaicarum ad Novum Testamentum. Assen: van Gorcum, 1976b), 420-463.

Attridge, H., 'Josephus and his Works', in M.E. Stone (ed.), *Jewish Writings of the Second Temple Period*, (Compendia Rerum Iudaicarum ad Novum Testamentum II.2, Assen: van Gorcum/ Philadelphia: Fortress Press, 1984), 185-232.

Arndt, W.F., and F.W. Gingrich *A Greek-English Lexicon of the New Testament and other Early Christian Literature* (Chicago, Illinois: The University of Chicago Press, fourth revised and augmented edition, 1952).

Aune, D.E., *Prophecy in Early Christianity and the Ancient Mediterranean World* (Grand Rapids, Michigan: Eerdmans, 1983).

—, 'Intertextuality and the Genre of the Apocalypse', in E.H. Lovering, Jr. (ed.), (SBL Seminar Papers. Atlanta, Georgia: 1991), 142-160.

—, *Revelation 1-5* (Word Bible Commentary 52A. Waco: Word Books, 1997).

—, *Revelation 17-22* (Word Bible Commentary 52C. Waco: Word Books, 1998).

Bailey, D.P., 'The Suffering Servant: Recent Tübingen Scholarship on Isaiah 53', in W.H. Bellinger Jr and W.R. Farmer (eds.), *Jesus and the Suffering Servant: Isaiah 53 and Christian Origins* (Harrisburg, PA: Trinity Press International, 1998), 251-259

Baldwin, B., *Suetonius* (Amsterdam: Hakkert, 1983).

Baldwin, J.G., *Haggai, Zechariah, Malachi* (Tyndale New Testament Commentaries. Leicester: Tyndale Press, 1972).

Bammel, E., 'The Revolution Theory from Reimarus to Brandon', in E. Bammel and C.F.D. Moule (eds.), *Jesus and the Politics of His Day* (Cambridge/London/New York: CUP, 1984), 11-68.

Barbé, D., *A Theology of Conflict: and other writings on Nonviolence* (Maryknoll, NY: Orbis Books, 1989).

Barclay, J.M.G., 'Deviance and Apostasy: Some applications of deviance theory to first-century Judaism and Christianity', in P. F. Esler, (ed.), *Modelling early Christianity: Social-scientific studies of the New Testament in its context* (London/New York: Routledge, 1995), 114-127.

—, *Jews in the Mediterranean Diaspora: From Alexander to Trajan (323 BCE-117 CE)* (Edinburgh: T & T, 1996).

Barclay, W., *The Revelation of John* (2 Vols. Daily Study of the Bible. Edinburgh: St. Andrews Press, 1976).

Barker, M., *The Older Testament* (London: SPCK, 1987).

—, *The Lost Prophet* (London: SPCK, 1988).

—, *The Gate of Heaven: The History and Symbolism of the Temple in Jerusalem* (London: SPCK, 1991).

—, *The Great Angel: A Study of Israel's Second God*, (London: SPCK, 1992).

—, *The Risen Lord: The Jesus of History as the Christ of Faith* (Edinburgh: T & T, 1996).

Barnard, L.W., 'Clement of Rome', *New Testament Studies* 10 (1963-64), 271-260.

Barrett, C.K., 'The Lamb of God', *New Testament Studies 1* (1954/55), 210-218.

Bartlett, A.W., *Cross Purposes: The Violent Grammar of Christian Atonement* (Harrisburg, Pennsylvania: Trinity Press International, 2001).

Barton, J., *Reading the Old Testament: Method in Biblical Study* (London: Darton Longman and Todd, 1984).

Bauckham, R.J., 'The Martyrdom of Enoch and Elijah: Jewish or Christian?' *Journal of Biblical Literature* 95 (1976), 447-458.

—, *Jude, 2 Peter* (Word Bible Commentary 50. Waco, Texas: Word Books, 1983).

—, *The Bible in Politics: How to Read the Bible Politically* (Louisville, Kentucky: Westminster/John Knox Press 1989).

—, *Jude and the Relatives of Jesus in the Early Church* (Edinburgh: T&T Clark, 1990).

—, *The Climax of Prophecy: Studies on the Book of Revelation* (Edinburgh: T&T Clark Press, 1993a).

—, *The Theology of the Book of Revelation.* (Cambridge: CUP, 1993b).

— 'God in the Book of Revelation', *Proceedings of the Irish Biblical Association* 18 (1995), 40-53.

—, 'The Relevance of Extra-Canonical Jewish Texts to New Testament Study', in J.B. Green (ed.), *Hearing the New Testament: Strategies for Interpretation*, (Carlisle: Paternoster, 1995), 90-108.

—, 'Life, Death, and the Afterlife in Second Temple Judaism', in R.N. Longenecker (ed.), *Life in the Face of death: The Resurrection Message of the New Testament*, (Grand Rapids, Michigan/Cambridge, UK: Eerdmans, 1998), 80-95.

Bauckham, R. and T. Hart, *Hope Against Hope: Christian Eschatology in Contemporary Context* (London: DLT, 1999).

Beagley, A.J., *The "Sitz im Leben" of the Apocalypse with Particular Reference to the Church's Enemies* (Beihefte zur Zeitschrift für Theologie und Kirche 50. Berlin/New York: de Gruyter, 1987).

Beale, G.K. 'The Origin of the Title "King of Kings and Lord of Lords" in Revelation 17.14', *New Testament Studies* 31 (1985), 618-620.

—, *The Use of Daniel in Jewish Apocalyptic Literature and in the Revelation of St John* (Lanham/New York/London: University of America Press, 1994).

—, 'The Old Testament Background of Rev 3.14', *New Testament Studies* 42 (1996), 133-152.

—, *The Book of Revelation: The New International Greek New Testament Commentary* (Grand Rapids, Michigan: Eerdmans, 1999/Cambridge: Paternoster, 1999).

Beall, T., *Josephus' Description of the Essenes Illustrated by the Dead Sea Scrolls* (Society for New Testament Studies Monograph Series 58. Cambridge: CUP, 1988).

Beasley-Murray, G.R., *The Book of Revelation* (New Century Bible. London: Marshall, Morgan & Scott, 1983).

Beck, D.M., 'The Christology of the Apocalypse of John', in E.P. Booth (ed.), *New Testament Studies: Critical Essays in New Testament Interpretation, with Special Reference to the Meaning and Worth of Jesus* (New York: Abingdon-Cokesbury Press (1942)), 253-277.

Beckwith, I.T., *The Apocalypse of John* (New York: The Macmillan Company, 1919).

Bell, A.A., 'The Date of the Apocalypse. The Evidence of some Roman Historians Reconsidered ', *New Testament Studies* 25 (1979), 93-102.

Berger, P. L., *Invitation to Sociology: A Humanistic Perspective* (Harmondsworth: Penguin, 1986 revised edition).

—, *The Sacred Canopy: Elements of A Sociological Theory of Religion* (New York/London/Toronto/Sydney/Auckland: Anchor Book, revised edition 1990).

Best, E., *The Temptation and the Passion: The Markan Soteriology* (Society for New Testament Studies Monograph Series 2. Cambridge: CUP, 1965).

—, *Mark: The Gospel as Story* (Edinburgh: T&T Clark, 1988).

Betz, O., 'Jesus and Isaiah 53', in W.H. Bellinger Jr and W.R. Farmer (eds.), *Jesus and the Suffering Servant: Isaiah 53 and Christian Origins* (Harrisburg, PA: Trinity Press International, 1998), 70-87.

Black, M., *The Scrolls and Christian Origins* (London: Thomas Nelson and Sons, 1961).

—, '"Not peace but a sword": Matt. 10.34ff; Luke 12.5ff', in Bammel and Moule (eds.), *Jesus and the Politics of His Day* (Cambridge/London/New York: CUP, 1984), 287-294.

—, *The Book of Enoch or 1 Enoch* (Studia in Veteris Testamenti Pseudepigrapha V11. Leiden: Brill, 1985).

Blaiklock, E.M., *Acts* (Tyndale New Testament Commentaries. Leicester: Tyndale Press, 1977).

Blass, F., and A. Debrunner, *A Greek Grammar of the New Testament and Other Early Christian Literature* (tr. R.W. Funk. Chicago/London: The University of Chicago Press, 1961).

Bloom, H., *The Revelation of St. John the Divine* (New York: Chelsea House Publishers, 1988).

Bondurant, J., *Conquest of Violence: the Gandhian Philosophy of Conflict* (Berkeley/Los Angeles: University of California Press, 1965).

Borgen, P., *Early Christianity and Hellenistic Judaism* (Edinburgh: T&T Clark, 1996).

Boring, M.E. 'How May We Identify Oracles of Christian Prophets in the Synoptic Tradition. Mark 3.28-29 as a Test Case', *Journal of Biblical Literature* 91 (1972), 501-521.

—, 'The Theology of Revelation: "The Lord Our God the Almighty Reigns"', *Interpretation* 40 (1986), 257-269.

Bovon, F., 'Le Christ de L'Apocalypse ', *Revue de Théologie et de philosophie* 21 (1972), 65-80.

Bowker, J., *The Targums and Rabbinic Literature: An Introduction to Jewish Interpretation of Scripture* (Cambridge: CUP, 1969).

Boyle, I. (ed.), *The Ecclesiastical History of Eusebius Pamphilius* (Tr. S. E. Parker. Grand Rapids, Michigan: Guardian Press, 1976).

Bowersock, G. W., *Martyrdom and Rome* (Cambridge: CUP, 1995).

Brandon, S. F. G., *Jesus and the Zealots* (Manchester: Manchester University Press, 1967).

Braver, S.L., 'When Martyrdom Pays: The Effects of Information Concerning the Opponents' Past Game Behavior', *Journal of Conflict Resolution* vol 19, No. 4 (1975), 652-662.

Bredin, M.R., 'The Influence of the Aqedah on Revelation 5.6-9', *Irish Biblical Studies* 18 (1996a), 26-43.

—, 'Gentiles and the Davidic Tradition in Matthew', in A. Brenner (ed.), *A Feminist Companion to the Hebrew Bible in the New Testament* (Sheffield: Sheffield Academic Press, 1996b), 95-111.

—, 'The Synagogue of Satan Accusation in Revelation 2.9', *Biblical Theological Bulletin* 28 (1998), 160-164.

Brett, M.G., 'Intratextuality', in R.J. Coggins and J.L. Houlden (eds.), *A Dictionary of Biblical Interpretation* (London: SCM, 1990), 320-321.

Brownlee, W.H., 'Messianic Motifs of Qumran and the New Testament', *New Testament Studies* 3/3 (1957), 195-210.

—, *The Meaning of the Qumran Scrolls for the Bible: with special attention to the Book of Isaiah* (New York: OUP, 1964).

—, 'From Holy War to Holy Martyrdom', in H.B. Huffmon, F.A.Spina, A.R.W. Green, (eds.), *The Quest for the Kingdom of God: Studies in honor of G.E. Mendenhall* (Winona Lake: Eisenbrauns, 1983), 281-292.

—, *Ezekiel* 1-19 (Word Bible Commentary 28; Dallas: Word Books, 1986).

Brox, N., *Zeuge und Märtyrer* (Studien zum Alten und Neuen Testament 5. Munich: Kosel-Verlag, 1961).

Bruce, F.F., *Biblical Exegesis in the Qumran Texts* (London: The Tyndale Press, 1960).

—, 'Qumran and Early Christianity', *New Testament Studies* 2/3 (1955-1956), 176-190.

Buchanan, G.W., *The Book of Revelation: Introduction and Prophecy* (Mellon Biblical Commentary, New Testament Series. Lewiston: Mellon, 1993).

Bultmann, R., *Theology of the New Testament* (vols.1 and 2. Tr. K. Grobel. London: SCM, 1955).

—, 'New Testament and Mythology', in H.W. Bartsch (ed.), *Kerygma and Myth: A Theological Debate* (Tr. R.H. Fuller, London: SPCK, 1957).

Caird, G.B., *War and the Christian* (London: The Fellowship of Reconciliation, 1955)

—, *Principalities and Powers* (Oxford: Clarendon Press, 1956).

—, *The Language and Image of the Bible* (London: G. Duckworth & Co., 1980).

—, *A Commentary on the Revelation of St John the Divine* (Black New Testament Commentaries. London: A & C Black, 1984 second edition).

Campenhausen, H.F. von, *Die Idee des Martyriums in der alten Kirche* (Göttingen: Vandenhoeck & Ruprecht, 1964).

Carnegie, D. R., 'Worthy is the Lamb: The hymns in Revelation', in H.H. Rowden (ed.) *Christ the Lord: Studies in Christology presented to Donald Guthrie*, (Leicester: IVP, 1982).

Carradice, I., *Coinage and Finances in the Reign of Domitian AD 81-96* (Oxford: BAR International Series 178, 1983).

—, 'Coin Types and Roman History: The Example of Domitian', in M. Price, A. Burnett and R. Bland (eds.), *Essays in Honour of Robert Carson and Kenneth Jenkins*, (London: Spink, 1993), 161-175.

Carrell, R.R., *Jesus and the Angels* (Society of New Testament Studies Monograph Series 95. Cambridge. CUP, 1997).

Carroll, R.P., *Jeremiah* (Old Testament Library. London: SCM, 1986).

Carson, R.A.G., *Coins of the Roman Empire* (London/New York: Routledge, 1990).

Casey, J., *Exodus Typology in the Book of Revelation* (PhD dissertation, Southern Baptist Theological Seminary, 1981-82).

—, 'The Exodus Theme in the Book of Revelation against the Background of the New Testament ', *Concilium* 189 (1987), 34-43.

Casey, M., *Son of Man: The Interpretation and Influence of Daniel 7* (London: SPCK, 1979).

Charles, J., 'An Apocalyptic Tribute to the Lamb (Rev 5.1-14) ', *Journal of the Evangelical Theological Society* 34/4 (December 1991), 461-473.

Charles, R.H., *The Revelation of St. John* (International Critical Commentary. 2 vols. Edinburgh: T&T Clark, 1920).

Charles, R.H., *The Apocrypha and Pseudepigrapha of the Old Testament in English 2 vols* (Oxford: Clarendon Press, 1913).

Charlesworth, J.H., (ed.) *The Old Testament Pseudepigrapha* (Vol. 1. New York/London/Toronto/Sydney/Auckland: Douleday, 1983).

Charlesworth, J.H., (ed.) *The Old Testament Pseudepigrapha* (Vol. 2. New York/London/Toronto/Sydney/Auckland: Douleday, 1983).

Charlesworth, M.P., 'Some Observations on the Ruler-Cult Especially in Rome ', *Harvard Theological Review* 28 (1935), 1-42.

Chavasse, C., 'The Suffering Servant and Moses', *Church Quarterly Review* 165 (1964), 152-163.

Childs, B.S., *Exodus* (Old Testament Library. London: SCM, 1974).

Chilton, D. *The Days of Vengeance: An exposition of the Book of Revelation* (Texas: Dominion Press, 1990).

Clements, R.E., 'Isaiah 53 and the Restoration of Israel', in W.H. Bellinger Jr and W.R. Farmer (eds.), *Jesus and the Suffering Servant: Isaiah 53 and Christian Origins*, (Harrisburg, PA: Trinity Press International, 1998), 39-54.

Coggins, J., and S. Paul Re'emi, *Nahum, Obadiah, Esther: Israel among the Nations* (International Theological Commentary. Edinburgh: The Handsel Press, 1985).

Cohen, S., *From the Maccabees to the Mishnah* (Library of Early Christianity 7. Philadelphia: Westminster, 1987).

Cohen, S.J.D., 'Crossing the Boundary and becoming a Jew', *Harvard Theological Review* 82:1(1989), 13-33.

Coker, G., 'Peace and the Apocalypse: Stanley Hauerwas and Miroslav Volf on the Eschatological Basis for Christian Nonviolence', *Evangelical Quar erly* 71 (1999), 261-268.

Collins, J.J., *A Commentary on the Book of Daniel* (Minneapolis: Fortress Press, 1993).

Comblin, J., *Le Christ dans l'Apocalypse* (Bibliothèque de Théologie; Théologie biblique 3/6. Paris: Desclée, 1965).

Cooke, G.A., *The Book of Ezekiel* (International Critical Commentary. Edinburgh: T&T Clark, 1936).

Court, J.K., *Myth and History in the Book of Revelation* (London: SPCK, 1979).

—, *Revelation: New Testament Guides* (Sheffield: Journal for the Study of the Old Testament, 1994).

Corsini, E., *The Apocalypse: The Perennial Revelation of Jesus Christ* (Tr. F.J. Moloney. Dublin: Veritas, 1983/Wilmington, Delaware: Glazier, 1983).

Crone, T.M., *Early Christian Prophecy: A Study of its Origin and Function* (Baltimore: St. Mary's University Press, 1973).

Croy, N.C., *Endurance in Suffering: Hebrews 12.1-13 in its rhetorical, religious and Philosophical Context* (Society for New Testament Monograph Series 98. Cambridge: CUP, 1998).

Dahl, N. A., *The Crucified Messiah, and other Essays* (Minneapolis: Augsburg Publishing House, 1974).

Daly, R.J., 'The Soteriological Significance of the Sacrifice of Isaac', *Catholic Biblical Quarterly* 39 (1977), 45-75.

—, *The Origins of the Christian Doctrine of Sacrifice* (Philadelphia: Fortress Press, 1978).

D'Angelo, M.R., *Moses in the Letter to the Hebrews* (Society of Biblical Literature Dissertation Series 42. Missoula, Montana: Scholars Press, 1979).

Davis, D.R., *The Heavenly Court Judgement of Revelation* 4-5 (Lanham: University Press of America, 1992).

Davies, P.R. and B.D. Chilton, 'The Aqedah: A Revised Tradition History ', *Catholic Biblical Quarterly* 40 (1978), 514-546.

Dear, J., *Our God is Nonviolent: Witnesses in the Struggle for Peace and Justice* (New York: The Pilgrim Press, 1990).

Delehaye, H., 'Martyr et Confesseur', *Analecta Bollandiana* 39 (1921), 20-49.

de Ste. Croix, G.E.M., 'Why were the Early Christians Persecuted?', *Past and Present* 26 (1963), 6-38.

Dehandschutter, B., 'The Meaning of Witness in the Apocalypse', in J. Lambrecht (ed.), *L' Apocalypse johannique et l'Apocalyptique dans le Nouveau Testament* (Bibliotheca ephemeridum theogicarum Lovaniensium 53. Gembloux: Duculot/Leuven: University Press, 1980), 283-288.

Desilva, D.A., 'The Social Setting of the Revelation to John: conflict within, tears without ', *West Theological Journal* 54 (1992), 273-302.

Deutsch, C., 'Transformation of Symbols: The New Jerusalem in Rev 21.3-22.5 ', *Zeitschrift für Theologie die neutestamentliche Wissenschaft* 78 (1987), 106-126.

Desjardins, M., *Peace, Violence and the New Testament* (The Biblical Seminar 46. Sheffield: Sheffield Academic Press, 1997).

Dodd, C.H., *The Epistle of Paul to the Romans* (The Moffatt New Testament Commentary. London: Hodder & Stoughton, 1932).

—, *The Interpretation of the Fourth Gospel* (Cambridge: CUP, 1963).

Downing, F.G., 'Pliny's Prosecutions of Christians: Revelation and 1 Peter', *Journal for the Study of the New Testament* 34 (1988), 105-123.

Downing, J., 'Jesus and Martyrdom', *Journal of Theological Studies* 14 (1963), 279-293.

Dunn, J.D.G., *Romans* (Word Bible Commentary 38. Dallas: Word, 1988).

Eaton, J.H., *Psalms* (Torch Bible. London: SCM, 1967).

Eichrodt, W., *Ezekiel: A Commentary* (Old Testament Library. London: SCM, 1970).

Eissfeldt, O. *The Old Testament: An Introduction* (Tr. P.R. Ackroyd, London: Blackwell, 1964).

Ektor, J., 'L'Impassibilité et L'Objectivité de Suétone', *Les Etudes Classiques* (1980) 317-326.

Ellacuría, I., 'Violence and Non-Violence in the Struggle for Peace and Liberation', *Concilium* 195 (1988), 69-77.

Ellwanger, W.H., 'The Christology of the Apocalypse', *Concordia Theological Monthly* 1 (1930), 512-528.

Engnell, I., *Critical Essays on the Old Testament* (Tr. J.T. Willis. London: SPCK, 1970).

Esler, P.F., *Trade and Sorcery in the Book of Revelation* (unpublished 1991).

—, *The First Christians in their Social World: Social Scientific approaches to New Testament interpretation* (London/New York: Routledge, 1994).

—, *Modelling early Christianity: Social-Scientific studies of the New Testament in its context* (London/New York: Routledge, 1995).

Farrer, A., A Rebirth of Images: The Making of St John's Apocalypse (Westminster: Dacre Press, 1949).

—, Revelation of St John the Divine (Oxford: Clarendon Press, 1964).

Fekkes, J., Isaiah and Prophetic Traditions in the Book of Revelation: Visionary Antecedents and their Development (Journal for the Study of the New Testament Supplement Series 93. Shefifield: JSOT Press, 1993).

Feldman, L.H., 'Josephus' Version of the Binding of Isaac', SBL 1982 Seminar Papers (Chico, CA: Scholars Press), 113-128.

—, Jew and Gentile in the Ancient World. Attitudes and Interactions from Alexander to Justinian (Princeton: Princeton University Press, 1993).

Finley, M.I., The Ancient Economy (London: Penguin Books, 1992).

Fischel, H.A., 'Martyr and Prophet', *Jewish Quarterly Review* 37 (1946-47), 265-280, 363-386.

Fishbane, M., Biblical Interpretation in Ancient Israel (Oxford: Clarendon Press, 1985).

Ford, J.M., Revelation (The Anchor Bible 38. Garden City, New York: Doubleday, 1975).

—, My Enemy is my Guest: Jesus and Violence in Luke (Maryknoll, NY: Orbis Books, 1984).

France, R.T., Jesus and The Old Testament: his application of Old Testament Passages to himself and his mission (London: Tyndale Press, 1971).

—, Matthew (Tyndale New Testament Commentaries. Leicester: Tyndale Press, 1987).

Fraser, A. 'Nahum', in Guthrie, Motyer, Stibbs and Wiseman (eds.), The New Bible Commentary Revised (Leicester: Tyndale Press, 1979).

Frend, W.H.C., 'The Persecutions: Some links between Judaism and the Early Church', The *Journal of Ecclesiastical History* 9 (1958), 141-158.

—, Martyrdom and Persecution in the Early Church (Oxford: Basil Blackwell, 1965).

Friesen, S.J., Twice Neokoros: Ephesus, Asia and the cult of the Flavian imperial family (Leiden/New York/Köln: Brill, 1993).

—, 'Revelation, Realia, and Religion: Archaeology in the Interpetation of the Apocalypse', *Harvard Theological Review* 88:3 (1995), 291-314.

Gager, J.G., Kingdom and Community: The Social World of Early Christianity (Englewood, New Jersey: Prentice-Hall, 1975).

—, The origns of Anti-Semitism: Attitudes Toward Judaism in Pagan and Christian Antiquity (New York/Oxford: OUP, 1983).

Gandhi, M., Non-violence in Peace and War vols.1-2 (Ahmedabad: Navajivan Publishing House, 1948).

Garnet, P., Salvation and Atonement in the Qumran Scrolls (Wissenschaftliche Untersuchungen zum Neuen Testament, 2. Tübingen: J.C.B. Mohr, 1977).

Garnsey, P. and R. Saller, The Roman Empire: Economy, Society and Culture (London: Duckworth, 1996).

Garrett, S., 'Revelation', in C.A. Newson and S.H. Ringe (eds.), The Women's Bible Commentary, (London/Lousville: SPCK/John Knox Press, 1992), 377-382.

Gelston, A., 'Universalism in Second Isaiah', *Journal of Theological Studies* 43 (1992), 377-398.

Georgi, D., Weisheit Salomos (Jüdische Schriften aus hellenistisch römischer zeit IIII.4, Gütersloh: Gerd Mohn, 1980).

Geyer, J.B., 'Mythology and Culture in the Oracles against the Nations', *Vetus Testamentum* 36 (1986), 129-145.

Giblin, C. H., 'Revelation 11.1-13: Its Form, Function and Contextual Integration', *New Testament Studies* 30 (1984), 433-456.

—, The Book of Revelation: The Open Book of Prophecy (Good News Studies 34. Collegeville, Minnesota: The Liturgical Press, 1991).

Ginsberg, G.L., 'The Oldest Interpretation of the Suffering Servant', *Vetus Testamentum* 3/4 (1953), 400-404.

Girard, R., I see Satan Fall Like Lightning (Maryknoll, NY: Oribis Books, 2001).

Glasson, T.F., Moses in the Fourth Gospel (Studies in Biblical Theology 40. London: SCM Press, 1963).

Golb, N., 'The Problem of Origin and Identification of the Dead Sea Scrolls', *Proceedings of the American Philosophical Society* 124 (1980), 1-24.

Goldingay, J. E., Daniel (Word Bible Commentary 30. Dallas: Word Books, 1987).

Goodenough, E.R., Jewish Symbols in the Graeco-Roman World (New York: Pantheon Books/Princeton University Press).

Goodman, M., 'Nerva, the fiscus Judaicus and Jewish Identity', *Journal of Roman Studies* 79 (1989), 41-44.

—, 'Jewish Proselytizing in the First Century', in J. Lieu, J. North and T. Rajak, (eds.), The Jews among Pagans and Christians In the Roman Empire (London/New York: Routledge, 1992), 53-78.

—, Mission and Conversion. Proselytizing in the Religious History of the Roman Empire (Oxford: Oxford University Press, 1994).

Grabbe, L.L., 'The Jannes/Jambres Tradition in Targum Pseudo-Jonathan and its Date', *Journal of Biblical Literature* 98/3 (1979), 393-401.

—, Wisdom of Solomon (Sheffield: Sheffield Academic Press, 1997).

Grant, M., The Ancient Historians (London: Weidenfield and Nicolson, 1970).

—, Greek and Roman Historians: Information and misinformation (London/New York: Routledge: 1994).

Graves, R., *Suetonius' The Twelve Caesars* (Harmondsworth: Baltmore, Penguin Books, 1957).

Green, B., *Mikhail Bakhtin and Biblical Scholarship: An Introduction* (SBL. Atlanta, Georgia, 2000).

Greene, T.M., The Light in Troy: Imitation and Discovery in Renaissance Poetry (Yale: Yale University Press, 1982).

Grelot, P., 'Les Targums du Pentatuque - Étude comparative d'après Genèse 4', *Semitica* 9 (1959), 59-88.

Grimsrud, T., 'Scapegoating No More: Christian Pacifism and New Testament Views of Jesus' Death', in W.M. Swartley (ed.), Violence Renounced: René Girard, Biblical Studies and Peacemaking, (Studies in Peace and Scripture 4. Institute of Mennonite Studies. Telford, Pennsylvania: Pandora Press, 2000), 49-69.

Günter, E., 'Zeuge und Märtyrer', *Zeitschrift für Theologie die neutestamentliche Wissenschaft* 47 (1956), 145-161.

Habel, N.C., *The Book of Job* (Old Testament Library. London: SCM, 1985).

Hadas, M., *The Third and Fourth Books of Maccabees* (New York: Harper & Brothers, 1953).

Hafemann, S. J. 'Moses in the Apocrypha and Pseudepigrapha: A survey', *Journal for the Study of the Pseudepigrapha* 7 (1990), 79-104.

Hall, S., *Melito of Sardis on Pascha and fragments* (Oxford: Oxford Early Christian Texts. 1979).

Hanson, A.T., *The Wrath of the Lamb* (London: SCM, 1957).

Hanson, P.D., 'The World of the Servant of the Lord in Isaiah 40-55', in W.H. Bellinger Jr and W.R. Farmer (eds.), *Jesus and the Suffering Servant: Isaiah 53 and Christian Origins*, (Harrisburg, PA: Trinity Press International, 1998), 9-22.

Harrington, W., *Revelation* (Sacra Pagina 16. Collegeville: The Liturgical Press, 1993).

—, 'Worthy is the Lamb', *Proceedings of the Irish Biblical Association* 18 (1995), 54-70.

Harris, B.F., 'Domitian, The Emperor Cult and Revelation', *Prudentia* 11/1 (1979), 15-25.

Hayes, R.B., *The Moral Vision of the New Testament: A Contemporary Introduction to New Testament Ethics* (Edinburgh: T&T Clark, 1996).

Hayes, J.H., 'The Usage of Oracles Against Foreign Nations in Ancient Israel', *Journal of Biblical Literature* 87 (1968), 81-92.

Hayward, R., 'The Present State of Research into the Targumic Account of the Sacrifice of Isaac', *Journal of Jewish Studies* 32 (1981), 127-150.

—, 'The Sacrifice of Isaac and Jewish Polemic against Christianity', *Catholic Biblical Quarterly* 52 (1990), 292-306.

Hemer, C.J., 'The Edfu Osraka and the Jewish Tax', *Palestinian Exploration Quarterly* 105 (1973), 6-12.

—, *The Letters to the Seven Churches of Asia in their Local Setting* (Journal for the Study of the New Testament Supplement Series 11. Sheffied: JSOT Press, 1986).

Henderson, B.W., *Five Roman Emperors: Vespasian-Trajan, AD 69-117* (Cambridge: CUP, 1927).

Hengel, M., *Was Jesus a Revolutionist?* (Tr. W. Klassen. Philadelphia, PA: Fortress Press, 1971).

—, *Judaism and Hellenism* (London: SCM, 1974).

—, *The Atonement: The Origins of the Doctrine of the Atonement in the New Testament* (Tr. J. Bowden, London: SCM, 1981).

—, *The Zealots: Investigations into the Jewish Freedom Movement in the Period from Herod 1 until 70 AD* (Tr. D. Smith, Edinburgh: T. & T. Clark, 1989).

Hick, J., *Evil and the God of Love* (The Fontana Library. Thetford: Collins, 1974).

—, *The Fifth Dimension: An Exploration of the Spiritual Realm* (Oxford: One World, 1999).

Hill, D., 'Prophecy and Prophets in the Revelation of St. John', *New Testament Studies* 18 (1972-1972), 401-418.

Hillyer, N., "'The Lamb" in the Apocalypse ', *The Evangelical Quarterly Review* Vol 1, 39, No 4 (1967), 228-236.

Holtz, T., *Die Christologie der Apokalypse des Johannes* (Text und Untersuchungen zur Geschichte der Altchristlichen Literatur 85. Berlin: Akademie Verlag, 1962).

Hope, M. and J. Young, *The Struggle for Humanity: Agents of Nonviolent Change in a Violent World* (Maryknoll, NY: Orbis Books, 1977).

Horsley, R.A., *Jesus and the Spiral of Violence: Popular Jewish Resistance in Roman Palestine* (San Francisco: Harper & Row, 1987).

Hurtado, L.W., 'Revelation 4-5 in the Light of Jewish Apocalyptic Analogies ', *Journal for the Study of the New Testament* 25 (1985), 105-124.

Hyatt, J.P., *Exodus* (New Century Bible. Eerdmans: Marshall, Morgan & Scott: London, 1983).

Ikeda, Y., 'Solomon's Trade in Horses and Chariots', in T. Ishida (ed.) *Studies in the Period of David and Solomon and other Essays*, (Tokyo: Yamakawa-Shuppanisha, 1982,), 215-238

Inman, A., 'This is the Lamb of God ', *New Blackfriars* 74/870 (April 1993), 191-196.

Isenberg, S., 'An Anti-Sadducee Polemic in the Palestininan Targum Tradition', *Harvard Theological Review* 63 (1970), 433-444.

Jaeger, W., *Paideia: The Ideals of Greek Culture* (3 vols, tr .G. Highet, New York: OUP, 1939-44).

Janzen, E.P., 'The Jesus of the Apocalypse Wears the Emperor's Clothes', in *SBL 1994 Seminar Papers*, (Atlanta, Georgia: Scholars Press), 637-661.

Jauss, H.R., 'Reception Theory and Reader-Response Criticism', in K.M. Newton (ed.) *Twentieth-Century Literary Theory: A Reader*, (New York, N.Y: St. Martin's Press, 1997), 189-194.

Jeremias, J., *The Eucharistic Words of Jesus* (New Testament Library, London: SCM Press Limited, 1966).

—, *New Testament Theology: The Proclamation of Jesus, vol.1* (New Testament Library. London: SCM, 1971).

—, *The Parables of Jesus* (Tr. S.H. Hooke. London: SCM, 1972).

—, 'Μωυσης', in G. Kittel (ed.), , *Theological Dictionary of the New Testament vol. 1V*, (Tr. G.W. Bromiley. Grand Rapids, Michigan: Eerdmans, 1967a), 848-873.

—, 'παῖς θεοῦ', in G. Kittel (ed),. *Theological Dictionary of the New Testament vol. V*, (Tr. G.W. Bromiley. Grand Rapids, Michigan: Eerdmans, 1967b), 654-717.

Jesudasan, I., *A Gandhian Theology of Liberation* (MaryKnoll, NY: Orbis Books, 1984).

Johnson, H., *The International Book of Trees* (London: Mitchell Beazley, 1973).

Johnson, S.E., 'Asia Minor and Early Christianity', in J. Neusner (ed.) *Christianity, Judaism and Other Greco-Roman Cults: Studies for Morton Smith at Sixty*, (Studies in Judaism in Late Antiquity 12 part 2. Leiden: Brill, 1975), 77-145.

Jones, B.W., *The Emperor Domitian* (London/New York: Routledge, 1992).

—, *Suetonius: Domitian* (Bristol: Bristol Classical Press, 1996).

Jones, D.R., *Haggai, Zechariah and Malachi* (Torch Bible Commentaries. London: SCM, 1962).

Jung, C.G., *Answer to Job* (Tr. R.F.C. Hull. London: Hodder and Stoughton, 1965).

Kaïser, O., *Isaiah 13-39* (Old Testament Library. London: SCM, 1980).

Kennedy, G., *Quintilian* (Twayne's World Author Series 66. New York: Twayne Publishers, 1969).

Keresztes, P., 'The Jews, the Christians, and Emperor Domitian', *Vigilae Christianae* 27 (1973), 1-28.

Kiddle, M., *The Revelation of St. John* (Moffat's New Testament Commentary. London: Hodder & Stoughton, 1940).

Kim, S., 'The sayings of Jesus in Paul's Letters', in G. Hawthorne, R. Martin and D. Reid (eds.), *Dictionary of Paul and His Letters: A Compendium of Contemporary Biblical Scholarship* (Leicester: Tyndale Press, 1993).

Klassen, W., 'Vengeance in the Apocalypse of John', *Catholic Biblical Quarterly* 28, (1966) 300-311.

—, *Love of Enemies: The Way to Peace* (Overtures to Biblical Theology 15. Philadelphia, PA: Fortress Press, 1984).

—, '"Peace" and "War in the New Testament', in D.N. Freedman *et al* (eds.), *The Doubleday Anchor Bible Dictionary* (New York: Doubleday, 1992), vol.5, 206-212 and vol.6, 867-875.

—, 'Jesus and the Zealot Option', in S. Hauerwas *et al* (eds.), *The Wisdom of the Cross: essays in honor of John Howard Yoder* (Grand Rapids, Michigan/Cambridge, UK: Eerdmans, 1999) 131-149

Knibb, M.A., *The Ethiopic Book of Enoch* (Vol. 2. Oxford: Clarendon Press, 1978).

Knight, D., *Rediscovering the Traditions of Israel* (SBL Dissertation Series 9; Missoula: Scholars Press, 1975).

Knight, J., *Revelation* (Readings: A New Biblical Commentary. Sheffield: Sheffield University Press, 1999).

Koch, K., 'Das Lamm, das Agypten vernichtet', *Zeitschrift für Theologie die neutestamentliche Wissenschaft* 57 (1966), 79-93.

Kolarcik, M. *The Ambiguity of Death in the Book of Wisdom: A Study of Literary Structure and Interpretation* (Analecta Biblica 127. Roma: Editrice Pontificio Instituto, 1991).

Kraabel, A. T., 'Melito the Bishop and the Synagogue at Sardis: Text and Context', in D. G. Martin, J. G. Pedley and J. A, Scott (eds.) *Studies Presented to George M.A. Hanfmann* (Mainz: Verlag Philipp von Zabern, 1971), 77-85.

Kraft. H. *Die Offenbarung des Johannes* (Handbuch zum Neuen Testament 16a. Tübingen: Mohr [Siebeck], 1974).

Kraybill, J.N., *Imperial Cult and Commerce in John's Apocalypse* (Journal for the Study of the New Testament Supplement Series 132. Sheffield: Sheffield Academic Press, 1996).

Kristeva, J. 'Word, Dialogue and Novel', in *Desire in Language: A Semiotic Approach to Literature and Art* (Tr. L.S. Roudiez; New York: Columbia University Press, 1980).

Krodel, G. A., *Revelation* (Augsburg Commentary on the New Testament. Minneapolis: Augsburg, 1989)

Kumar, S., *Non-Violence or Non-Existence: the Gandhian ideology of a non-violent society* (London: Christian Action, 1969).

Ladd, G.E., *A Commentary on the Revelation of John* (Michigan: Eerdmans, 1978).

Lampe, G.W.H., 'Martyrdom and Inspiration', in W. Horbury and B. McNeil (eds.), *Suffering and Martyrdom in the New Testament: Studies presented to G.M. Styler*, (Cambridge: CUP, 1981), 118-135.

Lampe, P., *Die Stadtrömischen Christen in den ersten beiden Jahrhunderten* (Wissenschafliche Untersuchungen zum Neuen Testament 2.18. Tübingen: Mohr [Siebeck] 1982).

Lange, S. 'The Wisdom of Solomon and Plato', *Journal of Biblical Literature* 55 (1936), 293-302.

Larkin, K., *The Eschatology of Second Zechariah: A Study of the Formation of a Mantological Wisdom Anthology* (Kampen-the Netherlands: Pharos, 1994).

Laqueur, R., *Der jüdische Historiker Flavius Josephus* (Studia 68. Roma: Bretshneider, 1970 [originally published 1920]).

Lawrence, D. H., *Apocalypse* (Harmondsworth: Penguin Books, reprint 1960).

Laws, S., *In the Light of the Lamb: Imagery, Parody, and Theology in the Apocalypse of John* (Good New Studies vol 31. Wilmington, Delaware: M. Glazier, 1988).

Leaney, A.R.C., *Cambridge Commentaries on the Writings of the Jewish and Christian World 200 BC to 200 CE* (Cambridge: CUP, 1989).

Leske, A.M., 'Isaiah and Matthew: The Prophetic Influence in the First Gospel', in W.H. Bellinger Jr and W.R. Farmer (eds.), *Jesus and the Suffering Servant: Isaiah 53 and Christian Origins*, (Harrisburg, PA: Trinity Press International, 1998), 152-170.

Le Déaut, R., *La Nuit Pascale: Essai sur la signification de la Pâque juive à partir du Targum d'Exode XII 4* (Analecta Biblica 22. Rome: Institut Biblique Pontifical, 1963).

Levenson, J.D. *The Death and Resurrection of the Beloved Son* (New Haven/London: Yale University Press, 1993).

Licht, J., 'Taxo or the Apocalyptic Doctrine of Vengeance', *Journal of Biblical Literature* 12 (1961) 95-103.

Lieu, J.M., 'History and theology in Christian views of Judaism', in J. Lieu, J. North and T. Rajak, (eds.), *The Jews among Pagans and Christians In the Roman Empire*, (London/New York: Routledge, 1992), 79-96.

—, '"The Parting of the Ways": Theological Construct or Historical Reality', *Journal for the Study of the New Testament* 56 (1994), 101-119.

—, *Image and Reality: The Jews in the World of the Christians in the Second Century* (Edinburgh: T&T Clark, 1996).

—, 'They Speak across the Centuries: Melito of Sardis', *Expository Times* 110/2 (1998), 43-46.

Lindars, B., 'A Bull, a Lamb and a Word: 1 Enoch XC. 38', *New Testament Studies* 22 (1975-76), 483-486.

—, *Jesus Son of Man: A fresh Examination of the Son of Man Sayings in the Gospels* (London: SPCK, 1983).

Lindbeck, G.A., *The Nature of Doctrine: Religion and Theory in Postliberal Age* (London: SPCK, 1984).

Lohmeyer, E., *Die Offenbarung des Johannes* (Tübingen: Mohr, 1927).

Lohse, E., *Märtyrer und Gottesknecht* (Göttingen: Vandenhoeck & Ruprecht, 1955).

Longenecker, B.W., *2 Esdras* (Sheffield: Sheffield Academic Press, 1995).

Lyonnet, S., and L., Sabourin, *Sin, Redemption, and Sacrifice, A Patristic Study* (Analecta Biblica 48. Rome: Biblical Institute Press, 1970).

Mack, B.L., and R.E. Murphy, 'Wisdom Literature', in R.A. Kraft and G.W.E. Nickelsburg (eds.), *Early Judaism and its Modern Interpreters* (Atlanta, Georgia: Scholars Press, 1986), 371-410.

Malina, B.J., *The New Testament World: Insights from Cultural Anthropology* (London: SCM, 1986).

—, 'Wealth and Poverty in the New Testament', *Interpretation* 41 (1987), 354-367.

—, 'First-Century Personality: Dyadic, not Individual', in J.H. Neyrey (ed.), *The Social World of Luke-Acts*, (Peabody, MA: Hendricksons Publishers, 1991), 67-96.

Malina, B.J and J.H. Neyrey, 'Conflict in Luke-Acts: Labelling and Deviance Theory', in J.H. Neyrey (ed.), *The Social World of Luke-Acts*, (Peabody, MA: Hendricksons Publishers, 1991), 97-124.

Mann, T.W., 'Theological Reflections on the denial of Moses', *Journal of Biblical Literature* 98/4 (1979), 481-494.

Manson, T.W., 'Martyrs and Martyrdom', *Bulletin of John Ryland's Library* 39 (1957), 463-484.

Marshall, I.H., *Acts* (Tyndale New Testament Commentaries. Leicester: Tyndale Press, 1980).

Martin-Achard, R., *From Death to Life: A Study of the Development of the Doctrine of the Resurrection in the Old Testament* (Tr. J.P. Smith; Edinburgh/London: Oliver & Boyd, 1960).

Mazzaferri, F.D., *The Genre of the Book of Revelation from a Source-critical Perspective* (Beihefte zur Zeitschrift für die neutestamentliche Wissenschaft 54. Berlin/New York: de Gruyter, 1989).

McFayden, D., 'The Occasion of the Domitianic Persecution', *Asian Journal of Theology* 24 (1920), 46-66.

McKay, H.A., 'Old Wine in New Wineskins', in A. Brenner (ed.), *A Feminist Companion to the Hebrew Bible in the New Testament*, (Sheffield: Sheffield Academic Press, 1996).

McNamara, M., *The New Testament and the Palestinian Targum to the Pentateuch* (Analecta Biblica 27. Rome: Pontifical Biblical Institute, 1966).

Meeks, W.A., *The Prophet-King: Moses Traditions and the Johannine Christology* (Supplements to Novum Testamentus XIV. Leiden: Brill, 1967).

Meeks, W.A., 'A Hermeneutics of Social Embodiment', *Harvard Theological Review* 79:1-3 (1986), 176-186.

Merton, T., 'Principles of Non-Violence', in T. Merton (ed.), *Gandhi on Non-Violence* (Boston/London: Shambhala, 1996), 69-70.

Merton, T., 'The Spirtual Dimensions of Non-Violence', in T. Merton (ed.), *Gandhi on Non-Violence*, (Boston/London: Shambhala, 1996), 108-109.

Merrill, E.T., 'The Persecution of Domitian', *Church Quarterly* (January-March, 1945), 154-164.

Millar, F., *A Study of Cassius Dio* (Oxford: Clarendon Press, 1964).

Miller, K.E., 'Nuptial Eschatology of Revelation 19-22', *Catholic Biblical Quarterly* 60 (1998), 301-318.

Miller, M.E., 'Girardian Perspectives and Christian Atonement' in W.M. Swartley, (ed.), *Violence Renounced: René Girard, Biblical Studies and Peacemaking*, (Studies in Peace and Scripture, vol.4. Telford, Pennsylvania: Pandora Press, 2000) 31-48.

Minear, P. S., *I Saw a New Earth: An Introduction to the Visions of the Apocalypse* (Washington/Cleveland: Corpus Books, 1967).

Mitchell, H. G., *Haggai, Zechariah, Malachi and Jonah* (Edinburgh: International Critical Commentary, 1912).

Moore, G.F., *Judaism* vol 1 (Cambridge: Harvard University Press, 1927).

Morris, L., *Revelation* (Tyndale New Testament Commentaries. London: Tyndale Press, 1979).

Moule, C.F.D., *The Origin of Christology* (Cambridge/New York//Melbourne/Sydney: CUP, 1990).

Mounce, R.H., *The Book of Revelation* (Grand Rapids: Eerdmans, 1977).

Moyise, S., *The Old Testament in Revelation* (Journal for the Study of the New Testament Supplement Series 115. Sheffield: Sheffield Academic Press, 1995).

—, 'Does the Lion lie down with the Lamb?' in S. Moyise (ed.), *Studies in the Book of Revelation*, (Edinburgh/New York: T&T Clark, 2001).

Müller, U.B., *Die Offenbarung des Johannes* (Gütersloh: Ökumenischer Taschenbuckerommentar zum Neuen Testament 19, 1984).

Murphy, F.L., *Pseudo Philo: Rewriting the Bible* (New York/Oxford: OUP, 1993).

Musaph-Andriesse, R.C., *From Torah to Kabbalah: A Basic Introduction to the Writings of Judaism* (Tr. J. Bowden. London: SCM, 1981).

Mussies, G., *The Morphology of Koine Greek: As Used in the Apocalypse of St. John. A study in Bilingualism* (Leiden: Brill, 1971).

Myers, C., *Binding the Strong Man: A Political Reading of Mark's Story of Jesus* (Maryknoll, NY: Orbis Books, 1988).

Nickelsburg, G.W.E., *Resurrection, Immortality, and Eternal Life in Intertestamental Judaism* (Harvard Theological Studies 26. Cambridge, 1972: Harvard University Press and London: OUP, 1972).

—, *Jewish Literature Between the Bible and the Mishnah* (London: SCM, 1981).

Neil, W., and S. Travis, *More Difficult Sayings of Jesus* (London/Oxford: Mowbray, 1981).

Niditch, S., *War in the Hebrew Bible: A study in the Ethics of Violence* (Oxford: OUP, 1993).

Nolland, J., *Word Biblical Commentary: Luke 9.21-18.34* (Word Bible Commentary 35b. Dallas: Word Books, 1993).

North, C.R., *The Suffering Servant in Deutero-Isaiah: An Historical and Critical Study* (London: OUP, 1956).

Oakman, D.E., 'The Ancient Economy and St. John's Apocalypse', *Listening: Journal of Religion and Culture* 28/3 (1993), 200-214.

O'Day, G., 'Jeremiah 9.22-23 and 1 Corinthians 1.26-31: A Study in Intertextuality', *Journal of Biblical Literature* 109 (1990), 259-267.

O'Hagan, A.P., 'The Martyrs in the Fourth Book of Maccabees ', *Studii biblici franciscani liber Testament* 24 (1974), 94-120.

O'Neill, J.C., 'Did Jesus teach that his death would be vicarious?' in W. Horbury and B. McNeil (eds.), *Suffering and Martyrdom in the New Testament: Studies presented to G.M. Styler*, (Cambridge: CUP, 1981), 9-27.

—, 'The Lamb of God in the Testaments of the Twelve Patriarchs', *Journal for the Study of the New Testament* 2 (1979), 2-30.

Onesti, K.L., and T. Brauch., 'Righteousness, Righteousness of God', in G. Hawthorne, R. Martin, D. Reid (eds.), in *Dictionary of Paul and His Letters* (A Compendium of Contemporary Biblical Scholarship. Leicester: Tyndale Press, 1993).

Parekh, B., *Gandhi* (Past Masters. Oxford/New York: OUP, 1997).

Parker, A.J., 'Trade Within the Empire and Beyond the Frontiers', in J. Wacher (ed.), *The Roman World* 11 (New York: Routledge & Kegan Paul, 1987), 635-657.

Parkes, J., *The Conflict of the Church and the Synagogue* (London: The Soncino Press, 1934).

Peels, H.G.L., *The Vengeance of God: The Meaning of the Root NQM and the Function of the NQM - Texts in the Context of Divine Revelation in the Old Testament* (Tr. W. Koopmans. Oudtestamentische Studiën 31, Leiden/New York/Köln: Brill, 1995).

Perelmann, C., and L. Olbrechts-Tyteca, *The New Rhetoric. A Treatise on Argumentation* (Notre Dame: University of Notre Dame Press, 1969).

Petersen, D.L. *Zechariah 9-14 and Malachi* (Old Testament Library. London: SCM, 1995).

Pfuhl, E.H., *The Deviance Process* (New York: van Nostrand, 1980).

Piper, J., *Love Your Enemies: Jesus' Love Command in the Synoptic Gospels and the Early Christian Paraenesis* (Society for New Testament Studies Monograph Series 38. Cambridge: University Press, 1979).

Pippin, T., *Death and Desire: The Rhetoric of Gender in the Apocalypse of John* (Literary Currents in Biblical Interpretation. Louisiville, KY/Westminster: John Knox Press, 1992).

Pleket, H.W. 'Domitian, the Senate and the Provinces', *Mnemosyne* 4th series, 14 (1961), 296-315.

Pobee, J.S., *Persecution and Martyrdom in the Theology of Paul* (Journal for the Study of the New Testament Supplement Series 6. Sheffield: JSOT Press, 1985).

Price, S.R.F., *Rituals and Power: The Roman Imperial Cult in Asia Minor* (Cambridge: Cambridge University, 1984).

Provan, I., 'Foul Spirits, Fornication and Finance: Revelation 18 from an Old Testament Perspective', *Journal for the Study of the New Testament* 64 (1996), 81-100.

Pucci Ben Zeez, M., 'Caesar and Jewish Law', *Revue Biblique* 102 (1995), 28-37.

Puech, E., 'Messianism, Resurrection and Eschatology at Qumran and in the New Testament', in E. Ulrich and J. VanderKam (eds.), *The Community of the New Covenant: The Notre Dame Symposium on the Dead Sea Scrolls*, (Notre Dame, Indiana: University of Notre Dame Press, 1994), 235-256.

Quell, G., and G. Shrenk, 'δικη κτλ', in G. Kittel and G. Friedrich (eds.), *Theological Dictionary of the New Testament* Vol. II, (Tr. G.W. Bromily. Grand Rapids, Michigan: Eerdmans, 1964), 174-225.

Rad, G., von, *Old Testament Theology* vol.2 (Tr. D.M.G. Stalker, Norwich: SCM, 1975).

Reddish, M.G., *The Theme of Martyrdom in the Book of Revelation* (PhD. dissertation, The Southern Baptist Theological Seminary, 1982).

—, 'Martyr Christology in the Apocalypse', *Journal for the Study of the New Testament* 33 (1988), 85-89.

Redditt, P.L., *Haggai, Zechariah, Malachi* (New Bible Commentary. London: Marshall, Morgan & Scott 1995)

Reese, J.M., *Hellenistic Influence on the Book of Wisdom and its Consequences* (Analecta Biblica 41. Rome: Biblical Institute Press, 1970).

Reventlow, H.G., 'Basic Issues in the Interpretation of Isaiah 53', in W.H. Bellinger Jr and W.R. Farmer (eds.), *Jesus and the Suffering Servant: Isaiah 53 and Christian Origins*, (Harrisburg, PA: Trinity Press International, 1998), 23-39.

Riddle, D.W., 'From Apocalypse to Martyrology', *Anglican Theological Review* 9/3 (1927), 260-280.

—, *The Martyrs: A Study in Social Control* (Chicago: University of Chicago Press, 1931).

Rissi, M., *Time and History: A study on the Revelation* (Tr. G.C. Winsor, Virginia: John Knox Press, 1966).

Roberts, A and J. Donaldson, (eds.), *The Apostolic Fathers* vol 1 (Ante-Nicene Christian Library. Translations of the writings of the Fathers. Edinburgh: T&T Clark, 1866).

Roberts, J.H., 'The Lamb of God', *Neotestamenica* 2 (1968) 41-56.

Robertson, A.S., *Roman Imperial Coins in the Hunter Coin Cabinet: 1. Augustus to Nerva* (London/Glasgow/New York: OUP, 1962).

Robinson, A.T., *Redating the New Testament* (London: SCM, 1976).

Robinson, B.P., 'The Two Persecuted Prophet-Witnesses of Rev.11', *Scripture Bulletin* 19 (1988), 14-19.

Rogers, P.M., 'Domitian and the finances of State', *Historia* 33 (1984), 60-78.

Roloff, M.G., *The Revelation of John: A Continental Commentary* (Tr. J. Alsup. Minneapolis: Fortress Press, 1993).

Rosenberg, R.A., 'Jesus, Isaac, and the "Suffering Servant"', *Journal of Biblical Literature* 84 (1965), 381-388.

Rostovtzeff, M., *The Social and Economic History of the Roman Empire* (Oxford: Clarendon Press, 1926).

Rowley, H.H., *The Faith of Israel* (London: SCM, 1956).

—, *The Relevance of Apocalyptic: A Study of Jewish and Christian Apocalypses from Daniel to the Revelation* (London: Lutterworth Press, 1963).

Ruiz, J-P., *Ezekiel in the Apocalypse: The Transformation of Prophetic Language in Revelation 16.17-19.10* (Frankfurt am Main: Peter Lang, 1989).

Russell, D.S., *Between the Testaments* (London: SCM, 1960).

Rutgers, L.V., 'Attitudes to Judaism in the Greco-Roman Period: Reflections on Feldman's Jew and Gentile in the Ancient World', *Jewish Quarterly Review* 85 (1995), 361-395.

Sanders, E.P., *Paul and Palestinian Judaism* (London: SCM, 1977).

Sapp, D.A., 'The LXX, 1QIsa, and MT Versions of Isaiah 53 and the Christian Doctrine of Atonement', in W.H. Bellinger Jr and W.R. Farmer (eds.), *Jesus and the Suffering Servant: Isaiah 53 and Christian Origins*, (Harrisburg, PA: Trinity Press International, 1998), 170-192.

Sasson, J. M., *Jonah* (The Anchor Bible 24B. New York/London/Toronto/Sydney/Auckland: Doubleday, 1990).

Satake, A., *Die Gemeindeordnung in der Johannesapokalpse* (Neukirchen-Vluyn: Neukirchener Verlag, 1966).

Schaberg, J. 'Major Midrashic Traditions in Wisdom 1, 1-6, 25', *Journal for the Study of Judaism in the Persian Hellenistic and Roman Period* Vol.12.1-2 (1982), 75-101.

Schillebeeckx, E., *The Church: The Human Story of God* (London: SCM, 1990).

Schoff, W.H., *The Ship "Tyre": A Symbol of Conquerors as Prophesied by Isaiah, Ezekiel and John and Fulfilled at Nineveh, Babylon and Rome. A Study in the Commerce of the Bible* (New York/London: Longmans, Green and Co., 1920).

Schüssler Fiorenza, E., *Priester für Gott. Studien zum Herrschafts und Pristermotiv in der Apokalypse* (Münster: Aschendorff, 1972).

—, 'Apokalypsis and Propheteia: The Book of Revelation in the Context of Early Christian Prophecy', in J. Lambrech (ed.), *L'Apocalypse johannique et l'Apocalyptique dans led Nouveau Testament*, (Leuven: Leuven University Press, 1980), 105-128.

—, *Invitation to the Book of Revelation* (Doubleday & Co. 1981).

—, *The Book of Revelation: Justice and Judgement* (Philadelphia: Fortress Press, 1985).

—, 'The Followers of the Lamb: Visionary Rhetoric and Social-Political Situation ', *Semeia* 36 (1986), 123-146

—, *Revelation: Vision of a Just World* (Edinburgh: T&T Clark, 1991).

Schwager, R., *Must there be Scapegoats? Violence and Redemption in the Bible* (Tr. M.L. Assad. New York: Crossroad publishing company/ Leominster, UK: Gracewing, 2000).

Scott, K., 'Statius' Adulation of Domitian ', *American Journal of Philology* 54 (1933), 247-259.

Seeley, D., 'Was Jesus like a Philosopher? The Evidence of Martyrological and Wisdom Motifs in Q, Pre-Pauline Traditions, and Mark ', *SBL 1989 Seminar Papers*, (Atlanta, Georgia: Scholars Press), 540-549.

—, *The Noble Death: Graeco-Roman Martyrology and Paul's Concept of Salvation* (Journal for the Study of the New Testament Supplement Series 28. Sheffield: JSOT Press, 1990).

Segal, A.F., 'The Akedah: Some Reconsiderations', in H. Cancile, H. Lichtenberger and P. Schäfer (eds.), *Geschichte-Tradition-Reflection: Festschrift für Martin Hengel zum 70 Geburstag*,(vol 1 Judentum, Tübingen: Mohr, 1996).

Segal, J.B., *The Hebrew Passover: From the Earliest Times to AD 70* (London Oriental Seriesl 12. London: OUP, 1963).

Seitz, C.R., 'The Prophet Moses and the Canonical Shape of Jeremiah', *Zeitschrift für die Alten Wissenschaft* 101 (1989), 3-27.

—, 'How is the Prophet Isaiah present in the Latter half of the Book? The Logic of chapters 40-66 within the Book of Isaiah', *Journal of Biblical Literature* 115/2 (1996), 219-240.

Selvidge, M. J., 'Powerful and Powerless Women in the Apocalypse', *Neotestamentica* 26 (1992), 157-167.

—, 'Reflections on Violence and Pornography: Misogyny in the Apocalypse and Ancient Hebrew Prophecy', in A. Brenner (ed.), *A Feminist Companion to the Hebrew Bible in the New Testament* (Sheffield: Sheffield Academic Press, 1996), 274-285.

Seneca, *Ad Lucilium Epistulae Morales* (Tr. R.M. Gummere. Loeb Classical Library. Cambridge, Mass: Harvard University Press, 1947).

Setzer, C.J., *Jewish Responses to Early Christians: History and Polemics, 30-150 CE* (Minneapolis: Fortress Press, 1994).

Sharp, G., *Gandhi as a Political Strategist: with essays on ethics and Politics* (Boston, MA: Extending Horizons Books, 1979).

Slater, T.B., 'On the Social Setting of the Revelation to John', *New Testament Studies* 44 (1998), 232-256.

Smallwood, E.M., 'Domitian's Attitude toward the Jews and Judaism', *Classical Philology* 51 (1956), 1-13.

Sobrino, J., 'The Crucified Peoples: Yahweh's Suffering Servant Today', *Concilium* 6 (1990), 120-129.

Sobrino, J., 'Latin America: Guatemala/El Salvador', in W. Beuken and K-J. Kuschel (eds.), *Religion as a Source of Violence* (Tr. P. Burns. Concilium 4. London/New York: SCM and Orbis Books, 1997), 38-54.

Sommer, B. D., 'Exegesis, allusion and Intertextuality in the Hebrew Bible: A response to Lyle Eslinger', *Vetus Testamentum* 46.4 (1996), 479-489.

Sordi, M., *The Christians and the Roman Empire* (Tr. A. Bedini, London/Sydney: Croom Helm, 1983).

Southern, P., *Domitian: Tragic Tyrant* (London/New York: Routledge, 1997).

Spieckermann, H., 'The Conception and Pre-history of the Idea of Vicariousness in the Old Testament', in W.H. Bellinger Jr and W.R. Farmer (eds.), *Jesus and the Suffering Servant: Isaiah 53 and Christian Origins*, (Harrisburg, PA: Trinity Press International, 1998), 253-254.

Spiegel, S., *The Last Trial* (tr. J. Goldin. New York: Pantheon Books, 1967).

Stanton, G.N., 'Aspects of Early Christian-Jewish Polemic and Apologetic', *New Testament Studies* 31 (1985), 377-392.

Starr, C.G., *The Roman Empire 27 BC-AD 476: A Study in Survival* (New York/Oxford: OUP, 1982).

Strand, K.A., 'Review of *The Book of Revelation: Apocalypse and Empire*, by L. Thompson ', *Andrews University Seminary Studies* 29 (1991) 188-90.

Stern, M., *Greek and Latin Authors on Jews and Judaism* (3 vols. Jerusalem: Israel Academy of Sciences and Humanities, 1974-84).

Stevenson, G.M., 'Conceptual Background to the Golden Crown Imagery in the Apocalypse of John (4.4, 10; 14:14)', *Journal of Biblical Literature* 114/2 (1995), 257-272.

Strelan, R., *Paul, Artemis and the Jews in Ephesus* (Berlin/New York: Walter de Gruyter, 1996).

Suggs, M.J. 'Wisdom of Solomon 2.10-5: A Homily on the Fourth Servant Song', *Journal of Biblical Literature* 76 (1957), 26-33.

Swartley, W.M., 'Discipleship and Imitation of Jesus/Suffering Servant: The Mimesis of New Creation', in W.M. Swartley (ed.), *Violence Renounced: René Girard, Biblical Studies and Peacemaking* (Studies in Peace and Scripture, vol. 4. Institute of Mennonite Studies. Telford, Pennsylvania: Pandora Press, 2000) 218-245.

Sweet, J.P.M., 'Maintaining the Testimony of Jesus: the suffering of Christians in the Revelation of St John ', in W. Horbury and B. McNeil (eds.), *Suffering and Martyrdom in the New Testament: Studies presented to G.M. Styler* (Cambridge: CUP, 1981), 101-117.

—, *Revelation*, (SCM Pelican Commentaries. London: SCM, 1979).

Swete, H.B., *The Apocalypse of St John* (Third Edition. London: Macmillan, 1922).

Swetnam, J., *Jesus and Isaac. A Study of the Epistle to the Hebrews in the Light of the Aqedah* (Analecta Biblica 94, Rome: Biblical Institute Press 1981).

Tabor, J.D., and M.O. Wise, '4Q521 "On Resurrection" and the Synoptic Gospel Tradition: A Preliminary Study', *Journal for the Study of the Pseudepigrapha* 10 (1992), 149-162.

Talbert, C.H., *The Apocalypse: A reading of the Revelation of John* (Kentucky: Westminster John Knox Press, 1994).

Tamari, M. *'With All Your Possessions': Jewish Ethics and Economic Life* (New York: The Free Press, 1987).

Taylor, J.B., *Ezekiel* (Tyndale Old Testament Commentary Series. London: Tyndale Press, 1969).

Taylor, V., *Jesus and his Sacrifice: A study of the passion-sayings in the Gospels* (London/Melbourne/Toronto: St Martin's Press, 1965).

Thackery, H. St. J. and Marcus, R., *Josephus* (Loeb Classical Library, 9 vols., London: Heinemann, 1926-65).

Thompson, L.A., 'Domitian and the Jewish Tax ', *Historia* 31 (1982), 329-342.

Thompson, L.L., *The Book of Revelation: Apocalypse and Empire* (New York/ Oxford: OUP, 1990).

Thompson, M., *Clothed with Christ* (Journal for the Study of the New Testament Supplement Series 59. Sheffield: JSOT, 1991).

Thompson, S., *The Apocalypse and Semitic Syntax* (Cambridge/London/New York/New Rochelle/Melbourne/Sydney: CUP, 1985).

Tigchelaar, J.C., *Prophets of old and the Day of the End: Zechariah, the Book of Watchers and Apocalyptic* (Oudtestamentische Studien 35. Leiden: Brill, 1996).

Tiller, P.A., *A Commentary On the Animal Apocalypse of 1 Enoch* (Atlanta, Georgia: Scholars Press, JBL Early Judaism and Its Literature, 1993).

Trebilco, R.R., *Jewish Communities in Asia Minor* (Society for New Testament Studies Monograph Series 69. Cambridge: CUP, 1991).

Trites, A.A., 'Martuj and Martyrdom in the Apocalypse: A Semantic Study', *Novum Testamentum* 1 (1973), 72-80.

—, *The New Testament Concept of Witness* (Society for New Testament Studies Monograph Series 31. Cambridge: CUP, 1977).

—, 'Witness and the Resurrection in the Apocalypse of John', in R.N. Longenecker (ed.), *Life in the Face of death: The Resurrection Message of the New Testament* (Grand Rapids, Michigan/Cambridge, UK: Eerdmans, 1998), 270-288.

Tromp, J., *The Assumption of Moses: A Critical Edition with Commentary* (Studia in Veteris Testamenti Pseudepigraph. Leiden/New York/ Köln: Brill, 1993)

Trudinger, P., 'Some observations concerning the Text of the Old Testament in the Book of Revelation', *Journal of Theological Studies* 17 (1966), 82-88.

—, 'The Apocalypse and the Palestinian Targums', *Biblical Theological Bulletin.* 16 (1986) 78-79.

Turner, V., *Drama, Fields and Metaphors* (Ithaca: Cornell University, 1974).

Usher, S., *The Historians of Greece and Rome* (London: Hamish Hamilton, 1969).

van der Horst, P.W., 'The Birkat ha-minim in Recent Research', *Expository Times* 105 (1993-1994), 363-368.

VanderKam, J. C., *The Dead Sea Scrolls Today* (Michigan: Eerdmans, 1994).

—, 'The Aqedah, Jubilees, and Pseudo-Jubilees', in C. Evans and S. Talman (eds.), *The Quest for Context and Meaning: Studies in Biblical Intertextuality in Honor of J.A. Sanders* (Biblical Interpretation Series 28. Leiden: Brill, 1997), 241-261.

van Henten, J. W. *The Maccabean Martyrs as Saviours of the Jewish People: A Study of 2 and 4 Maccabees* (Supplement Series of the Journal for the Study of Judaism 57. Leiden/New York/Köln: Brill, 1997).

van Unnik, W.C., '"Worthy is the Lamb": The Background of Apoc.5', in A. Descamps and A. de Halleux (ed.), *Mélanges biblique en hommage au R. P. Béda Rigaux* (Gembloux: Duculot, 1970), 445-461.

Vermes, G., *Scripture and Tradition in Judaism* (Haggadic Studies. Studia post-biblica 4, Leiden: Brill, 1961).

—, 'The Targumic Versions of Genesis 4.3-16', *Studies in Judaism in Late Antiquity* 8 (1975), 92-138.

—, 'New Light on the Sacrifice of Isaac from 4Q225' *Journal of Biblical Literature* 47 (1996), 140-145.

—, *The Dead Sea Scrolls in English* (fourth edition. London: Penguin, 1995).

Vos, L. A., *The Synoptic Traditions in the Apocalypse* (Kampen: J.H. Kok, 1965).

Vree, D., 'Stripped Clean - Berrigans and Politics of Guilt and Martyrdom', *Ethics vol* 85.4 (1974-75), 271-287.

Wacher, J., *The Roman Empire* (London/Melbourne: J.M. Dent & Sons Ltd., 1987).

Wall, R. W., *Revelation* (New International Bible Commentary 18; Peabody, MA: Hendrickson, 1991).

Wallace, K.G., 'The Flavii Sabini in Tacitus', *Historia* 36 (1987), 343-358.

Wallace-Hadrill, A., *Suetonius: The Scholar and his Caesars* (London: Duckworth, 1983).

Walsh, J.J, 'On Christian Atheism', *Vigilae Christianae* 45 (1991), 255-277.

Waltke, B.K. and O'Connor, M.O., *An Introduction to Biblical Hebrew Syntax* (Winona Lake, Indiana: Eisenbrauns, 1990).

Waterman, L., 'The Martyred Servant Motif of Is. 53', *Journal of Biblical Literature* 56 (1937), 27-34.

Watts, R.E., 'Jesus' Death, Isaiah 53, and Mark 10.45: A Crux Revisited', in W.H. Bellinger Jr and W.R. Farmer (eds.), *Jesus and the Suffering Servant: Isaiah 53 and Christian Origins* (Harrisburg, PA: Trinity Press International, 1998), 112-151.

Weaver, D.W., *The Nonviolent Atonement* (Grand Rapids, Michigan/Cambridge, UK: Eedmans, 2001).

Weiner, E. and A. Weiner, *A Martyr's Conviction: A Sociological Analysis* (Brown Judaic Studies 203. Atlanta, Georgia: Scholars Press, 1990).

Weinrich, W.C., *Spirit and Martyrdom: A study of the work of the Holy Spirit in the Contexts of Persecution and Martyrdom in the New Testament and Early Christian Literature* (Washington, D.C.: University Press of America, 1981).

Weiser, A., *The Psalms* (Old Testament Library. London: SCM, 1962).

Wells, C., *The Roman Empire* (Fontana History of the Ancient World. Glasgow: Fontana Paperbacks, 1984).

Wenham, G., Violence in the Pentateuch (unpublished paper to the British Old Testament Society in 2001).

Wengst, K., *Pax Romana: and the Peace of Jesus Christ* (Tr. J. Bowden. London: SCM, 1987).

Westermann, C., *The Living Psalms* (Tr. J.R. Porter. Edinburgh: T&T Clark, 1989).

Wheeler Robinson, H., *The Cross in the Old Testament* (London: SCM, 1955).

Whybray, R.N., *Isaiah 40-66* (New Century Bible. London: Marshall, Morgan & Scott, 1990).

Wilken R.L., 'Melito, The Jewish Community at Sardis, and the Sacrifice of Isaac', *Theological Studies* 37 (1976), 53-69

—, *The Christians as the Romans Saw them* (Yale: Yale University Press, 1984).

Williams, J.G., *The Bible, Violence, and the Sacred: Liberation from the myth of sanctioned violence* (SanFrancisco: Harper Collins, 1991).

—, (ed.), *The Girard Reader* (New York: A Crossroad Herder Book, 2000).

Williams, M.H., 'Domitian, the Jews and the "Judaizers" - A Simple Matter of Cupiditas and Maiestas?' *Historia* 39 (1990), 196-211.

Williams, S.K., *Jesus' Death as Saving Event: The Background and Origin of a Concept* (Harvard Dissertations in Religion 2. Missoula, Montana: Scholars Press, 1975).

Wilson, B., *Magic and the Millennium* (New York: Harper & Row, 1973).

Wilson, S.G., *Related Strangers: Jews and Christians* 70-170CE (Minneapolis: Fortress Press, 1995).

Wink, W., 'Neither Passivity nor Violence: Jesus' Third Way', *Forum* 7 (1991), 5-28.

—, *Engaging the Powers. Discernment and Resistance in a World of Domination* (Minneapolis: Fortress Press, 1992).

Wright, N. T., *Jesus and the Victory of God* (London: SPCK, 1996).

Wood, J.E., 'Isaac Typology in the New Testament', *New Testament Studies* 14 (1967-68), 583-589.

Yarbro Collins 'The Political Perspective of the Rev to John', *Journal of Biblical Literature* 96/2 (1977), 241-256.

—, *The Apocalypse* (Dublin: Veritas Publications, New Testament Message 22, 1979).

—, 'Dating the Apocalypse of John', *Biblical Research* 26 (1981a), 33-45.

—, 'Myth and History in the Book of Revelation: the Problem of its Date', in B Halpern and J.D. Levenson, (eds.), *Traditions in Transformation: Turning Points in Biblical Faith* (Winona Lake: Eisenbrauns, 1981b), 377-403.

—, 'Numerical Symbolism in Jewish and Early Christian Apocalyptic Literature', in W. Haase (ed.), *Aufsteig und Niedergang der römischen Welt*, vol. 2/21/1 (New York/Berlin: de Gruyter, 1984a), 1221-1287.

—, *Crisis and Catharsis: The Power of the Apocalypse* (Philadelphia: The Westminster Press, 1984b).

Yoder, J. H., *The Politics of Jesus: Behold the Man! Our Victorious Lamb* (Carlisle, UK: The Paternoster Press & Grand Rapids, Michigan: Eerdmans, 1994).

Young, E.J., *Studies in Isaiah* (Grand Rapids, Michigan: Eerdmans, 1954).

Zimmerli, W. and J. Jeremias, *The Servant of God* (Studies in Biblical Theology 20. Chatham: SCM, 1957).

—, Ezekiel 2: A commentary on the Book of the Prophet Ezekiel 25-48 (Tr. J.D. Martin, Philadelphia: Fortress Press, 1983).

Index of Passages Cited

Index of Modern Authors

Paternoster Biblical Monographs

(All titles uniform with this volume)
Dates in bold are of projected publication

Joseph Abraham
Eve: Accused or Acquitted?
A Reconsideration of Feminist Readings of the Creation Narrative Texts in Genesis 1–3

Two contrary views dominate contemporary feminist biblical scholarship. One finds in the Bible an unequivocal equality between the sexes from the very creation of humanity, whilst the other sees the biblical text as irredeemably patriarchal and androcentric. Dr Abraham enters into dialogue with both camps as well as introducing his own method of approach. An invaluable tool for any one who is interested in this contemporary debate.

2002 / 0-85364-971-5 / xxiv + 272pp

Octavian D. Baban
Mimesis and Luke's on the Road Encounters in Luke-Acts
Luke's Theology of the Way and its Literary Representation

The book argues on theological and literary (mimetic) grounds that Luke's on-the-road encounters, especially those belonging to the post-Easter period, are part of his complex theology of the Way. Jesus' teaching and that of the apostles is presented by Luke as a challenging answer to the Hellenistic reader's thirst for adventure, good literature, and existential paradigms.

2005 */ 1-84227-253-5 / approx. 374pp*

Paul Barker
The Triumph of Grace in Deuteronomy

This book is a textual and theological analysis of the interaction between the sin and faithlessness of Israel and the grace of Yahweh in response, looking especially at Deuteronomy chapters 1–3, 8–10 and 29–30. The author argues that the grace of Yahweh is determinative for the ongoing relationship between Yahweh and Israel and that Deuteronomy anticipates and fully expects Israel to be faithless.

2004 / 1-84227-226-8 / xxii + 270pp

Jonathan F. Bayes
The Weakness of the Law
God's Law and the Christian in New Testament Perspective

A study of the four New Testament books which refer to the law as weak (Acts, Romans, Galatians, Hebrews) leads to a defence of the third use in the Reformed debate about the law in the life of the believer.

2000 / 0-85364-957-X / xii + 244pp

Mark Bonnington
The Antioch Episode of Galatians 2:11-14 in Historical and Cultural Context
The Galatians 2 'incident' in Antioch over table-fellowship suggests significant disagreement between the leading apostles. This book analyses the background to the disagreement by locating the incident within the dynamics of social interaction between Jews and Gentiles. It proposes a new way of understanding the relationship between the individuals and issues involved.

2005 / 1-84227-050-8 / approx. 350pp

David Bostock
A Portrayal of Trust
The Theme of Faith in the Hezekiah Narratives
This study provides detailed and sensitive readings of the Hezekiah narratives (2 Kings 18–20 and Isaiah 36–39) from a theological perspective. It concentrates on the theme of faith, using narrative criticism as its methodology. Attention is paid especially to setting, plot, point of view and characterization within the narratives. A largely positive portrayal of Hezekiah emerges that underlines the importance and relevance of scripture.

2005 / 1-84227-314-0 / approx. 300pp

Mark Bredin
Jesus, Revolutionary of Peace
A Non-violent Christology in the Book of Revelation
This book aims to demonstrate that the figure of Jesus in the Book of Revelation can best be understood as an active non-violent revolutionary.

2003 / 1-84227-153-9 / xviii + 262pp

Robinson Butarbutar
Paul and Conflict Resolution
An Exegetical Study of Paul's Apostolic Paradigm in 1 Corinthians 9
The author sees the apostolic paradigm in 1 Corinthians 9 as part of Paul's unified arguments in 1 Corinthians 8–10 in which he seeks to mediate in the dispute over the issue of food offered to idols. The book also sees its relevance for dispute-resolution today, taking the conflict within the author's church as an example.

2006 / 1-84227-315-9 / approx. 280pp

Daniel J-S Chae
Paul as Apostle to the Gentiles
His Apostolic Self-awareness and its Influence on the Soteriological Argument in Romans

Opposing 'the post-Holocaust interpretation of Romans', Daniel Chae competently demonstrates that Paul argues for the equality of Jew and Gentile in Romans. Chae's fresh exegetical interpretation is academically outstanding and spiritually encouraging.

1997 / 0-85364-829-8 / xiv + 378pp

Luke L. Cheung
The Genre, Composition and Hermeneutics of the Epistle of James

The present work examines the employment of the wisdom genre with a certain compositional structure and the interpretation of the law through the Jesus tradition of the double love command by the author of the Epistle of James to serve his purpose in promoting perfection and warning against doubleness among the eschatologically renewed people of God in the Diaspora.

2003 / 1-84227-062-1 / xvi + 372pp

Youngmo Cho
Spirit and Kingdom in the Writings of Luke and Paul

The relationship between Spirit and Kingdom is a relatively unexplored area in Lukan and Pauline studies. This book offers a fresh perspective of two biblical writers on the subject. It explores the difference between Luke's and Paul's understanding of the Spirit by examining the specific question of the relationship of the concept of the Spirit to the concept of the Kingdom of God in each writer.

2005 / 1-84227-316-7 / approx. 270pp

Andrew C. Clark
Parallel Lives
The Relation of Paul to the Apostles in the Lucan Perspective

This study of the Peter-Paul parallels in Acts argues that their purpose was to emphasize the themes of continuity in salvation history and the unity of the Jewish and Gentile missions. New light is shed on Luke's literary techniques, partly through a comparison with Plutarch.

2001 / 1-84227-035-4 / xviii + 386pp

Andrew D. Clarke
Secular and Christian Leadership in Corinth
A Socio-Historical and Exegetical Study of 1 Corinthians 1–6
This volume is an investigation into the leadership structures and dynamics of first-century Roman Corinth. These are compared with the practice of leadership in the Corinthian Christian community which are reflected in 1 Corinthians 1–6, and contrasted with Paul's own principles of Christian leadership.

2005 / 1-84227-229-2 / 200pp

Stephen Finamore
God, Order and Chaos
René Girard and the Apocalypse
Readers are often disturbed by the images of destruction in the book of Revelation and unsure why they are unleashed after the exaltation of Jesus. This book examines past approaches to these texts and uses René Girard's theories to revive some old ideas and propose some new ones.

2005 / 1-84227-197-0 / approx. 344pp

David G. Firth
Surrendering Retribution in the Psalms
Responses to Violence in the Individual Complaints
In *Surrendering Retribution in the Psalms*, David Firth examines the ways in which the book of Psalms inculcates a model response to violence through the repetition of standard patterns of prayer. Rather than seeking justification for retributive violence, Psalms encourages not only a surrender of the right of retribution to Yahweh, but also sets limits on the retribution that can be sought in imprecations. Arising initially from the author's experience in South Africa, the possibilities of this model to a particular context of violence is then briefly explored.

2005 / 1-84227-337-X / xviii + 154pp

Scott J. Hafemann
Suffering and Ministry in the Spirit
Paul's Defence of His Ministry in II Corinthians 2:14–3:3
Shedding new light on the way Paul defended his apostleship, the author offers a careful, detailed study of 2 Corinthians 2:14–3:3 linked with other key passages throughout 1 and 2 Corinthians. Demonstrating the unity and coherence of Paul's argument in this passage, the author shows that Paul's suffering served as the vehicle for revealing God's power and glory through the Spirit.

2000 / 0-85364-967-7 / xiv + 262pp

Scott J. Hafemann
Paul, Moses and the History of Israel
The Letter/Spirit Contrast and the Argument from Scripture in 2 Corinthians 3
An exegetical study of the call of Moses, the second giving of the Law (Exodus 32–34), the new covenant, and the prophetic understanding of the history of Israel in 2 Corinthians 3. Hafemann's work demonstrates Paul's contextual use of the Old Testament and the essential unity between the Law and the Gospel within the context of the distinctive ministries of Moses and Paul.
2005 / 1-84227-317-5 / xii + 498pp

Douglas S. McComiskey
Lukan Theology in the Light of the Gospel's Literary Structure
Luke's Gospel was purposefully written with theology embedded in its patterned literary structure. A critical analysis of this cyclical structure provides new windows into Luke's interpretation of the individual pericopes comprising the Gospel and illuminates several of his theological interests.
2004 / 1-84227-148-2 / xviii + 388pp

Stephen Motyer
Your Father the Devil?
A New Approach to John and 'The Jews'
Who are 'the Jews' in John's Gospel? Defending John against the charge of antisemitism, Motyer argues that, far from demonising the Jews, the Gospel seeks to present Jesus as 'Good News for Jews' in a late first century setting.
1997 / 0-85364-832-8 / xiv + 260pp

Esther Ng
Reconstructing Christian Origins?
The Feminist Theology of Elizabeth Schüssler Fiorenza: An Evaluation
In a detailed evaluation, the author challenges Elizabeth Schüssler Fiorenza's reconstruction of early Christian origins and her underlying presuppositions. The author also presents her own views on women's roles both then and now.
2002 / 1-84227-055-9 / xxiv + 468pp

Robin Parry
Old Testament Story and Christian Ethics
The Rape of Dinah as a Case Study

What is the role of story in ethics and, more particularly, what is the role of Old Testament story in Christian ethics? This book, drawing on the work of contemporary philosophers, argues that narrative is crucial in the ethical shaping of people and, drawing on the work of contemporary Old Testament scholars, that story plays a key role in Old Testament ethics. Parry then argues that when situated in canonical context Old Testament stories can be reappropriated by Christian readers in their own ethical formation. The shocking story of the rape of Dinah and the massacre of the Shechemites provides a fascinating case study for exploring the parameters within which Christian ethical appropriations of Old Testament stories can live.

2004 / 1-84227-210-1 / xx + 350pp

Ian Paul
Power to See the World Anew
The Value of Paul Ricoeur's Hermeneutic of Metaphor in Interpreting the Symbolism of Revelation 12 and 13

This book is a study of the hermeneutics of metaphor of Paul Ricoeur, one of the most important writers on hermeneutics and metaphor of the last century. It sets out the key points of his theory, important criticisms of his work, and how his approach, modified in the light of these criticisms, offers a methodological framework for reading apocalyptic texts.

2006 / 1-84227-056-7 / approx. 350pp

Robert L. Plummer
Paul's Understanding of the Church's Mission
Did the Apostle Paul Expect the Early Christian Communities to Evangelize?

This book engages in a careful study of Paul's letters to determine if the apostle expected the communities to which he wrote to engage in missionary activity. It helpfully summarizes the discussion on this debated issue, judiciously handling contested texts, and provides a way forward in addressing this critical question. While admitting that Paul rarely explicitly commands the communities he founded to evangelize, Plummer amasses significant incidental data to provide a convincing case that Paul did indeed expect his churches to engage in mission activity. Throughout the study, Plummer progressively builds a theological basis for the church's mission that is both distinctively Pauline and compelling.

2006 / 1-84227-333-7 / approx. 324pp

David Powys
'Hell': A Hard Look at a Hard Question
The Fate of the Unrighteous in New Testament Thought
This comprehensive treatment seeks to unlock the original meaning of terms and phrases long thought to support the traditional doctrine of hell. It concludes that there is an alternative—one which is more biblical, and which can positively revive the rationale for Christian mission.

1997 / 0-85364-831-X / xxii + 478pp

Sorin Sabou
Between Horror and Hope
Paul's Metaphorical Language of Death in Romans 6.1-11
This book argues that Paul's metaphorical language of death in Romans 6.1-11 conveys two aspects: horror and hope. The 'horror' aspect is conveyed by the 'crucifixion' language, and the 'hope' aspect by 'burial' language. The life of the Christian believer is understood, as relationship with sin is concerned ('death to sin'), between these two realities: horror and hope.

2005 / 1-84227-322-1 / approx. 224pp

Rosalind Selby
The Comical Doctrine
The Epistemology of New Testament Hermeneutics
This book argues that the gospel breaks through postmodernity's critique of truth and the referential possibilities of textuality with its gift of grace. With a rigorous, philosophical challenge to modernist and postmodernist assumptions, Selby offers an alternative epistemology to all who would still read with faith *and* with academic credibility.

2005 / 1-84227-212-8 / approx. 350pp

Kiwoong Son
Zion Symbolism in Hebrews
Hebrews 12.18-24 as a Hermeneutical Key to the Epistle
This book challenges the general tendency of understanding the Epistle to the Hebrews against a Hellenistic background and suggests that the Epistle should be understood in the light of the Jewish apocalyptic tradition. The author especially argues for the importance of the theological symbolism of Sinai and Zion (Heb. 12:18-24) as it provides the Epistle's theological background as well as the rhetorical basis of the superiority motif of Jesus throughout the Epistle.

2005 / 1-84227-368-X / approx. 280pp

Kevin Walton
Thou Traveller Unknown
The Presence and Absence of God in the Jacob Narrative
The author offers a fresh reading of the story of Jacob in the book of Genesis through the paradox of divine presence and absence. The work also seeks to make a contribution to Pentateuchal studies by bringing together a close reading of the final text with historical critical insights, doing justice to the text's historical depth, final form and canonical status.
2003 / 1-84227-059-1 / xvi + 238pp

George M. Wieland
The Significance of Salvation
A Study of Salvation Language in the Pastoral Epistles
The language and ideas of salvation pervade the three Pastoral Epistles. This study offers a close examination of their soteriological statements. In all three letters the idea of salvation is found to play a vital paraenetic role, but each also exhibits distinctive soteriological emphases. The results challenge common assumptions about the Pastoral Epistles as a corpus.
2005 / 1-84227-257-8 / approx. 324pp

Alistair Wilson
When Will These Things Happen?
A Study of Jesus as Judge in Matthew 21–25
This study seeks to allow Matthew's carefully constructed presentation of Jesus to be given full weight in the modern evaluation of Jesus' eschatology. Careful analysis of the text of Matthew 21–25 reveals Jesus to be standing firmly in the Jewish prophetic and wisdom traditions as he proclaims and enacts imminent judgement on the Jewish authorities then boldly claims the central role in the final and universal judgement.
2004 / 1-84227-146-6 / xxii + 272pp

Lindsay Wilson
Joseph Wise and Otherwise
The Intersection of Covenant and Wisdom in Genesis 37–50
This book offers a careful literary reading of Genesis 37–50 that argues that the Joseph story contains both strong covenant themes and many wisdom-like elements. The connections between the two helps to explore how covenant and wisdom might intersect in an integrated biblical theology.
2004 / 1-84227-140-7 / xvi + 340pp

Stephen I. Wright
The Voice of Jesus
Studies in the Interpretation of Six Gospel Parables
This literary study considers how the 'voice' of Jesus has been heard in different periods of parable interpretation, and how the categories of figure and trope may help us towards a sensitive reading of the parables today.
2000 / 0-85364-975-8 / xiv + 280pp

Paternoster
9 Holdom Avenue,
Bletchley,
Milton Keynes MK1 1QR,
United Kingdom
Web: www.authenticmedia.co.uk/paternoster

July 2005

Paternoster Theological Monographs

(All titles uniform with this volume)
Dates in bold are of projected publication

Emil Bartos
Deification in Eastern Orthodox Theology
An Evaluation and Critique of the Theology of Dumitru Staniloae

Bartos studies a fundamental yet neglected aspect of Orthodox theology: deification. By examining the doctrines of anthropology, christology, soteriology and ecclesiology as they relate to deification, he provides an important contribution to contemporary dialogue between Eastern and Western theologians.

1999 / 0-85364-956-1 / xii + 370pp

Graham Buxton
The Trinity, Creation and Pastoral Ministry
Imaging the Perichoretic God

In this book the author proposes a three-way conversation between theology, science and pastoral ministry. His approach draws on a Trinitarian understanding of God as a relational being of love, whose life 'spills over' into all created reality, human and non-human. By locating human meaning and purpose within God's 'creation-community' this book offers the possibility of a transforming engagement between those in pastoral ministry and the scientific community.

2005 */ 1-84227-369-8 / approx. 380 pp*

Iain D. Campbell
Fixing the Indemnity
The Life and Work of George Adam Smith

When Old Testament scholar George Adam Smith (1856–1942) delivered the Lyman Beecher lectures at Yale University in 1899, he confidently declared that 'modern criticism has won its war against traditional theories. It only remains to fix the amount of the indemnity.' In this biography, Iain D. Campbell assesses Smith's critical approach to the Old Testament and evaluates its consequences, showing that Smith's life and work still raises questions about the relationship between biblical scholarship and evangelical faith.

2004 / 1-84227-228-4 / xx + 256pp

Tim Chester
Mission and the Coming of God
Eschatology, the Trinity and Mission in the Theology of Jürgen Moltmann
This book explores the theology and missiology of the influential contemporary theologian, Jürgen Moltmann. It highlights the important contribution Moltmann has made while offering a critique of his thought from an evangelical perspective. In so doing, it touches on pertinent issues for evangelical missiology. The conclusion takes Calvin as a starting point, proposing 'an eschatology of the cross' which offers a critique of the over-realised eschatologies in liberation theology and certain forms of evangelicalism.
2006 / 1-84227-320-5 / approx. 224pp

Sylvia Wilkey Collinson
Making Disciples
The Significance of Jesus' Educational Strategy for Today's Church
This study examines the biblical practice of discipling, formulates a definition, and makes comparisons with modern models of education. A recommendation is made for greater attention to its practice today.
2004 / 1-84227-116-4 / xiv + 278pp

Darrell Cosden
A Theology of Work
Work and the New Creation
Through dialogue with Moltmann, Pope John Paul II and others, this book develops a genitive 'theology of work', presenting a theological definition of work and a model for a theological ethics of work that shows work's nature, value and meaning now and eschatologically. Work is shown to be a transformative activity consisting of three dynamically inter-related dimensions: the instrumental, relational and ontological.
2005 / 1-84227-332-9 / xvi + 208pp

Stephen M. Dunning
The Crisis and the Quest
A Kierkegaardian Reading of Charles Williams
Employing Kierkegaardian categories and analysis, this study investigates both the central crisis in Charles Williams's authorship between hermetism and Christianity (Kierkegaard's Religions A and B), and the quest to resolve this crisis, a quest that ultimately presses the bounds of orthodoxy.
2000 / 0-85364-985-5 / xxiv + 254pp

Keith Ferdinando
The Triumph of Christ in African Perspective
A Study of Demonology and Redemption in the African Context
The book explores the implications of the gospel for traditional African fears of occult aggression. It analyses such traditional approaches to suffering and biblical responses to fears of demonic evil, concluding with an evaluation of African beliefs from the perspective of the gospel.
1999 / 0-85364-830-1 / xviii + 450pp

Andrew Goddard
Living the Word, Resisting the World
The Life and Thought of Jacques Ellul
This work offers a definitive study of both the life and thought of the French Reformed thinker Jacques Ellul (1912-1994). It will prove an indispensable resource for those interested in this influential theologian and sociologist and for Christian ethics and political thought generally.
2002 / 1-84227-053-2 / xxiv + 378pp

David Hilborn
The Words of our Lips
Language-Use in Free Church Worship
Studies of liturgical language have tended to focus on the written canons of Roman Catholic and Anglican communities. By contrast, David Hilborn analyses the more extemporary approach of English Nonconformity. Drawing on recent developments in linguistic pragmatics, he explores similarities and differences between 'fixed' and 'free' worship, and argues for the interdependence of each.
2006 */ 0-85364-977-4 / approx. 350pp*

Roger Hitching
The Church and Deaf People
A Study of Identity, Communication and Relationships with Special Reference to the Ecclesiology of Jürgen Moltmann
In *The Church and Deaf People* Roger Hitching sensitively examines the history and present experience of deaf people and finds similarities between aspects of sign language and Moltmann's theological method that 'open up' new ways of understanding theological concepts.
2003 / 1-84227-222-5 / xxii + 236pp

John G. Kelly
One God, One People
The Differentiated Unity of the People of God in the Theology of
Jürgen Moltmann
The author expounds and critiques Moltmann's doctrine of God and highlights the systematic connections between it and Moltmann's influential discussion of Israel. He then proposes a fresh approach to Jewish–Christian relations building on Moltmann's work using insights from Habermas and Rawls.
2005 / 0-85346-969-3 / approx. 350pp

Mark F.W. Lovatt
Confronting the Will-to-Power
A Reconsideration of the Theology of Reinhold Niebuhr
Confronting the Will-to-Power is an analysis of the theology of Reinhold Niebuhr, arguing that his work is an attempt to identify, and provide a practical theological answer to, the existence and nature of human evil.
2001 / 1-84227-054-0 / xviii + 216pp

Neil B. MacDonald
Karl Barth and the Strange New World within the Bible
Barth, Wittgenstein, and the Metadilemmas of the Enlightenment
Barth's discovery of the strange new world within the Bible is examined in the context of Kant, Hume, Overbeck, and, most importantly, Wittgenstein. MacDonald covers some fundamental issues in theology today: epistemology, the final form of the text and biblical truth-claims.
2000 / 0-85364-970-7 / xxvi + 374pp

Keith A. Mascord
Alvin Plantinga and Christian Apologetics
This book draws together the contributions of the philosopher Alvin Plantinga to the major contemporary challenges to Christian belief, highlighting in particular his ground-breaking work in epistemology and the problem of evil. Plantinga's theory that both theistic and Christian belief is warrantedly basic is explored and critiqued, and an assessment offered as to the significance of his work for apologetic theory and practice.
2005 / 1-84227-256-X / approx. 304pp

Gillian McCulloch
The Deconstruction of Dualism in Theology
With Reference to Ecofeminist Theology and New Age Spirituality
This book challenges eco-theological anti-dualism in Christian theology, arguing that dualism has a twofold function in Christian religious discourse. Firstly, it enables us to express the discontinuities and divisions that are part of the process of reality. Secondly, dualistic language allows us to express the mysteries of divine transcendence/immanence and the survival of the soul without collapsing into monism and materialism, both of which are problematic for Christian epistemology.

2002 / 1-84227-044-3 / xii + 282pp

Leslie McCurdy
Attributes and Atonement
The Holy Love of God in the Theology of P.T. Forsyth
Attributes and Atonement is an intriguing full-length study of P.T. Forsyth's doctrine of the cross as it relates particularly to God's holy love. It includes an unparalleled bibliography of both primary and secondary material relating to Forsyth.

1999 / 0-85364-833-6 / xiv + 328pp

Nozomu Miyahira
Towards a Theology of the Concord of God
A Japanese Perspective on the Trinity
This book introduces a new Japanese theology and a unique Trinitarian formula based on the Japanese intellectual climate: three betweennesses and one concord. It also presents a new interpretation of the Trinity, a co-subordinationism, which is in line with orthodox Trinitarianism; each single person of the Trinity is eternally and equally subordinate (or serviceable) to the other persons, so that they retain the mutual dynamic equality.

2000 / 0-85364-863-8 / xiv + 256pp

Eddy José Muskus
The Origins and Early Development of Liberation Theology in Latin America
With Particular Reference to Gustavo Gutiérrez
This work challenges the fundamental premise of Liberation Theology, 'opting for the poor', and its claim that Christ is found in them. It also argues that Liberation Theology emerged as a direct result of the failure of the Roman Catholic Church in Latin America.

2002 / 0-85364-974-X / xiv + 296pp

Jim Purves
The Triune God and the Charismatic Movement
A Critical Appraisal from a Scottish Perspective
All emotion and no theology? Or a fundamental challenge to reappraise and realign our trinitarian theology in the light of Christian experience? This study of charismatic renewal as it found expression within Scotland at the end of the twentieth century evaluates the use of Patristic, Reformed and contemporary models of the Trinity in explaining the workings of the Holy Spirit.
2004 / 1-84227-321-3 / xxiv + 246pp

Anna Robbins
Methods in the Madness
Diversity in Twentieth-Century Christian Social Ethics
The author compares the ethical methods of Walter Rauschenbusch, Reinhold Niebuhr and others. She argues that unless Christians are clear about the ways that theology and philosophy are expressed practically they may lose the ability to discuss social ethics across contexts, let alone reach effective agreements.
2004 / 1-84227-211-X / xx + 294pp

Ed Rybarczyk
Beyond Salvation
Eastern Orthodoxy and Classical Pentecostalism on Becoming Like Christ
At first glance eastern Orthodoxy and classical Pentecostalism seem quite distinct. This ground-breaking study shows they share much in common, especially as it concerns the experiential elements of following Christ. Both traditions assert that authentic Christianity transcends the wooden categories of modernism.
2004 / 1-84227-144-X / xii + 356pp

Signe Sandsmark
Is World View Neutral Education Possible and Desirable?
A Christian Response to Liberal Arguments
(Published jointly with The Stapleford Centre)
This book discusses reasons for belief in world view neutrality, and argues that 'neutral' education will have a hidden, but strong world view influence. It discusses the place for Christian education in the common school.
2000 / 0-85364-973-1 / xiv + 182pp

Hazel Sherman
Reading Zechariah
The Allegorical Tradition of Biblical Interpretation through the Commentary of Didymus the Blind and Theodore of Mopsuestia

A close reading of the commentary on Zechariah by Didymus the Blind alongside that of Theodore of Mopsuestia suggests that popular categorising of Antiochene and Alexandrian biblical exegesis as 'historical' or 'allegorical' is inadequate and misleading.

2005 / 1-84227-213-6 / approx. 280pp

Andrew Sloane
On Being a Christian in the Academy
Nicholas Wolterstorff and the Practice of Christian Scholarship

An exposition and critical appraisal of Nicholas Wolterstorff's epistemology in the light of the philosophy of science, and an application of his thought to the practice of Christian scholarship.

2003 / 1-84227-058-3 / xvi + 274pp

Damon W.K. So
Jesus' Revelation of His Father
A Narrative-Conceptual Study of the Trinity with Special Reference to Karl Barth

This book explores the trinitarian dynamics in the context of Jesus' revelation of his Father in his earthly ministry with references to key passages in Matthew's Gospel. It develops from the exegeses of these passages a non-linear concept of revelation which links Jesus' communion with his Father to his revelatory words and actions through a nuanced understanding of the Holy Spirit, with references to K. Barth, G.W.H. Lampe, J.D.G. Dunn and E. Irving.

2005 / 1-84227-323-X / approx. 380pp

Daniel Strange
The Possibility of Salvation Among the Unevangelised
An Analysis of Inclusivism in Recent Evangelical Theology

For evangelical theologians the 'fate of the unevangelised' impinges upon fundamental tenets of evangelical identity. The position known as 'inclusivism', defined by the belief that the unevangelised can be ontologically saved by Christ whilst being epistemologically unaware of him, has been defended most vigorously by the Canadian evangelical Clark H. Pinnock. Through a detailed analysis and critique of Pinnock's work, this book examines a cluster of issues surrounding the unevangelised and its implications for christology, soteriology and the doctrine of revelation.

2002 / 1-84227-047-8 / xviii + 362pp

Scott Swain
God According to the Gospel
Biblical Narrative and the Identity of God in the Theology of Robert W. Jenson
Robert W. Jenson is one of the leading voices in contemporary Trinitarian theology. His boldest contribution in this area concerns his use of biblical narrative both to ground and explicate the Christian doctrine of God. *God According to the Gospel* critically examines Jenson's proposal and suggests an alternative way of reading the biblical portrayal of the triune God.
2006 / 1-84227-258-6 / approx. 180pp

Justyn Terry
The Justifying Judgement of God
A Reassessment of the Place of Judgement in the Saving Work of Christ
The argument of this book is that judgement, understood as the whole process of bringing justice, is the primary metaphor of atonement, with others, such as victory, redemption and sacrifice, subordinate to it. Judgement also provides the proper context for understanding penal substitution and the call to repentance, baptism, eucharist and holiness.
2005 / 1-84227-370-1 / approx. 274 pp

Graham Tomlin
The Power of the Cross
Theology and the Death of Christ in Paul, Luther and Pascal
This book explores the theology of the cross in St Paul, Luther and Pascal. It offers new perspectives on the theology of each, and some implications for the nature of power, apologetics, theology and church life in a postmodern context.
1999 / 0-85364-984-7 / xiv + 344pp

Adonis Vidu
Postliberal Theological Method
A Critical Study
The postliberal theology of Hans Frei, George Lindbeck, Ronald Thiemann, John Milbank and others is one of the more influential contemporary options. This book focuses on several aspects pertaining to its theological method, specifically its understanding of background, hermeneutics, epistemic justification, ontology, the nature of doctrine and, finally, Christological method.
2005 / 1-84227-395-7 / approx. 324pp

Graham J. Watts
Revelation and the Spirit
A Comparative Study of the Relationship between the Doctrine of Revelation and Pneumatology in the Theology of Eberhard Jüngel and of Wolfhart Pannenberg

The relationship between revelation and pneumatology is relatively unexplored. This approach offers a fresh angle on two important twentieth century theologians and raises pneumatological questions which are theologically crucial and relevant to mission in a postmodern culture.

2005 / 1-84227-104-0 / xxii + 232pp

Nigel G. Wright
Disavowing Constantine
Mission, Church and the Social Order in the Theologies of John Howard Yoder and Jürgen Moltmann

This book is a timely restatement of a radical theology of church and state in the Anabaptist and Baptist tradition. Dr Wright constructs his argument in dialogue and debate with Yoder and Moltmann, major contributors to a free church perspective.

2000 / 0-85364-978-2 / xvi + 252pp

Paternoster
9 Holdom Avenue,
Bletchley,
Milton Keynes MK1 1QR,
United Kingdom
Web: www.authenticmedia.co.uk/paternoster

July 2005